THE FIRST PART

OF

JACOBS' LATIN READER.

ADAPTED TO

BULLIONS' LATIN GRAMMAR:

WITH AN INTRODUCTION, ON THE IDIOMS OF THE LATIN LANGUAGE; AN IMPROVED VOCABULARY; AND EXERCISES IN LATIN PROSE COMPOSITION, ON A NEW PLAN.

REVISED EDITION,

With New Marginal Notes and References.

BY REV. PETER BULLIONS, D. D.,

LATE PROFESSOR OF LANGUAGES IN THE ALBANY ACADEMY; AND AUTHOR OF THE SERIES OF GRAMMARS, GREEK, LATIN AND ENGLISH, ON THE SAME PLAN, ETC., ETC.

NEW YORK:

SHELDON AND COMPANY, PUBLISHERS,

498 BROADWAY.

1866.

Manufactured by Case, Lockwood & Co., Hartford, Conn.

PREFACE.

THIS work has been prepared at the request of many teachers who use the author's Latin Grammar, and is intended to follow it as a "First Reading Book." The body of the work consists of the first part of Jacobs' Latin Reader—a work already well known in this country, and which appears to be well adapted to the end for which it was intended. The introductory exercises, however, are arranged a little differently, and a few sentences have been introduced from other sources, for the purpose of illustrating some constructions more fully.

The object of such a work as this is to furnish to the beginner, who is supposed to have become acquainted with the leading principles of the Grammar, a *praxis* on those principles, both in Etymology and Syntax, by which they may be rendered perfectly familiar to his mind, so as to be applied with more success and ease, when he comes to read and analyze the writings of the Roman authors. It is in fact a Supplement to the Grammar, and the foundation of thorough scholarship must be laid here.

In order more fully to meet the wants of the beginner, and to render the study of the Latin language more pleasant and easy to pupils of every capacity, an INTRODUCTION is prefixed, containing explanations of the leading idioms of the language, arranged under proper heads, and illustrated by numerous examples, all of which are numbered, so as to be easily referred to for the purpose of illustrating similar modes of expression which occur in the course of reading, as is more fully explained p. 54. Though this part is intended chiefly for reference, much advantage will be derived from studying it in course in short lessons, simultaneously with lessons in reading and parsing, and rendering the whole familiar by frequent reviews.

The Introductory Exercises consist of short and simple sentences classed in such a way as to illustrate the leading grammatical principles in the construction of sentences, both simple and compound, and by a sufficient number of examples to render these principles familiar and easy of application. In these, as well as throughout the body of the work, constant reference is made to the Grammar itself, as well as to the preceding Introduction, to illustrate and explain the principles of the language as they occur, and, by repeated reference, to render them familiar to the pupil, and impress them indelibly on his mind. These references are more numerous at first; but when any construction or idiom may be supposed to have become familiar, the references to it are less frequent; and the pupil is left to exercise the knowledge acquired, in applying the principles without the aid of references. The construction and use of the subjunctive mood being one of the greatest difficulties and niceties of the language, and all important to be well understood, references for explanation, to the Grammar and Introduction, are more numerous and longer continued on this point than on any other.

These references also form a sort of *index*, by which the pupil may be able to find at once other constructions of a similar kind in the portion of the work previously studied, and so compare the one with the other. For example, the letter [t], p. 103, refers to the Grammar, 627, 5; by running the eye back along the references at the foot of the page, the same construction will be found at the letter [l], p. 95; at [c], p. 90; at [d], p. 89; at [d], p. 87, &c.; all of which may thus be compared with great facility.

The method of reference and explanation here adopted entirely supersedes the use of notes, by rendering them unnecessary, and it is believed will prove vastly more profitable to the student than any number of notes could be, which generally do nothing more than give the meaning of an idiom or phrase in a free translation, without any explanation of its construction. Though this sort of aid enables the pupil to get along with the translation of a sentence, it leaves him as much in the dark as ever respecting its construction. The consequence is, that when he meets with a similar construction again in different words, he is as much at a loss as ever, and finds his progress arrested, unless he is again lifted over blindfold by the aid of another friendly note. It is obvious that persons, in this way, may go over much surface; and if they have a memory capable of bringing to their aid the translation in the note when it is wanted, they may be able to give a good translation of what they have gone over, and yet know nothing, or next to nothing, of the construction of what they have read; and hence it happens, that knowing but little of principles, or of the method of analyzing the idioms and more difficult constructions of the language, whenever they come to an author or passage where the wonted supply of notes is wanting, they find themselves unable to proceed; or if they do, it is so much in the dark that it is with them a mere peradventure whether they are right or wrong. It is therefore not without reason that many of our best teachers think that such notes, like translations, do more evil than good.

This evil, it is hoped, is in a great measure avoided by the method here pursued; for while all needful assistance is furnished, it can be attained only by referring to the grammatical principle which contains the explanation needed; and which soon becomes so familiar, that it can be readily applied to the analyzing of every sentence in which it is involved.

Besides the application of the principles of Grammar in the analysis of sentences, no less important is the study of the words themselves of which these sentences are composed. This belongs to the department of Etymology, and, to the enquiring and philosophical mind, presents a most interesting and pleasing field of investigation. A proper selection of words is no less necessary to the expression of our thoughts than their proper arrangement in sentences. Much, accordingly, of the interest and advantage of studying the models of antiquity, lies in the study of the words selected by these writers for conveying their sentiments to others. The derivation and composition of words, and the variety of meanings which they assume in the expression of thought, should therefore form an important part of study to the classical student from the very beginning, and, if properly conducted, will prove as pleasing as it is profitable. It may be laid down as a principle capable of abundant illustration, that every word has one primitive and radical signification, to which all its other significations and uses are related, and from which they are drawn. This may be regarded as its strict and proper meaning, and should constantly be associated in the mind of the learner with the word itself. Once in possession of this, and accustomed to trace the varied shades of meaning which the words assume as they diverge from their radical and primary signification, he will feel an interest and see a beauty in the study of language, which he would otherwise never be likely to attain.

This primary meaning of a word is not always indeed its most common meaning: this may even have passed into disuse; but still it is necessary to be known, in order to have a clue to its various derived significations, both in its simple and compound forms. If instead of the primary, a secondary and distant meaning, though a more common one, should be associated in the mind with the word, it will be found impossible in many instances to account for, or to perceive any sort of propriety or analogy in its use in certain cases. Take, as an example, the verb *emo*, the more common but not the primary meaning of which is, "to buy," and it will be impossible to trace any sort of connection between such a meaning and that of its compounds, *adĭmo, exĭmo, interĭmo, perĭmo, dirĭmo*, and the like. But assign to *emo* its primary meaning, "to take," and the whole is perceived at once to be clear and consistent. This one example will show how important it is that not only the derivation and composition of words should be fully exhibited in a good dictionary, but also, that the radical and primary signification of all words, where that can be ascertained, should be first stated, and then the secondary and more distant meanings in that order which appears the most natural. In this respect, our school dictionaries are generally defective. This defect I have endeavored to supply in the Vocabulary appended to this work, in which the plan just stated has been followed; so that the pupil is here furnished with the means of tracing every derivative and compound word to its source, if that is in the Latin language, (derivations from the Greek not being given,) and of ascertaining what is the primary signification of each word, from the best authorities within my reach, as well as those significations which are more common, or which belong to the words in the various places where they occur in this work. Care has been taken in connection with this also to distinguish those words usually considered as synonymes. An earlier and more special attention to this part of study than is usual, it is believed would amply repay the labor bestowed upon it.

A few Exercises in Composition are appended, drawn, as will be perceived, from the reading lessons indicated both by the number of the page and the paragraph. Lessons in composition, of the simplest character and to any extent, may be framed in the same way from every reading lesson, or even from every sentence, and rendered into Latin, either orally in the class, or as an exercise in writing, as suggested in the remarks prefixed to the Exercises themselves.

A few suggestions have been introduced at the beginning of the work, respecting what is supposed to be the best method of using it, especially with young pupils. These, I am well aware, are of no importance to the experienced teacher; nevertheless they may be of some use to the young and inexperienced, and especially to those who pursue the study of the Latin without the aid of a teacher.

For explanation of references, see p. 54.

TROY, N. Y., Feb. 11, 1863.

INTRODUCTION.

SENTENCES.

1. A sentence is such an assemblage of words as makes complete sense; as, *Man is mortal.*

2. Sentences are of two kinds, *simple* and *compound.*

3. A simple sentence contains only a single affirmation; as, *Life is short. Time flies.*

4. A compound sentence contains two or more simple sentences combined; as, *Life, which is short, should be well employed.*

5. In the combining of words to form a sentence, observe carefully the following

General Principles of Syntax.

1. In every sentence there must be a *verb* in the indicative, subjunctive, imperative, or infinitive mood, and a *subject*, expressed or understood.

2. Every adjective, adjective pronoun, or participle, must have a substantive expressed or understood, with which it agrees, § 98 and § 146.*

3. Every relative must have an antecedent or word to which it refers, and with which it agrees, § 99.

4. Every nominative has its own verb expressed or understood, of which it is the subject, §§ 100, 101, 102. Or it is placed after the substantive verb in the predicate, § 103.

5. Every finite verb; i. e., every verb in the indicative, subjunctive, or imperative mood, has its own nominative, expressed or understood, §§ 101, 102, and when the infinitive has a subject, it is in the accusative, § 145. The infinitive without a subject does not form a sentence or proposition, § 143.

6. Every oblique case is governed by some word, expressed or understood, in the sentence of which it forms a part.

---

* The references with § prefixed are to the sections in the Latin Grammar.

Resolution or Analysis.

Every simple sentence consists of two parts, the subject and the predicate, § 94, 6. 7. 8. In analyzing a sentence, it is necessary to distinguish between the *Grammatical* subject and predicate, and the *Logical* subject and predicate.

The *Grammatical subject* is the person or thing spoken of, without, or separated from, all modifying words or clauses, and which stands as the nominative to the verb, or the accusative before the infinitive.

The *Logical subject* is the same word, in connection with the qualifying or restricting expressions which go to make up the full and precise idea of the thing spoken of.

The *Grammatical predicate* is the word or words containing the simple affirmation made respecting the subject.

The *Logical predicate* is the grammatical predicate, combined with all those words or expressions that modify or restrict it in any way; thus:

In the sentence, "An inordinate desire of admiration often produces a contemptible levity of deportment;" the Grammatical subject is "*desire;*" the Logical, "*An inordinate desire of admiration.*" The Grammatical predicate is "*produces;*" the Logical, "*produces often a contemptible levity of deportment.*"

In Latin and English, the *general* arrangement of a sentence is the same; i. e., the sentence commonly begins with the subject and ends with the predicate. But the order of the words in each of these parts, is usually so different in Latin from what it is in English, that one of the first difficulties a beginner has to encounter with a Latin sentence is to know how "to take it in," or to arrange it in the proper order of the English. This is technically called *construing* or *giving the order.* To assist in this, some advantage may be found by carefully attending to the following

Directions for Beginners.

DIRECTION I. As all the other parts of a sentence depend upon the two leading parts, namely, the subject or NOMINATIVE, and the predicate or VERB; the first thing to be done with every sentence, is to find out these. In order to this,

1. Look for the leading verb, which is always in the present, imperfect, perfect, pluperfect, or future of the indicative, or in the imperative mood,* and usually at or near the end of the sentence.

2. Having found the verb, observe its number and person; this will aid in finding its nominative, which is a noun or pronoun in the same number and person with the verb, commonly before it, and near the beginning of the sentence, though not always so, 739 R. I. with exceptions.

DIRECTION II. Having thus found the nominative and verb, and ascertained their meaning, the sentence may be resolved from the Latin into the English order, as follows:

1. Take the *Vocative*, *Exciting*, *Introductory*, or *Connecting words*, if there are any.

2. The NOMINATIVE.

3. Words *limiting* or *explaining* it, i. e., words agreeing with it, or governed by it, or by one another, where they are found, till you come to the *verb*.

4. The VERB.

5. Words *limiting* or *explaining* it, i. e., words which modify it, are governed by it, or depend upon it.

6. Supply every where the words *understood*.

7. If the sentence be compound, take the parts of it severally as they depend one upon another, proceeding with each of them as above.

DIRECTION III. In arranging the words for translation, in the subordinate parts of a sentence, observe the following

Rules for Construing.

I. An oblique case, or the infinitive mood, is put after the word that governs it.

EXC. The relative and interrogative are usually put before the governing word, unless that be a preposition; if it is, then after it.

II. An adjective, if no other word depend upon it or be coupled with it, is put *before* its substantive; but if another word depend upon it, or be governed by it, it is usually placed after it.

* All the other parts of the verb are generally used in subordinate clauses. So, also, is the pluperfect indicative. In oblique discourse, the leading verb is in the infinitive. 650. *Rule* VI.

III. The participle is usually construed after its substantive, or the word with which it agrees.

IV. The relative and its clause should, if possible, come immediately after the antecedent.

V. When a question is asked, the nominative comes after the verb; (in English, between the auxiliary and the verb.) Interrogative words, however, such as *quis, quotus, quantus, uter*, &c., *come before the verb.*

VI. After a transitive active verb, look for an accusative, and after a preposition for an accusative or ablative, and arrange the words accordingly.

VII. Words in apposition must be construed as near together as possible.

VIII. Adverbs, adverbial phrases, prepositions with their cases, circumstances of time, place, cause, manner, instrument, &c., should be placed, in general, after the words which they modify:—The case absolute commonly before them, and often first in the sentence.

IX. The words of different clauses must not be mixed together, but each clause translated by itself, in its order, according to its connection with, or dependence upon, those to which it is related.

X. Conjunctions should be placed before the last of two words or sentences connected.

LATIN IDIOMS.*

PARTICULAR DIRECTIONS AND MODELS FOR TRANSLATION.

The following explanations and directions are intended chiefly for reference. But it will be of great advantage for the pupil to become familiar with them by going through them two or three times, *in course*, simultaneously with his reading lessons.

1. BEFORE translating, every sentence should be read over till it can be read correctly and with ease, paying special attention to the quantity and pronunciation. The words should then be arranged according to the preceding general directions, and translated as they are arranged, separately or in clusters, as may be found convenient; always remembering to place adjectives and adjective pronouns with their substantives before translating. The sense and grammatical construction being thus ascertained, the translation may then be read over without the Latin, and due attention paid to the English idiom. The whole sentence, whether simple or compound, may then be analyzed as directed § 152, and last of all, every word parsed separately as directed, § 153.

2. In order to arrange and translate with ease, it is necessary to be familiar with, and readily to distinguish the different cases, genders, and numbers of nouns, pronouns, adjectives and participles, and to translate them correctly and promptly, in these cases and numbers, &c.; and also to distinguish and correctly translate the verb in its various moods, tenses, numbers, persons, &c. This can be acquired only by continual practice and drilling, which should be kept up till the utmost readiness is attained.

3. The English prepositions used in translating the different cases in Latin, for the sake of convenience, may be called SIGNS of those cases; and in translating these, the English *definite* or *indefinite* article is to be used as the sense requires. The signs of the cases are as follows:

Nom. (No sign.)	Acc. (No sign.)
Gen. *Of.*	Voc. *O*, or no sign.
Dat. *To* or *for.*	Abl. *With, from, in, by,* &c.

* A *Latin idiom*, strictly speaking, is a mode of speech peculiar to the Latin language. It is here used in a more extended sense, to denote a mode of speech different from the English, or which, if rendered word for word, and with the ordinary signs of cases, moods, tenses, &c., would not make a correct English sentence.

In certain constructions the idiom of the English language requires the oblique cases in Latin to be translated in a manner different from the above. The chief of these constructions are the following:

4. *The Genitive.*

1. The genitive denoting the place where, 548, R. XXXVI., is translated by *at;* as, *Romæ*, "*At* Rome."

2. Denoting *price*, sometimes by *for;* as, *Vendĭdit* *pluris*, "He sold it *for more;*" or without a sign; as, *Constĭtit* *pluris*, "It cost *more.*"

5. *The Dative.*

1. After a verb of taking away, 501 R. XXIX.; the dative is translated by *from;* as, *Eripuit me* *morti*, "He rescued me *from death;*" *Eripĭtur* *morti*, "He is rescued *from death.*" 522–III. See 502.

2. Denoting the doer after a passive verb, 528, R. XXXIII., it is translated by *by;* as, *Vix audior* *ulli*, "I am scarcely heard *by any one.*"

3. Denoting the possessor, 380, it is translated as the genitive; as, *Ei in mentem venit*, "It came into the mind *to him,*" i. e., *of him*, or into *his* mind.

4. After verbs signifiing "to be present," by *at;* as, *Adfuit* *precĭbus*, He was present *at prayers.* 393.

6. *The Ablative.*

1. The ablative denoting a property or quality of another substantive, R. VII., is translated by *of;* as, *Vir* *mirâ magnitudĭne*, "A man *of wonderful size.*"

2. The place where, 549, is commonly translated by *at*, sometimes by *in.*

3. After the comparative degree, 467, R. XXIV., by *than;* as, *Dulcior* *melle*, "Sweeter *than honey.*"

4. Denoting the material of which a thing is made, 541, by *of;* as, *Factus* *ebŏre*, "Made *of ivory.*"

5. After *dignus* and words denoting origin; also after *opus and usus*, signifying need, by *of;* as, *Dignus* *honōre*, "Worthy *of honor.*"

6. Denoting time how long,—sometimes by *in;* as, *Uno die fecit*, "He did it *in one day;*" sometimes without a sign; as, *Uno die abfuit*, "He was absent *one day.*"

7. Time when—by *at*, *on;* as, *Solis occāsu*, "*At the setting* of the sun;" *Idĭbus Aprīlis*, "*On the ides* of April."

8. After verbs of depriving, 514—by *of;* as, *Eum veste spoliāvit*, "He stripped him *of his garment.*"

Cases without Signs.

7. When the genitive, dative, or ablative, is governed by an intransitive verb which is translated by a transitive verb in English (132, Obs. 4.), or by an adjective denoting likeness, the sign of the case is omitted; as,

1. Gen. *Miserēre mei*,	Pity *me.*
2. Dat. *Præfuit exercĭtui*,	He commanded *the army.*
3. " *Placuit regi*,	It pleased *the king.*
4. Abl. *Utĭtur fraude*,	He uses *deceit.*
5. " *Potītus est imperio*,	He obtained the *government.*
6. Dat. *Simĭlis patri*,	Like his *father.*

Obs. But when rendered by an intransitive verb in English, the sign of the case must be used; as,

7. *Insidiantur nobis*,	They lie in wait *for us.*

8. When a verb governs two datives, by R. XIX., 427, the dative of the end or design is sometimes rendered without the sign; as,

1. *Est mihi voluptāti*,	It is to me [for] *a pleasure;* i. e., It is [*or* it brings] a pleasure to me.

9. The ablative absolute, 690, R. LX., (See No. 109,) and frequently time how long, R. XLI., are without the sign; as,

1. *Bello finīto*,	*The war* being ended.
2. *Sex mensĭbus abfuit*,	He was absent *six months.*

10. When the ablative is governed by a preposition, the English of that preposition takes the place of the sign of the ablative, and no other will be used; thus,

1. *Ab exercĭtu*,	*From* the army.	4. *Cum dignitāte*,	*With* dignity.
2. *Ex urbe*,	*Out of* the city.	5. *Pro castris*,	*Before* the camp.
3. *In agro*,	*In* the field.	6. *Tenus pube*,	*Up to* the middle.

11. In order to specify more particularly, the English idiom sometimes requires the possessive pronouns, *my*, *thy*, *his*, *her*, *its*, *our*, *your*, *their*, (not expressed in Latin unless contrasted with others), to be supplied before a noun, and especially if

they refer to the subject of the sentence. The sense will show when this is to be done, and what pronoun is to be used; as,

1. *Filius similis patri,*	A son like *his* father.
2. *Reverēre parentes,*	Reverence *your* parents.

12. Nouns in apposition, (251, R. I.,) must be brought as near together as possible, and the sign of the case, when used, prefixed to the first only; as,

1. Nom. *Cicĕro orātor,*	Cicero the orator.
2. Gen. *Cicerōnis oratōris,*	*Of* Cicero the orator.
3. Dat. *Cicerōni oratōri,*	*To* Cicero the orator.
4. Abl. *Cicerōne oratōre,*	*With* Cicero the orator.

13. The noun in apposition is sometimes connected with the noun before it by the words *as*, *being*, &c.; as,

1. *Misit* *me comĭtem,*	He sent *me as a companion.*
2. *Hic puer venit,*	*He* came, *when* [or *being*] *a boy.*

Adjectives and Substantives.

14. In translating an adjective or adjective pronoun and a substantive together, the adjective is commonly placed first, and the sign of the case is prefixed to it, and not to the noun, 263, R. II.; as,

1. Nom. *Altus mons,*	A high mountain.
2. Gen. *Alti montis,*	Of a high mountain.
3. Dat. *Alto monti,*	To [for] a high mountain.
4. Abl. *Alto monte,*	With a high mountain.

15. When two or more adjectives, coupled by a conjunction, belong to one substantive, they may be placed either before or after it; as,

1. *Jupĭter optĭmus et maxĭmus,*	Jupiter the best and greatest; *or*
Optĭmus et maxĭmus Jupĭter,	The best and greatest Jupiter.
2. *Viri sapientis et docti,*	Of a man wise and learned; *or*
Sapientis et docti viri,	Of a wise and learned man.

16. The adjective must be placed after its substantive when the former has a negative joined with it, or another word in the sentence governed by it, or dependent upon it. So also *solus*; as,

1. *Dux perĭtus belli,*	A general skilled in war.
2. *Filius simĭlis patri,*	A son like his father.
3. *Poēta dignus honōre,*	A poet worthy of honor.
4. *Homĭnes soli sapiunt,*	Men alone are wise.
5. *Avis tam parum decōra,*	A bird so little beautiful.
6. *Littŏre non molli neque arenōso,*	With a shore not soft nor sandy.

17. The adjectives *primus, medius, ultĭmus, extrēmus, infĭmus, imus, summus, suprēmus, relĭquus, ceter*, or *cetĕrus*, and some others describing a *part* of an object, are translated as substantives, with the sign of the case prefixed, and *of* before the substantive following, 273; as,

1. *Mediâ nocte,*	*In the middle of* the night.
2. *Ad summum montem,*	*To the top of* the mountain.

18. When these adjectives (No. 17) describe the whole, and not a part only, they are translated as in No. 14; as,

Summum bonum,	The chief good.
Suprēmus dies,	The last day.

19. An adjective without a substantive usually has a substantive understood, but obvious from the connection, 269. Masculine adjectives (if plural) commonly agree with *homĭnes*, or, if possessives, with *amīci, cives*, or *milĭtes*, understood; and neuters, with *factum, negotium, verbum, tempus*, &c.; as,

1. *Boni (homĭnes) sunt rari,*	Good men are rare.
2. *Cæsar misit suos (milĭtes),*	Cæsar sent his soldiers.
3. *Cocles transnāvit ad suos (cives),*	Cocles swam over to his fellow-citizens.
4. *Labor vincit omnia (negotia),*	Labor overcomes all things.
5. *In postĕrum (tempus),*	In time to come,—for the future.
6. *In eo (loco) ut,*	In such a situation that.

20. Adjectives commonly used without a substantive, (but still belonging to a substantive understood,) may be regarded as substantives. They are such as *mortāles, boni, mali, supĕri, infĕri, Græcus, Romānus*, &c. (See 269); as,

1. *Mali odĕrunt bonos,*	*The wicked* hate *the good.*
2. *Græcos Romāni vicĕrunt,*	*The Romans* conquered *the Greeks.*

21. Adjective words, when partitives, or used partitively, take the gender of the noun expressing the whole, and govern it in the genitive plural, (if a collective noun, in the genitive singular), 355, Rule X. In this case, verbs and adjectives agree with the partitive as if it were a noun; as,

1. *Alĭquis philosophōrum dixit,*	*Some one of the philosophers* has said.
2. *Una musārum veniet,*	*One of the muses* will come.
3. *Multi nobilium juvĕnum,*	*Many noble young men.*

22. The comparative degree not followed by an ablative, or the conjunction *quam* (than), is usually translated by the positive with *too* or *rather* prefixed. For explanation see 473; as.

1. *Iracundior est*, (scil. *æquo*,) He is *too* (or *rather*) *passionate*.
2. *Ægrius ferēbat*, He took it *rather ill*.
3. *Altius volāvit*, He flew *too high*.

Obs. In a comparison, *eò* or *tanto* with a comparative in one clause, and *quò* or *quanto* in the other, may be rendered "the" (See No. 44. 7. 8.); as,

4. *Quò plures, eò feliciōres*, *The* more, *the* happier.

23. The superlative degree expressing comparison, is usually preceded by the article *the* in English (110); as,

1. *Doctissĭmus Romanōrum*, *The most learned* of the Romans.
2. *Fortissĭmus miles in exercĭtu*, *The bravest* soldier in the army.

24. When the superlative does not express comparison, but only eminence or distinction, it is translated with the article *a* or *an* prefixed in the singular, and without an article in the plural; or by the positive, with *very*, *eminently*, &c., prefixed (110); as,

1. *Homo doctissĭmus*, *A* most learned (or *a very learned*) man.
2. *Homĭnes doctissĭmi*, Most learned (or *very learned*) men.

25. *Alius* repeated with a different word in the same clause, renders that clause double, and requires it to be translated as in the following examples:

1. *Alius aliâ viâ*, One by one way, another by another.
2. *Aliud aliis vidētur*, One thing seems good to some, another to others; i. e., Some think one thing, and some another. (See other varieties, 275.)

The same usage occurs with words derived from *alius*. See Gr. 276.

26. The distributive numeral adjectives are usually translated by the cardinal number indicated, with "each," or "to each," annexed; sometimes by repeating the cardinal thus, "one by one," "two by two," &c., 107, 11; as,

1. *Consŭles binas naves habēbant*, The consuls had *each two* ships, or, had *two* ships *each*.
2. *Quâ singŭli carri ducerentur*, Where wagons could be led *one by one*.
3. *Tigna bina*, Beams *two by two*, or in pairs.
4. *Singŭlis singŭlas partes distribuit æquāles*, He distributed equal parts, *one to each*.
5. *Singŭlis mensĭbus hoc fecit*, This he did *every* (or *each*) *month*.
6. *Plures singŭli uxōres habent*, They have *each* many wives.

Pronouns.

27. 1st. The adjective pronoun, *hic, hæc, hoc,* with a noun following, is used as an adjective, and means, in the singular, "*this,*"—in the plural, "*these.*"—*Ille, illa, illud,*—*is, ea, id,*—*iste, ista, istud,* with a noun, in the singular, mean "*that,*"—in the plural, "*those.*"

2d. Without a noun following, they are all used substantively, and mean, in the singular, *he, she, it;* in the plural, *they;* thus,

1. *Hic vir,* This man.
2. *Illa femĭna,* That woman.
3. *Ea urbs,* That city.
4. *Hic fecit, He* did it.
5. *Illa vēnit, She* came.
6. *Ea* (Dido) *condĭdit eam, She* built *it,* (Carthage.)

Obs. In sentences containing an enumeration of particulars, the same pronoun is sometimes used in successive clauses, but they require to be translated differently, (276); thus,

7. *Hic,* 8. *Is,* 9. *Ille,* 10. *Alter,* } "one," "the one." —*hic,* —*is,* —*ille,* —*alter,* } "another," "the other."

When antithesis or contrast is stated, *hic* is translated "this," and refers to the nearer antecedent; *ille,* "that," and refers to the more distant; as,

11. *Hic minor natu est, ille major, This* is the younger, *that* the older.

28. *Is, ea, id,* followed by *ut,* or the relative, *qui, quæ, quod,* in the next clause, means "*such,*" and implies comparison. The relative after it may be translated, *that I, that thou, that he, that they,* &c., according as the antecedent requires, or it may be translated *as,* and its verb by the infinitive, (123, 2); thus,

1. *Is homo erat ut, &c.,* He was *such* a man that, &c.
2. *Neque is sum qui terrear,* I am not *such that* I may be frightened. Or better thus, I am not *such a one as* to be frightened.

Obs. The adverb *eò* with *ut* following it, means "so far," "to such a degree," to such a point," "in such a state;" as,

3. *Eò pervēnit ut,* "He came *so far,* (i. e., made such progress,) that,"

Possessive Pronouns.

29. The possessive pronoun is equivalent in meaning to the genitive of the substantive pronoun, and may often be so translated; as,

1. *Beneficio* s u o *populīque Romāni*, By the kindness *of himself* and of the Roman people.
2. *Cum* m e a *nemo scripta legat, vulgo recitāre timentis*, Since no one reads the writings *of me* fearing to recite them publicly.

30. The possessive, *suus, sua, suum*, in Latin, agrees in gender, number, and case, with the noun denoting the *object possessed*, but in English must be translated by a pronoun denoting the *possessor;* thus,

1. *Pater dilĭgit* s u o s *libĕros*,	A father loves *his* children.
2. *Parentes dilĭgunt* s u a m *sobŏlem*,	Parents love *their* offspring.
3. *Frater dilĭgit* s u a m *sorōrem*,	A brother loves *his* sister.
4. *Soror dilĭgit* s u u m *frātrem*,	A sister loves *her* brother.

Obs. In the first sentence, "*suos*" agrees with "*libĕros*," but must be translated "*his*," denoting "*pater*," the possessor. In the second, *suam*, though singular, to agree with *sobŏlem*, must be translated "*their*," so as to denote the possessors, "*parentes*," &c.

Usage of Sui, Suus,—Ille, Iste, Hic, Is.

31. The reflexive, *sui*, and its possessive, *suus*, generally refer to the subject of the leading verb* in the sentence; *ille, iste, hic, is*, never refer to that subject, but to some other person or thing spoken of; thus,

1. C a t o *occīdit* s e,	*Cato* killed *himself*.
2. P a t e r *dilĭgit* s u o s *libĕros*,	A *father* loves *his* (own) children.
3. P a r e n t e s *dilĭgunt* s u a m *sobŏlem*,	*Parents* love *their* (own) offspring.
4. *Dicit* s e *valēre*,	*He* says that *he* is well.

Obs. In the second and third sentence, "his," made by *suos*, and "their," made by *suam*, referring to some other person than *pater* or *parentes*, would be made by the genitive of *ille, iste, hic, is*. In the first and fourth, *se* would be made *eum*. For the difference between these words usually translated "he," see Gr. 118, 3.

---

* See Gr. 118, 3, 1st, with note.

Note. If a second subject and verb be introduced, the reflexive governed by that verb will belong to the new subject, unless the whole clause refer to the words, wishes, or actions, of the first subject; as,

5. *Scipio civitatĭbus Italiæ reddĭdit omnia quæ* s u a *recognoscēbant,*	Scipio restored to the States of Italy, all the things which they recognised as *their own.*

Usage of Ipse.

32. *Ipse* renders the word with which it is joined emphatic, whether expressed or understood, and is equal to the English, *myself, thyself, himself, themselves,* &c., annexed to it; sometimes to the word *very* prefixed. With *numbers* it denotes exactness, and sometimes it is used by itself as a reflexive instead of *sui,* 118, 3, 2d.; as,

1. *I p s e faciam,* (i. e. *ego ipse,*)	I will do it *myself.*
2. *I p s e fruĕris otio,* (i. e. *tu ipse,*)	Thou *thyself* enjoyest ease.
3. *Jacŭlo cadit i p s e,* (i. e. *ille ipse,*)	He *himself* falls by a dart.
4. *Cæsar i p s e vēnit,*	Cæsar *himself* came.
5. *Tempus i p s u m convēnit,*	The *very* time was agreed on.
6. *Ad i p s a s portas,*	To the *very* gates.
7. *Decem i p s i dies,*	Ten *whole* days.
8. *Precātus est ut i p s u m liberāret,*	He begged that he would liberate *him.*
9. *Donum i p s i datum,*	A present given *to him.*

33. When joined with the personal pronouns, used in a reflexive sense, and in an oblique case, it sometimes agrees with them in case, but more commonly with the subject of the verb in the nominative or accusative. It is always, however, to be translated with the oblique case, to which it adds the force of the word *self,* or simply of emphasis (282); thus,

1. *Se ipse interfēcit* (or *se ipsum*),	He slew him*self.*
1. *Nosce te i p s e* (or *te i p s u m*),	Know thy*self.*
2. *Mihi i p s e* (or *i p s i,*) *faveo,*	I favor my*self.*
3. *Agam per me i p s e,*	I will do it my*self.*
4. *Virtus est per se i p s a laudabĭlis,*	Virtue is to be praised for it*self.*
5 *Se i p s o s omnes natūrâ dilĭgunt,*	All men naturally love them*selves.*

RELATIVE AND ANTECEDENT.

General Principle.

34. Every sentence containing a relative and its antecedent is a compound sentence, of which the relative with its clause

forms one of the parts, and is used further to describe or limit its antecedent word in the other part. That word may be the subject, or belong to the predicate, or to some circumstance connected with either. But to whichsoever of these it belongs, the relative and its clause must all be translated *together*, and in immediate connection with its antecedent word. Hence the following

General Rule of Arrangement.

35. The relative with its clause should be placed immediately after, or as near as possible to the antecedent, and, unless unavoidable, another substantive should not come between them; thus;

Latin Arrangement.

1. *Urbi immĭnet* **mons**, *qui ad Arcadiam procurrit.* Here "*qui*" with its clause, "*ad Arcadiam procurrit,*" belongs to, and further describes the antecedent subject "*mons.*" As then the subject with all that belongs to it must be taken before the verb, (Gr. 770, 2d, 3d,) the above sentence should be arranged for translation, thus: *Mons qui procurrit ad Arcadiam, immĭnet urbi,* A *mountain, which* extends to Arcadia, hangs over the city.

Or, the English order may be inverted, thus: *Urbi immĭnet mons, qui procurrit ad Arcadiam,* Over the city hangs *a mountain, which,* &c.

But not, *Mons immĭnet urbi, qui,* &c., because this arrangement would place "*urbi*" between the antecedent, "*mons,*" and the relative, "*qui,*" and so lead to a false translation. The following sentence also affords an example:

2. *Proxĭme urbem Eurōtas fluvius delabĭtur, ad cujus ripas Spartāni se exercēre solēbant.* Arrange, *Proxĭme urbem delabĭtur,* &c., Close to the city flows; or, *Eurōtas fluvius, ad cujus ripas,* &c. *delabĭtur proxĭme urbem.*

36. When another noun necessarily comes between the relative and its antecedent, there is more danger of ambiguity in English than in Latin, as the gender and number of the Latin relative will generally direct to the proper antecedent, to which in English we are directed chiefly by the sense.

The following sentence affords an example of this kind: *Ad Byzantium fugit, oppĭdum naturâ munītum et arte, quod copiâ abundat.*

37. The antecedent in Latin is often understood when the English idiom requires it to be supplied. It is generally understood, and should be supplied in the proper case:

1st. When it is intentionally left indefinite, or is obvious from the gender and number of the relative, and the connection in which it stands, as in No. 19; as,

1. *Sunt (homĭnes) quos juvat,*	There are *men* whom it delights.
2. *Hic est (id) quod quærĭmus,*	*That* which we seek is here.
" *Hic sunt, (ea) quæ quærĭmus,*	*Those* things which we seek are here.
3. *(Is) qui cito dat, bis dat,*	*(He)* who gives promptly, gives twice.

Note. In the preceding sentences the antecedent supplied is in parentheses.

2d. The antecedent is usually understood before the relative, when it is expressed after it, and in the same case, (286, Obs. 1, 2d.); as,

4. *(Pars) quæ pars terrēna fuit,*	The *part* which was earthy.
5. *(Locus) in quem locum venit,*	The *place* into which he came.
" *Apud Actium (locum) qui locus est, &c.*	At Actium a *place* which is, &c.

Note 1. When the antecedent word is expressed in the relative clause, as in the examples Nos. 4, and 5, or is repeated, as in the following, No. 6, (286, Obs. 1, 3d.,) it is omitted in translating; as,

6. *Erant omnīno duo itinĕra, quibus itinerĭbus domo exīre possent,*	There were only two ways by which they could go from home.

Note 2. *Quisquis, quidquid, or quicquid,* (and also *quicunque, quæcunque, quodcunque,*) "whoever, whatever," used as a relative without an antecedent, includes a general or indefinite antecedent, in such case as the construction requires, and is equivalent to *omnis,* or *quivis qui,—omne,* or *quidvis quod;* as,

7. *Fortūnam quæcunque* (i. e. *quamvis fortūnam quæ*) *accĭdat experiantur,*	They would hazard *whatever* fortune (i. e. *any* fortune *which*) might happen.
8. *Quidquid tetigĕrat aurum fiēbat,*	*Whatever* (i. e. *everything which*) he had touched became gold.

Note 3. When the antecedent is a proposition, or clause of a sentence, 285, the relative is put in the neuter gender, and sometimes has *id* before it referring to the same clause; as,

9. *Servi, quod* (or *id quod*) *nunquam ante factum, manumissi et milĭtes facti sunt;*	The slaves, *which* never had been done before, were set free and made soldiers.

38. In the beginning of a sentence, a relative, with or without *quum*, or other conjunctive term, and referring to some word, clause, or circumstance, in a preceding sentence, usually has the antecedent word repeated, or, if evident, understood; and instead of *who* or *which*, may be rendered *this*, *that*, *these*, *those*, or, *and this*, *and that*, &c., according as the closeness of the connection may require, 295; as,

1. *Quæ urbs quum infestarētur,*	*And* since (or because) *this* city was infested.
" *Qui legāti quum missi essent,*	When *these* ambassadors had been sent.
2. *Quæ contentio cuncta permiscuit,*	*This* contention threw all things into confusion.
3. *Quibus nunciis acceptis,*	*These* tidings being received.
4. *Quod quum ille cernĕret,*	*And* when he saw *this*.
5. *Quo facto,*	*This* being done, (or accomplished.)
6. *Quæ dum omnia contemplabantur,*	*And* while they were contemplating all *these* things.
7. *Quod quum impetrâsset,*	*And* when he had obtained *this*.
8. *A quo consilio quum revocāret,*	When he recalled him from *this* design.
9. *Quo ictu ille extinctus est,*	*And* by *this* blow he was killed.

Note. To this construction belongs *quod*, (apparently for *propter* or *ad quod*, 539,) in the beginning of a sentence, referring to something previously stated, and meaning, "*on account of*, *with respect to*, or *as to*, THIS THING;" as,

10. *Quod diis gratias habeo,*	*On account of this*, (*for this thing*, *wherefore*,) I give thanks to the gods.
11. *Quod dicĕret se venturum,*	*As to what* (as to that thing which) he said, that he would come.

39. When the antecedent word is not repeated, as in No. 38, the relative, with or without *quum*, or other conjunctive term, may be rendered *he*, *she*, *it*, *they*, or *and he*, *and she*, &c., according as the antecedent word requires, 295; as,

1. *Qui quum admittĕret,*	*And* when *he* admitted.
2. *Quæ quum vidisset,*	*And* when *she* had seen.
Quæ quum visa esset,	When *she* had been (*or* was) seen.
3. *Quam quum dare nollet,*	*And* when he would not give *it*.
4. *Quibus quum occurrisset,*	When he had met *them*.
5. *Qui (quæ; pl. qui, quæ,) respondit,*	*And he (she, they,)* replied.
6. *Qui (or quæ) quum adessent,*	*And* when *they* were present.
7. *Quem Meleăger interfēcit,*	*And* Meleager slew *him*.
8. *Quam quum ducĕret,*	*And* when he was leading *her*.
9. *Ad quem quum venissent,*	*And* when they had come to *him*.
10. *Quem ut vidit,*	As soon as (or when) he saw *him*.

40. When the relative in any case is followed by the subjunctive mood, and the two clauses, viz.: the antecedent and relative, involve a *comparison;* or the latter expresses the *purpose*, *object*, or *design* of something expressed by the former, the relative is better translated by the conjunction *that*, and the personal pronoun; thus, *that I, that thou, that he, that they*, &c., as the antecedent word may require. (See Gr. 642.)

1. *Missus sum qui te adducĕrem,*	I have been sent *that I* might bring you.
2. *Neque is qui facias id,*	You are not such a person *that you* should do that.
3. *Quis est tam lynceus qui, &c.,*	Who is so sharp sighted *that he*.
4. *Misit legātos qui cognoscĕrent,*	He sent ambassadors *that they* might find out.
5. *Fruges mandāvit quas dissemināret,*	She gave him fruits *that* he might scatter *them*.

41. In the expressions, *quippe qui, ut qui, utpŏte qui*, the relative is better translated by the personal pronoun which represents the antecedent, (647); as,

1. *Quippe qui nunquam legĕrim,*	For (or because) *I* have never read them.

42. After *dignus, indignus, idoneus*, and the like, in the predicate, the relative and subjunctive mood may be rendered by the infinitive, (643, 1st,); as,

1. *Dignus qui amētur,*	Worthy *to be loved.*
2. *Si dignum qui numerētur creavĭtis,*	If you shall elect a person worthy *to be reckoned*, &c.

43. Sometimes the natural order of the sentence is inverted, so that the relative clause stands first and the antecedent follows it. In translating, the antecedent clause should generally be placed first; as,

1. *Qui bonis non recte utĭtur, ei bona mala fiunt,*	Good things become evil to *him who* does not use good things well.
2. *Qui cito dat, (is) bis dat,*	*He* gives twice *who* gives quickly.

Correlative Adjectives.

44. The demonstratives, *tot*, so many, and *totĭdem*, just so many; *tantus*, as great, so great, as much, so much; *talis*, such; are followed by their relatives, *quot*, *quantus*, *qualis*, signifying *as*, to denote comparison; as,

1. *Tot homĭnes quot,*	*As many* men *as.*
2. *Totĭdem naves quot,*	*Just so many* ships *as.*
3. *Tantus exercĭtus quantus,*	*As great* (or *so great*) an army *as.*
4. *Talis homo qualis,*	*Such* a man *as.*

So also the correlative adverbs.

5. *Toties,*	—— *quoties,*	As often	—— as.
6. *Tam,*	—— *quam,*	So	—— as.
7. *Eò,*	—— *quò,*	By so much	—— as.
8. *Tanto,*	—— *quanto,*	By so much	—— as; or,
		In proportion	—— as.

45. Instead of the relative in such sentences, the conjunctions *ac*, *atque*, (728,) *ut*, and the relative *qui*, *quæ*, *quod*, are sometimes used, and may generally be translated, "as," or "that."

1. *Honos talis paucis est delātus ac mihi,*	Such honor has been bestowed upon few persons *as* upon me.
2. *Cum totĭdem navĭbus atque profectus erat rediit,*	He returned with just as many ships *as* he had departed with.
3. *Nulla est tanta vis quæ non frangi possit,*	No power is so great *as* (or, *that it*) can not be broken.

46. When the relative only is expressed in sentences implying comparison, the *demonstrative* (No. 44,) must be supplied, and the sentence translated as above; as,

1. *Crocodīlus parit (tanta) ova quanta ansĕres,*	The crocodile lays (*as large*) eggs *as* geese lay.
2. *(Tot) millia quot unquam venēre Mycēnis,*	*As many* thousands *as* ever came from Mycenæ.

47. Sometimes, as in No. 43, the natural order of the sentence is inverted, so that the relative clause stands first and the antecedent follows it. In translating, the antecedent clause should be placed first; as,

1. *Quot homĭnes tot causæ,* arrange *Tot causæ quot homĭnes,*	*As* many causes *as* there are men.

48. The relatives, *quot*, *quoties*, *quantus*, *qualis*, used *interrogatively*, or *in an exclamation*, or *indefinitely*, in the indirect interrogation, and without implying comparison, have no reference to an antecedent term either expressed or understood, and are translated respectively, "how many," "how often," "how great," or "how much," "what," or "of what kind;" as,

1. *Inter.* *Quot annos habet?*	*How many* years has he? i. e., how old is he?
2. *Indef.* *Nescio quot,*	I know not *how many.*
3. *Excl.* *Cum quantâ gravitāte!*	With *how much* gravity!
4. *Indef.* *Doce quales sint,*	Tell us *of what kind* they are.

THE VERB AND ITS SUBJECT.

General Principle.

49. Every finite verb (244, 5,) has its own subject, expressed or understood, in the nominative case.

Obs. The subject of the verb is the person or thing spoken of, and may be a *noun*, a *pronoun*, a *verb in the infinitive mood*, a *clause of a sentence*, or any thing which, however expressed, is the subject of thought or speech. (304.)

General Rule of Arrangement.

50. The subject and all the words agreeing with it, governed by it, connected with it, or dependent upon it, must be arranged in the order of their connection and dependence, and translated before the verb.

1. *Canis latrat,*	*The dog* barks.
2. *Ego scribo,*	*I* write.
3. *Ludĕre est jucundum,*	*To play* is pleasant.
4. *Dulce est pro patriâ mori,*	*To die for one's country* is sweet.
5. *Totus Græcōrum exercĭtus Aulĭde convenĕrat,*	*The whole army of the Greeks* had assembled at Aulis.
6. *Vir sapit qui pauca loquĭtur,*	*The man who speaks little* is wise.

51. When the subject of the verb is the infinitive, either alone or with its subject; or a clause of a sentence, connected by *ut*, *quod*, or other conjunctive term, the English pronoun, *it*, is put with the verb referring to that infinitive or clause following it, and which is the proper subject of the verb; as,

1. *Facile est jubēre,*	*It* is easy to command.
2. *Nuntiātum est classem devinci,*	*It* was announced that the fleet was conquered.
3. *Semper accĭdit ut absis,*	*It* always happens that you are absent.
4. *Qui fit ut metuas,*	How happens *it* that you fear.
5. *Nunquam Romānis placuisse imperatōrem a suis milit-ĭbus interfĭci,*	That *it* never had pleased the Romans, *that a commander should be killed by his own soldiers.*

52. The verb must always be translated in its proper tense, and in the same person and number with its nominative. (See paradigms of the verb, §§ 54–70.) But when it has two or more nouns or pronouns in the singular, taken together, or a collective noun expressing many as individuals, as its subject, the verb must be translated in the plural; as,

1. *Et pater et mater venērunt,*	Both his father and mother *have come.*
2. *Turba quoquoversum ruunt,*	The crowd *rush* in every direction.

53. The nominative to a verb in the first or second person, being evident from the termination, is seldom expressed in Latin, but must be supplied in translating; as,

1. *Scribo, I* write.
2. *Legis, Thou* readest.
3. *Scribĭmus, We* write.
4. *Legĭtis, You* read.

54. When the verb in the third person has no nominative expressed, it refers to some noun or pronoun evident from the connection; and, both in translating and parsing, the pronoun *ille*, or *is*, in the *nominative* case, and in the *gender* and *number* of the noun or pronoun referred to, must be supplied; as,

1. *(Ille) scribit,* (He) writes.
2. *(Illi) scribunt,* (They) write.

55. When the same word is the subject of several verbs closely connected in the same construction, it is expressed with the first and understood to the rest, both in Latin and English; thus,

1. *Cæsar venit, vidit, et vicit,*	*Cæsar* came, saw, and conquered.
2. *Dicĭtur Cæsărem venisse, vidisse, et vicisse,*	It is said that *Cæsar* came, saw, and conquered.

Interrogative Sentences.

56. A question is made in Latin in four different ways, as follows:

1st. By an interrogative pronoun; as, *Quis venit?* "*Who* comes?" *Quem misit?* "*Whom* did he send?" *Cujus pecus hoc?* "*Whose* flock is this?" &c.

2d. By an interrogative adverb; as, *Unde venit?* "*Whence* came he?" *Cur venit?* "*Why* did he come?"

3d. By the interrogative particles, *num*, *an*, and the enclitic, *ne*. Thus used these particles have no corresponding English word in the translation; they merely indicate a question; as, *Num venit*, or *an venit*, or *venitne?* "Has he come?" *Num vidētur?* "Does it seem?"

4th. By simply placing an interrogation mark at the end of the question; as, *Vis me hoc facere?* "Do you wish me to do this?"

57. The interrogative pronoun or adverb, in all cases, is translated before the verb; as,

1. *Quis fecit?*	*Who* did it? or *who* has done it?
2. *Quem misit?*	*Whom* did he send?
3. *Quanto constĭtit?*	*How much* did it cost?
4. *Qualis fuit?*	*What sort of* a man was he?

This is true also of the indirect question; i. e., when the substance of a question is stated but not in the interrogative form; as,

5. *Nescio quanto constitĕrit,*	I know not *how much* it cost.
6. *Docuit quam firma res esset concordia,*	He showed them *how* firm a thing agreement was.

Note. When the verb in the direct or indirect question comes under 319, R. V., the predicate, or nominative *after* the verb, is translated *first*, and the subject or nominative, in the direct question after the verb, as in Ex. 4; but in the indirect, before it, as in Ex. 6. Thus, in Ex. 4, *qualis* is the predicate, and *ille* understood, the subject; in Ex. 6, *res* is the predicate, and *concordia* the subject.

58. In all forms of interrogation not made by an interrogative pronoun, as in No. 57, the nominative or subject is translated *after the verb* in English, in the simple forms, and *after the first auxiliary* in the compound forms; as,

1. *Videsne?*	Seest *thou?* or dost *thou* see?
2. *An Venisti?*	Hast *thou* come? or have *you* come?
3. *Scribetne?*	Will *he* write?
4. *Num ibĭmus?*	Shall *we* go?
5. *Nonne fecit?*	Has *he* not done (it)?

6. *An egisset melius?* — Would *he* have done better?
7. *Nosne alēmus?* — Shall *we* support?
8. *Nonne Dei est?* — Does *it* not belong to God?
9. *Iste est frater?* — Is *that* your brother?

59. When a sentence not interrogative is introduced by *nec* or *neque*, not followed by a corresponding conjunction, (See No. 124,) in a connected clause, the verb will be translated by an auxiliary, and the English nominative will stand after the first auxiliary; as,

1. *Neque hoc intellĭgo,* — Neither do *I* understand this.
2. *Nec venisset,* — Neither would *he* have come.
3. *Nec adeptus sum,* — Nor have *I* attained.

The object of the verb.

60. In translating, the object of a transitive verb in the accusative is arranged after the verb, and as near to it as possible. That object may be a *noun*, a *pronoun*, an *infinitive*, or *a clause of a sentence*, (439); as,

1. *Romŭlus condĭdit urbem,* — Romulus built a *city*.
2. *Vocāvit eam Romam,* — He called *it* Rome.
3. *Disce dicĕre vera,* — Learn to *speak the truth*.
4. *Obtŭlit ut captīvos redimĕrent,* — He offered *that they should redeem the captives*.

61. The interrogative or relative pronoun is always translated *before* the verb that governs it; as,

1. *Quem mittēmus?* — *Whom* shall we send?
2. *Cui dedisti?* — To *whom didst* thou give it?
3. *Deus quem colĭmus,* — God *whom* we worship.
4. *Cui omnia debēmus,* — To *whom* we owe all things.

62. When a transitive verb governs two cases, the immediate object in the accusative, according to the natural order, is usually translated first, and after that the remote object in the genitive, § 122; dative, § 123; accusative, § 124; or ablative, § 125; as,

1. *Arguit me furti,* — He accuses *me* of theft.
2. *Compăro Virgilium Homēro,* — I compare *Virgil* to Homer.
3. *Poscĭmus te pacem,* — We beg *peace* of thee.
4. *Onĕrat naves auro,* — He loads the *ships* with gold.

Note. The accusative of the person after verbs of asking, is translated by *of*, or *from;* as,

5. *Pyrrhum auxilium poposcĕrunt,* — They demanded aid *of* (or *from*) Pyrrhus.

63. But when the remote object is a *relative*, or when the immediate object is an *infinitive*, or a clause of a sentence, or a noun further described by other words, the remote object must be translated first; as,

1. *Cui librum dedĭmus,*	*To whom* we gave the book.
2. *Da mihi fallĕre,*	Give *me* to deceive.
" *Dixit ei, confiteor meum peccātum,*	He said *to him,* I confess my fault.
3. *Eum rogavērunt, ut ipsos defendĕret,*	They entreated *him,* that he would defend them.
4. *Docuit illos quam firma esset,*	He showed *them* how firm it was.
5. *Civitātem, antea solicitātam, armis ornat,*	He supplies *with arms,* the city already excited.

64. When a verb, which in the active voice governs two cases, is used in the passive form, that which was the immediate object in the accusative, becomes the subject in the nominative; and the remote object in its own case immediately follows the verb. Thus, the examples No. 62, may be arranged and translated as follows, § 126.

1. *Arguor furti,*	*I* am accused of theft.
2. *Virgilius comparātur Homēro,*	*Virgil* is compared to Homer.
3. *Pax poscĭtur te,*	*Peace* is begged of thee.
4. *Naves onerantur auro,*	*The ships* are loading with gold.

So also the participles

5. *Accusātus furti,*	Accused *of theft.*
6. *Comparātus Homēro,*	Compared *to Homer.*
7. *Onerāta auro,*	Loaded *with gold.*
8. *Nudāta homĭnĭbus,*	Stripped *of men.*
9. *Erĕptus morti,*	Saved *from death.*

Impersonal Verbs.

65. The impersonal verb has no nominative before it in Latin. It is translated by placing the pronoun *it* before it in English; as, (223, 2.)

1. *Decet,*	*It* becomes.	4. *Pugnātur,*	*It* is fought.
2. *Constat,*	*It* is evident.	5. *Itur,*	*It* is gone.
3. *Tonat,*	*It* thunders.	6. *Currĭtur,*	*It* is run.

66. Impersonal verbs governing the dative or accusative in Latin, may be translated in a personal form by making the word in the dative or accusative the nominative to the English verb, taking care always to express the same idea (223, 6, and § 113); thus,

	Impersonally.	*Personally.*
1. *Placet mihi,*	It pleases *me;*	*I* am pleased.
2. *Licet tibi,*	It is permitted to *you;*	*You* are permitted.
3. *Decet eum,*	It becomes *him;*	*He* ought.
4. *Pudet nos,*	It shames *us;*	*We* are ashamed.
5. *Tædet vos,*	It wearies *you;*	*You* are wearied.
6. *Favĕtur, illis,*	Favor is done to *them;*	*They* are favored.
7. *Nocĕtur hosti,*	Hurt is done *to the enemy;*	The *enemy* is hurt.
8. *Misĕret me tui,*	It moves *me* to pity of you;	*I* pity you.
9. *Pœnĭtet eos,*	It repents *them;*	*They* repent.
10. *Pœnitet me peccâsse,*	It repents *me,* that I have sinned;	*I* repent of having sinned.

67. When the doer of an action denoted by an impersonal verb, or by a passive verb used impersonally, is expressed by the ablative with *a*, (223, 6,) the verb may be translated personally in the active voice, and the doer, in the ablative, be made its English subject or nominative; as,

	Impersonally.	*Personally.*
1. *Pugnătur a me,*	It is fought by *me;*	*I* fight.
2. *Currĭtur a te,*	It is run by *thee;*	*Thou* runnest.
3. *Favĕtur a nobis,*	It is favored by *us;*	*We* favor.
4. *Favĕtur tibi a nobis,*	It is favored to you by *us;*	*We* favor you; *or,* you are favored by *us.*

Note. The doer in the ablative with *a*, is frequently understood, (especially when no definite person or thing is intended,) and must be supplied as the context requires; as,

5. *Ubi perventum est (ab illis,)*	When it was come by them, i. e., when they came.
6. *Descendĭtur (ab hominĭbus,)*	Men (or people,) go down.
7. *Conveniebătur (ab hominĭbus,)*	People assembled.

68. Some verbs, not impersonal, are used impersonally, when used before the infinitive of impersonal verbs, (411,); as,

	Impersonally.	*Personally.*
1. *Potest credi tibi,*	*It can* be trusted to you;	You *can* be trusted; 66, 2.
2. *Non potest nocĕri hosti,*	*It cannot* be hurt to the enemy;	The enemy *cannot* be hurt; 66, 7.
3. *Ut fĭĕri solet,*	As *it is wont* to be done; or, As is usual.	

69. Verbs usually impersonal are sometimes used personally, and have their subject in the nominative, (412,); as,

1. *Doleo*, I grieve, (Impersonally, *Dolet mĭhi*,) It grieves me.
2. *Candĭda pax homĭnes decet*, Candid *peace becomes* men.
3. *Ista gestamĭna nostros humĕros decent*, These *arms become* my shoulders.

Usage of Videor, "*I seem.*"

70. *Videor*, "I seem," though never impersonal in Latin, is often rendered impersonally in English; and the dative following it, seems properly to come under 528, Rule XXXIII. to denote the person to whom any thing seems or appears, i. e., by whom it is seen; thus, *Videor tibi esse pauper*, I seem to you, (i. e., I am seen by you,) to be poor. *Videor mihi esse pauper*, I seem to myself, (i. e., I am seen by myself,) to be poor; or, I think that I am poor. So the following:

1. *Videor esse liber*,	I seem to be free; or, *It seems* that I am free.
2. *Videor mihi esse liber*,	I seem to myself to be free; or, *It seems* to me, (or, I think) that I am free.
3. *Vidēris esse*,	You seem to be; or, *It seems* that you are.
4. *Vidēris tibi esse*,	You seem to yourself to be; or, *It seems* to you, (i. e., you think) that you are.
5. *Vidēris mihi esse*,	You seem to me to be; or, *It seems* to me, (i. e., I think) that you are.
6. *Tu, ut vidēris, non scribis*,	You, as you seem, (or, as *it seems*) do not write.

Obs. The third person singular of *videor* followed by an infinitive, with its subject in the accusative, or by a dependent clause after *ut*, or *quod*, may be said to be used impersonally; though, strictly speaking, that infinitive with its accusative, or that clause, is the subject, (See No. 51,); as,

7. *Vidētur mihi te valēre*,	It appears to me that you are well; strictly rendered, That you are well appears to (or, is seen by) me.
8. *Illi vidētur ut valeat*,	It appears to him, (or, he thinks,) that he (*another person*) is well.
9. *Vidētur sibi valēre*,	It appears to him, (or, he thinks,) that he (*himself*) is well. He seems to himself to be well.

Verbs.—Indicative Mood.

71. Verbs in the indicative mood are translated as in the paradigm in the Grammar. Care must be taken, however, to notice when the sense requires the *simple*, or *emphatic*, or *progressive* form.

72. When the perfect tense expresses a past action or event extending to, or connected with the present, in itself or in its consequences, it is used *definitely*, and must be rendered by the auxiliaries, *have*, *hast*, *has*, or *hath;* as,

1. *Regem* vidi *hodie,*	I *have seen* the king to-day.

73. When the perfect tense expresses a past action or event, without reference to the present, it is used *indefinitely*, (Gr. 163,) and can not be rendered by *have*, *hast*, *has*, or *hath;* as,

1. *Regem* vidi *nuper,*	I *saw* the king lately.

Subjunctive Mood.

The subjunctive mood is used in two different ways, viz.: *subjunctively* and *potentially*. (Gr. § 42, II. and §§ 139–141.)

Subjunctive used Subjunctively.

74. This mood is used subjunctively, but for the most part translated as the indicative, when it expresses what is actual and certain, though not directly asserted as such. This it does,

1st. When it is subjoined to some adverb, conjunction, or indefinite term in a dependent clause, for the purpose of stating the existence of a thing, (without directly asserting it), as something supposed, taken for granted, or connected with the direct assertion as a cause, condition, or modifying circumstance, (631,); as,

1. *Ea cum ita* sint *discēdam,*	Since these things *are* so, I will depart.
2. *Si* madeat,	If it is *wet.*
3. *Quum Cæsar* redīret,	When Cæsar *returned—was returning.*
4. *Ita perterrĭtus est ut* morirĕtur,	He was so frightened that *he died.*
5. *Gratŭlor tibi quod* redi*ĕ*ris,	I am glad that you *have returned.*

6. *Si imperitavĕrint,*	If they *have commanded.*
7. *Si reliquissem, iniqui dicĕrent,*	If I *had left* him, &c.
8. *Quum Cæsar profectus esset,*	When Cæsar *had departed.*

Obs. In the first of the above examples, the direct assertion is *discēdam,* "I will depart." The dependent clause, *ea cum ita sint,* "since these things are so," expresses the existence of certain things referred to without directly asserting it, but taking it for granted as a thing admitted or supposed, but still affecting in some way the event directly asserted. This holds good of all the other examples above.

The dependent clause connected by *ut,* or *ubi,* "when;" *dum,* "whilst;" *priusquam,* "before;" *postquam,* "after;" and other conjunctions, (629 and 630,); and also by *quum* or *cum,* "when," (631), sometimes take the indicative mood.

2d. The subjunctive mood is used subjunctively, as above, after an interrogative word used indefinitely, in a dependent clause, or in what is called the *indirect* question, i. e., an expression containing the substance of a question without the form. All interrogative words may be used in this way, (See 627, 5,); thus,

9. *Nescio quis sit—quid fiat,*	I know not *who* he *is—what is doing.*
10. *Doce me ubi sint dii,*	Tell me *where* the gods *are.*
11. *Nescio uter scribĕret,*	I know not *which* of the two *wrote.*
12. *Nescio quid scriptum esset,*	I know not *what was written.*
13. *Scio cui, (a quo) scriptum esset,*	I know *to whom (by whom)* it *was written.*
14. *An scis quis hoc fecĕrit?*	Do you know *who has done* this?
15. *An scis a quo hoc factum fuĕrit?*	Do you know *by whom* this *has been done?*
16. *Nemo sciēbat quis hæc fecisset,*	None knew *who had done* these things.
17. *Percunctātus quid vellet,*	Having enquired *what* he *wished.*

Note. The direct question requires the indicative; as, *Quis fēcit?* "Who *did* it?" The indirect requires the subjunctive; as, *Nescio quis fecĕrit,* "I know not who *did* it."

75. This mood is used subjunctively, and usually translated as the indicative in a relative clause, after an indefinite general expression (636), a negation, or a question implying

a negation; and also after the relative in oblique narration, (650,); as,

1. *Est qui dicat,*	There is one who *says*.
2. *Nullus est qui neget,*	There is no one who *denies*.
3. *Quis est qui hoc faciat,*	Who is there that *does* this?
4. *Antonius inquit, artem esse eārum rerum quæ sciantur,*	Antonius says that art belongs to those things which *are known*.

The Subjunctive used Potentially.

76. The subjunctive mood is used *potentially;* 1st, in interrogative sentences; and 2d, to express a thing not as actual and certain, but contingent and hypothetical, (Gr. 142, 2d, and 143). Thus used, it is much less definite with respect to time, and is translated with some variety; as follows:

1. *Present,* by *may, can, shall, will, could, would, should.*
2. *Imperfect,* by *might, could, would,* or *should.*
3. *Perfect,* by *may have, can have, must have, &c.*
4. *Pluperfect,* by *might have, could have, would have, should have;* and, denoting futurity, *should.*

The most usual renderings of each tense are the following:

77. *Present.* The present subjunctive used potentially, expresses present liberty, power, will, or obligation, usually expressed by the English auxiliaries, *may, can, shall, will, could, would, should.* (§ 45, I.)

1. *Licet eas,*	You *may go*.
2. *An sic intelligat?*	*Can* he so *understand* it?
3. *Men' moveat cimex Pantilius?*	*Shall* (or *should*) the insect Pantilius *discompose* me?
4. *Quis istos ferat?*	Who *could bear* those men?
5. *Si hic sis, aliter sentias*	If you were here, you *would think* otherwise.

Imperatively.

6. *Sic eat,*	Thus *let her* (or *him*) *go*.
7. *Eāmus,*	*Let us go.*
8. *Pugnētur, (Impersonally,)*	*Let it be fought.*
9. *Dii faciant,*	*May* the gods *grant*.

78. *Imperfect.* The imperfect subjunctive used potentially, is preceded by a past tense, and expresses *past* liberty, power, will, or duty, but still in its use expresses time very indefinitely. It is usually rendered by the English auxiliaries,

might, could, would, should; sometimes *had, would have, should have;* as,

1. *Legēbat ut discĕret,* He read that he *might learn.*
2. *Quid facĕrem,* What *could* I *do?*
3. *Iret si jubēres,* He *would go* if you *should order* it.
4. *Cur venīret,* Why *should* he *come.*
5. *Rogavērunt ut venīret,* They entreated that he *would come.*
6. *Si quis dicĕret, nunquam putārem,* If any one *had said* it, I *would* not *have thought* it.

Note. After verbs denoting to hinder, forbid, and the like, *quo minus* with the subjunctive, may be rendered by *from* and the present participle, (172, 3,); thus,

7. *Impedīvit quo minus iret,* He hindered him *from going.*

Obs. An action or state which would, or would not exist, or have existed, in a case supposed, but the contrary of which is implied, is expressed in Latin by the imperfect or pluperfect subjunctive, without an antecedent verb or conjunction, 625, 4th. (See An. & Pr. Eng. Gr. 864,); as,

8. *Scribĕrem, si necesse esset,* I *would write,* if it were necessary.
9. *Scripsissem, si necesse fuisset,* I *would have written,* had it been necessary.

79. *Perfect.* The perfect subjunctive properly expresses what is supposed to be past, but of which there exists uncertainty. Thus used it is commonly rendered by the auxilaries, *may have, can have,* &c. It is also used sometimes in a present and sometimes in a future sense, with much variety of meaning, according to its connection, (§ 45, III.); as,

1. *Fortasse erravĕrim,* Perhaps I *may have erred.*
2. *Etsi non scripsĕrit,* Though he *cannot have written.*
3. *Ut sic dixĕrim,* That I *may* so *speak.*
4. *Citius credidĕrim,* I *would* sooner *believe.*
5. *Facĭle dixĕrim,* I *could* easily *tell.*
6. *Quasi affuĕrim,* As if I *had been present.*

80. *Pluperfect.* The pluperfect (§ 45, IV.) is usually rendered by the auxiliaries, *might have, could have, would have, should have,* as in the paradigm of the verb. But when an action is related as having been future at a certain past time, it is expressed in Latin in the pluperfect subjunctive, and translated *should;* as,

1. *Quodcunque jussisset me factūrum dixi,* I said that I would do whatsoever he *should order.*

2. *Promisisti te scriptūrum, si rogavissem,*	You promised that you would write, if I *should desire* it.
3. *Dum convaluisset,*	Until he *should get well.*

81. the pluperfect subjunctive active, with *quum*, in verbs not deponent, is used instead of a past participle active, (182, 8,) and may be rendered by the compound perfect participle in English; as,

1. *Cæsar, quum hæc dixisset,*	Cæsar *having said* these things; (literally, Cæsar, when he had said these things.)

82. When the subjunctive has a relative for its subject, and the relative and antecedent clause involve a comparison, they may be rendered as in No. 40; or the sense will be expressed if we render the relative by *as*, and the subjunctive by the infinitive; thus,

1. *Quis tam esset amens qui semper vivĕret,*	Who would be so foolish *as to live* always.
2. *Neque tu is es qui nescias,*	You are not such a one *as* not *to know.*

83. When the relative and subjunctive follow such adjectives as *dignus*, *indignus*, *idoneus*, (643, Obs. 5.) and the like; or when they express the end or design of something expressed in the antecedent clause, their meaning will be expressed as in No. 40, or by the infinitive alone, or preceded by the phrase "in order to;" thus,

1. *Dignum qui secundus ab Romŭlo numerētur,*	Worthy *to be ranked* next after Romulus.
2. *Legatos misērunt qui eum accusārent,*	They sent legates *to accuse* (or, *in order to accuse*) him.
3. *Virgas iis dedit quibus agĕrent,*	He gave them rods *to drive, (in order to drive;* or, *so that with these they might drive.)*

84. The subjunctive with or without *ut*, after verbs signifying to *bid, forbid, tell, allow, hinder, command,* and the like, (627, 1, 3d, and 632,) may be rendered by the English infinitive preceded by the subject of the verb in the objective case; as,

1. *Precor venias,*	I pray *that you may come;* i. e., I pray *you to come.*
2. *Dic veniat,*	Tell *her to come.*
3. *Sine eat,*	Permit *him to go.*
4. *Non patiĕris ut eant,*	You will not suffer *them to go.*
5. *Non patiĕris ut vescāmur,*	You do not suffer *us to eat.*

85. When several verbs in the same mood and tense, have the same nominative, and are connected in the same construction, the *auxiliary* and "*to*," the sign of the infinitive, in the translation is used with the first only, and understood to the rest; as,

1. *Et vidisset et audivisset,*	He might have both seen and heard.
2. *Et visus et audĭtus esset,*	He might have been both seen and heard.
3. *Cupĭmus et vidēre et audīre,*	We wish both to see and hear.

The Infinitive Mood.

86. When the infinitive is without a subject, it is to be considered as a verbal noun, (659,) and translated as in the paradigm of the verb; as,

1. *Volo scribĕre,*	I wish *to write.*
2. *Dicĭtur didicisse,*	He is said *to have learned.*
3. *Dicĭtur itūrus esse,*	He is said *to be about to go.*
4. *Dicĭtur itūrus fuisse,*	He is said *to have been about to go.*

87. When the verbs *possum, volo, nolo, malo,* in the indicative or subjunctive, are translated by the English auxiliaries, *can, will, will not, will rather,* and sometimes, in the past tense, by *could, would,* &c., the infinitive following is translated without *to* before it; as,

1. *Potest fiĕri,*	It can *be done.*
2. *Volo ire,*	I will *go.*
3. *Nolo facĕre,*	I will not *do* it.
4. *Malo facĕre,*	I will rather *do* it.
5. *Ut se volucrem facĕre vellet,*	That he would *make* her a bird.
6. *Nihil jam defendi potuit,*	Nothing could now *be defended.*
7. *Hoc facĕre non potuit,*	He could not *do this.*
8. *Nolīte timēre,*	Do not *fear.*

88. The present infinitive is generally translated as the perfect without "to," after the imperfect, perfect or pluperfect tense of *possum, volo, nolo, malo,* when translated *could, would, would not, would rather;* and with "to" after the same tenses of *debeo* and *oportet,* translated *ought;* as,

1. *Melius fiĕri non potuit,*	It could not *have been done* better.
2. *Volui dicĕre,*	I would *have said.*
3. *Sumĕre arma noluit,*	He would not *have taken* arms.
4. *Maluit augēre,*	He would rather *have increased.*
5. *Quam potuisset edĕre,*	Than he could *have caused.*
6. *Debuisti mihi ignoscĕre,*	You ought *to have pardoned* me.
7. *Divĭdi oportuit,*	It ought *to have been divided.*

Note. A strictly literal translation of most of the above sentences would not express the precise idea intended; thus, in the third sentence, "He would not have taken arms," and "He was not willing to take arms," manifestly do not mean the same thing.

89. After verbs denoting to *see*, *hear*, *feel*, and the like, the present infinitive is often translated by the English present participle; as,

1. *Audīvi eum dicĕre,*	I heard him *saying.*
2. *Surgĕre videt lunam,*	He sees the moon *rising.*
3. *Terram tremĕre sensit,*	He felt the earth *trembling.*

Obs. So also when the infinitive alone, or as part of a clause, is the subject of another verb; as,

4. *Morāri periculōsum est,*	Delaying *is dangerous.*
5. *Morāri periculōsum (esse) arbitrantur,*	They think that *delaying* is dangerous.

The Infinitive with a subject.

90. The infinitive with its subject in the accusative, though but seldom, is sometimes translated in the same form in English; as,

1. *Cupio te venīre,*	I wish *you to come.*
2. *Quos discordāre novĕrat,*	*Whom* he had known *to differ.*
3. *Hoc optĭmum esse judicāvit,*	He decided *this to be* the best.
4. *Eum vocāri jussit,*	He ordered *him to be* called.

91. The infinitive with a subject, usually is, and always may be, translated by the English indicative or potential, according to the sense intended. When so rendered, its subject must always be translated in the nominative; and this, if not a relative, is usually preceded by the conjunction *that*, (§ 145,); as,

1. *Cupio te venīre,*	I wish *that you would come.*
2. *dicit me scribĕre,*	He says *that I write.*
3. *Eos ivisse putābat,*	He thought *that they had gone.*
4. *Quem nunquam risisse ferunt,*	*Who* they say never *laughed.*
5. *Rogāvit quid faciendum (esse) putāret,*	He asked *what* he thought *ought to be done.*

92. Both the Latin and the English infinitive, by their tenses, represent an act, &c., as present, past or future, *at the time of the governing verb.* Hence, when the one is translated by the other; that is, the Latin infinitive by the English infinitive, (Nos. 86 and 90,) any tense of the one

will be correctly translated by the same tense in the other, (except as in No. 88,) no matter what be the tense of the governing verb; as,

		Pres.	Past.	Future.
1. Pres. *Dicĭtur,*		*habēre;*	*habuisse;*	*habitūrus esse.*
2. Past, *Dicebātur,*				
3. Fut. *Dicētur,*				

1. Pres. He is said,	to have;	to have had;	to be about to have.
2. Past, He was said,			
3. Fut. He will be said,			

93. But when the Latin infinitive, with its subject, is translated by the English *indicative* or *potential*, the tense used in these moods must be that which will correctly express the time of the act expressed by the Latin infinitive as estimated, not from the time of the governing verb, as in Latin, but as estimated from the present. That is, events present at the same time, or past at the same time, will be expressed in English by the same tense; an event represented in Latin as prior to the present time, (perfect infinitive after the present tense,) will be expressed by the English imperfect or perfect indefinite; and an event represented in Latin as prior to a past event, (perfect infinitive after a past tense,) will be expressed by the English pluperfect; thus,

1. Pres. *Dicunt eum* v e n ī r e,	They say *that* he *is coming*, or *comes*.
2. Past, *Dixērunt eum* v e n ī r e,	They said *that* he *came*.
3. Pres. *Dicunt eum* v e n i s s e,	They say *that* he *came*.
4. Past, *Dixērunt eum* v e n i s s e,	They said *that* he *had come*.
5. Past, *Cœpērunt suspicāri illam* v e n ī r e,	They began to suspect *that* she *came*.

Note. The infinitive after the future does not follow this analogy, but is always translated in its own tense; as,

	Pres.	Perf.	Future.
6.	*Dicent eum* v e n ī r e,	v e n i s s e,	v e n t ū r u m e s s e.
	They will say that he *comes*,	*has come*,	*will come*.

94. 1. Present, past, and future time, are variously expressed as follows:

1st. *Present time* is expressed by the *present tense*, and generally by the *perfect definite*.

2d. *Past time* is expressed by the *imperfect*, *perfect indefinite*, and *pluperfect*,—by the *perfect participle*,—the *present infinitive after a past tense*,—the *present tense used to express a past event*, 157, 3,—and by the *present partici-*

ple, agreeing with the subject of the governing verb in any of these tenses, 182, 5.

3d. Future time is expressed by the *future* and *future perfect.*

2. The infinitive of deponent verbs, is translated in the same manner as the infinitive active in the following examples in Nos. 95 to 100.

3. After verbs denoting to *promise, request, advise, command*, and the like, implying a reference to something future, the present infinitive, with its subject, is usually translated as the future, by *should*, or *would*, (See No. 100, 1, 2, 3, 7, 8, 9,); as, *Jussit, eos per castra duci*, He ordered that they *should be led* through the camp.

4. The Latin words for "*he said*," "*saying*," or the like, introducing an oblique narration, are often omitted, and the infinitive takes the form of translation corresponding to the *time* expressed by the word to be supplied.

From these principles are deduced the following directions for translating the infinitive with a subject.

Present Infinitive after Present or Future Time.

95. Direction I. When the preceding verb is in the *present*, the *perfect* used indefinitely, or *future tense*, the present infinitive is translated as the present; as,

Active Voice.

1. *Dico eum laudāre*, I say that he *praises*.
2. *Dixi eum laudāre*, I have said that he *praises*.
3. *Dicam eum laudāre*, I will say that he *praises*.

Passive Voice.

1. *Dico eum laudāri*, I say that he *is praised*.
2. *Dixi eum laudāri*, I have said that he *is praised*.
3. *Dicam eum laudāri*, I will say that he *is praised*.

Present Infinitive after Past Time.

96. Direction II. When the preceding verb is in the *imperfect, perfect indefinite*, or *pluperfect*, or in the *present infinitive after a past tense*, the present infinitive is translated as the imperfect, or perfect indefinite; as,

Present Infinitive Active.

1. *Dicēbam eum laudāre,* I said that he *praised.*
2. *Dixi eum laudāre,* I said that he *praised.*
3. *Dixĕram eum laudāre,* I had said that he *praised.*
4. *Cœpi dicĕre eum laudāre,* I began to say that he *praised.*

Present Infinitive Passive.

5. *Dicēbam eum laudāri,* I said that he *was praised.*
6. *Dixi eum laudāri,* I said that he *was praised.*
7. *Dixĕram eum laudāri,* I had said that he *was praised.*
8. *Cœpi dicĕre eum laudāri,* I began to say that he *was praised.*

EXC. 1. When the present infinitive expresses that which is always true, it must be translated in the *present,* after any tense, 157, 1; as,

9. *Doctus erat Deum gubernāre mundum,* He had been taught that God *governs* the world.

EXC. II. When the present infinitive expresses an act subsequent to the time of the governing verb, it is translated after any tense, by the potential with *should; would;* as,

10. *Jubet* } *te ire,* He orders } that you *should go.*
11. *Jussit* } *te ire,* He ordered } that you *should go.*
12. *Jussĕrat* } *te ire,* He had ordered } that you *should go.*

Perfect Infinitive after Present or Future Time.

97. DIRECTION III. When the preceding verb is in the *present, perfect definite,* or *future tense,* the perfect infinitive is translated as the imperfect or perfect indefinite; as,

Active Voice.

1. *Dico eum laudavisse,* I say that he *praised.*
2. *Dixi eum laudavisse,* I have said that he *praised.*
3. *Dicam eum laudavisse,* I will say that he *praised.*

Passive Voice.

4. *Dico eum laudātum esse,* I say that he *was praised.*
5. *Dixi eum laudātum esse,* I have said that he *was praised.*
6. *Dicam eum laudātum esse,* I will say that he *was praised.*

7. *Dico eum laudātum fuisse,* I say that he *has been praised.*
8. *Dixi eum laudātum fuisse,* I have said that he *has been praised.*
9. *Dicam eum laudātum fuisse,* I will say that he *has been praised.*

Perfect Infinitive after Past Tenses.

98. DIRECTION IV. When the preceding verb is in the *imperfect*, *perfect indefinite*, or *pluperfect*, or in the *present infinitive after a past tense*, the perfect infinitive is translated as the pluperfect; as,

Active Voice.

1. *Dicēbam eum* laudavisse,	I said that he *had praised.*
2. *Dixi eum* laudavisse,	I said that he *had praised.*
3. *Dixĕram eum* laudavisse,	I had said that he *had praised.*
4. *Cœpi dicĕre eum* laudavisse,	I began to say that he *had praised.*

Passive Voice.

5. *Dicēbam eum* laudātum esse,	I said that he *had been praised.*
6. *Dixi eum* laudātum esse,	I said that he *had been praised.*
7. *Dixĕram eum* laudātum esse,	I had said that he *had been praised.*
8. *Cœpi dicĕre eum* laudātum esse,	I began to say that he *had been praised.*
9. *Dicēbam eum* laudātum *fu*isse,	I said that he *had been praised.*
10. *Dixi eum* laudātum *fuisse*,	I said that he *had been praised.*
11. *Dixĕram eum* laudātum *fu*isse,	I had said that he *had been praised.*
12. *Cœpi dicĕre eum* laudātum *fuisse*,	I began to say that he *had been praised.*

Future Infinitive after the Present Tense.

99. DIRECTION V. When the preceding verb is in the *present*, or *perfect definite*, or *future tense*, the future infinitive with *esse* is translated as the future indicative; and with *fuisse*, by *would have*, or *should have*, in the pluperfect potential in a future sense; and *fore*, for *futūrum esse*, is translated by *will be.*

Active Voice.

1. *Dico eum* laudatūrum esse,	I say that he *will praise.*
2. *Dixi eum* laudatūrum esse,	I have said that he *will praise.*
3. *Dicam eum* laudatūrum esse,	I will say that he *will praise.*
4. *Dico eum* laudatūrum *fu*isse,	I say that he *would have praised.*
5. *Dixi eum* laudatūrum *fu*isse,	I have said that he *would have praised.*
6. *Dicam eum* laudatūrum *fu*isse,	I will say that he *would have praised.*

Passive Voice.

7. *Dico eum laudātum iri,* — I say that he *will be praised.*
8 *Dixi eum laudātum iri,* — I have said that he *will be praised.*
9. *Dicam eum laudātum iri,* — I will say that he *will be praised.*

Future Infinitive after Past Tenses.

100. DIRECTION VI. When the preceding verb is of the *imperfect*, *perfect indefinite*, or *pluperfect*, the future of the infinitive with *esse* is rendered by *would* or *should;* and with *fuisse*, by *would have*, and *should have;* and *fore*, for *futūrum esse*, after any past tense, by *would be;* as,

Active Voice.

1. *Dicēbam eum laudatūrum esse,* — I said that he *would praise.*
2. *Dixi eum laudatūrum, &c.,* — I said that he *would praise.*
3. *Dixĕram eum laudatūrum, &c.* — I had said that he *would praise.*
4. *Dicēbam eum laudatūrum fuisse,* — I said that he *would have praised.*
5. *Dixi eum laudatūrum, &c.,* — I said that he *would have praised.*
6. *Dixĕram eum laudatūrum fuisse,* — I had said that he *would have praised.*

Passive Voice.

7. *Dicēbam eum laudātum iri,* — I said that he *would be praised.*
8. *Dixi eum laudātum iri,* — I said that he *would be praised.*
9. *Dixĕram eum laudātum iri,* — I had said that he *would be praised.*
10. *Dicēbam (dixi) eum fore tutum,* — I said that he *would be* safe.

Usage of Fore.

Obs. Fore is used for *futurum esse*, and, with a subject after present tenses, means "*will be;*" after past tenses, "*would be.*" Both of them when followed by a subjunctive with *ut*, (678,) after a present tense, may be translated by the future indicative of that verb; and after a past tense, by the imperfect potential; as,

11 *Credo eum fore tutum,* — I believe that he *will be* safe.
12. *Credēbam* or *credĭdi, (credidĕram) eum fore tutum,* — I believed, (had believed) that he *would* be safe.
13. *Credo fore* (or *futūrum esse*) *ut discas,* — I believe that you *will learn.*
14. *Credēbam* or *credĭdi (credidĕram) fore* (or *futūrum esse*) *ut discĕres,* — I believed, (had believed) that you *would learn.* (lit. *it would be that you would learn.*)

Participles.

101. Participles are usually translated after their nouns, as in the paradigms of the verb; thus,

1. Present active,	*Homo carens fraude,*	A man *wanting* guile.
2. Future active,	*Homo scriptūrus,*	A man *about to write.*
3. Perfect passive,	*Vita bene acta,*	A life well *spent.*
4. ———— ————,	*Cæsar coactus,*	Cæsar *being* (or *having been*) *compelled.*
5. (Deponent,)	*Cæsar regressus,*	Cæsar *having returned.*
6. Future passive,	*Mala vitanda,*	Evils *to be avoided,* i. e., which ought to be avoided.

Exc. But when a participle is used as an adjective, (182, 3,) it is translated, like the adjective, before its substantive; as,

7. *Tigrin ostendit mansuefactam,* He exhibited a *tamed tiger.*
8. *In ferventĭbus arēnis insistens,* Standing on the *burning sands.*

Future Participle Active.

102. When the future participle active is used to express a *purpose, end, or design* of another action, (685,) it is rendered by "to," or the phrase "in order to," instead of "about to;" as,

1. *Pergit consultūrus oracŭla,* He goes *to consult* (or, *in order to consult*) the oracle.

Obs. The present participle is also sometimes used in this sense; as,

2. *Venērunt postulantes cibum,* They came *to* (or, *in order to*) *ask* food.

Perfect Participle Passive.

103. As the Latin verb has no perfect participle in the active sense (except in deponent verbs), its place is usually supplied by the perfect participle passive in the case absolute, (692,); thus, "Cæsar having consulted his friends," rendered into Latin, will be, *Cæsar, amīcis consultis,* literally, "Cæsar, *his friends being consulted.*" Hence,

104. When the action expressed passively by the perfect participle in the case absolute, or agreeing with the object of a verb, is something done by the subject of the leading verb in

the sentence, the participle is rendered more in accordance with English idiom, by the perfect participle in the active voice in English, agreeing with the subject of the verb, and followed by its noun in the objective case (182, 8, and 692,); thus,

1. *Cæsar* *his dictis*, *profectus est*, translated in the
   Latin idiom, Cæsar, *these things being said*, departed.
   English idiom, Cæsar, *having said these things*, departed.
2. *Opĕre peracto*, *ludēmus*,
   Latin idiom, *Our work being finished*, we will play.
   English idiom, *Having finished our work*, we will play.
3. *Pythiam ad se vocātum pecuniā instruxit*,
   Latin idiom, He supplied with money Pythias *being called* to him.
   English idiom, *Having called* Pythias to him, he supplied him with money.

105. The perfect participle of deponent verbs having an active signification, accords with the English idiom, and is best translated literally; as,

1. *Nactus navicŭlum*, — *Having found* a boat.
2. *Cohortātus exercĭtum*, — *Having exhorted* the army.

106. When the perfect participle of deponent or common verbs, expresses an act nearly or entirely contemporaneous with the leading verb, it may be translated by the English present participle in *ing*, (182, 5, Note,); as,

1. *Rex hoc facĭnus mirātus juvĕnem dimīsit*, — The king, *admiring* this act, dismissed the youth.
1. *Columba delapsa refert sagittam*, — The dove *falling* brings back the arrow.

The Future Participle Passive.

107. After verbs signifying *to give, to deliver, to agree* or *bargain for; to have, to receive, to undertake*, and the like, the participle in *dus* generally denotes *design* or *purpose*, and is rendered simply as in the paradigm, or with the phrase "in order to," prefixed (686,); as,

1. *Testamentum tibi tradit legendum*, — He delivers his will to you *to* (or *in order to*) *be read*.
2. *Attribuit nos trucidandos Cethēgo*, — He has given us over to Cethegus *(in order) to be slain*.

108. The participle in *dus*, especially when agreeing with the subject of a sentence or clause, generally denotes *propriety, necessity*, or *obligation*, and is rendered variously, as the

tense of the accompanying verb and the connection require (687,); the following are examples:

1. *Legātus mittendus est,*	An ambassador *must* (or *should*) be sent.
2. *Legātus mittendus erat* or *fuit,*	An ambassador *had to be sent.*
3. *Legātus mittendus erit,*	An ambassador *will have to be sent.*
4. *Legātum mittendum esse,*	That an ambassador *should be sent.*
5. ——— *mittendum fuisse,*	——— ——— ——— *ought to* or *should have been sent.*
6. *Dissimulanda loquĭtur,*	He speaks things that *ought to be concealed.*
7. *Dissimulanda loquebātur,*	He spake things which *ought to have been concealed.*
8. *Quæ dissimulanda erunt,*	Which *will have to be concealed.*
9. *Dic, quid statuendum sit,*	Say, what is *to be* (or *must be*) *thought.*

Ablative Absolute.

109. When a participle stands with a substantive in the ablative absolute, R. LX., the substantive is translated without a sign, No. 9, and after it the participle, as in the paradigm of the verb; as,

1. *Romŭlo regnante,*	Romulus *reigning.*
2. *Hac oratione habĭtâ,*	This oration *being delivered.*
3. *Cæsăre ventūro,*	Cæsar (being) *about to come.*
4. *Præceptis tradendis,*	Rules being *to be delivered.*
5. *Bello orto,*	War *having arisen.*

Note. The future participles, Ex. 3, 4, are seldom used in the case absolute.

110. When two nouns,—a pronoun and a noun,—a noun or a pronoun and an adjective, are used in the ablative without a participle, (695,) they are translated in the nominative without a sign, and the English participle "*being,*" inserted between them; as,

1. *Adolescentŭlo duce,*	A young man *being* leader.
2. *Mario consŭle,*	Marius *being* consul.
3. *Me suasōre,*	I *being* the adviser.
4. *Annibăli vivo,*	Hannibal *being* alive.
5. *Se invīto,*	He *being* unwilling.

Gerunds and Gerundives.

111. The gerund, being a verbal noun, is translated in the

same manner as other nouns of the same case, and at the same time may govern the case of its own verb 698; as,

1. N.	*Petendum pacem,*	Seeking peace.
2. G.	*Petendi pacem*	*Of* seeking peace.
3. D.	*Utendo libris,*	*To* (or *for*) using books.
4. Ac.	*Obliviscendum injuriārum,*	Forgetting injuries.
5. Abl.	*Parendo magistratui,*	*By* obeying the magistrate.
6. Abl.	*Petendo pacem.*	*With, from, in, by* seeking peace.

112. Of verbs that govern the accusative, instead of the gerund in the oblique cases, the Latins commonly used the participle in *dus*, in the sense of the gerund, and agreeing with its object in gender, number, and case; the case being governed by the same word that would have governed the gerund. When thus used, it is called a *gerundive.* (707, R. LXII.)

Gerunds.	*Gerundives.*
1. *Ars librum* *legendi,*	5. *Ars libri legendi,* The art *of reading a book.*
2. *Utile vulnĕra curando,*	6. *Utile vulnerĭbus curandis,* Useful *for healing wounds.*
3. *Ad litĕras scribendum,*	7. *Ad litĕras scribendas,* For *writing a letter.*
4. *De captīvos commutando,*	8. *De captīvis commutandis,* Respecting *exchanging captives.*

113. When the gerund is the subject of the verb *est*, governing the dative, it implies necessity, and is variously translated into the English idiom, as the tense of the verb requires (699,); as,

Latin Idiom.	*English Idiom.*
1. *Legendum est mihi,* Reading is to me; i. e.,	I must read; I ought to read; I should read.
2. *Legendum erat (fuit) mihi,* Reading was to me;	I had to read; I ought to have read; I should have read.
3. *Legendum fuĕrat mihi,* Reading had been to me;	I had been obliged to read.
4. *Legendum erit mihi,* Reading will be to me;	I will have to read; it will be necessary for me to read.
5. *Dicit legendum esse mihi,* He says that reading is to me;	He says that I must read—ought to read—should read.
6. *Dicit legendum fuisse mihi,* He says that reading was to me;	He says that I had to read—ought to—or should—have read.

Obs. The dative is frequently omitted, and generally when it denotes persons or things, in a general or indefinite sense.

In such cases, *homĭni, hominĭbus, nobis*, or the like, must be supplied; as,

7. *Vivendum est recte, (scil. hominĭbus,)*	Living honestly is, viz.: to men; i. e. men ought to live honestly.
8. *Dicit vivendum esse recte. (scil. homĭni,)*	He says that living honestly is, viz.: to a man; i. e., a man ought to live honestly.

Supines.

114. The supines are rendered without variation, as in the paradigm, and under the rules, (§ 148,); as,

1. *Abiit deambulātum,*	He has gone *to walk.*
2. *Facĭle dictu,*	Easy *to tell,* or *to be told.*

Passive Voice.

115. The passive voice, in the indicative mood, is translated as in the paradigms. The subjunctive mood is subject to all the variety of construction and translation used in the active voice, Nos. 74–84, acting on the verb *to be*, which, as an auxiliary with the perfect participle, makes up the passive form of the verb in English.

In the compound tenses, (186, 3,) when two or more verbs in a sentence are in the same tense, and have the same nominative, or are in the same construction, the verb *sum* is commonly expressed with the last and understood to the rest, as in the following Ex. 1. But when the nominative is changed, the verb "to be" should be repeated as in Ex. 2.

1. *Nisus a Minōe victus et occīsus est,*	Nisus *was* conquered and killed by Minos.
2. *Tres naves captæ, decem demersæ, duo millia hostium capta, tredĕcim millia occīsa sunt.*	Three ships *were* taken, ten sunk; two thousand of the enemy *were* taken, thirteen thousand killed.

Passive Voice in a Middle Sense.

116. The Latin passive voice is often used to represent its subject, not as acted upon by another, but as acting on itself, or for itself, or intransitively, by its own impulse; and so corresponds in sense to the middle voice in Greek. Thus used, it is best translated by the active voice followed by the reflexive pronoun as an object, or by an intransitive verb expressing the idea intended, (136, 3.) The following are examples:

1. *Paludĭbus abdĭti sunt,*	They *concealed themselves* in the marshes.
2. *Cum omnes in omni genĕre scelĕrum volutentur,*	Since all *give themselves up* to every kind of wickedness.
3. *Fertŭr in hostes,*	*Rushes* against the enemy.
4. *Volutāti super poma,*	*Rolling themselves* over the apples.
5. *Cingĭtur armis,*	*Girds himself* with his armor.
6. *Sternuntur tumŭlo,*	*Throw themselves* on the grave.
7. *Gallus victus occultātur,*	The cock, when conquered, *hides himself.*

117. The verb *sum* governing the genitive by R. XII., 364, may generally be translated by the phrase "belongs to," "is the part," "is the property," &c. See explanation under Rule; as,

1. *Est regis,*	It *belongs to* the king.
2. *Pecus est Melibœi,*	The flock *belongs to* Melibœus.
3. *Prudentia est senectūtis,*	Prudence *is the characteristic* of old age.

118. The verb *sum,* (also *desum,*) in the third person, governing the dative by 394, Rule II., may generally be translated by the corresponding tenses of the verb "to have," with the Latin dative for its subject, and the Latin subject for its object; as,

	Latin Idiom.	*English Idiom.*
1. *Liber est mihi,*	A book is to me,	I have a book.
2. *Liber erat mihi,*	A book was to me,	I had a book.
3. *Liber fuit mihi,*	A book was (or has been) to me,	I had, or have had a book.
4. *Liber fuĕrat mihi,*	A book had been to me,	I had had a book.
5. *Liber erit mihi,*	A book will be to me,	I will have a book.
6 *Libri sunt mihi,*	Books are to me,	I have books.
7. *Est mihi,*	It is to me,	I have it.
8. *Liber deest mihi,*	A book is not to me,	I have not a book.

119. When a compound verb, rendered by the simple verb and a preposition, is followed by two cases, the simple verb with the immediate object (always in the accusative,) is usually translated first, and then the preposition with the remote object.

1. *Flumen copias transduxit,*	He *led* his forces *across* the river.
2. *Circumdăre mœnia oppĭdo,*	*To build* walls *around* the city.
3. *Caput dejēcit saxo,*	He *threw* the head *down* from the rock.

120. An adverb, adverbial phrase, or clause expressing some circumstance, in translating may often be arranged in different situations in a sentence, due regard being paid to the sense and harmony of the whole; thus, *Magna debēmus suscipĕre dum vires suppĕtunt*, may be arranged variously for translating, as follows:

1. Debēmus suscipĕre magna, *dum vires suppĕtunt*, or,
2. *Dum vires suppĕtunt*, debēmus suscipĕre magna, or,
3. Debēmus, *dum vires suppĕtunt*, suscipĕre magna.

121. The negative conjunction *ne*, is variously rendered *lest, lest that, that–not, not;* and after verbs signifying to *fear, forbid*, and the like, it is translated *that*, while *ut* in the same situation, means *that not.*

1. *Ne quis eat,*	*Lest* (or *that not*) any one may go.
2. *Orat ne se perdat,*	She entreats *that* he would *not* destroy her.
3. *Egi ne interessem,*	I managed *that* I should *not* be present.
4. *Dum ne veniat,*	Provided he do *not* come,
5. *Respondit ne cogitāta quidem latent,*	He replied *that not* even the thoughts are concealed.
6. *Vereor ne cadas,*	I am afraid *that* you may fall.
7. *Timui ut venīret,*	I feared *that* he would *not* come.

Note 1. But when the fear expressed, refers to such things *as we wish, ne* means *that–not;* as, *Paves ne ducas illam,* You are afraid *that* you do *not* get her to wife.

Ne, after a command implying a negative, or prohibition, is often omitted; as, *cave titŭbes*, take care *that* you do *not* stumble.

Note 2. *Ne quidem*, (always separate,) is an emphatic negative, and has the emphatic word between; as, *ne hoc quidem*, not even *this; ne tum quidem*, not even *then.*

122. When a verb is translated into English by the aid of an auxiliary, an adverb, or clause modifying it, will often have to be placed *between* the auxiliary and the verb, (Eng. Gr. 413, An. & Pr. Gr. 936,); as,

1. *Dixit ne ob hoc alios contemnā-mus,*	He said that we should not *on this account* despise others.

123. Some prepositions are variously translated according to the meaning of the words, or the case with which they are connected; thus,

1. *In*, followed by an accusative, means *to, into, towards, for, against*, &c. (607, R. L.)
2. *In*, followed by the ablative, means *in, upon, among, in, in the case of*, (608, R. LI.)
3. *Inter*, referring to *two*, means *between*; to more than two, *among*.
4. *Sub* means *under, at the foot of, close up to.*
5. *Præ* means *before, in comparison of*,—sometimes, *more than.*

124. When the following conjunctions, adjectives, and adverbial particles, are placed, one before each of two successive words or clauses, the first is commonly translated differently from the second, and usually in the following manner, (726.)

1.	*Et*	—— *et,*	Both	—— and.
2.	*Que*	—— *que,*	Both	—— and.
3.	*Aut, vel, sive,*	—— *aut, vel, sive,*	Either	—— or.
4.	*Nec*	—— *nec,*	Neither	—— nor.
5.	*Neque*	—— *neque,*		
6.	*Sive, seu*	—— *sive, seu,*	Whether	—— or.
7.	*Tum*	—— *tum,*	Not only Both	—— but also. —— and.
8.	*Cùm or quum*	—— *tum,*	Not only Both	—— but also. —— and.
9.	*Jam*	—— *jam,*	Now At one time	—— then. —— at another.
10.	*Nunc*	—— *nunc,*		
11.	*Simul*	—— *simul,*	Not only No sooner As soon as	—— but also. —— than. —— instantly.
12.	*Modo, alias,*	—— *modo, alias,*	At one time Sometimes	—— at another. —— sometimes.

Corresponding Conjunctive Terms.

13.	*Ne*	—— *an,*	Whether	—— or.
14.	*Utrum*	—— *an,*	Whether	—— or.
15.	*Ita, sic, tam, adeo,*	—— *ut,*	So	—— that; so —— as.
16.	*Talis, tantus*	—— *ut,*	Such, so great	—— that.
17.	*Is, ejusmŏdi*	—— *ut,*	Such, of such a kind	—— that.
18.	*Simul*	—— *ac,* or *atque,*	As soon	—— as.
19.	*Tamdiu*	—— *quamdiu,*	As long	—— as.
20.	*Ut*	—— *sic,*	As	—— so.

Ne is frequently omitted with the first word or clause, and must be supplied when *an* stands with the second; as,

21. *Rectè an perpĕram,* (*Whether*) right or wrong.

Preliminary Suggestions and Explanations.

1. There can be no pleasure either to the teacher or pupil in reciting, unless the lesson is thoroughly prepared. Pupils who are anxious to go over a great space in a short time should remember that a short lesson well prepared is vastly more profitable than a long one ill prepared. Nothing is more injurious than superficial learning. *Festina lentè.* Hence,

2. No lesson should be assigned longer than can be thoroughly got by all the class. And no lesson should be allowed to pass, unless it is thoroughly prepared.

3. Every word, at first, should be looked out in the vocabulary or dictionary, and its primary meaning, at least, fixed in the memory. And if more meanings than one are given, the pupil should try which will answer best in the sentence he is reading. Nor should he pass to another till he know all about this one—its class, gender, declension, &c., as directed, Gr. 774. And if he forget, he should look it out again, and if necessary, again, till he know it thoroughly.

4. Frequent and accurate reviews of the portion previously studied, are of great importance. This is the best way to fix permanently in the memory, the acquisitions made.

5. Every instance of false quantity, either in reading or parsing, should be instantly corrected. Bad habits in this particular are easily formed, and, if ever, are corrected with great difficulty. If proper attention has been paid to this in going through the grammar, there will be less difficulty now. In order to assist in this, the pupil should commit to memory and apply the few following—

General Rules for the Quantity of Syllables.

1. A vowel before another vowel is short; as, *vĭa, dĕus.*

2. A vowel before two consonants, or a double consonant, is long by position; as, *arma, fallo, axis.*

3. A vowel before a mute and a liquid, (*l* and *r*,) is common; i. e., either long or short; as, *volŭcris,* or *volūcris.*

4. A diphthong is always long; as, *Cæsar, aūrum.*

Note. In this work, when the quantity of the penult is determined by any of these rules, it is not marked; otherwise it is marked.

6. The pupil should never satisfy himself with being able to read and translate his lesson, or even to parse it *tolerably*, but should try to understand the construction of every word, and the connection and dependence of every part; and moreover, should hold himself ready, if called upon, to answer such questions as the following, viz.:

1. *Questions that may be asked concerning every sentence.*

Has this sentence any connection with the preceding? If so—What is the connecting word? In arranging or construing this sentence, which word do you take first?—which next?—which next? &c, Why? (See introduction—directions, &c.) In this sentence, what is the grammatical subject? What is the grammatical predicate? What is the logical subject? What is the logical predicate? Which should be taken first? (§ 152.) In what voice, mood, and tense, is the verb? Why?

2. *Questions that may be asked when the words or the sentence render them proper.*

Is this sentence simple or compound? If compound—What are the simple sentences composing it? By what words are they connected? Analyze the whole, and each part, (§ 152.) Is this word simple or compound? If compound—Of what is it compounded? What is the meaning of each part? What is the meaning of the compound? Form other compounds and tell their meaning. Is this word primitive or derivative? If derivative—From what is it derived? What is its primary meaning? What is its meaning here? (If different)—How came it to have this meaning? What English words are derived from it? Change the verb, if active, into passive, and express the same idea—If passive, change it into the active, and express the same idea. Change the verb into different tenses, &c.

Nouns. How do you know this word to be a noun? Proper? or common? Why? In what case? Why? For what purpose is the nominative used? Is it the subject or predicate here? For what purpose is the genitive commonly used?—the dative?—the accusative?—the vocative?—the ablative? For what purpose is it used, and by what is it governed here?

Adjectives. How do you know this word to be an adjective? What noun or pronoun does it qualify or limit here? Is it compared? Why? Why not? (If a numeral)—To what class does it belong?

Pronouns. How do you know this to be a pronoun? To what class of pronouns does it belong? (If used substantively)—Instead of what noun does it here stand? (If adjectively) With what noun does it agree? (If a relative)—What is its antecedent?

Verbs. How do you know this word to be a verb? Of what class? In what mood, tense, number, person? For what purpose is the indicative mood used?—the subjunctive?—the imperative?—the infinitive? For what purpose is it used here? For what purpose is the present tense used?—the imperfect?—the perfect definite?—indefinite?—the pluperfect?—the future?—the future perfect?

From what point is the time of the infinitive mood reckoned? (§ 47.) How is the present infinitive translated after a verb denoting present time?—past time?—future time? How is the perfect translated (the future—the future-perfect) after a verb denoting present time?—past time?—future time? (§ 47.) In what mood is the leading verb in oblique narration? (651.) In what mood are verbs in dependent clauses in oblique narration? (634.) For what purpose is the participle used? How does it become an adjective? How are gerunds used?—supines?

Adverbs, Prepositions, Interjections, Conjunctions.—What is the use of the adverb? What word does it modify here? What is the use of the preposition? Between what words does it show the relation here? What is the use of the interjection? What emotion does it express here? What is the use of the conjunction? What words or sentences does it join here?

7. If the lesson contain names of persons or places, or allusions to events or fables, in history or mythology, or to the manners or customs of any people, let the pupil inquire into them and be ready to tell something respecting them. This however should be only a secondary matter with the beginner, as it properly belongs to a more advanced stage; but still a little attention to it may serve to interest and stimulate him to further research.

EXPLANATION OF REFERENCES.

The references at the foot of each page which have Gr. prefixed, are to the running paragraph numbers and their subdivisions in the Grammar, and are intended chiefly to explain the *construction*.

In the references which have Id. (Idioms) prefixed, the first number directs to the corresponding number in the preceding introduction, and the second to the example under that number. Thus, for example, 42, 1, directs to the example, *Dignus qui amētur*, (p. 23,) and shows how the words *qui amētur*, in that, and all similar constructions, are to be translated. The words particularly referred to and intended to be noticed in the reference, are distinguished by being printed in a different character. The references are intended to explain *particular phrases* and *idioms*, and to give an example of the mode of translating them. This will be found a more valuable aid in translating than notes, as it reduces the idioms of the language to a sort of system, with every part of which the attentive pupil will soon become familiar.

In many cases there is a reference both to the Grammar and to the Introduction. All of these should be carefully looked out and applied.

In the references to the Rules of Syntax in the Grammar, if there is only one Rule in the section, it is indicated simply by the letter R.; if there are more than one, the number of the Rule is annexed.

Exp. refers to the Explanation under the rule. Words to be supplied are indicated by the syllable "Sup." for "supply," prefixed.

INTRODUCTORY EXERCISES.

Substantives, Adjectives, and Adjective Pronouns.

Decline the following adjectives and substantives separately—then together—translate them in each case and number. (See Nos. 3 and 14.) Tell the case and number here, and translate them. Give the rule for their agreement. (§ 98.) Show how they agree.

Bonus vir. Ingenui puĕri. Prima hora. Summum bonum. In omnĭbus terris. In toto orbe. Decĭmo anno ætātis (No. 11). Meliōris natūræ. Præsens pericŭlum. Muliebri habĭtu. Ad quintum diem. Fugāces anni. Breve tempus. Altus mons. Arbor altissĭma.

Omnĭbus viris. Primo anno. Præsente tempŏre. Meliōre habĭtu. Ad omnem ætātem. Summi pericŭli. Totum annum. Brevis ætātis. Fugāces horæ. Omnĭbus temporĭbus. Mediâ nocte (No. 17.) Ultĭma via. Ad imam vallem.

Ille dies. Hoc tempŏre. Ipsi fontes. Tuum nomen. Hic caper. Ista carmĭna. Lupus ipse. His montĭbus. Re ipsâ. Ex tuis libris. Ad hunc ignem. Tua facta. Carminĭbus nostris. Hoc apri setōsi caput. Pater noster. Eōdem tempŏre.

The Verb and its Nominative. (243, 7.)

Translate each noun or pronoun according to its number and case; and each verb according to its voice, mood, tense, number, and person. Parse each word as directed, 774, and show how the verb agrees with its nominative, according to 303, Rule IV.

Indicative Mood.

Present. Amo.* Amāmus. Legĭmus. Ventus spirat. Domĭnus jubet. Servus paret. Tempus fugit. Aves volant. Bonus homo amātur. Stella vidētur. Nos monēmus. Ignis urit. Luna lucet. Homĭnes dormiunt.

2. *Imperfect.* Monebāmus. Rex regēbat. Vigil vocābat. Canis custodiēbat. Sol occidēbat. Stellæ videbantur. Camēli currēbant. Equus hinniēbat. Boni homĭnes amabantur.

3. *Perfect.* Nos amavĭmus. Illi monuērunt. Domĭnus jussit. Servus paruit. Homĭnes docuērunt. Scripsistis. Arbŏres crevērunt. Venisti. Amāvi.

4. *Pluperfect.* Sol occidĕrat. Hostes fugĕrant. Puĕri legĕrant. Vos viderātis. Tu scripsĕras. Ille bibĕrat. Amāti erāmus. Monĭtus eram. Aves volavĕrant. Illi jussĕrant. Vos legerātis. Illi docuĕrant.

5. *Future.* Scribēmus. Amabĭtis. Umbra fugiet. Viātor cantābit. Erĭmus. Uret ignis. Deus dabit. Tempŏra venient. Illi monēbunt. Nos monebĭmur.

6. *Future-Perfect.* Amavĕro. Hannibal vicĕrit. Nos venerĭmus. Monĭti erĭmus. Hora fugĕrit. Docuĕro. Risĕris. Pomum cecidĕrit. Ambulaverĭmus. Legĕro.

Subjunctive Mood.

1. *Present.* Canis latret. Sim. Amēmus. Ager arētur. Vos videātis. Tempus fugiat. Luna luceat. Ventus spiret. Dormiāmus. Ille capiātur. Illi equi currant.

2. *Imperfect.* Capĕrem. Monerēmus. Puĕri legĕrent. Sol lucēret. Luna occidĕret. Illi amārent. Philomēla cantāret. Amor vincĕret. Amarēmur.

* The nominatives of the first and the second person, *ego, tu, nos, vos,* are usually omittted, (305.)

3. *Perfect.* Misĕrim. Duxerĭmus. Si deus dedĕrit. Quum hiems venĕrit. Nos fuerĭmus. Miles pugnavĕrit. Domus ædificāta fuĕrit. Sol occidĕrit. Vos amiserĭtis. Monuerĭmus. Illi cepĕrint.

4. *Pluperfect.* Fuissēmus. Bella finītà essent. Amavissem. Mercatōres venissent. Poma pependissent. Vos vendidissētis. Risissem. Illi mansissent. Puĕri scripsissent. Fuissem. Litĕræ scriptæ essent.

Imperative Mood.

Ama. Manēto. Regunto. Avis volāto. Canes latranto. Scribe. Illi scribunto. Time. Currĭto. Auditōte. Tene. Faciunto. Amāte. Amanto. Litĕræ leguntor. Dies abīto.

Miscellaneous Exercises.

Ego eram. Sylva stabat. Musa canēbat. Nox erat. Dormiēbas. Arma sonābant. Ego vidēbo. Tempus erit. Rura manēbunt. Troja fuit. Prata bibērunt. Non jurāvi. Umbra fugĕrat. Cicĕro scripsĕrat. Cæsar vicit. Surge. Legĭto. Studēte. Disce aut discēde. Vox audītur. Præmia dentur. Bellum parabĭtur. Hostes capti essent. Portæ panduntur. Verba legebantur. Leges datæ sunt. Puĕri ducuntur. Tempŏra mutantur, et nos mutāmur.

Transitive Verbs, Active Voice, and their Object.

Translate and parse as in the preceding. Point out the *subject* of the verb, i. e., the person or thing that *acts.* Point out the *object* of the verb, i. e., the person or thing acted upon. State what case it is in, and give the rule.

Audīvi sonum. Hi puĕri legunt Homērum. Cæsar vicit Galliam. Vidi patrem (11). Romāni bella parābant. Vicērunt hostes. Vulpes vidĕrat leonem. Pavo explĭcat pennas (No. 11). Canis arcēbat boves. Accipĭter rapuit lusciniam. Boni mortem non timent. Bacchus duxit exercĭtum in Indiam. Scipio delēvit Carthagĭnem. Mummius cepit Corinthum. Divitiæ non semper felicitātem præstant.

Verbs Modified by Adverbs.

Pugnat bene. Veniēbant celerĭter. Pugnātum est acriter. Res prospĕrè gestæ sunt. Corvus fortè repĕrit caseum. Libenter bonas artes sequĕre. Fortè errāvit, fortasse erravĕrit. Gallīna quotidie ovum parit. Semper esto parātus. Nunquam dice mendacium. I cito, statim reverte. Egredior mane. Elephanti maxĭmè odērunt murem; gregātim ingrediuntur.

Prepositions and their Cases.

Sub solem. Infra lunam. In urbem venit. In urbe habĭtat. Sedēbat in loco aprīco. E sylvâ rediit. Trans Tibĕrim natat. Ex illo die Cæsar tendit in Galliam. In rus abiit. Niŏbe locūta est in Apollĭnem et Diānam. Flumĭna in mare currunt. In forum descendit. In aureo sæcŭlo flores nascebantur sine semĭne. Hannĭbal bellum in Italiâ gessit.

SIMPLE SENTENCES.

General Remarks.

1. A simple sentence consists of two parts; the subject, or thing spoken of, and the predicate, or that which is affirmed of the subject, § 152. In the natural order, the subject is translated first, and the predicate last.

2. Nouns and pronouns, either in the subject or predicate, may be limited by nouns in apposition—by nouns in the genitive case, and by adjectives and their regimen.*

3. Verbs belong to the predicate, and are limited by the noun or pronoun governed by them as their object, by adverbs, and adverbial phrases.

4. Both subject and predicate may be further modified and limited by circumstances of time, place, manner, &c., by a preposition and its regimen, or by a dependent clause or phrase connected by a relative or connective term;—and all these should occupy that place in the sentence in which their effect will be best perceived, and the meaning of the whole sentence be most clearly exhibited.

N. B. Before proceeding with the following sentences, the pupil should now be made perfectly familiar with § 152 of the Grammar, and commit to memory, so thoroughly as to have always ready at hand the "directions for beginners," p. 299, and the Rules for construing, p. 300. This being done, these rules should be applied in the analysis of every sentence for some time, till the exercise becomes perfectly familiar and easy. This requires some attention on the part both of teacher and pupil for a short time at first, and the quantity read will necessarily be small; but both will be rewarded tenfold for this labor by the ease, rapidity and certainty with which the pupil, even without the aid of his teacher, will soon analyze and translate the most intricate sentences. Let the trial be properly made, and success is certain.

* By "regimen," is meant the noun or pronoun governed by any word. Thus in the phrases, *Amor patriæ, avĭdus gloriæ, ama deum, ad patrem,* the words *patriæ, gloriæ, deum, patrem,* are the regimen of *Amor, avĭdus, ama, ad,* respectively.

1. *Subject and Predicate.*

The *subject* or thing spoken of, before a finite verb, is always in the nominative case, and has a verb agreeing with it by R. IV. (303).

The *predicate*, or the thing affirmed or denied of the subject, is usually placed after it, and is expressed two ways, as follows:

1. The predicate consists of a *noun*, an *adjective*, or a *participle*, in the same case with the subject, and connected with it by an intransitive verb, or a transitive verb of naming, appointing, &c., called the *copula*. In all such sentences the predicate word, if a noun, comes under R. V. (319): —if an adjective or participle, it agrees with the subject, and comes under R. II. (263) (See Gr. 322;) or

2. The predicate consists of a verb, either alone or with its limiting or modifying words.

1. *The Predicate a Noun.*

Eurōpa est *Peninsŭla.*[a] Tu eris *rex.*[a] Plurĭmæ[b] stellæ sunt *soles.*[a] Boni puĕri egregii *viri*[a] fient. Castor et Pollux erant[c] *fratres.*[a] Ego sum *discipŭlus.*[a] Cicĕro factus est *consul.*[a] Ego salūtor *poēta.*[a]

2. *Predicate an Adjective or Participle.*

Terra est *rotunda.*[d] Vita *brevis*[d] est. Vera amicitĭa est *sempiterna.*[d] Fames et sitis sunt[c] *molestæ.*[d] Nemo semper *felix*[d] est. Non omnes milĭtes sunt *fortes.*[d] Mundi *innumerabĭles*[d] sunt. Nemo nimium *beātus*[d] est. Avārus[e] nunquam est *contentus.*[d] Pater *reversūrus*[d] est. Virtus *laudanda,*[f] ebriĕtas *vitanda*[f] est.

3. *The Predicate a Verb, &c.—Active Voice.*

Elephanti semper gregātim *ambŭlant.*[g] Cornīces *ambŭlant,*[g] passĕres et merŭlæ *saliunt;*[g] perdīces *currunt;*[g] plurĭmæ[h] etiam *nidifĭcant.*

Democrĭtus *explĭcat*[g] cur ante lucem galli canunt.[g] Etiam infantes *somniant.*[g] Parvæ res *crescunt.*[g]

---

[a] Gr. 319, R. V.
[b] Gr. 113 and Id. 24.
[c] Gr. 312, R. I.
[d] Gr. 322.
[e] Id. 19, 1.
[f] Id. 108. 1.
[g] Gr. 303, R. IV.
[h] Id. 19, Sup. *aves.*

4. *Passive Voice.*

Oves non ubīque *tondentur.*[a]

In Indiâ[b] *gignuntur* maxĭma animalia.

In Afrĭcâ[b] nec cervi, nec apri, nec ursi *inveniuntur.*[a]

In Syriâ[b] nigri leōnes *reperiuntur.*

Apud Romānos mortui[c] plerumque *cremabantur.*

Fortes[c] *laudabuntur*, ignāvi[c] *vituperabuntur.*

Littĕræ a Phœnicĭbus *inventæ*[d] *sunt.*

Carthāgo, Corinthus, Numantia, et multæ aliæ urbes a Romānis *eversæ sunt.*

5. *Deponent Verbs.*

Formīcæ etiam noctu *operantur.*[e]

Ursi interdum bipĕdes[f] *ingrediuntur.*

Aquĭlæ semper solæ[f] *predantur.*

Apud Æthiŏpes[g] maxĭmi elephanti in silvis[b] *vagantur.*

Sturni et psittăci humānas voces[h] *imitantur.*

6. *The Accusative after Transitive Verbs, Active Voice, and Transitive Deponents.*

Diem[i] perdĭdi. Terra parit *flores.*[i]

Crocodīlus *ova*[i] parit. Elephantus odit *murem*[i] et[j] *suem.*[i]

Camēli diu *sitim*[k] tolĕrant.

Lanæ nigræ *nullum colōrem*[i] bibunt.

Senes minĭmè sentiunt *morbos*[i] *contagiōsos.*

Cervi *cornua*[i] *sua* quotannis amittunt.

Ceres *frumentum*[i] *invēnit;* Bacchus[l] *vinum;*[i] Mercurius[l] *littĕras.*[i]

---

[a] Gr. 303, R. IV.
[b] Gr. 608, R. LI.
[c] Id. 19, 1.
[d] Gr. 164, *Note.*
[e] Gr. 207, 1.
[f] Gr. 274.
[g] Gr. 602, R. XLVIII.
[h] Gr. 437, R. I.
[i] Gr. 436, R. XX.
[j] Gr. 720, R. LXV.
[k] Gr. 90, 1.
[l] Gr. 308.

Canes soli[a] *domĭnos*[b] *suos* bene novēre, soli *nomĭna sua* agnoscunt.

Hystrix *aculeos*[h] longè jaculātur.

Sturni et[c] psittăci *humānas voces*[h] imitantur.

Miltiădes *Athēnas*[b] *totam*que *Græciam* liberāvit.

The Genitive.

The genitive is used to limit the signification of the word which governs it, by connecting with that word the idea of origin, property, or possession (331). It is commonly governed,

1st. By substantives, § 106. Rules VI., VII., and VIII.

2d. By adjectives, § 107, viz: verbals, partitives, and adjectives of plenty or want; Rules IX., X., XI.

3d. By verbs, §108, Rules XII., XIII., XIV.; also, Rules XXVII., XXVIII.; § 126, Rules I., and II., § 113, Exc. I., and II. See also 245, 7, 4th, and 5th.

7. *The Genitive governed by Substantives.*

Crescit amor *nummi.*[d]

Infinīta[f] est multitūdo *morbōrum.*[d]

Litterārum[d] usus est antiquissĭmus.[f]

Asia et[c] Afrĭca greges[b] *ferōrum asinōrum* alit.[g]

Magna[f] est *linguārum* inter homĭnes[i] variĕtas.

Innumerabilia[f] sunt *mortis*[d] signa, *salūtis*[j] paucissĭma.[f]

Cyrus *omnium* in exercĭtu[k] suo *milĭtum*[d] nomĭna[b] tenebat memoriâ.

Canis vestigia[h] *ferārum*[d] diligentissĭmè scrutātur.

Nemo non benignus est *sui*[d] judex.[e]

Leōnum[d] *anĭmi*[d] index[e] cauda est.

8. *Genitive governed by Adjectives.*

Semper *fragilitātis*[l] humānæ sis memor.[f]

---

[a] Id. 16, 4.
[b] Gr. 436, R. XX.
[c] Gr. 720, R. LXV.
[d] Gr. 332, R. VI.
[e] Gr. 319, R. V.
[f] Gr. 322.
[g] Gr. 312, R. I. & 313.
[h] Gr. 437, R. I.
[i] Gr. 602, R. XLVIII.
[j] Gr. 336.
[k] Gr. 608, R. LI.
[l] Gr. 349, R. IX.

Elephanti *frigŏris*[a] impatientes[b] sunt.

Stultissĭma[c] *animalium*[d] sunt lanāta.[b]

Velocissĭmum[c] *omnium animalium*[d] est delphīnus.

Stultōrum[d] neque quisquam beātus[b] est.

Gallōrum[d] *omnium* fortissĭmi[b] sunt Belgæ.

9. *Genitive governed by Verbs.*

Omnia[e] erant *hostium*.[f] Hoc[e] non *nostri moris*[f] est. Miserēre *nostri*.[g] *Amīci*[f] est recordāri *amicōrum*.[j] Platōnem *magni*[h] æstĭmo, sed Socrătem *pluris*.[h] Monuisti me *diei*[i] *natālis*. *Bonōrum*[f] est *injuriārum*[j] oblivisci, et *beneficii*[j] recordāri. *Stulti*[f] est dicĕre[k] "non putâram." Est[l] *magni labōris*[f] multum scribĕre.[k]

The Dative.

The dative denotes the remote object to which any thing is done or *given*, or that to which any quality, action, or state tends or refers, without directly acting upon it, and is governed chiefly,

1. By substantives, § 110.
2. By adjectives, § 111.
3. By verbs, § 112, 123, and 126; R. III. and R. XXXIII.

10. *The Dative governed by Substantives and Adjectives.*

Clodius semper *virtutĭbus*[m] hostis[n] erat.

Vir bonus *amīcis*[m] et *patriæ*[o] decus[n] est.

Nox *somno*[p] opportūna[b] est.

Nero primò *bonis*[m] amīcus,[n] et *studio*[p] musārum[q] dedĭtus[b] fuit; sed postea *monitorĭbus*[p] asper et irātus fuit, *genĕri*[p] *humāno* infestus, *omnĭbus*[r] inimīcus, *diis* invīsus, et multa *illi*[p] adversa fuērunt.

[a] Gr. 349, R. IX. [b] Gr. 322. [c] Gr. 355, R. X. & Id. 21. [d] Gr. 355, R. X. [e] Id. 19, 4. [f] Gr. 364, R. XII.

[g] Gr. 369, R. XIII. [h] Gr. 495, R. XXVIII. [i] Gr. 489, R. XXVII. [j] Gr. 373, R. XIV. [k] Gr. 660, R. LVI. [l] Gr. Id. 51, 1.

[m] Gr. 378, R. XV. [n] Gr. 319, R. V. [o] Gr. 720, R. LXV. [p] Gr. 382, R. XVI. [q] Gr. 332, R. VI. [r] Id. 19, 1.

Æquus *cunctis*[a] et benignus esto, *paucis*[a] familiāris, *hostĭbus*[b] mitis, et *nemĭni* molestus; sic *omnĭbus*[a] carus eris, et invīsus *nulli.*[b]

Asĭno[b] *segni* nullum onus gratum, et *puĕro*[b] *ignāvo* omnis labor molestus est.

11. *The Dative governed by Verbs.*

Natūra *animalĭbus*[c] varia tegumenta[d] tribuit, testas,[d] coria, spinas, villos, setas, pennas, squamas.

Homĭni[e] *soli*[f] avaritia[g] et ambitio data[h] est.

Leōni[i] vis summa est[j] in pectŏre.

Antiquissĭmis hominĭbus[i] specus erant[k] pro domĭbus.

Nulli animāli[i] memoria major est, quàm *cani.*[g]

Gallinacei *leonĭbus*[m] *terrōri*[m] sunt.

Homĭni[e] plurĭma ex homĭne[l] fiunt[n] mala.

Homo furiōsus ne *libĕris*[o] quidem *suis*[p] parcit.

Via mali[q] *omnĭbus*[r] semper vitanda[s] est.

The Accusative.

The accusative is used for the most part to express the object of a transitive active verb, or of some relation, and is governed,

1. By transitive verbs in the active voice, or by transitive deponent verbs, No. 6. 2. By prepositions.

12. *The Accusative governed by Prepositions.*

Camēlus naturāle odium adversùs *equos*[t] gerit.

Pictæ vestes jam apud *Homērum*[t] commemorantur.

Multa animalia congregantur et contra *alia*[u] dimĭcant.

---

[a] Id. 19, 1.
[b] Gr. 382, R. XVI.
[c] Gr. 501, R. XXIX.
[d] Gr. 436, R. XX.
[e] Gr. 522.
[f] Id. 16, 4.
[g] Gr. 720, R. LXV.
[h] Gr. 164, *Note.*
[i] Gr. 394, R. II.
[j] Id. 118, 1.
[k] Id. 118, 2.
[l] Gr. 603, R. XLIX.
[m] Gr. 427, R. XIX.
[n] Gr. 221, 8, Obs. 3.
[o] Gr. 403, R. V. and Id. 7, 2.
[p] Id. 30, 1.
[q] Gr. 332, R. VI.
[r] Id. 5, 2; and 19, 1.
[s] Id. 108, 1, and Gr. 322.
[t] Gr. 602, R. XLVIII.
[u] Gr. 97, 4, and Gr. 602, R. XLVIII.

Hippopotămus segĕtes circa *Nilum*[a] depascĭtur.

Apud *Romānos*[a] mortui plerumque cremabantur.

Inter *omnes bestias*[a] simia homĭni[b] simillĭma est.

The Ablative.

The ablative generally denotes that from which something is separated or taken, or by or with which something is done or exists. It is governed,

1. By nouns, §118, or adjectives, §§ 107, 119, 120.
2. By verbs, § 121, R. XXV., and XXVI., § 125, R. XXXVI., and § 126, R. V.
3. By prepositions.
4. It is used to express various circumstances. See No. 17, p. 67.

13. *The Ablative governed by Nouns and Adjectives.*

Gratiâ[c] opus est nobis[d] *tuâ*, *tuâ*que *auctoritāte.*[e]

Nunc *virĭbus*[c] opus est vobis,[d] nunc prudenti consilio.

Reperiuntur interdum cervi *candĭdo colōre.*[f]

Catilīna *nobĭli genĕre*[g] natus erat, *magnâ vi*[f] et anĭmi[h] et corpŏris,[e] sed *ingenio*[f] *malo pravō*que.

Anĭmus per somnum est *sensĭbus*[i] et *curis*[e] vacuus.

Est philosophia *paucis* contenta *judicĭbus.*[g]

Nihil video in Sullâ *odio*[g] dignum, misericordiâ[g] digna multa. Natūra *parvo*[g] contenta est.

14. *The Ablative governed by Verbs.*

Leænæ *jubâ*[j] carent. Leōnes facĭlè per triduum *cibo*[j] carent.

Eliphanti maxĭmè *amnĭbus*[k] gaudent.

Apes *tinnītu*[k] æris gaudent.

Numĭdæ plerumque *lacte*[l] et *ferīnâ carne*[m] vescuntur.

---

[a] Gr. 602, R. XLVIII.
[b] Gr. 382, R. XVI.
[c] Gr. 456, R. XXII., & Id. 6, 5.
[d] Gr. 394, R. II.
[e] Gr. 720, R. and 721.
[f] Gr. 339, R. VII., & Id. 6, 1.
[g] Gr. 462, R. XXIII.
[h] Gr. 332, R. VI.
[i] Gr. 361, R. XI.
[j] Gr. 480, R. XXV.
[k] Gr. 485.
[l] Gr. 484, R. XXVI.
[m] Gr. 78, *Note.*

Plurĭmis bonis[a] fruĭmur atque utĭmur.[b]

Hispania *viris*,[c] *equis*, *ferro*, *plumbo*, *œre*, *argento*, *aurō*que abundat.

15. *The ablative governed by Prepositions.*

Quidam homĭnes nati sunt cum *dentĭbus*.[d]

Xerxes cum *paucissĭmis militĭbus*[d] ex *Grœciâ*[d] aufūgit.

Lucius Metellus primus[e] elephantos ex *primo Punĭco bello*[d] duxit in *triumpho*.

Cantābit vacuus coram *latrōne*[d] viātor.

Sidĕra ab *ortu* ad occāsum commeant.

Britannia a *Phœnicĭbus* inventa[f] est.

Apes sine *rege* esse non possunt.

Infans nihil sine *aliēnâ ope* potest.

Dulce[g] est[h] pro *patriâ* mori.[i]

Venēnum aliquando pro *remedio* fuit.

Littĕræ a *Phœnicĭbus* inventæ[f] sunt.

16. *The Accusative and Ablative with In and Sub,* § 136, *R. L. and LI.*

Aquĭlæ nidifĭcant[j] in *rupĭbus* et *arborĭbus*.

Coccyx semper parit in *aliēnis nidis*.

In *senectūte* hebescunt[k] sensus; visus, audītus debilitātur.[l]

In *Indiâ* gignuntur maxĭma animalia.

Hyænæ plurĭmæ in *Afrĭcâ* gignuntur.

In *Afrĭcâ*, nec[m] cervi, nec apri, nec ursi reperiuntur.

In *Syriâ* nigri leōnes reperiuntur.

---

[a] Gr. 484, R. XXVI.
[b] Gr. 720, R. & 721.
[c] Gr. 480, R. XXV.
[d] Gr. 603, R. XLIX.
[e] Gr. 274.
[f] Gr. 164, *Note.*
[g] Gr. 270.
[h] Id. 51, 1.
[i] Gr. 660, R. LVI.
[j] Gr. 157, I. 1.
[k] Gr. 227, 2.
[l] Gr. 313.
[m] Gr. 726 and Id. 124, 4.

Serus in *cœlum* redeas.[a]

Victi Persæ in *naves* confugĕrunt.

Numa Pompilius annum in *duodĕcim menses* distribuit.

Pontius Thelesīnus Romānos sub *jugum* misit.

Gallia sub *septentrionĭbus* posĭta est.

17. *The Ablative used to express various circumstances without a Preposition.*

The circumstances commonly denoted by the ablative without a preposition, are *Respect wherein*, § 128; *Cause, manner, means*, or *instrument*, § 129; *Place*, § 130; *Time*, § 131; *Measure*, § 132; *Price*, § 133.

Apri in morbis sibi[b] medentur *hedĕrâ*.[c]

Pyrrhus rex,[d] *tactu*[c] pollĭcis in dextro pede, lienōsis[e] medebātur.

Oleo insecta exanimantur.

Feræ domantur *fame* atque *verberĭbus*.

Anacreon poēta[d] *acĭno*[c] uvæ passæ exstinctus est.

Crocodīlus *pelle*[c] *durissĭmâ* contra omnes ictus munītur.

In Afrĭcâ elephanti capiuntur *foveis*.[c]

Elephanti spirant, bibunt, odorantur *proboscĭde*.[c]

Dentes *usu* atteruntur, sed *igne* non cremantur.

Mures Alpīni *binis pedĭbus* gradiuntur.

Apes *tinnītu* æris convocantur.

Quibusdam in locis[f] ansĕres bis *anno*[g] velluntur.

Color lusciniārum *autumno*[h] mutātur.

Hiĕme[g] ursi in antris dormiunt.

Nemo mortalium *omnĭbus horis*[h] sapit.

Primōres dentes *septĭmo mense* gignuntur; *septĭmo* iīdem decĭdunt *anno*.[h]

---

[a] Gr. 171, I. 1; and Gr. 144 and 145.
[b] Gr. 403, & Id. 7, 2.
[c] Gr. 542, R. XXXV.
[d] Gr. 251, R. I.
[e] Gr. 403, & Id. 19, 1.
[f] Gr. 608, R. LI.
[g] Gr. 565, R. XLI.
[h] Gr. 565, R. XL.

Antipăter Sidonius, poēta,[a] quotannis, *die natāli suo*[b] *febre* corripiebātur.

Æstāte dies sunt longiōres quàm *hiĕme*.

Isocrătes orātor unam oratiōnem *viginti talentis*[c] vendĭdit.

Luscinia candĭda, *sex sestertiis*[c] Romæ venit.

18. *Nouns in Apposition.*

Plurĭmi Scythæ, *bellicosissĭmi homĭnes*,[a] lacte[d] vescuntur.

Delphīnus, *anĭmal*[a] homĭni[e] *amīcum*, cantu[f] gaudet.

Carthāgo atque Corinthus, *opulentissĭmæ urbes*,[g] eōdem anno a Romānis eversæ[h] sunt.

Quàm brevi tempŏre[i] popŭli Romāni, omnium gentium *victōris*,[a] libertas fracta[h] est!

Mithridātem, Ponti *regem*, Tigrānes, *rex Armenius*, excēpit.

Circa Cyllēnen, *montem* in Arcadiâ, merŭlæ nascuntur.

19. *The Infinitive Mood without a Subject.*

The infinitive without a subject is usually regarded as the subject of a verb, § 144, R. LVI., or as the object of another verb, R. LVII.; and in this case always expresses an act or state of the subject of the verb that governs it.

In the following, let the pupil state whether the infinitive is the subject or the object of the verb with which it is connected.

Errāre[j] est humānum.[k]

Turpe[k] est beneficium *repetĕre*.[j]

Beneficiis[l] gratiam non *referre* etiam turpius est.

Parentes suos non *amāre* est impium.[k]

---

[a] Gr. 251, R. I.
[b] Gr. 565, R. XL.
[c] Gr. 581, R. XLIV.
[d] Gr. 484, R. XXVI.
[e] Gr. 382, R. XVI.
[f] Gr. 485.
[g] Gr. 254.
[h] Gr. 164, 5, *Note.*
[i] Gr. 565, R. XLI.
[j] Gr. 660, R. LVI.
[k] Gr. 270.
[l] Gr. 501, R. XXIX.

Te cupio *vidēre.*[a] Volui *dormīre.*[a]

Aude *contemnĕre*[a] opes. Carmĭna possŭmus *donāre.*

Potĕram *contingĕre* ramos.

Nihil amplius *scribĕre* possum.

Ego cupio ad te *venīre*. *Intelligĕre* non possum.

Cessātor[b] *esse* noli. Cur timet flavum Tibĕrim *tangĕre?*

Philippus volēbat[c] *amāri*. Alexander *metui* volēbat.

Tecum[d] *vivĕre* amo. Natūram *mutāre* pecunia nescit.

Benè *ferre* disce magnam fortūnam.

Angustam pauperiem *pati* puer discat.[c]

Dici beātus[b] ante obĭtum nemo debet.

Æquam memento[f] rebus in arduis *servāre* mentem.

Aurum vestĭbus[g] *intexĕre* invēnit rex Attălus.

Non omnes homĭnes æquo amōre[h] *complecti* possŭmus.

Illecebras voluptātis *vitāre* debēmus.

Romæ[i] elephantes per funes *incedĕre* docebantur.

20. *Gerunds.*

Gerunds are construed like substantives, and, at the same time, govern the case of their own verbs, § 147.

Etiam post malam messem *serendum*[j] est.

Omnĭbus[j] aliquando *moriendum*[j] est.

Semper *pugnandum*[j] est contra cupiditātes et lubidĭnem.

Plurĭmæ[k] sunt illecebræ *peccandi.*[l]

Artem *scribendi*[l] Phœnīces, artem acu *pingendi*[l] Phryges invenērunt.

Cupidĭtas *vivendi* nunquam immensa[b] esse debet.

---

[a] Gr. 663, R. LVII.
[b] Gr. 326.
[c] Gr. 160, 1.
[d] Gr. 235, 2.
[e] Gr. 171, 1, & 145.
[f] Gr. 222, 2.
[g] Gr. 501, R. XXIX.
[h] Gr. 542, R. XXXV.
[i] Gr. 548, R. XXXVI. & Id. 4, 1.
[j] Gr. 699, R. LXI. & 701.
[k] Gr. 322.
[l] Gr. 702.

Honestissĭma est contentio beneficiis[a] beneficia *vincendi*.

Homo natūrâ[a] est cupĭdus nova semper *videndi* et *audiendi*.

Libri sunt inutĭles ignāro[b] *legendi*.

Olim calămus adhibebātur *scribendo*.[c]

Aqua marīna inutĭlis est *bibendo*.

Culex habet telum et[d] *fodiendo* et *sorbendo* idoneum.

Non omnes æqualĭter ad *discendum*[e] proni sumus.

Simiæ catŭlos sæpe *complectendo*[f] necant.

Beneficia *exprobrando*[f] corrumpĭmus.

Amīcus amīcum semper alĭquâ re[a] juvābit, aut re, aut consilio, aut *consolando*[f] certè.

21. *Gerundives.*

Gerundives are participles in *dus*, with the sense of the gerund, and agreeing in gender, number, and case, with their nouns, § 49, 7, and § 147, R. LXII.

Inĭtum est consilium urbis *delendæ*,[g] civium *trucidandōrum*,[g] nomĭnis Romāni *exstinguendi*.[g]

Puer par est *onĕri*[h] *ferendo*.

Omnes civitātes Greciæ pecuniam ad *classem ædificandam* et *exercĭtum comparandum* dedērunt.

Vir bonus, in *malis* aliōrum *amovendis*, seipsum sublĕvat.

Compound Sentences.

A compound sentence consists of two or more simple sentences, connected together by *conjunctions, relatives,* or *adverbs,* §§ 149, 99, 140, and 141.

---

[a] Gr. 542, R. XXXV.
[b] Id, Sup. *homĭni.*
[c] Gr. 703.
[d] Gr. 726, & Id. 124, 1.
[e] Gr. 704.
[f] Gr. 705.
[g] Gr. 707, R. LXII. & Id. 112.
[h] Gr. 382, R. XVI.

22. *Conjunctions.*

Sol ruit, *et*[a] montes umbrantur.

Vir[b] bonus *et* prudens dici delector ego.

Immensa est, finem*que*[c] potentia Dei non habet.

Accipĕre[d] præstat *quàm*[a] facĕre injuriam.

Rapĕre *atque* abīre semper assuēvit lupus.

Semper honos, nomen*que*[c] tuum, laudes*que* manēbunt.

Sapientem *neque*[e] paupertas, *neque* mors, *neque* vincŭla terrent.

Juno erat Jovis *et*[f] soror *et* conjux.

Nox erat, *et* fulgēbat luna.

In prælio cita mors venit, *aut* victoria læta.

Marius *et* Sylla civīle bellum gessērunt.[g]

Leti vis rapuit, rapiet*que* gentes.

Non formōsus erat, *sed* erat facundus Ulysses.

Si[h] divitiæ felicitātem præstant, avaritia prima virtus est.

23. *Adverbs.*

Quoties litĕras tuas lego, omnem mihi[i] præteritōrum tempŏrum memoriam in mentem revŏco.

Magna[j] debēmus suscipĕre, *dum* vires suppĕtunt.

Cervi, *quamdiu* cornĭbus[k] carent, noctu ad pabŭla procēdunt.

Quidam crocodīlum,[l] *quamdiu* vivat,[m] crescĕre[n] existĭmant, vivit autem multos annos.[o]

Gloria virtūtem, *tanquam* umbra,[p] sequĭtur.

---

[a] Gr. 720, R. LXV.
[b] Gr. 326.
[c] Gr. 242, Obs. 2.
[d] Gr. 660, R. LVI., & 662.
[e] Gr. 720, R. LXV. & 722.
[f] Id. 124, 1.
[g] Gr. 312, R. I.
[h] Gr. 630.
[i] Gr. 380, & Id. 5, 3.
[j] Id. 19, 4.
[k] Gr. 480, R. XXV.
[l] Gr. 671, R. LVIII.
[m] Gr. 656.
[n] Id. 95, 1.
[o] Gr. 565, R. XLI.
[p] Gr. 252, *ad fin.*

24. *Comparison with a Conjunction.*

Comparison is made in two ways, 1st By a conjunction, *quàm, ac, atque*, after the comparative, connecting the words denoting the things compared in the same case, 466;—and 2d, By the ablative after the comparative without a conjunction, § 120.

Canes Indĭci grandiōres sunt *quàm* cetĕri.[a]

Nullum malum est vehementius[b] et importunius[d] *quàm* invidia.[c]

Interdum ferārum anĭmos mitiōres invenīmus *quàm* homĭnum.[d]

Latro feræ[e] est similior *quàm* homĭni.[c]

Major est anĭmi voluptas *quàm* corpŏris.[d]

In montĭbus aër purior est, et tenuior *quàm* in vallĭbus.

Comparison without a Conjunction.

Nihil est *clementiâ*[f] divinius.

Aurum gravius est *argento*.[f]

Adămas durior est *ferro*,[f] ferrum durius cetĕris *metallis*.

Luna terræ propior est *sole*.

Quid magis est durum *saxo*, quid mollius *aquâ?*

25. *Relative Pronouns.* (§ 99.)

Non omnis *ager*, *qui*[g] serĭtur, fert fruges.

Psittăcus, *quem* India mittit, reddit *verba quæ* accēpit.

Achilles, *cujus* res gestas Homēri carmĭna celebrant, ad Hellespontum sepultus est.

Myrmecĭdes quidam *quadrīgam* fecit et ebŏre, *quam* musca alis[h] integēbat.

Qui[i] bonis non rectè utĭtur, *ei*[j] bona mala fiunt.[k]

---

a Gr. 720, R. LXV., & Id. 19.
b Gr. 322.
c Gr. 720, R. LXV.
d Gr. 336.
e Gr. 382, R. XVI.
f Gr. 467, R. XXIV., & Id. 6, 3.
g Gr. 284, R. III.
h Gr. 542, R. XXXV.
i Gr. 285, & Id. 43, 1.
j Gr. 522, R. III.
k Gr. 221, Obs. 3: p. 188.

Beneficium reddit, *qui*[a] ejus[b] bene memor est.

Grues in itinerĭbus *ducem*, *quem* sequantur,[c] elĭgunt.

Copias suas Cæsar in proxĭmum collem subduxit, *equitatum*que, *qui* sustinēret[d] hostium impĕtum, misit.

Subjunctive Mood.

The subjunctive mood is used in dependent clauses, connected with the leading clause by conjunctive particles, adverbs, or by the relative pronoun. When it expresses a fact, real or supposed, but not directly asserted or vouched for, it is translated by the English *indicative*. When it expresses a thing as not actual and certain, but only as conditional or contingent, as what *may*, *can*, *might*, or *should* take place, it is translated by the English potential, § 42, II. and § 140 and 141.

26. *The Subjunctive with* CUM *or* QUUM.

Platea, *cŭm* devorātis se *implēvit*[e] conchis,[f] testas evŏmit.

Ceres frumenta invēnit, *cŭm* antea homĭnes glandĭbus[g] *vescerentur.*[e]

Nave[h] primus[i] in Græciam Danăus advēnit, *cŭm* antea ratĭbus[h] *navigarētur.*[j]

Alexander, rex[k] Macedoniæ, *cŭm* Thebas *cepisset*,[l] Pindări vatis[k] familiæ[m] pepercit.

27. *The Subjunctive after Conjunctive Particles.* (§ 140.)

Tanta est in Indiâ ubertas soli, *ut* sub unâ ficu[n] turmæ equĭtum *condantur.*[o]

Ursi per hiĕmem tam gravi somno[h] premuntur, *ut* ne vulnerĭbus[h] quidem *excitentur.*[o]

---

[a] Id. 37, 1st, 3.
[b] Gr. 349, R. IX.
[c] Gr. 641, R. & Id. 40, 5.
[d] Gr. 641, R. & Id. 40, 4.
[e] Gr. 630.
[f] Gr. 514, R. XXXI.
[g] Gr. 484, R. XXVI.
[h] Gr. 542, R. XXXV.
[i] Gr. 274.
[j] Gr. 223, 3, & 630.
[k] Gr. 251, R. I.
[l] Gr. 631, & Id. 74, 8.
[m] Gr. 403, R. V.
[n] Gr. 608, R. LI.
[o] Gr. 627, 1, 1st.

Delphīni tantâ interdum vi e mari exsiliunt, *ut* vela[a] navium *transvŏlent.*[b]

In Indiâ serpentes ad tantam magnitudĭnem adolescunt, *ut* integros *hauriant*[b] cervos taurosque.

Fac,[c] *ut* homĭnes anĭmum tuum pluris *faciant,*[d] quàm omnia, quæ illis[e] tribuĕre possis.[f]

Alexander edixit, *ne* quis ipsum[g] præter Apellem *pingĕret.*[h]

Pythagorēis[i] interdictum fuit,[j] *ne*[k] fabis[l] *vescerentur.*[h]

Ocŭli palpebris[m] sunt munīti, *ne*[n] quid *incĭdat.*[h]

Nihil ferè tam recondĭtum est, *quin*[o] quærendo[m] inveniri *possit.*

Nunquam tam manè egredior, neque tam vespĕri domum[p] revertor, *quin*[o] te in fundo *conspĭcer* fodĕre,[q] aut arāre,[q] aut alĭquĭd facĕre.

Xerxes non dubitābat, *quin*[o] copiis suis Græcos facĭlè *superatūrus esset.*[r]

28. *The Subjunctive with words expressing an indirect question.* (§ 140, 5.)

Quærĭtur, unus *ne*[s] *sit*[t] mundus, an plures.

Disputābant vetĕres philosŏphi, casu[m] *ne*[s] *factus sit*[t] mundus, an mente[m] divinâ.

Augustus cum amīcis suis consultābat, *utrùm* imperium *servāret,*[t] *an deponĕret.*

Perpĕram quærĭtur, *num* in amīci gratiam, jus violāri *possit.*[t]

---

[a] Gr. 613, R. LII.
[b] Gr. 627, 1, 1st.
[c] Gr. 214, 4.
[d] Gr. 627, 1, 3d.
[e] Gr. 501, R. XXIX.
[f] Gr. 656.
[g] Id. 32, 8.
[h] Gr. 619, R. LIII. 620, & Gr. 627, 1, 3d.
[i] Gr. 522, R. III.
[j] Id. 51, 3.
[k] Id. 121, 6.
[l] Gr. 484, R. XXVI.
[m] Gr. 542, R. XXXV.
[n] Id. 121, 1.
[o] Gr. 627, 3.
[p] Gr. 558, R. XXXIX.
[q] Id. 89, 1.
[r] Gr. 170.
[s] Id. 124, 13.
[t] Gr. 627, 5.

Ciconiæ *quonam* e loco *veniant*, aut in *quas* se regiōnes *confĕrant*, incompertum est.[a]

Quis numerāre potest, *quoties* per totam vitam lacrўmas *fudĕrit?*

29. *Subjunctive after the Relative.* (§ 141.)

Quis est *qui nesciat*[b] quid voluptas sit?[c]

Non invenies qui Demosthĕnem oratōrem maxĭmum esse *neget.*[b]

Nemo felix est, *qui* eâ lege *vivat,*[b] ut impūnè necāri posset.[d]

Cæsar legātos misit, *qui* iter *cognoscĕrent.*[e]

Sunt *qui* amicitiam molestam *reddant.*[b]

Hos libros non contemno, quippe *qui* nunquam *legĕrim.*[f]

Verba, *quæ* sententias *indĭcent,*[e] reperta sunt.

Peccavisse mihi videor,[g] *qui* a te *discessĕrim.*[h]

Decemvĭri creāti sunt, *qui* civitāti leges *scribĕrent.*[e]

Regŭlus dixit se desiisse Romānum esse, ex illâ die *quâ* in potestātem Pœnōrum *venisset.*[i]

30. *The Infinitive with a Subject.* § 145.

The infinitive with a subject is translated by the indicative or potential in English. Its subject, which is always in the accusative, is translated in the nominative, and usually has the conjunction *that* before it. It forms a distinct but dependent proposition, which, like the infinitive without a subject, forms either the subject or object of the verb on which it depends. (See § 145.)

Aristotĕles tradit, in Latmo, Cariæ monte, *hospĭtes* a scorpionĭbus non *lœdi, indigĕnas interĭmi.*[k]

[a] Id. 51, 3.
[b] Gr. 636, R. I.
[c] Gr. 627, 5.
[d] Gr, 627, 1, 1st.
[e] Gr. 643, 4th.
[f] Gr. 647.
[g] Id. 70, 2.
[h] Gr. 645, R. III.
[i] Gr. 650, R. VI.
[j] Gr. 522, R. III.
[k] Gr. 670, & Id. 95, 4.

M. Varro narrat, a cunicŭlis *suffossum*[a] in Hispaniâ *oppĭdum*,[b] a talpis in Thessaliâ; ab ranis *incŏlas*[b] urbis in Galliâ pulsos,[a] ab locustis in Afrĭcâ; ex Gyăro insŭlâ *incŏlas*[b] a murĭbus *fugātos*, in Italiâ *Amyclas* a serpentĭbus *delētas esse*.

Observātum est,[c] *pestilentiam*[b] semper a meridiānis partĭbus ad occidentem *ire*.[d]

Homērus *Pygmæos*[b] popŭlum ad oceănum, a gruĭbus *infestāri*[e] prodĭdit; Aristotĕles *eosdem* in cavernis *vivĕre*[d] narrat.

Postĕri aliquando querentur nostrâ culpâ *mores*[b] *eversos esse*.[f]

Virgilius per testamentum jussĕrat *carmĭna*[b] *sua cremāri*,[g] *id*[b] Augustus *fiĕri*[g] vetuit.

Sertorius cervam alēbat candĭdam, *quam*[b] Hispaniæ gentes *fatidĭcam*[h] *esse*[i] credēbant.

Illustre est inter philosŏphos nomen Anaxagŏræ, *quem*[b] vetĕres nunquam in vitâ *risisse*[j] ferunt.

31. *Participles*. (§ 146.)

Participles are usually translated after their nouns, with which they agree in gender, number, and case, in the same manner as adjectives; and at the same time govern the case of their own verb.

Exempla fortūnæ *variantis*[k] sunt innumĕra.[h]

Galli diem *venientem* cantu nuntiant.

Cecrops urbem[l] a se *condĭtam*[h] appellābat Cecropiam.[l]

---

[a] Gr. 179, 6, & Id. 97, 4.
[b] Gr. 671, R. & 672.
[c] Id. 51, 2, & 94, 1.
[d] Id. 95, 1.
[e] Id. 95, 4.
[f] Id. 97, 6.
[g] Id. 96, 12, or 90, 4.
[h] Gr. 322.
[i] Id. 90, 2, or 91, 4.
[j] Id. 91, 4.
[k] Id. 101, 1.
[l] Gr. 440.

Augustus primus [a] Romæ [b] tigrin [c] ostendit *mansuefactum.* [d]

Gymnosophistæ in Indiâ toto die [e] *fervent̆ibus* [d] arēnis [f] insistunt, Solem [g] *intuentes.*

Epimenĭdes puer,[h] æstu [i] et itinĕre [j] fessus,[k] septem et quinquaginta annos [e] in specu dormivisse dicĭtur.

Julius Cæsar simul dictāre,[l] et *legentem* [m] audīre solēbat

Leo *prostrātis* [n] parcit.

Aves aduncos ungues *habentes* carne [o] vescuntur, nec unquam congregantur.

Canis venatĭcus venatōrem *comitantem* loro [i] ad ferārum lustra trahit.

Beneficium non in eo [h] consistit quod datur, sed in ipso *dantis* [m] anĭmo.

Struthiocamēli Afrĭci altitudĭnem equĭtis equo [q] *insidentis* excēdunt.

Interdum delphīni conspecti sunt, *defunctum* [d] delphīnum *portantes*, et quasi funus *agentes.*

Multa, quæ de infantĭbus ferārum lacte *nutritis* [k] produntur, fabulōsa [r] videntur.

Homo quidam, lapĭde *ictus*,[k] oblītus est litĕras; [s] alius, ex præalto tecto *lapsus*, matris et affinium nomĭna dicĕre non potuit.

L. Siccius Dentātus, centies vicies *prœliātus*, quadraginta quinque cicatrīces adverso corpŏre [f] habēbat, nullam in tergo.

---

[a] Gr. 274.
[b] Gr. 548, R. XXXVI.
[c] Gr. 90, 13.
[d] Id. 101, 7 & 8.
[e] Gr 565, R. XLI, & Id. 6, 6.
[f] Gr. 611, (*in*).
[g] Gr. 437, R. I.
[h] Id. 13, 2.
[i] Gr. 542, R. XXXV.
[j] Gr. 720, R. LXV.
[k] Id. 101, 4.
[l] Gr. 663, R. LVII.
[m] Id. 19, 1.
[n] Gr. 403, & Id. 19, 1.
[o] Gr. 484, R. XXVI.
[p] Id. 19, 4.
[q] Gr. 399, R. IV
[r] Gr. 322.
[s] Gr. 373, R. XIV.

Leōnes *satiāti* innoxii sunt.

Elephantes nemĭni[a] nocent, nisi *lacessīti.*

Elephantes amnem[b] *transitūri*[c] minĭmos præmittunt.

Pavo *laudātus*[c] *gemmātam* pandit caudam.

Gallus, ab adversario *victus*,[c] occultātur[d] *silens*, et servitium patĭtur.

Leo *vulnerātus*[c] percussōrem intellĭgit, et in quantâlĭbet multitudĭne appĕtit.

Olōres iter *facientes*[c] colla impōnunt *præcedentĭbus;*[e] fessos duces ad terga recipiunt.

Testudĭnes in mari *degentes* conchyliis[f] vivunt; in terram *egressæ*,[g] herbis.[f]

Sarmătæ longinqua itinĕra *factūri*,[c] inediâ pridie præpărant equos, potum exiguum *impertientes;* atque ita longissĭmam viam contĭnuo cursu conficiunt.

Elephanti, equitātu *circumventi*, infirmos aut fessos *vulneratos*que in medium agmen recipiunt.

Multos *morientes* cura sepultūræ angit.

Danăus, ex Ægypto in Græciam *advectus*, rex[h] Argivōrum factus est.

Alexander, Bucephălo equo[i] *defuncto*, duxit exequias, urbemque Bucephălon *appellātam* ejus tumŭlo[j] circumdĕdit.

P. Catiēnus Plotīnus patrōnum adeò dilexit, ut, heres omnĭbus ejus bonis[k] *institūtus*,[c] in rogum ejus se conjicĕret[l] et concremarētur.[m]

---

[a] Gr. 403, R. V.
[b] Gr. 613, R. LII.
[c] Gr. 688.
[d] Id. 116, 7.
[e] Gr. 501, R. & Id. 19.
[f] Gr. 485.
[g] Id. 105, 1.
[h] Gr. 319, R. V. & 320.
[i] Gr. 690, R. LX. & Id. 9, 1.
[j] Gr. 501, R. & 505, & Id. 119, 2.
[k] Gr. 380, R.
[l] Gr. 627, 1, 1st.
[m] Gr. 720, R. LXV.

Erinacei *volutāti*[a] super poma, humi[b] *jacentia*, illa spinis[c] *affixa* in cavas arbŏres portant.

Indĭcum mare testudĭnes tantæ magnitudĭnis[d] alit, ut singŭlæ tugurio *tegendo*[e] sufficiant.[f]

Leōnes, senes *facti*, appĕtunt homĭnes, quoniam ad *persequendas* feras vires non suppĕtunt.

Struthiocamēlis[h] ungŭlæ sunt cervīnis[i] simĭles, *comprehendendis*[j] lapidĭbus utĭles, quos[k] in fugâ contra *sequentes*[l] jaculantur.

32. *Ablative Absolute.* (§ 146, R. LX.)

Senescente Lunâ[m] ostrea tabescĕre dicuntur, *crescente eâdem*, gliscunt. Cepe contrà, *Lunâ deficiente*, revirescĕre, *adolescente*, inarescĕre dicĭtur.

Geryŏne[n] *interemto* Hercŭles in Italiam venit.

Sabīnis[n] *debellātis*, Tarquinius triumphans Romam rediit.

Jasŏne[m] *Lycio interfecto*, canis, quem habēbat, cibum capĕre noluit, inediâque confectus est.

Regis Lysimăchi canis, *domĭno*[m] accensæ pyræ[c] *imposĭto*, in flammas se conjēcit.

Nicomēde[m] rege *interfecto*, equus ejus vitam finīvit inediâ.

Chilo, unus e septem sapientĭbus,[o] *filio victōre*[p] Olympiæ,[q] præ gaudio exspirāvit.

---

a Id. 116, 4.
b Gr. 559.
c Gr. 522, R. III.
d Gr. 339, R. VII.
e Gr. 703 and 707, R. LXII. and Gr. 399, R. IV. & Id. 112, 6.
f Gr. 627, 1 1st.
g Id. 112, 7.
h Gr. 394, R. II.
i Gr. 337, & Id. 19.
j Id. 112, 6.
k Gr. 437, R. I.
l Id. 19, 1.
m Gr. 690, R. LX. & 694.
n Gr. 694, & Id. 104, 1.
o Gr. 360.
p Gr, 695, & Id. 110, 4.
q Gr. 548, R. XXXVI. & Id. 4, 1,

FABLES FROM ÆSOP.

1. *Accipĭter et Columbæ.*

COLUMBÆ milvii metu accipĭtrem[a] rogavērunt,* ut eas[b] defendĕret.[c] Ille[b] annuit. At in[d] columbāre receptus, uno die[e] majorem stragem edĭdit, quàm milvius longo tempŏre[e] potuisset edĕre.[f]

Fabŭla docet, malōrum[g] patrocinium vitandum[h] esse.[i]

2. *Mus et Milvius.*

Milvius laqueis irretītus muscŭlum[a] exorāvit, ut eum, corrōsis plagis[j] liberāret.[c] Quo[k] facto, milvius liberātus murem arripuit et devorāvit.

Hæc fabŭla ostendit, quam gratiam mali[g] pro beneficiis reddĕre soleant.[l]

3. *Hœdus et Lupus.*

Hœdus, stans in[m] tecto domûs, lupo[n] prætereunti[o]

---

* The remote object of *rogavērunt* here is *accipĭtrem;* the immediate, *ut eas defendĕret.* (R. XXX. § 124.) So, generally, in these fables, after *inquit, dixit, respondit,* and the like, the immediate object of the verb is a clause expressing the thing said or replied, and, if in direct discourse, (651), is printed in *italics.*

[a] Id. 63, 3.
[b] Id. 27, 6.
[c] Id. 78, 5; Gr. 627, 1, 3d.
[d] Id. 123, 2.
[e] Id. 6, 6.
[f] Id. 88, 5.
[g] Id. 20, 1.
[h] Id. 108, 4.
[i] Id. 95, 1.
[j] Id. 109, 2, & 104, 1.
[k] Id. 38, 5.
[l] Id. 74, 9.
[m] Id. 123, 2.
[n] Gr. 397, R., Id. 7, 3.
[o] Id. 101, 1.

maledixit. Cui[a] lupus, *Non tu,*[b] inquit, *sed tectum mihi*[c] *maledĭcit.*

Sæpe locus et tempus homĭnes timĭdos audāces reddit.[d]

4. *Grus et Pavo.*

Pavo, coram grue pennas suas[e] explĭcans, *Quanta*[f] *est,* inquit,[u] *formosĭtas mea et tua deformĭtas!* At grus evŏlans, *Et quanta est,* inquit, *levĭtas mea et tua tardĭtas!*

Monet[u] hæc fabŭla, ne[g] ob alĭquod bonum, quod nobis natūra tribuit,[k] alios contemnāmus,[h] quibus[a] natūra alia[i] et fortasse majōra[i] dedit.[k]

5. *Pavo.*

Pavo gravĭter conquerebātur[l] apud Junōnem, domĭnam suam,[e] quòd vocis suavĭtas sibi[m] negāta esset,[n] dum luscinia, avis tam parum decōra,[o] cantu excellat.[n] Cui[a] Juno, *Et merĭtò,* inquit; *non enim omnia bona*[v] *in unum conferri oportuit.*

6. *Ansĕres et Grues.*

In eōdem quondam prato pascebantur[l] ansĕres et grues. Adveniente domĭno[p] prati, grues facĭlè avolābant; sed ansĕres, impedīti corpŏris gravitāte,[q] deprehensi[r] et mactāti sunt.

Sic sæpe paupĕres,[s] cum potentiorĭbus in eōdem crimĭne deprehensi, soli[t] dant pœnam, dum illi salvi evādunt.

---

[a] Id. 63, 1 & Gr. 504.
[b] Gr. 315.
[c] Gr. 397, R. & Id. 7, 3.
[d] Gr. 313.
[e] Id. 30, 1.
[f] Id. 48.
[g] Id. 121, 3.
[h] Id. 77, 3, & Gr. 627, 1, 3d.
[i] Id. 19, 4.
[k] Id. 72, 1.
[l] Gr. 160, 1.
[m] Id. 64, 2.
[n] Gr. 655.
[o] Id. 16, 5.
[p] Id. 9, & 109, 1.
[q] Gr. 542, R. XXXV.
[r] Id. 115, 1.
[s] Id. 20.
[t] Id. 16, 4.
[u] Gr. 445.
[v] Gr. 423, Exc. III.

7. *Capra et Lupus.*

Lupus capram in[a] altâ rupe stantem conspicātus, *Cur non,* inquit, *relinquis*[b] *nuda illa et sterilia loca, et huc descendis in*[c] *herbĭdos campos, qui tibi lætum pabŭlum offĕrunt?* Cui[d] respondit capra: *Mihi*[e] *non est in anĭmo, dulcia*[f] *tutis*[f] *præponĕre.*

8. *Venter et Membra.*

Membra quondam dicēbant ventri:[d] *Nosne*[g] *te semper*[h] *ministerio nostro alēmus, dum ipse*[i] *summo otio*[j] *fruĕris? Non faciēmus.** Dum igĭtur ventri[k] cibum subdūcunt, corpus debilitātur, et membra[l] serò invidiæ suæ pœnituit.[m]

9. *Canis et Boves.*

Canis jacēbat[n] in[a] præsēpi bovesque latrando[o] a pabŭlo arcēbat. Cui[d] unus[p] boum, *Quanta ista,*[q] inquit, *invidia est, quòd non patĕris, ut eo cibo*[j] *vescāmur,*[r] *quem tu ipse*[i] *capĕre nec velis*[s] *nec possis!*[s]

Hæc fabŭla invidiæ indŏlem declārat.

10. *Vulpes et Leo.*

Vulpes, quæ nunquam leōnem vidĕrat, quum ei[t] forte occurrisset,[u] ita est[v] perterrĭta, ut pæne morerētur[w] for-

---

[a] Id. 123, 2.
[b] Id. 56, 2d, 3d.
[c] Id. 123, 1.
[d] Id. 63, 1.
[e] Id. 118, 7 & 51.
[f] Id. 19, 4 & Gr. 501, R.
[g] Id. 58, 7.
[h] Id. 120.
[i] Id. 32, 2.
[j] Gr. 484, R. XXVI.
[k] Id. 5, 1.
[l] Gr. 419, Exc. II.
[m] Id. 66, 9.
[n] Gr. 160, 1.
[o] Id. 111, 5.
[p] Id. 21, 2.
* Supply *hoc*, Id. 19, 4.
[q] Gr. 123, 2.
[r] Id. 84, 4.
[s] Gr. 656.
[t] Gr. 399, R. & Id. 7, 2.
[u] Id. 74, 8.
[v] Id. 124, 15.
[w] Gr. 627, 1, 1st and Id. 74, 4.

midĭne.[a] Eundem conspicāta[b] itĕrum, timuit quidem, sed nequāquam,[c] ut antea.[c] Tertiò illi[d] obviâm facta, ausa est etiam propiùs accedĕre, eumque[e] allŏqui.

11. *Cancri.*

Cancer dicēbat[f] filio[g]: *Mi*[h] *fili,*[i] *ne*[j] *sic oblīquis semper gressĭbus*[a] *incēde, sed rectâ viâ*[a] *perge.* Cui ille, *Mi pater*, respondit, *libenter tuis præceptis*[k] *obsĕquar, si te priùs idem facientem vidĕro.*[l]

Docet hæc fabŭla, adolescentiam[m] nullâ re[a] magis quàm exemplis[n] instrui.[o]

12. *Boves.*

In eōdem prato pascebantur[f] tres boves in maxĭmâ concordiâ, et sic ab omni[p] ferārum incursiōne tuti erant. Sed dissidio[q] inter illos orto, singŭli a feris petīti[r] et laniāti sunt.

Fabŭla docet, quantum boni[s] sit[t] in concordiâ.

13. *Asinus.*

Asĭnus, pelle[u] leōnis indūtus, territābat homĭnes et bestias, tanquam leo esset.[v] Sed fortè, dum se celeriùs[w]

---

[a] Gr. 542, R. XXXV.
[b] Id. 105, 1.
[c] —, Sup. *timuit.*
[d] Gr. 600, R. XLVII.
[e] Gr. 613, R. LII.
[f] Gr. 159 & 504.
[g] Id 11.
[h] Gr. 98, 1, *Note* 1.
[i] Gr. 69, Exc. 5.
[j] Gr. 657, 2.
[k] Id. 7, 2.
[l] Gr. 168, VI.
[m] Gr. 671, R. LVIII.
[n] Gr. 469.
[o] Id. 95, 4.
[p] Gr. 740, 2d.
[q] Id. 9, 1, & 109, 5.
[r] Id. 115, 1.
[s] Gr. 343, R. VIII.
[t] Gr. 627, 5.
[u] Id. 64, 7.
[v] Gr. 627, 2.
[w] Id. 22, 3, & Gr. 473.

movet, aures eminēbant; unde agnĭtus in[a] pistrīnum abductus est, ubi pœnas petulantiæ dedit.

Hæc fabŭla stolĭdos[b] notat, qui immerĭtis honorĭbus[c] superbiunt.

14. *Mulier et Gallīna.*

Mulier quædam habēbat gallīnam, quæ ei quotidie ovum pariēbat aureum. Hinc suspicāri[d] cœpit, illam[e] auri massam intus celāre,[f] et gallīnam occīdit. Sed nihil in eâ repĕrit, nisi quod[g] in aliis gallīnis reperīri solet. Ităque dum majorĭbus divitiis[h] inhiābat, etiam minōres[i] perdĭdit.

15. *Viatōres et Asĭnus.*

Duo[h] qui unâ iter faciēbant, asĭnum oberrantem in solitudĭne conspicāti,[j] accurrunt læti, et uterque eum sibi vindicāre cœpit, quòd eum prior[k] conspexisset.[l] Dum verò contendunt et rixantur, nec[m] a[n] verberĭbus abstĭnent, asĭnus aufŭgit, et neuter eo[o] potītur.

16. *Corvus et Lupi.*

Corvus partem prædæ petēbat a lupis, quòd eos totum diem[p] comitātus esset.[l] Cui illi, *Non tu nos*, inquiunt, *sed prædam sectātus es, idque*[q] *eo anĭmo,*[c] *ut ne nostris quidem corporĭbus*[r] *parcĕres,*[s] *si exanimarentur.*[t]

---

[a] Id. 123, 1.
[b] Id. 19, 1.
[c] Gr. 542, R. XXXV.
[d] Gr. 663, R. LVII.
[e] Gr. 671, R. LVIII.
[f] Id. 96, 4.
[g] Id. 37, 2.
[h] Gr. 399, R. IV.
[i] Id. 19. Sup. *divitias.*
[j] Id. 105, 1.
[k] Gr. 274.
[l] Gr. 655.
[m] Gr. 242, 1.
[n] Gr. 615.
[o] Id. 7, 3, and Gr. 484, R. XXVI.
[p] Gr. 565, R. XLI.
[q] Gr. 123, 2, a (fecisti.)
[r] Gr. 403, R. V., Id. 7, 1.
[s] Gr. 627, 1, 1st.
[t] Gr. 627, 2

Merĭtò in actionĭbus non spectātur, quid fiat,[a] sed quo anĭmo fiat.[a]

17. *Pastōres et Lupus.*

Pastōres cæsâ ove[b] convivium celebrābant. Quod[c] quum lupus cernĕret,[d] *Ego*, inquit, *si agnum rapuissem*,[e] *quantus tumultus fiĕret!*[f] *At isti*[g] *impūne ovem comĕdunt!* Tum unum illōrum,[h] *Nos enim*,[z] inquit, *nostrâ, non aliēnâ ove*[i] *epulāmur.*

18. *Carbonarius et Fullo.*

Carbonarius, qui spatiōsam habēbat domum, invitāvit fullōnem, ut ad se commigrāret.[j] Ille respondit; *Quœnam inter nos esse possit*[k] *sociĕtas? quum tu vestes, quas ego nitĭdas reddidissem*,[l] *fuligĭne et macŭlis inquinatūrus esses.*[m]

Hæc fabŭla docet dissimilia[n] non debēre[o] conjungi.[p]

19. *Tubĭcen.*

Tubĭcen ab hostĭbus captus, *Ne*[q] *me*, inquit, *interficĭte; nam inermis sum, neque*[r] *quidquam habeo prœter hanc tubam.* At hostes, *Propter hoc ipsum*, inquiunt, *te interimēmus, quòd, quum ipse*[s] *pugnandi*[t] *sis*[u] *imperĭtus, alios ad pugnam incitāre soles.*

Fabŭla docet, non solùm malefĭcos[v] esse puniendos,[w] sed[x] etiam eos, qui alios ad malè faciendum[y] irrītent.[l]

[a] Gr. 627, 5 & Id. 74, 9.
[b] Id. 9, 1, & 109, 2.
[c] Id. 38, 4, & Gr. 295.
[d] Id. 74, 3.
[e] Id. 74, 7, & Gr. 627, 2.
[f] Gr. 627, 5.
[g] Gr. 118, 3, 3d.
[h] Id. 21, 2.
[i] Gr. 485.
[j] Id. 78, 5 and Gr. 627, 1, 3d.
[k] Id. 77, 4.
[l] Gr. 656.
[m] Gr. 214, 8.
[n] Id. 19, 4, and Gr. 671, R. LVIII.
[o] Id. 95, 1.
[p] Gr. 665.
[q] Gr. 657, 2.
[r] Gr. 242, 1.
[s] Id. 32, 2.
[t] Gr. 702, and Gr. 349, R. IX.
[u] Gr. 630.
[v] Id. 19, 1.
[w] Id. 108, 4, and Gr. 687.
[x] Gr. 720, R. LXV.
[y] Gr. 704.
[z] Gr. Sup. *verum est.*

20. *Accipitres et Columbæ.*

Accipitres quondam acerrĭmè inter se belligerābant. Hos columbæ in[a] gratiam reducĕre conātæ[b] effecērunt, ut illi pacem inter se[c] facĕrent.[d] Quâ[e] firmātâ, accipitres vim suam[f] in ipsas columbas convertērunt.

Hæc fabŭla docet, potentiōrum discordias imbecilliorĭbus[g] sæpe prodesse.

21. *Mulier et Gallīna.*

Mulier vidua gallīnam habēbat, quæ ei quotidie unum ovum pariēbat. Illa existimābat, si gallīnam diligentiùs sagināret,[h] fore,[i] ut illa bina aut terna ova quotidie parĕret. Quum autem cibo superfluo gallīna pinguis esset facta,[j] planè ova parĕre desiit.

Hæc fabŭla docet, avaritiam sæpe damnōsam esse.

22. *Vulpes et Uva.*

Vulpes uvam in vite conspicāta[b] ad illam subsiliit omnium virium suārum[f] contentiōne,[k] si eam fortè attingĕre posset.[h] Tandem defatigāta ināni labōre[k] discēdens dixit: *At nunc etiam acerbæ sunt, nec*[l] *eas in viâ repertas*[m] *tollĕrem.*[n]

Hæc fabŭla docet, multos[o] ea[o] contemnĕre, quæ se assĕqui posse desperent.[p]

---

[a] Id. 123, 1.
[b] Id. 105, 2.
[c] Id. 31, *Note.*
[d] Gr. 627, 1, 3d.
[e] Id. 38, 3.
[f] Id. 31, 3.
[g] Gr. 393, R. I.
[h] Gr. 627, 2.
[i] Gr. 678.
[j] Id. 74, 8.
[k] Gr. 542. R. XXXV.
[l] Gr. 242, 1.
[m] Id. 101, 4.
[n] Id. 78, 8.
[o] Id. 19, 1 and 4.
[p] Gr. 656.

23. *Vulpes et Leæna.*

Vulpes leænæ[a] exprobrābat, quòd nonnĭsi unum catŭlum parĕret.[b] Huic dicĭtur respondisse, *Unum. sed leōnem.*

Hæc fabŭla, non copiam sed bonitātem rerum æstimandam[c] esse, docet.

24. *Mures.*

Mures aliquando habuērunt consilium, quomŏdo sibi a fele cavērent.[d] Multis aliis[e] proposĭtis, omnĭbus[f] placuit,[g] ut ei[h] tintinnabŭlum annecterētur;[i] sic enim ipsos[j] sonĭtu admonĭtos eam fugĕre posse.[k] Sed quum jam inter mures quærerētur,[l] qui feli[m] tintinnabŭlum annectĕret,[n] nemo repertus est.

Fabŭla docet, in suadendo plurĭmos esse audāces,[o] sed in ipso pericŭlo timĭdos.[p]

25. *Canis Mordax.*

Cani[h] mordāci paterfamilias jussit tintinnabŭlum ex ære appendi,[q] ut omnes eum cavēre possent.[i] Ille verò æris tinnītu gaudēbat, et, quasi virtūtis suæ præmium[r] esset,[s] alios canes præ se contemnĕre cœpit. Cui unus senior,[t] *O te*[u] *stolĭdum,* inquit, *qui ignorāre vidēris,*[w] *isto tinnītu pravitātem morum tuōrum indicāri!*[v]

---

[a] Id. 63, 2, and Gr. 501, R. XXIX.
[b] Gr. 629.
[c] Id. 108, 4.
[d] Gr. 627, 5.
[e] Id. 9, 1, & 19, 4.
[f] Gr. 409, R. XVIII.
[g] Id. 65.
[h] Gr. 522, R. III.
[i] Gr. 627, 1, 4th.
[j] Id. 32, 8.
[k] Gr. 679, Sup. *existimavērunt.*
[l] Id. 65, & 74, 3.
[m] Gr. 501, R. XXIX.
[n] Id. 76, 2, & Gr. 127, 1.
[o] Gr. 322.
[p] Gr. 720, R. LXV.
[q] Id. 90, 1.
[r] Gr. 319, R. V.
[s] Gr. 627, 2. Sup. *id.* sc. *tintinnabŭlum.*
[t] Id. 6, 3. Sup. *cetĕris.*
[u] Gr. 451.
[v] Id. 95, 4.
[w] Id. 70, 3.

Hæc fabŭla scripta est in[a] eos, qui sibi[b] insignĭbus flagitiōrum suōrum placent.

26. *Canis et Lupus.*

Lupus canem videns benè saginātum, *Quanta est*, inquit, *felicĭtas tua! Tu, ut vidēris*,[c] *lautè vivis, at ego fame enĕcor.* Tum canis, *Licet*, inquit *mecum*[d] *in urbem venias*,[e] *et eâdem felicitāte*[f] *fruāris.* Lupus conditiōnem accēpit. Dum unà eunt, animadvertit lupus in collo canis attrītos[g] pilos. *Quid hoc est?* inquit.* *Num*[h] *jugum sustĭnes?*[i] *cervix enim tua tota est glabra. Nihil est*, canis respondit. *Sed interdiu me allĭgant, ut noctu sim vigilantior; atque hæc sunt vestigia collāris, quod cervīci*[j] *circumdări solet.* Tum lupus, *Vale*, inquit, *amīce!*[k] *nihil*[l] *moror felicitātem servitūte emptam!*

Hæc fabŭla docet, libĕris[t] nullum commŏdum tanti[m] esse, quod[n] servitūtis calamitātem compensāre possit.[o]

27. *Lupus et Grus.*

In faucĭbus lupi os inhæsĕrat. Mercēde igĭtur condūcit gruem, qui[n] illud extrăhat.[p] Hoc[q] grus longitudĭne colli facĭlè effēcit. Quum autem mercēdem postulāret, subrīdens lupus et dentĭbus infrendens, *Num*[h] *tibi*, inquit, *parva merces*[r] *vidētur*,[u] *quòd caput incolŭme ex lupi faucĭbus extraxisti?*[s]

---

[a] Id. 123, 1.
[b] Gr. 403, R. V.
[c] Id. 70, 6.
[d] Gr. 118, 4.
[e] Gr. 632.
[f] Gr. 484, R. XXVI.
[g] Gr. 179, 6; Id. 97, 4.
[h] Id. 56, 3d.
[i] Id. 58, 1.
[j] Gr. 522, R. III.
[k] Gr. 448.
[l] Gr. 500.
[m] Gr. 582, & Gr. 496.
[n] Id. 40, 1.
[o] Gr. 643, 2.
[p] Gr. 643, 4th.
[q] Id. 19, 4.
[r] Gr. 319, R. V.
[s] Gr. 624, 1, 2.
[t] Gr. 378, R. XV.
[u] Id. 51 and 70.

* Supply *lupus.*

28. *Agricŏla et Anguis.*

Agricŏla anguem repĕrit frigŏre pæne extinctum. Misericordiâ motus eum fovit sinu,[a] et subter alas[b] recondĭdit. Mox anguis recreātus vires recēpit, et agricŏlæ[c] pro beneficio letāle vulnus inflixit.

Hæc fabŭla docet, qualem[d] mercēdem mali pro beneficiis reddĕre soleant.[d]

29. *Asĭnus et Equus.*

Asĭnus equum beātum prædicābat, qui[c] tam copiōse pascerētur,[e] quum sibi post molestissĭmos labōres ne paleæ quidem satis præberentur.[f] Fortè autem bello[g] exorto equus in[h] prœlium agĭtur, et circumventus ab hostĭbus, post incredibĭles labōres tandem, multis vulnerĭbus confossus, collabĭtur. Hæc omnia asĭnus conspicātus,[i] *O me*[j] *stolĭdum*, inquit, *qui*[e] *beatitudĭnem ex præsentis tempŏris fortūnâ æstimavĕrim!*[e]

30. *Agricŏla et Filii.*

Agricŏla senex, quum mortem sibi[k] appropinquāre[l] sentīret, filios convocāvit, quos, ut fiĕri solet,[m] interdum discordāre[n] novĕrat, et fascem virgulārum afferri[n] jubet. Quibus[o] allātis, filios hortātur, ut hunc fascem frangĕrent.[p] Quod[q] quum facĕre non possent, distribuit singŭlas virgas, iisque celerĭter fractis, docuit

[a] Gr. 611.
[b] Gr. 608, R. LI.
[c] Gr. 501, R. XXIX.
[d] Gr. 627, 5.
[e] Gr. 645, R. III.
[f] Id. 74, 3 & Gr. 630.
[g] Id. 9, 1, & 109, 5.
[h] Id. 123, 1.
[i] Id. 105, 1.
[j] Gr. 449, R. XXI.
[k] Gr. 399, R. IV.
[l] Id. 96, 1.
[m] Id. 68, 3.
[n] Id. 90, 2.
[o] Id. 38, 3.
[p] Gr. 627, I. 3d.
[q] Id. 38, 4.

illos,[a] quàm firma res[b] esset[c] concordia, quàmque imbecillis discordia.

31. *Equus et Asĭnus.*

Asĭnus onustus sarcĭnis equum[a] rogāvit, ut alĭquâ parte[d] onĕris se[e] levāret, si se[e] vivum vidēre vellet.[f] Sed ille asĭni preces repudiāvit. Paulò pòst igĭtur asĭnus labōre consumptus in viâ corruit, et efflāvit anĭmam. Tum agitātor omnes sarcĭnas, quas asĭnus portavĕrat, atque insŭper etiam pellem asĭno[g] detractam in[h] equum imposuit. Ibi ille serò priōrem superbiam deplōrans, *O me misĕrum*, inquit, *qui parvŭlum onus in*[h] *me recipĕre noluĕrim*,[i] *quum nunc cogar*[j] *tantas sarcĭnas ferre, unà cum pelle comĭtis mei, cujus preces tam superbè contempsĕram.*

32. *Mulier et Ancillæ.*

Mulier vidua, quæ texendo[k] vitam sustentābat, solēbat ancillas suas[l] de nocte excitāre ad opus, quum primùm galli cantum audivisset. At illæ diuturno labōre fatigātæ statuērunt gallum interficĕre.[m] Quo[n] facto, deteriōre conditiōne[o] quam priùs* esse cœpērunt. Nam domĭna, de horâ noctis incerta[p] nunc famŭlas sæpe jam primâ nocte[q] excitābat.

* Supply *fuĕrant.*

[a] Id. 63, 4, 3.
[b] Id. 57, 6, & *Note.*
[c] Gr. 627, 5.
[d] Gr. 514, R. XXXI.
[e] Gr. 118, 3, 1st.
[f] Gr. 627, 2.
[g] Gr. 524, R. V.
[h] Id. 123; 1.
[i] Gr. 645, R. III.
[j] Id. 74, 1.
[k] Gr. 705.
[l] Id. 30, 1.
[m] Gr. 663, R. LVII.
[n] Id. 38, 5, & 109.
[o] Gr. 611.
[p] Id. 16.
[q] Gr. 565, R. XL.

33. *Testūdo et Aquĭla.*

Testūdo aquĭlam magnopĕre orābat, ut sese[a] volāre docēret. Aquĭla ei ostendēbat quidem, eam[b] rem petĕre[c] natūræ[d] suæ contrariam; sed illa nihĭlo[e] minùs instābat, et obsecrābat aquĭlam, ut se[a] volucrem facĕre[f] vellet. Ităque ungŭlis arreptam* aquĭla sustŭlit in sublīme, et demīsit illam, ut per aërem ferrētur. Tum in saxa incĭdens comminūta interiit.

Hæc fabŭla docet, multos[g] cupiditatĭbus suis occœcātos consilia prudentiōrum respuĕre[g] et in exitium ruĕre[g] stultitiâ suâ.[h]

34. *Luscinia et Accipĭter.*

Accipĭter esuriens rapuit lusciniam. Quæ,[i] quum intelligĕret sibi[j] mortem[g] impendēre, ad preces conversa orat accipitrem, *ne*[k] *se perdat sine causâ. Se*[g] *enim avidissĭmum ventrem illius non posse explēre, et suadēre adeò, ut grandiōres alĭquas volucres venētur.*[l] Cui accipĭter, *Insanīrem,*[m] inquit, *si partam prœdam amittĕre,*[n] *et incerta*[o] *pro certis*[o] *sectāri vellem.*[p]

35. *Senex et Mors.*

Senex in silvâ ligna cecidĕrat, iisque[q] sublātis, domum[r]

---

* Supply *illam.*

[a] Gr. 118, 3, 1st.
[b] Id. 27, 2, 6, & 91, & Gr. 673 & 674.
[c] Id. 96, 1.
[d] Gr. 382, R. XVI.
[e] Gr. 579, R. XLIII.
[f] Id. 87, 5.
[g] Id. 91, 2.
[h] Id. 31, 3.
[i] Id. 39, 5.
[j] Gr. 399, R. IV.
[k] Id. 121, 2.
[l] Gr. 656.
[m] Id. 78, 8.
[n] Id. 87, 5.
[o] Id. 19, 4.
[p] Gr. 627, 2.
[q] Id. 9, 1 & 109.
[r] Gr. 558, R. XXXIX.

redīre cœpit. Quum aliquantum[a] viæ[b] progressus esset,[c] et[d] onĕre et viâ defatigātus fascem deposuit, et secum ætātis et inopiæ mala contemplātus[e] Mortem clarâ voce invocāvit, quæ[f] ipsum[g] ab omnĭbus his malis[h] liberāret.[f] Tum Mors senis precĭbus audītis[i] subĭtò adstĭtit,* et, quid vellet,[j] percunctātur.[k] At Senex, quem[l] jam votōrum[m] suōrum pœnitēbat,[l] *Nihil,*† inquit, *sed requīro qui*[n] *onus paulŭlùm allĕvet*[f] *dum ego rursus subeo.*‡

36. *Inimīci.*

In eâdem navi vehebantur duo,[o] qui inter se[p] capitalia odia exercēbant. Unus eōrum[q] in prorâ, alter in puppi residēbat. Ortâ tempestāte ingenti, quum omnes de vitâ desperārent, interrŏgat is,[r] qui in puppi sedēbat, gubernatōrem, *Utram partem navis priùs submersum iri*[s] *existimāret.*[j] Cui gubernātor, *Proram,*‖ respondit. Tum ille, *Jam mors mihi non molesta est, quum inimīci mei mortem adspectūrus sim.*[t]

37. *Hinnuleus et Cervus.*

Hinnuleus quondam patrem suum his verbis interrogâsse dicĭtur: *Mi*[u] *pater, quum multo*[v] *sis*[w] *major canĭbus,*[x]

* Supply *seni,* Gr. 399, R. IV. † Supply *volo.* ‡ Supply *id,* viz: *onus.*
‖ Supply *priùs submersum iri,*

[a] Gr. 573, R. XLII.
[b] Gr. 343, R. VIII.
[c] Id. 74, 8.
[d] Id. 124, 1.
[e] Id. 106, 1.
[f] Id. 40, 4.
[g] Id. 32, 8.
[h] Gr. 517.
[i] Id. 104, 1.
[j] Id. 74, 16.
[k] Gr. 621.
[l] Id. 66, 9.
[m] Gr. 419, Exc. II.
[n] Id. 37, 1; Gr. 286, 4th.
[o] Id. 19, 1.
[p] Id. 123, 3, & Gr. 118, 5.
[q] Id. 21, 2.
[r] Id. 34 and 35.
[s] Id. 100, 7.
[t] Gr. 170, 1, & 214, 8.
[u] Gr. 98, *Note* 1.
[v] Gr. 579, R. XLIII.
[w] Id. 74, 1.
[x] Id. 6, 3.

et tam ardua cornua habeas,[a] *quibus a te vim propulsāre possis,*[b] *quî fit,*[c] *ut canes tantopĕre metuas?* Ibi cervus ridens, *Mi nate,* inquit, *vera*[d] *memŏras; mihi*[e] *tamen, nescio quo pacto, semper accĭdit,*[c] *ut audītâ canum voce, in fugam statim convertar.*

Hæc fabŭla docet, natūrâ[f] formidolōsos nullis rationĭbus[f] fortes reddi posse.

38. *Hœdus et Lupus.*

Quum hœdus evasisset lupum, et confugisset in caulam ovium, *Quid tu, stulte,* inquit ille, *hìc te salvum futūrum*[g] *speras, ubi quotidie pecŭdes rapi*[h] *et diis*[i] *mactāri*[h] *videas?*[b] *Non curo,* inquit hœdus; *nam si moriendum*[j] *sit, quanto*[k] *præclarius*[l] *mihi*[m] *erit, meo cruōre aspergi aras deōrum immortalium, quàm irrigāri siccas lupi fauces.*

Hæc fabŭla docet, bonos[n] mortem, quæ omnĭbus[e] immĭnet, non timēre,[o] si cum honestāte et laude conjuncta sit.[p]

39. *Corvus et Vulpes.*

Corvus alicunde caseum rapuĕrat, et cum illo in altam arbŏrem subvolârat.[q] Vulpecŭla illum caseum appĕtens corvum blandis verbis[f] adorĭtur; quumque

[a] Gr. 720, R. LXV.
[b] Gr. 656.
[c] Id. 51, 4.
[d] Id. 19, 4.
[e] Gr. 399, R. IV.
[f] Gr. 542, R. XXXV.
[g] Gr. 179, 4, *Note* 1.
[h] Id. 95, 4.
[i] Gr. 522, R. III.
[j] Gr. 699, R. LXI. & 701.
[k] Gr. 579, R. XLIII.
[l] Gr. 270.
[m] Gr. 382, R. XVI.
[n] Id. 91, 2.
[o] Id. 95, 1.
[p] Gr. 627, 2.
[q] Gr. 214, 1.

primùm formam ejus[a] pennarumque nitōrem laudâsset, *Pol*, inquit, *te avium regem esse dicĕrem*,[b] *si cantus pulchritudĭni*[c] *tuæ respondēret*. Tum ille laudĭbus vulpis inflātus etiam cantu se[a] valēre[d] demonstrāre voluit. Ita verò e rostro aperto caseus delapsus est, quem vulpes arreptum devorāvit.

Hæc fabŭla docet, vitandas[e] esse adulatōrum voces, qui blanditiis suis nobis[f] insidiantur.

40. *Leo.*

Societātem junxĕrant leo, juvenca, capra, ovis. Prædâ[g] autem, quam cepĕrant, in quatuor partes æquāles divīsâ, leo, *Prima*,[h] ait, *mea*[h] *est; debētur enim hæc*[h] *præstantiæ*[i] *meæ. Tollam et secundam, quam merētur robur meum. Tertiam*[j] *vindĭcat sibi egregius labor meus. Quartam qui sibi arrogāre voluĕrit, is*[k] *sciat*,[l] *se habitūrum*[m] *me inimīcum sibi*.[n] Quid facĕrent[o] imbecilles bestiæ, aut quæ* sibi[n] leōnem infestum habēre vellet?[o]

41. *Mus et Rustĭcus.*

Mus a rustĭco in caricārum acervo deprehensus tam[p] acri morsu ejus[a] digĭtos vulnerāvit, ut[p] ille eum dimittĕret,[q] dicens: *Nihil, mehercŭle, tam pusillum est, quod*[r] *de salūte desperāre debeat, modò se defendĕre et vim depulsāre velit*.[s]

---

* Supply *bestia*, Id. 19.

a Id. 31, & Obs.
b Id. 78, 8.
c Gr. 405, 5th.
d Id. 96, 2.
e Id. 108, 4.
f Gr. 403, & Id. 7, 7.
g Id. 9, 1, & 109.
h Id. 19.
i Id. 64, 2, & Gr. 519, R.
j Id. 62, & Gr. 501, R.
k Gr. 118, 3, 3d.
l Gr. 171, 1.
m Gr. 179, 4. *Note* 1.
n Gr. 382, R. XVI.
o Gr. 142, 2d.
p Id. 124, 15.
q Gr. 627, 1, 1st.
r Id. 40, 3.
s Gr. 627, 4.

42. *Vultur et Avicŭlæ.*

Vultur aliquando avicŭlas invitāvit[a] ad convivium, quod illis datūrus esset[b] die[c] natāli suo. Quæ[d] quum ad tempus adessent, eas carpĕre et occidĕre, epulasque sibi de invitātis instruĕre cœpit.

43. *Ranæ.*

Ranæ lætabantur, quum nuntiātum esset[e] Solem uxōrem duxisse.[f] Sed una cetĕris[g] prudentior, *O vos stolĭdos,* inquit; *nonne meministis,*[h] *quantopĕre nos sæpe unius Solis æstus excruciet?*[i] *Quid igĭtur fiet, quum libĕros etiam procreavĕrit?*[j]

44. *Ranæ et Jupĭter.*

Ranæ aliquando regem sibi a Jove[k] petivisse dicuntur. Quarum ille precĭbus exorātus trabem ingentem in lacum dejēcit. Ranæ sonĭtu perterrĭtæ primùm refugĕre,[l] deinde verò trabem in aquâ natantem conspicātæ magno cum contemptu[m] in eâ consedērunt, aliumque sibi novis clamorĭbus regem expetivērunt. Tum Jupĭter eārum stultitiam punitūrus[n] hydrum illis misit, a quo[o] quum plurĭmæ captæ perĭrent, serò eas[p] stolidārum precum pœnituit.

45. *Lupi et Pastōres.*

Quum Philippus, rex Macedoniæ, cum Atheniensĭbus fœdus initūrus esset eâ conditiōne,[q] ut oratōres suos

---

[a] Id. 73.
[b] Gr. 655.
[c] Gr 565, R. XL.
[d] Id. 39, 6.
[e] Id. 51, 2.
[f] Id 98, 3.
[g] Id. 6, 3.
[h] Gr. 84, 2, & Id. 58, 1.
[i] Gr. 157, 1, & Gr. 627, 5.
[j] Gr. 168, VI.
[k] Gr. 511.
[l] Gr. 669.
[m] Gr. 545.
[n] Id. 102, 1.
[o] Gr. 530.
[p] Id. 66, 8, & Gr. 419.
[q] Gr. 542, R. XXXV.

ipsi[a] tradĕrent, Demosthĕnes popŭlo narrāvit fabŭlam, quâ iis[b] callĭdum regis consilium ante ocŭlos ponĕret.[c] Dixit enim lupos quondam cum pastorĭbus pactos esse,[d] se nunquam in postĕrum[e] greges esse impugnatūros,[f] si canes ipsis[g] dederentur. Placuisse stultis pastorĭbus[h] conditiōnem; sed quum lupi caulas excubiis[i] nudātas vidissent, eos[j] impĕtu facto omnem gregem dilaniâsse.

46. *Puer Mendax.*

Puer oves pascens crebrò per lusum magnis clamorĭbus opem rusticōrum imploravĕrat, lupos gregem suum aggressos esse[k] fingens. Sæpe autem frustrātus eos, qui auxilium latūri[l] advenĕrant, tandem lupo reverâ irruente, multis cum lacrȳmis vicīnos orāre cœpit, *ut sibi*[m] *et gregi*[m] *subvenīrent.* At illi eum parĭter ut antea ludĕre[n] existimantes preces ejus et lacrȳmas neglexērunt, ita ut lupus libĕrè in oves grassarētur,[o] plurimasque eārum[p] dilaniāret.

47. *Corvus.*

Corvus, qui caseum fortè reperĕrat, gaudium altâ voce[q] significāvit. Quo[r] sono[q] allecti plures corvi famelĭci advolavērunt,[s] impetūque in illum facto, opīmam ei[t] dapem eripuērunt.

---

[a] Gr. 501, R. XXIX.
[b] Id. 5, 3, & Gr. 380, 381.
[c] Gr. 641, R. II.
[d] Id. 98, 2, & 94, 3.
[e] Gr. 232, Obs. 1, & Id. 19, 5.
[f] Id. 100, 3.
[g] Gr. 522, R. III.
[h] Id. 7, 2.
[i] Id. 64, 8.
[j] Gr. 720, R. LXV.
[k] Id. 94, 1, 2d, 2 & 98, 2.
[l] Id. 102, 1.
[m] Id. 7, 2, & Gr. 403.
[n] Id. 94, 1, 2, & 96, 2.
[o] Gr. 627, 1, 1st.
[p] Gr. 355, R. X.
[q] Gr. 542, R. XXXV.
[r] Id. 38.
[s] — Sup. *ad eum.*
[t] Id. 5, 1.

48. *Cornix et Columba.*

Cornix columbæ[a] gratulabātur fœcunditātem,[b] quod singŭlis mensĭbus pullos excludĕret.[c] At illa, *Ne mei,* inquit, *dolōris causam commemŏres.*[d] *Nam quos pullos*[e] *edūco, eos*[f] *domĭnus raptos aut ipse comĕdit, aut aliis comedendos*[g] *vendit. Ita mihi mea fœcundĭtas novum semper luctum parit.*

49. *Leo, Asĭnus, et Vulpes.*

Vulpes, asĭnus, et leo, venātum[h] ivĕrant.[i] Amplâ prædâ factâ, leo asĭnum illam partīri jubet.[j] Qui[k] quum singŭlis singŭlas[l] partes ponĕret æquāles, leo eum correptum dilaniāvit, et vulpecŭlæ partiendi[m] negotium tribuit. Illa astutior leōni partem maxĭmam apposuit, sibi vix minĭmam reservans particŭlam. Tum leo subrīdens ejus prudentiam laudāre, et unde hoc didicĕret[n] interrogāre, cœpit. Et vulpes, *Hujus*[o] *me,* inquit, *calamĭtas docuit, quid minōres*[p] *potentiorĭbus debeant.*[n]

50. *Muscæ.*

Effūsa mellis copia est: Muscæ advŏlant:[q]
Pascuntur. At mox impedītis crurĭbus
Revolāre nequeunt. *Heu misĕram,* inquiunt, *vicem!*[r]

---

[a] Id. 7, 2, & Gr. 403.
[b] Gr. 539, & *Note.*
[c] Gr. 655.
[d] Gr. 171, 1.
[e] Id. 37, 2d, *Note,* & 6.
[f] — Supply *pullos.*
[g] Id. 107, 2.
[h] Id. 114, 1.
[i] Gr. 312, R. I.
[j] Gr. 157, 3.
[k] Id. 39, 1.
[l] Id. 26, 4.
[m] Gr. 702.
[n] Gr. 627, 5.
[o] —. viz., *asini.*
[p] Id. 19, 1.
[q] —. Sup. *ad id (mel.)*
[r] Gr. 451.

Cibus iste[a] *blandus, qui pellexit suavĭter,*
Nunc fraudulentus quàm crudelĭter necat!
Perfĭda voluptas fabŭlâ hac depingĭtur.

51. *Cancer.*

Mare cancer olim deseruit, in litŏre
Pascendi[b] cupĭdus. Vulpes hunc simul[c] adspĭcit
Jejūna, simul accurrit,[d] et prædam capit.
Næ, dixit ille, *jure plector, qui,* SALO*
Quum fuĕrim natus, voluĕrim[e] SOLO *ingrĕdi!*
Suus unicuīque[f] præfinītus est locus,
Quem præterīre sine periclo non licet.

52. *Culex et Taurus.*

In cornu tauri parvŭlus quondam culex
Consēdit; seque[g] dixit, mole si suâ[g]
Eum[g] gravāret, avolatūrum[h] illĭco.
At ille:[i] *Nec te considentem sensĕram.*

---

* There is a play upon the words *salo* and *solo,* which cannot be preserved in the translation;—a loss of but little importance.

[a] Gr. 118, 3, 3d.
[b] Gr. 702.
[c] Id. 124, 11.
[d] — Sup. *ad eum.*
[e] Gr. 645, R. III.
[f] Gr. 522, R. III.
[g] Id. 31.
[h] Gr. 302, 2, and Gr. 179, *Note* 1.
[i] Gr. 308.

MYTHOLOGY.

1. Cadmus, Agenŏris filius,[a] quòd dracōnem, Martis filium, fontis cujusdam in Bœotiâ custōdem,[a] occidĕrat, omnem suam prolem interemptam vidit, et ipse cum Harmoniâ,[b] uxōre[a] suâ in Illyriam fugit, ubi ambo[c] in dracōnes conversi sunt.

2. Amy̆cus, Neptūni filius,[a] rex Bebryciæ, omnes, qui in ejus regna venissent,[d] cogēbat cæstĭbus secum contendĕre, et victos occidēbat. Hic quum Argonautas ad certāmen provocâsset,[e] Pollux cum eo contendit, et eum interfēcit.

3. Otos et Ephialtes, Aloëi filii[f] mirâ magnitudĭne[g] fuisse dicuntur. Nám singŭlis[h] mensĭbus[i] novem digĭtis[j] crescēbant. Ităque quum essent annōrum novem,[g] in cœlum ascendĕre sunt conāti. Huc sibi adĭtum sic faciēbant,[k] ut montem Ossam super Pelion ponĕrent, aliosque præterea montes exstruĕrent. Sed Apollĭnis sagittis interempti sunt.

5. Dædălus, Euphēmi filius, artĭfex peritissĭmus, ob

[a] Id. 12, 1.
[b] Gr. 314.
[c] Gr. 265, 266.
[d] Gr. 636, R. I.
[e] Id. 74, 8.
[f] Gr. 254.
[g] Id. 6, 1, and Gr. 339, R. VII.
[h] Id. 26, 5.
[i] Gr. 565, R. XLI.
[j] Gr. 573, R. XLII.
[k] Gr. 160, 2.

cædem Athēnis[a] commissam in Cretam[b] abiit ad regem Minōëm. Ibi labyrinthum exstruxit. A Minōë[c] aliquando in custodiam conjectus, sibi et Icăro filio alas cerâ[d] aptāvit, et cum eo avolāvit. Dum Icărus altiùs[e] evolābat, cerâ solis calōre calefactâ, in mare decĭdit, quod ex eo Icarium pelăgus[f] est appellātum. Dædălus autem in Siciliam[b] pervēnit.

5. Æsculapius, Apollĭnis filius, medĭcus præstantissĭmus, Hippolўto, Thesei filio, vitam reddidisse dicĭtur. Ob id facĭnus Jupĭter eum fulmĭne percussit. Tum Apollo quòd filii mortem in Jove[g] ulcisci non potĕrat, Cyclōpes, qui fulmĭna fecĕrant, interēmit. Ob hoc factum, Apollĭnem Jupĭter Admēto, regi Thessaliæ, in servitūtem dedit.

6. Alcestim,[i] Peliæ filiam, quum multi in matrimonium petĕrent, Pelias promĭsit, se filiam ei esse datūrum,[j] qui feras currui junxisset.[k] Admētus, qui eam perdĭtè amābat, Apollĭnem rogāvit, ut se in hoc negotio adjuvāret. Is quum ab Admēto, dum ei[l] serviēbat, liberalĭter esset tractātus, aprum ei et leōnem currui junxit,[m] quibus[n] ille Alcestim avexit. Idem gravi morbo implicĭtus, munus ab Apollĭne accēpit, ut præsens pericŭlum effugĕret, si quis sponte pro eo morerētur.[o] Jam quum neque pater, neque mater Admēti pro eo mori voluissent[p] uxor se Alcestis morti obtŭlit, quam Hercules fortè adveniens Orci manĭbus[q] eripuit, et Admēto reddĭdit.

7. Cassiŏpe filiæ suæ Andromĕdæ formam Nereïdum

[a] Id. 6, 2.
[b] Id. 123, 1, & Gr. 562.
[c] Gr. 530.
[d] Id. 6, 4.
[e] Id. 22, 3.
[f] Gr. 319, R. V.
[g] Id. 123, 2, and Gr. 609 & 610.
[h] Gr. 501, R. XXIX.
[i] Gr. 90, 2.
[j] Id. 100, 2.
[k] Id. 80, 2.
[l] Gr. 408, R. V.; Id. 7, 2.
[m] Gr. 427, R. XIX., & Gr. 431.
[n] Gr. 291.
[o] Gr. 142, 2d, and Gr. 627, 2.
[p] Gr. 313.
[q] Id. 5, 1.

formæ[a] anteposuit. Ob hoc crimen illæ a Neptūno[b] postulavērunt, ut Andromĕda ceto[c] immāni, qui oras populabātur, objicerētur. Quæ[d] quum ad saxum alligāta esset, Perseus ex Libyâ, ubi Medūsam occidĕrat, advolāvit, et, belluâ devictâ[e] et interemptâ,[e] Andromĕdam lībērāvit.

8. Quam quum abducĕre vellet victor, Agēnor, cui antea desponsāta fuĕrat, Perseo insidias struxit, ut eum interficĕret, sponsamque eripĕret.[f] Ille, re cognĭtâ,[e] caput Medūsæ insidiantĭbus ostendit, quo[g] viso, omnes in saxa mutāti sunt. Perseus autem cum Andromĕdâ in patriam rediit.

9. Ceyx, Hespĕri filius, quum in naufragio periisset, Alcyŏne, conjŭgis morte audītâ,[e] se in mare præcipitāvit. Tum deōrum misericordiâ ambo in aves sunt mutāti, quæ Alycŏnes appellantur. Hæ aves pariunt hiberno tempŏre.[h] Per illos dies mare tranquillium esse dicĭtur; unde nautæ tranquillos et serēnos dies Alcyonēos appellāre solent.

10. Tantălus, Jovis filius, tam carus fuit diis,[i] ut Jupĭter ei consilia sua concredĕret, eumque ad epŭlas deōrum admittĕret.[f] At ille, quæ[j] apud Jovem audivĕrat, cum mortalĭbus communicābat. Ob id crimen dicĭtur[k] apud infĕros in aquâ collocātus esse, semperque sitīre. Nam, quoties haustum aquæ sumptūrus[l] est, aqua recēdit. Tum etiam poma ei[m] super caput pendent; sed, quoties ea decerpĕre conātur, rami vento moti

[a] Gr. 501, R. XXIX.
[b] Gr. 511.
[c] Gr. 522, R. III.
[d] Id. 39, 2.
[e] Id. 104, 1.
[f] Id. 85.
[g] Id. 38, 5.
[h] Gr. 365, R. XL.
[i] Gr. 382, R. XVI.
[j] Id. 37, 2.
[k] Gr. 676.
[l] Gr. 214, 8.
[m] Id. 5, 3, & Gr. 380. R.

recēdunt. Alii saxum ejus capĭti [a] impendĕre dicunt, cujus ruīnam timens perpetuo metu cruciātur.

11. In nuptiis [b] Pelei et Thetĭdis omnes dii invitāti erant præter Discordiam. Hæc irâ commōta malum misit in medium, cui [c] inscripta erant verba: *Pulcherrĭma me habēto.* Tum Juno, Venus et Minerva illud simul appetēbant; [d] magnâque inter eas discordiâ exortâ, Jupĭter Mercurio impĕrat, ut deas ad Parĭdem, Priămi filium, ducĕret,[e] qui in monte Idâ greges pascēbat;* hunc eārum litem diremptūrum esse.[f] Huic Juno, si se pulcherrĭmam judicâsset,[g] omnium terrārum regnum est pollicĭta; Minerva ei splendĭdam inter homĭnes famam promīsit; Venus autem Helĕnam, Ledæ et Jovis filiam, se ei in conjugium dare [h] spopondit. Paris, hoc dono priorĭbus [c] anteposĭto [i] Venĕrem pulcherrĭmam esse [j] judicāvit. Postea Venĕris hortātu Lacedæmŏnem [k] profectus, Helĕnam conjŭgi [l] suo [m] Menelāo eripuit. Hinc bellum Trojānum origĭnem cepit, ad quod tota ferè Græcia, duce [n] Agamemnŏne, Menelāi fratre, profecta est.

12. Thetis, Pelei conjux, quum sciret Achillem filium suum citò peritūrum esse,[f] si Græcōrum exercĭtum ad Trojam sequerētur,[g] eum misit in insŭlam Scyron,[o] regīque Lycomēdi commendāvit. Ille eum, muliebri habĭtu,[p] inter filias suas servābat. Græci autem quum audivissent eum ibi occultāri,[q] unus eōrum [r] Ulysses, rex Ithăcæ, in regio [s] vestibŭlo munĕra feminea [s] in calathiscis

* Supply *dicens*, agreeing with Jupiter, Id. 94, 4.

[a] Gr. 399, R. IV.
[b] Gr. 609.
[c] Gr. 522, R. III.
[d] Gr. 312, R. I.
[e] Gr. 627, 1, 3d.
[f] Id. 94, 1, 2d, & 100, 1.
[g] Gr. 627, 2.
[h] Id. 94, 3, & 100, 2.
[i] Id. 104, 1.
[j] Id. 90, 3.
[k] Gr. 547, 2.
[l] Id. 5, 1.
[m] Id. 30, 4, and Gr. 118, 3, *Exc.*
[n] Id. 110, 1.
[o] Gr. 74.
[p] Gr. 542, R. XXXV.
[q] Id. 96, 7.
[r] Id. 21, 2.
[s] Gr. 337.

posuit, simulque clypeum et hastam; mulieresque advocāri[a] jussit. Quæ[b] dum omnia contemplabantur, subĭtò tubĭcen cecĭnit; quo sono audīto, Achilles arma arripuit. Unde eum virum[c] esse[d] intellectum est.

13. Quum totus Græcōrum exercĭtus Aulĭde[e] convenisset, adversa tempestas eos ob iram Diānæ retinēbat. Agamemnon enim, dux illius expeditiōnis, cervam deæ[f] sacram[g] vulneravĕrat, superbiùsque[h] in Diānam locūtus erat. Is quum haruspĭces convocâsset, respondērunt, iram deæ expiāri[i] non posse,[d] nisi filiam suam Iphigenīam ei immolâsset.[j] Hanc ob causam Ulysses Argos[k] profectus mentītur[l] Agamemnŏnem filiam Achilli in matrimonium promisisse.[m] Sic eam Aulĭdem[k] abduxit. Ubi quum pater eam immolāre[n] vellet, Diāna virgĭnem miserāta[o] cervam ei[p] supposuit. Iphigenīam ipsam per nubes in terram Taurĭcam detŭlit, ibique templi sui sacerdōtem fecit.

14. Trojâ eversâ, quum Græci domum[q] redīre vellent, ex Achillis tumŭlo vox dicĭtur fuisse audīta, quæ Græcos monēbat, ne fortissĭmum virum sine honōre relinquĕrent.[r] Quare Græci Polyxĕnam, Priămi filiam, quæ virgo fuit formosissĭma, ad sepulcrum ejus immolavērunt.

15. Promētheus, Iapĕti filius, primus[s] homĭnes ex luto finxit, iisque[p] ignem e cœlo in ferŭlâ attŭlit, monstravitque quomŏdo cinĕre obrŭtum servārent.[t] Ob hanc rem Vulcānus eum in monte Caucăso Jovis jussu clavis

---

[a] Id. 90, 4.
[b] Id. 38, 6.
[c] Gr. 319, R. V.
[d] Id. 96, 2.
[e] Id. 6, 2.
[f] Gr. 382, R. XVI.
[g] Id. 16,
[h] Id. 22, 3.
[i] Id. 87, 1.
[j] Gr. 656, & Id. 80.
[k] Gr. 553, R. XXXVII.
[l] Gr. 157, 3.
[m] Id. 94, 1, 2d, & 98, 2.
[n] Id. 88, 2.
[o] Id. 106, 1.
[p] Gr. 501, R. XXIX., & 502.
[q] Gr. 558, R. XXXIX.
[r] Gr. 627, 1, 3d.
[s] Gr. 274.
[t] Gr. 627, 5.

ferreis alligāvit ad saxum, et aquĭlam ei apposuit, quæ [a] cor exedĕret. Quantum [b] verò interdiu exedĕrat, tantum [b] nocte crescēbat. Hanc aquĭlam insequenti tempŏre Hercŭles transfixit sagittis, Prometheumque liberāvit.

16. Pluto, inferōrum deus, a Jove fratre petēbat, ut sibi Proserpĭnam, Jovis et Cerĕris filiam, in matrimonium daret.[c] Jupĭter negāvit quidem Cerĕrem passūram esse,[d] ut filia in tenebris Tartări morarētur;[c] sed fratri permīsit, ut eam, si posset, rapĕret.[c] Quare Proserpĭnam, in nemŏre Ennæ in Siciliâ flores legentem, Pluto quadrīgis ex terræ hiātu proveniens rapuit.

17. Ceres quum nescīret ubi filia esset,[f] eam per tōtum orbem terrārum quæsīvit. In quo itinĕre ad Celeum venit, regem Eleusiniōrum, cujus uxor Metanīra puĕrum Triptolĕmum peperĕrat, rogavitque ut se tanquam nutrīcem in domum recipĕrent.[c] Quo facto, quum Ceres alumnum suum [g] immortālem reddĕre vellet,[h] eum interdiu lacte divīno alēbat, noctu clam igne obruēbat. Ităque mirum in modum crescēbat. Quod [i] quum mirarentur parentes, eam [j] observavērunt. Qui [k] quum vidērent Cerĕrem puĕrum in ignem mittĕre,[l] pater exclamāvit. Tum dea Celeum exanimāvit; Triptolĕmo autem currum dracōnĭbus [m] junctum tribuit, frugesque mandāvit, quas per orbem terrārum vectus dissemināret.[n]

18. Althæa, Thestii filia, ex Œneo pepĕrit Meleăgrum. Ei Parcæ ardentem titiōnem dedērunt, præfantes [o] Meleăgrum tam diu victūrum [d] quàm diu [p] is titio foret [q] in-

[a] Id. 40, 1; Gr. 643, 4th.
[b] Id. 44, 3 & 47.
[c] Gr. 627, 1, 3d.
[d] Id. 100, 2.
[e] Gr. 677, 5th.
[f] Gr. 656.
[g] Id. 30, 4.
[h] Id. 74, 3.
[i] Id. 38, 4.
[j] Id. 27, 6.
[k] Id. 39, 1.
[l] Id. 96, 1.
[m] Id, 64, 6.
[n] Id. 40, 5, and Gr. 641, R. II.
[o] Id. 94, 1, 2d.
[p] Id. 124, 19.
[q] Gr. 627, 6.

colŭmis. Hunc[a] ităque Althæa diligenter in arcâ clausum servāvit. Intĕrim Diāna Œneo[b] irāta quia eī sacra annua non fecĕrat, aprum mirâ magnitudĭne[c] misit, qui agrum Calydonium vastāret.[d] Quem[e] Meleāger cum juvenĭbus ex omni Græciâ delectis interfēcit, pellemque ejus Atalantæ donāvit. Cui[f] quum Althææ fratres eam eripĕre vellent, illa Meleāgri auxilium implorāvit, qui avuncŭlos occīdit. Tum Althæa, gravi irâ[g] in filium commōta, titiōnem illum fatālem in ignem conjēcit. Sic Meleāger periit. At sorōres ejus, dum fratrem insolabilĭter lugent, in aves mutātæ sunt.

19. Eurōpam, Agenŏris filiam, Sidoniam, Jupĭter in taurum mutātus Sidōne[h] Cretam[i] transvexit, et ex eâ procreāvit Minōëm, Sarpedŏnem, et Rhadamanthum. Hanc ut reducĕrent Agēnor suos filios misit, conditiōne addĭtâ, ut nec ipsi[j] redīrent, nisi sorōrem invenissent.[k] Horum unus, Cadmus nomĭne,[l] quum errāret, Delphos[i] venit, ibique responsum accēpit, bovem præcedentem sequerētur;[m] ubi ille decubuisset,[k] ibi urbem condĕret.* Quod quum facĕret,[n] in Bœotiam venit. Ibi aquam quærens ad fontem Castalium dracōnem invēnit, Martis filium, qui aquam custodiēbat.[o] Hunc Cadmus interfēcit, dentesque ejus sparsit et arāvit. Unde Sparti enāti sunt. Pugnâ inter illos exortâ, quinque superfuērunt, ex quibus quinque nobĭles Thebanōrum stirpes origĭnem duxērunt.

---

* *Condĕret* is in the same construction with *sequerētur*.

[a] Sup. *titionem*.
[b] Gr. 382, R. XVI.
[c] Id. 6, 1, and Gr. 339, R. VII.
[d] Id. 40, 4.
[e] Id. 39, 7.
[f] Id. 39, "*from her*," & Id. 5, 1.
[g] Gr. 542, R. XXXV.
[h] Gr. 556, R. XXXVIII.
[i] Gr. 553, R. XXXVII.
[j] Id. 32, 3.
[k] Gr. 656.
[l] Gr. 535, R. XXXIV.
[m] Gr. 632.
[n] Id. 38, 4.
[o] Gr. 160, 2.

20. Quum Bacchus, Jovis ex Semĕle filius, exercĭtum in Indiam ducĕret, Silēnus ab agmĭne aberrāvit. Quem[a] Midas, rex Mygdoniæ, hospitio[b] liberalĭter accēpit, eique ducem dedit, qui[c] eum ad Bacchum reducĕret. Ob hoc beneficium Bacchus Midæ optiōnem dedit, ut quicquid vellet[d] a se petĕret.[e] Ille petiit, ut quidquid[f] tetigisset[d] aurum fiĕret.[e] Quod[g] quum impetrâsset,[h] quidquid[f] tetigĕrat aurum fiēbat. Primò gavīsus est hâc virtūte[i] suâ; mox intellexit nihil ipsi[j] hoc munĕre[k] perniciosius esse. Nam etiam cibus et potio in aurum mutabātur.[l] Quum jam fame cruciarētur, petit a Baccho, ut donum suum revocāret.[e] Quem[a] Bacchus jussit in flumĭne Pactōlo se abluĕre, quumque aquam tetigisset, facta est colōre[m] aureo.

21. Schœneus Atalantam filiam formosissĭmam dicĭtur habuisse, quæ cursu viros superābat.[n] Hæc quum a plurĭbus[o] in conjugium peterētur, pater ejus conditiōnem proposuit, ut, qui eam ducĕre vellet,[d] priùs cursu cum eâ contendĕret;[c] si victus esset,[d] occiderētur.[e] Multos quum superâsset et interfecisset, tandem ab Hippomĕne victa est. Hic enim a Venĕre tria mala aurea accepĕrat. Dum currēbant, horum unum post altĕrum projēcit, iisque[b] Atalantæ cursum tardāvit. Nam dum mala collĭgit, Hippomĕnes ad metam pervēnit. Huic ităque Schœneus filiam uxōrem dedit. Quam[p] quum in patriam ducĕret, oblītus Venĕris beneficio[b] se vicisse,[q] grates ei[r] non egit.

---

[a] Id. 39, 7.
[b] Gr. 542, R. XXXV.
[c] Id. 40, 4, and Gr. 641, R. II.
[d] Gr. 656.
[e] Gr. 627, 1, 3d.
[f] Id. 37, 8.
[g] Id. 38, 7.
[h] Id. 74, 8, & Gr. 631.
[i] Gr. 611.
[j] Gr. 382, R. XVI.
[k] Id. 6, 3.
[l] Gr. 313.
[m] Id. 6, 1, and Gr. 339, R. VII.
[n] Gr. 160, 1.
[o] Id. 19, 1.
[p] Id. 39, 8.
[q] Id. 94, 1, 2d, & 98, 2.
[r] Id. 27, 2d, 6, and Gr. 501, R. XXIX.

Hanc ob causàm Hippomĕnes mutātus est in leōnem, Atalanta in leænam.

22. Nisus, rex Megarensium, in capĭte crinem purpureum habuisse dicĭtur,[a] eique prædictum[b] fuit, tam diu eum regnatūrum,[c] quàm diu[d] eum crinem custodîsset.[e] Hunc Minos, rex Cretensium, bello[f] aggressus est. Qui[g] quum urbem Megăram oppugnāret, Scylla, Nisi filia, amōre[f] ejus correpta est, et, ut ei victoriam parāret,[h] patri[i] dormienti fatālem crinem præcīdit. Ita Nisus a Minōë victus[j] et occīsus est. Quum autem Minos in Cretam redīret,[k] Scylla eum rogāvit, ut eam secum avehĕret. Sed ille negāvit Cretam tantum scelus esse receptūram.[c] Tum illa se in mare præcipĭtat, navemque persequĭtur. Nisus in aquĭlam marīnam conversus est, Scylla in piscem, quem Cirim vocant. Hodiēque, siquando illa avis hunc piscem conspexĕrit,[l] mittit se in aquam, raptumque unguĭbus[f] dilaniat.

23. Amphīon, Jovis et Antiŏpes filius, qui Thebas muris cinxit, Niŏben, Tantăli filiam, in matrimonium duxit. Ex quâ procreāvit filios septem totidemque filias. Quem partum Niŏbe Latōnæ libĕris anteposuit, superbiùsque[m] locūta est in Apollĭnem et Diānam. Ob id Apollo filios ejus venantes sagittis interfēcit, Diāna autem filias. Niŏbe libĕris[n] orbāta in saxum mutāta esse dicĭtur,[a] ejusque lacrȳmæ hodiēque manāre narrantur.[a] Amphīon autem, quum templum Apollĭnis expugnāre vellet,[o] ab Apollĭne sagittis est interfectus.

---

[a] Gr. 676.
[b] Id. 51, 2, & Gr. 309.
[c] Id. 100, 2.
[d] Id. 124, 19.
[e] Gr. 656.
[f] Gr. 542, R. XXXV.
[g] Id. 39, 1.
[h] Gr. 627, 1, 2d.
[i] Id. 5, 1.
[j] Id. 115, 1.
[k] Gr. 159, II.
[l] Gr. 173, 1, 2.
[m] Id. 22, 2.
[n] Id. 64, 8, & 5, 1.
[o] Gr. 631.

24. Phineus, Agenŏris filius, ab Apollĭne futurārum rerum scientiam accepĕrat. Quum verò hominĭbus[a] deōrum consilia enuntiāret,[b] Jupĭter eum excæcāvit, et immīsit ei[a] Harpyias, quæ Jovis canes[c] esse dicuntur, ut cibum ab ore* ei[d] auferrent.[e] Ad quem[f] quum Argonautæ venissent, ut eum iter[g] rogārent,[h] dixit se illis iter demonstratūrum esse,[i] si eum pœnâ[j] liberārent. Tum Zetes et Calaïs, Aquilōnis filii,[k] qui pennas in capĭte et in pedĭbus habuisse dicuntur, Harpyias fugavērunt in insŭlas Strophădas, et Phineum pœnâ[j] liberârunt.

---

* Ab ore ei, *from him, from his mouth*, i. e. "*from his very mouth.*"

[a] Gr. 501, R. XXIX.
[b] Gr. 631.
[c] Gr. 319, R. V.
[d] Id. 5, 1.
[e] Gr. 627, 1, 2d.
[f] Id. 39, 9.
[g] Gr. 508, R. XXX.
[h] Gr. 656.
[i] Id. 100, 2.
[j] Gr. 514, R. XXXI.
[k] Gr. 254.

ANECDOTES OF EMINENT PERSONS.

1. THALES, interrogātus an facta homĭnum deos[a] latērent,[b] respondit, ne[c] cogitāta quidem.

2. Solon, qui Atheniensĭbus leges scripsit, dicēbat nemĭnem, dum vivĕret,[d] beātum habēri posse, quòd omnes ad ultĭmum usque diem ancipĭti fortūnæ[e] obnoxii essent.[f]

3. Pythagŏræ philosŏphi tanta fuit apud discipŭlos suos auctorĭtas, ut, quæ ab eo audivissent,[d] ea in dubitatiōnem adducĕre non audērent.[g] Rogāti autem ut causam reddĕrent[h] eōrum, quæ dixissent,[d] respondēbant, *Ipsum dixisse.*[i] *Ipse* autem erat *Pythagŏras.*

4. Bias unus ex septem Sapientĭbus,[j] quum patriam Priēnen ab hostĭbus expugnātam et eversam fugĕret,[k] interrogātus, cur nihil ex bonis[j] suis secum ferret,[b] *Ego verò*, respondit,[l] *bona mecum porto omnia.*

5. Democrĭtus, cui pater ingentes divitias reliquĕrat, omne ferè patrimonium suum civĭbus donāvit, ne do-

---

a Gr. 436, R. XX.
b Id. 74, 12.
c Id. 121, 5.
d Gr. 656.
e Gr. 382, R. XVI.
f Gr. 655.
g Gr. 627, 1, 1st.
h Id. 78, 5.
i Id. 98, 1.
j Gr. 360, & Id, 19, 1, & 4.
k Id. 74, 3.
l Gr. 445, R.

mesticārum rerum curâ a philosophiæ studio avocarētur.[a]

6. Etiam Crates Thebānus bona sua inter Thebānos divīsit, nihil sibi servans præter peram et bacŭlum. Hæc enim Cynicōrum instrumenta erant. A quo[b] consilio quum amīci et propinqui eum avocāre studērent,[c] eos correpto bacŭlo[d] fugāvit, nihil pulchrius esse arbitrātus, quàm ab omnĭbus curis[e] vacuum[f] uni philosophiæ opĕram dare.[g]

7. Anaxagŏras, quum a longinquâ peregrinatiōne scientiæ augendæ[h] causâ susceptâ in patriam rediisset, agrosque suos neglectos et desertos vidēret, *Non essem*,[i] inquit, *salvus, nisi ista*[j] *periissent*.[k]

8. Carneădes usque ad extrēmam senectam nunquam cessāvit a philosophiæ studio. Sæpe ei accĭdit,[l] ut, quum cibi[h] capiendi causâ accubuisset, cogitationĭbus[m] inhærens manum ad cibos appositos porrigĕre oblivisceretur.[n]

9. Idem adversùs Zenōnem Stoĭcum scriptūrus caput hellebŏro purgābat, ne corrupti humōres sollertiam et acūmen mentis impedīrent.[a]

20. Anaxagŏras, philosŏphus, morte[d] filii audītâ, vultu nihil[o] immutāto dixit.[p] *Sciēbam me mortālem genuisse*.[q]

11. Archȳtas Tarentīnus, quum ab itinĕre reversus agros suos villĭci socordiâ neglectos vidēret, *Gravĭter te castigārem*,[i] inquit, *nisi irātus essem*.[k]

12. Plato quoque, quum in servum vehementiùs[i] ex-

[a] Gr. 627, 1, 2d.
[b] Id. 38, 8.
[c] Id. 74, 3, & Gr. 631.
[d] Id. 9, 1, & 104, 2.
[e] Gr. 361, R. XI. & 363.
[f] — Sup. *se*.
[g] Gr. 720, R. & 722.
[h] Id. 112, 1, & 5.
[i] Id. 78, 8.
[j] Gr. 118, 3, 3d.
[k] Gr. 629.
[l] Id. 51, 3, "*happened*."
[m] Gr. 399, R. IV.
[n] Gr. 627, 1, 4th.
[o] Gr. 539.
[p] Gr. 445, R.
[q] Id. 98, 1.
[r] Id. 22, 1.

arsisset, verĭtus ne[a] vindictæ modum excedĕret, Speusippo[b] adstanti mandāvit, ut de illiùs pœnâ statuĕret.[c]

13. Idem discendi[d] cupiditāte ductus, Ægyptum peragrāvit, et a sacerdotĭbus illius regiōnis geometriam et astronomiam didĭcit. Idem in Italiam trajēcit, ut ĭbi Pythagŏræ philosophiam et institūta discĕret.[e]

14. Athenienses Socrătem damnavērunt, quòd novos deos introducĕre videbātur. Protagŏram quoque philosŏphum, qui ausus[f] fuĕrat scribĕre, se ignorāre an dii essent,[g] Athenienses ex urbe pepulērunt.

15. Xanthippe, Socrătis uxor, morōsa admŏdum fuisse fertur. Quam[h] ejus indŏlem quum perspexisset Alcibiădes, Socrătem interrogāvit, quid esset,[g] quòd muliĕrem tam acerbam et jurgiōsam non exigĕret[i] domo.[j] Tum ille, *Quoniam*, inquit, *dum illam domi*[j] *perpetior, insuesco, ut ceterōrum quoque foris petulantiam et injurias faciliùs feram.*[e]

16. Xenocrătes philosŏphus, quum maledicōrum quorundam sermōni[k] interesset, neque quidquam ipse loquerētur,[l] interrogātus, cur solus tacēret,[g] respondit: *Quia dixisse*[m] *me aliquando pœnituit, tacuisse*[m] *nunquam.*

17. Hegesias philosŏphus in disputationĭbus suis[n] mala et cruciātus vitæ tam vivĭdis colorĭbus repræsentābat, ut multi, qui eum audivĕrant, sponte se occidĕrent.[o] Quare a Ptolemæo rege ulteriùs his de rebus disserĕre est prohibĭtus.

---

[a] Id. 121, 6, & Gr. 633.
[b] Gr. 501, R. XXIX.
[c] Gr. 627, 1, 3d.
[d] Gr. 702.
[e] Gr. 627, 1, 2d.
[f] Gr. 213, 1.
[g] Id. 74, 11, & Gr. 627, 5.
[h] Id. 38, 6.
[i] Gr. 656.
[j] Gr. 558, R. XXXIX.
[k] Gr. 393, R. I. & Id. 5, 4.
[l] Gr. 720, R. LXV.
[m] Id. 66, 10, & Gr. 421.
[n] Id. 30, 1.
[o] Gr. 627, 1, 1st.

18. Gorgiæ Leontīno,[a] qui eloquentiâ[b] et eruditiōne omnes suæ ætātis homĭnes superāre existimabātur, universa Græcia in templo Apollĭnis Delphĭci statuam auream collocāvit.

19. Idem, quum annum centesĭmum septĭmum agĕret, interrogātus, quapropter tam diu vellet[c] in vitâ remanēre, respondit: *Quia nihil habeo, quod*[d] *senectūtem meam accūsem.*[e]

20. Illustrissĭmi sæpe viri humĭli loco[f] nati fuērunt.[g] Socrătes, quem oracŭlum Apollĭnis sapientissĭmum omnium homĭnum[h] judicāvit,[i] obstetrīcis filius fuit. Euripĭdes, poëta tragĭcus, matrem habuit,[i] quæ olĕra venditābat,[j] et Demosthĕnis, oratōris eloquentissĭmi, patrem cultellos vendidisse[k] narrant.

21. Homērus, princeps poëtārum Græcōrum, dolōre absumptus esse credĭtur, quòd quæstiōnem a piscatorĭbus ipsi[l] proposĭtam solvĕre non posset.[m]

22. Simonĭdes, poëta præstantissĭmus, gloriātur in quodam poëmăte, se[n] octoginta annos[o] natum in certāmen musĭcum descendisse[k] et victoriam inde retulisse. Idem aliquandiu vixit apud Hipparchum, Pisistrăti filium, Athenārum tyrannum. Inde Syracūsas[p] se contŭlit ad Hierōnem regem, cum quo familiarĭter vixisse dicĭtur. Primus[q] carmĭna statūto pretio[r] scripsit; quare eum Musam venālem reddidisse dicunt.

23. Quum Æschȳlus Atheniensis, qui parens[s] tragœdiæ dicĭtur, in Siciliâ versarētur,[t] ibique in loco aprīco

[a] Gr. 501, R. XXIX.
[b] Gr. 535, R. XXXIV. Id. 74, 16.
[d] Gr. 492.
[e] Gr. 636, R. I.
[f] Id. 6, 5, and Gr. 462, R. XXIII.
[g] Id. 72.
[h] Gr. 355, R. X.
[i] Id. 73.
[j] Gr. 160, 1.
[k] Id. 97, 1.
[l] Id. 32, 9, & Gr.522,R.
[m] Gr. 655.
[n] Gr. 671, R. LVIII.
[o] Gr. 565, R. XLI.
[p] Gr. 553, R.
[q] Gr. 274.
[r] Gr. 581, R. XLIV.
[s] Gr. 319, R. V.
[t] Id. 74, 3.

sedēret, aquĭla testudĭnem glabro ejus capĭti[a] immīsit quod pro saxo habuit. Quo[b] ictu ille extinctus est.

24. Eurīpĭdes, qui et ipse magnum inter poëtas tragĭcos nomen habet, a cœnâ domum rediens a canĭbus lacerātus est.

25. Athenienses quondam ab Eurīpĭde postulābant, ut ex tragœdiâ sententiam quandam tollĕret.[c] Ille autem in scenam progressus dixit, se fabŭlas componĕre solēre,[d] ut popŭlum docēret,[e] non ut a popŭlo discĕret.

26. Philippĭdes, comœdiārum scriptor, quum in poëtārum certamĭne præter spem vicisset[f] et illâ victoriâ impensè gaudēret, eo ipso gaudio repentè exstinctus est.

27. Pindărus, poëta Thebānus, Apollĭni[g] gratissĭmus fuisse dicĭtur. Quare sæpe a sacerdotĭbus in templum Delphĭcum ad cœnam vocabātur, parsque ei[h] tribuebātur donōrum, quæ sacrificantes[i] deo obtulĕrant. Ferunt etiam Pana[j] Pindări hymnis[k] tantopĕre fuisse lætātum, ut eos in montĭbus et silvis canĕret.[l] Quum Alexander, rex Macedoniæ, Thebas diripĕret, unīus Pindări domo[m] et familiæ pepercit.

28. Diogĕnes Cynĭcus Myndum profectus, quum vidēret magnifĭcas portas et urbem exiguam, Myndios monuit, ut portas claudĕrent,[c] ne urbs egrederētur.[e]

29. Demosthĕnes Atheniensis incredibĭli studio et labōre eò[n] pervēnit, ut, quum[o] multi eum ingenio[p] parum valēre existimārent, omnes ætātis suæ oratōres superāret eloquentiâ.[p] Nunquam tamen ex tempŏre dicēbat, neque in conciōne volēbat assurgĕre, nisi rem, de quâ agerētur,[q]

---

[a] Gr. 501, R. XXIX.
[b] Id. 38, 9.
[c] Gr. 627, 1, 3d.
[d] Id. 96, 2.
[e] Gr. 627, 6, or 1, 2d.
[f] Id. 74, 8.
[g] Gr. 384, 2d.
[h] Gr. 522, R. III.
[i] Id. 19, 1.
[j] Gr. 90, 4.
[k] Gr. 485.
[l] Gr. 627, 1, 1st.
[m] Gr. 403, R. & Id. 7, 2.
[n] Id. 28, Obs.
[o] Gr. 631.
[p] Gr. 535, R. XXXIV.
[q] Gr. 656.

accurāte antea meditātus esset.[a] Unde plerīque eum timĭdum esse existimābant. Sed in hac re Periclis consuetudĭnem imitabātur, qui non facĭlè de quáque re dicĕre, nec existimatiōnem suam[b] fortūnæ committĕre solēbat.

30. Pericles in conciōnem itūrus, quum anĭmo perpendĕret, quantum pericŭli[c] inconsiderātè dicta[d] homĭnĭbus afferrent,[e] solēbat precāri a diis,[f] ne quod ipsi[g] verbum imprudenti excidĕret, quod reipublĭcæ officĕre posset.[h]

31. Minos, Cretensium rex, sæpe se in speluncam quandam conferēbat, ibique se cum Jove collŏqui[i] legesque ab eo accipĕre[i] dicebat. Etiam Lycurgus Lacedæmoniis[j] persuāsit, se leges suas[b] ab Apollĭne didicisse.[k]

32. Quum Lycurgus, Lacedæmoniōrum legislātor, Delphis[l] in templum Apollĭnis intrâsset, ut a deo[f] oracŭlum petĕret, Pythia eum his verbis allocūta est: *Nescio utrùm deus an homo appellandus*[m] *sis; sed deus potiùs videāris*[n] *esse.*

33. Leonĭdas, rex Lacedæmoniōrum, quum Persæ dicerentur sagittārum multitudĭne solem obscuratūri, respondisse fertur: *Meliùs ităque in umbrâ pugnabĭmus.*

34. Cyrus omnium suōrum milĭtum nomĭna memoriâ tenēbat. Mithridātes autem, rex Ponti, duārum et viginti gentium, quæ sub regno ejus erant, linguas ita didĭcerat, ut cum omnĭbus, quibus[o] imperābat, sine interprĕte loqui posset.

35. Themistŏcles interroganti[p] utrùm Achilles esse mallet,[e] an Homērus,[q] respondit: *Tu verò mallesne te in Olympĭco certamĭne victōrem renuntiāri*[r] *an præco esse, qui victōrum nomĭna proclāmat?*

---

[a] Gr. 629.
[b] Id. 30, 3.
[c] Gr. 343, R. VIII.
[d] Id. 19, 4.
[e] Id. 74, 11.
[f] Gr. 511.
[g] Gr. 401.
[h] Gr. 656.
[i] Id. 96, 1.
[j] Gr. 501, R. & 504.
[k] Id. 98, 2.
[l] Gr. 549, & Id. 6, 2.
[m] Id. 74, 9, & 108, 1.
[n] Id. 70, 3.
[o] Id. 7, 2, & Gr. 403, R.
[p] Id. 19, & Gr. 269.
[q] Gr. 319, R. V.
[r] Gr. 673, 675.

36. Epaminondas, Thebanōrum imperātor, in bello adversŭs Lacedæmonios, anĭmos suōrum religiōne excitandos[a] ratus, arma in templis affixa nocte[b] detraxit, persuasitque militĭbus, quum illa abesse[c] vidērent, deos iter suum sequi,[c] ut ipsis[d] prœliantĭbus adessent.

37. Idem in pugnâ ad Mantinēam gravĭter vulnerātus est. Quum anĭmam recepisset, interrogāvit cĭrcumstantes amīcos, an clypeus salvus esset;[e] deinde, an hostes fusi essent.[e] Illi utrumque affirmavērunt. Tum demum hastam e corpŏre edūci[f] jussit. Quo[g] facto statim exspirāvit.

38. Epaminondas tantâ fuit abstinentiâ[h] et integritāte, ut post plurĭma bella, quibus Thebanōrum potentiam incredibilĭter auxĕrat, nihil in supellectĭli habēret præter ahēnum et veru.

39. Lysander, dux Lacedæmoniōrum, milĭtem quendam viâ[i] egressum castigābat. Cui dicenti, ad nullĭus rei rapīnam se ab agmĭne recessisse,[j] respondit: *Ne*[k] *speciem quidem raptūri*[l] *prœbeas volo.*

40. Iphicrătes, dux Atheniensium, quum præsidio tenēret Corinthum, et sub adventum hostium ipse[m] vigilias circumīret, vigĭlem, quem dormientem invenĕrat, hastâ transfixit. Quod[n] factum quibusdam[o] ei[o] ut sævum exprobrantĭbus, *Qualem*[p] *invēni*, inquit, *talem relīqui.*

41. Quum quidam Thrasybūlo, qui civitātem Atheniensium a tyrannōrum dominatiōne liberāvit, dixisset: *Quantas*[q] *tibi gratias Athēnœ debent!* ille respondit: *Dii*

---

[a] Id. 108, 4, & Gr. 214, 9.
[b] Gr. 565, R. XL.
[c] Id. 96, 2.
[d] Gr. 393, R. I.
[e] Id. 74, 12, & Gr. 627, 5.
[f] Id. 90, 4.
[g] Id. 38, 5.
[h] Gr. 339, R. VII.
[i] Gr. 613, R. LII.
[j] Id. 94, 1, 2d, & 98, 2.
[k] Id. 121, 2, and Gr. 627, 1, 3d.
[l] Id. 19, & Gr. 269.
[m] Id. 32, 3.
[n] Id. 38.
[o] Gr. 501, R. XXIX.
[p] Id. 44, 4, & 47.
[q] Id. 48, 3.

faciant,[a] *ut quantas*[b] *ipse*[c] *patriæ debeo gratias, tantas et videar*[d] *retulisse.*

42. Philippus, rex Macedŏnum, monentĭbus[e] eum quibusdam, ut Pythiam quendam cavēret,[d] fortem milĭtem, sed ipsi[f] alienātum, quòd tres filias ægrè alĕret,[g] nec a rege adjuvarētur, dixisse fertur: *Quid?*[h] *si partem corpŏris habērem*[i] *ægram, abscindĕrem*[j] *potiùs, an curārem?* Deinde Pythiam ad se vocātum,[k] acceptâ[k] difficultāte rei domestĭcæ, pecuniâ[l] instruxit. Quo facto nullum rex milĭtem Pythiâ[m] fideliōrem habuit.

43. Mulier quædam ab eōdem Philippo, quum a convivio temulentus recedĕret, damnāta, *A Philippo,* inquit, *temulento ad Philippum sobrium provŏco.*

44. Philippus, rex Macedoniæ, predicāre solēbat, se oratorĭbus Atheniensium maxĭmam gratiam habēre.[n] *Nam conviciis suis,* inquit, *efficiunt, ut quotidie melior*[o] *evādam, dum eos dictis*[p] *factisque mendacii arguĕre conor.*

45. Ejusdem regis epistŏla fertur scripta ad Aristotĕlem philosŏphum, quâ filium sibi[q] natum esse nuntiāvit. Erat illa epistŏla verbis concepta ferè his: *Filium mihi*[q] *genĭtum esse scito. Quod*[r] *equĭdem diis habeo gratiam: non tam quòd natus est, quàm quòd ei*[s] *contĭgit nasci temporĭbus vitæ tuæ. Spero enim fore,*[t] *ut a te educātus et erudĭtus dignus evādat et nobis*[u] *et rebus, quas ipsi relictūri sumus.*

---

[a] Ik. 77, 9 and Gr. 144, 145.
[b] Id. 44, 3, & 47.
[c] Id. 32, 1.
[d] Gr. 627, 1, 3d, & Id. 70.
[e] Gr. 494.
[f] Id. 64, 9.
[g] Gr. 655.
[h] Gr. 730, 1.
[i] Gr. 627, 2.
[j] Id. 78, 4, Gr. 626, Id. 124, 13.
[k] Id. 104, 3, & 2.
[l] Gr. 514, R. XXXI.
[m] Id. 6, 3.
[n] Id. 94, 1, 2d, & 96, 1.
[o] Gr. 322.
[p] Gr. 542, R. XXXV.
[q] Gr. 522, R. III.
[r] Id. 38, 10.
[s] Gr. 409, R. XVIII.
[t] Gr. 678.
[u] Id. 6, 5, and Gr. 462, R. XXIII

46. Alexander Macĕdo, Philippi filius, quum puer a præceptōre suo audivisset innumerabĭles mundos esse.[a] *Heu me*[b] *misĕrum*, inquit, *qui ne uno*[c] *quidem adhuc potītus sum!*

47. Quum Alexander quondam Macedŏnum quorundam benevolentiam largitionĭbus sibi conciliāre conātus esset, Philippus eum his verbis increpuit: *Sperasne*[d] *eos tibi*[e] *fidēles esse futūros*,[f] *quos pecuniâ tibi conciliavĕris?*[g] *Scito amōrem non auro emi sed virtutĭbus.*

48. Alexandro[l] Macedŏni, Asiâ debellātâ, Corinthii per legātos gratulāti sunt, regemque civitāte[h] suâ donavērunt. Quod[j] officii genus quum Alexander risisset, unus ex legātis, *Nulli*[j] *unquam*, inquit, *civitātem dedĭmus alii quàm tibi*[k] *et Hercŭli.* Quo[i] audīto, Alexander honōrem sibi delātum lubentissĭmè accēpit.

49. Quum Alexander Græciæ popŭlis[l] imperâsset, ut divīnos ipsi honōres decernĕrent,[m] Lacedæmonii his verbis utebantur: *Quoniam Alexander deus esse voluit, esto deus;* Laconĭcâ brevitāte regis notantes vecordiam.

50. Lysimăchus, rex Thraciæ, Theodōrum Cyrenæum, virum libertātis[n] amantissĭmum et regiæ dominatiōni[e] infestum, cruci affīgi[o] jussit. Cui ille, *Hujus modi minis*, inquit, *purpurātos tuos terreas.*[p] *Mea*[q] *quidem nihil*[r] *intĕrest, humīne*[s] *an sublīmè putrescam.*

51. Mausōlus, rex Cariæ, Artemisiam habuit conjŭgem. Hæc, Mausōlo defuncto, ossa cineremque marīti contūsa et odorĭbus mixta cum aquâ potābat. Extruxit

---

[a] Id. 96, 9.
[b] Gr. 451.
[c] Id. 7, 5, and Gr. 484, R. XXVI.
[d] Id. 58, 1, & 56, 3.
[e] Gr. 382, R. XVI.
[f] Id. 99, 1.
[g] Gr. 656.
[h] Gr. 514, R. & 516.
[i] Id. 38, 7, & 38, 5.
[j] Gr. 501, R. XXIX.
[k] Gr. 720, R. LXV.
[l] Id. 7, 2, & Gr. 403, R.
[m] Gr. 627, 1, 3d.
[n] Gr. 349, R. IX.
[o] Id. 90, 4.
[p] Gr. 171, 1.
[q] Gr. 415.
[r] Gr. 500.
[s] Gr. 559.

quoque, ad conservandam[a] ejus memoriam, sepulcrum illud nobilissĭmum, ab ejus nomĭne appellātum, quod inter septem orbis terrārum miracŭla numerātur. Quod[b] quum Mausōli manĭbus[c] dicāret, certāmen instituit, præmiis amplissĭmis ei proposĭtis, qui defunctum regem optĭmè laudâsset.[d]

52. Dionysius, qui a patre Syracusārum et pæne totius Siciliæ tyrannĭdem accepĕrat, senex patriâ[e] pulsus Corinthi[f] puĕros littĕras docuit.[g]

53. Mithridātes, rex Ponti, sæpe venēnum hausĕrat, ut sibi a clandestīnis cavēret insidiis. Hinc factum est ut, quum a Pompeio superātus mortem sibi consciscĕre vellet, ne velocissĭma quidem venēna ei nocērent.[h]

54. Quum Gyges, rex Lydiæ ditissĭmus, oracŭlum Apollĭnis interrogāret, an quisquam mortalium[i] se[j] esset[k] felicior, deus, Aglaüm quendam Psophidium feliciōrem, prædicāvit. Is autem erat Arcădum[i] pauperrĭmus, parvŭli agelli possessor, cujus termĭnos quàmvis senex nunquam excessĕrat, fructĭbus[l] et voluptatĭbus angusti ruris contentus.

55. Pyrrhus, rex Epīri, quum in Italiâ esset, audīvit, Tarentīnos quosdam juvĕnes in convivio parum honorifĭcè de se locūtos esse.[m] Eos igĭtur ad se arcessītos percunctātus est, an dixissent[k] ea, quæ ad aures suas pervenissent.[n] Tum unus ex his, *Nisi*, inquit, *vinum nobis*[o] *defecisset,*[p] *multo*[q] *etiam plura*[r] *et graviōra in te locutūri erāmus.*[s] Hæc crimĭnis excusatio iram regis in risum convertit.

---

[a] Id. 112, 7.
[b] Id. 38, 4.
[c] Gr. 501, R. XXIX.
[d] Gr. 643, 2d.
[e] Gr. 524, R. V.
[f] Id. 4, 1, & Gr. 548, R.
[g] Gr. 508, R. XXX.
[h] Gr. 627, 1, 4th.
[i] Gr. 355, R. X.
[j] Id. 6. 3.
[k] Gr. 627, 5.
[l] Gr. 462, R. XXIII.
[m] Id. 98, 2.
[n] Gr. 656.
[o] Gr. 396.
[p] Gr. 629.
[q] Gr. 579, R. XLIII.
[r] Id. 19, 4.
[s] Gr. 214, 8.

56. Marsyas, frater Antigŏni, regis Macedoniæ, quum causam habēret cum privāto quodam, fratrem rogāvit, ut de eâ domi cognoscĕret.[a] At ille, *In foro potiùs*,* inquit. *Nam si culpâ* [b] *vacas, innocentia tua ibi meliùs apparēbit; sin damnandus es, nostra justitia.**

57. Clara sunt apud Catanenses nomĭnà fratrum Anāpi [c] et Amphinŏmi,[c] qui patrem et matrem humĕris per medios [d] ignes Ætnæ portârunt, eosque cum vitæ suæ [c] pericŭlo e flammis eripuērunt.

58. Spartānus quidam quum riderētur, quòd claudus in pugnam iret,[f] *At mihi*,[g] inquit, *pugnāre*,[h] *non fugĕre est propositum.*[i]

59. Spartānus quidam in magistrātûs petitiōne ab æmŭlis victus, maxĭmæ sibi lætitiæ esse,[j] dixit, quòd patria sua se [k] meliōres cives habēret.[f]

60. Quum homo quidam, qui diu in uno pede stare didicĕrat, Lacedæmonio [l] cuidam dixisset, se non arbitrari Lacedæmoniōrum [q] quemquam tamdiu idem facĕre posse, ille respondit: *At ausĕres** *te* [k] *diutiùs.*

61. Diagŏras Rhodius, quum tres ejus filii in ludis Olympĭcis victōres renuntiāti essent, tanto affectus est gaudio,[m] ut in ipso stadio, inspectante popŭlo, in filiōrum manĭbus anĭmam reddĕret.[n]

62. Scipio Africānus nunquam ad negotia publĭca accedēbat, antequam in templo Jovis precātus esset.[o]

63. Scipio dicĕre solēbat, hosti non solùm dandam [p]

* Supply the proper verb.

[a] Gr. 627, 1, 3d.
[b] Gr. 480, R. XXV.
[c] Gr. 251, R. & 257.
[d] Id. 17, 1.
[e] Id. 30, 2.
[f] Gr. 656.
[g] Gr. 522, R. III.
[h] Gr. 660, R. LVI.
[i] Id. 51, 1.
[j] Id. 8, 1, & Gr. 427, R.
[k] Id. 6, 3, & Gr. 467, R.
[l] Id. 63, & Gr. 501, R.
[m] Gr. 542, R. XXXV.
[n] Gr. 627, 1, 1st.
[o] Gr. 627, 4.
[p] Id. 108, 4.
[q] Gr. 355, R. X.

esse viam fugiendi, sed etiam muniendam. Similĭter Pyrrhus, rex Epīri, fugienti hosti[a] pertinacĭter instandum[b] esse negābat; non solùm, ne fortiùs ex necessitāte resistĕret,[c] sed ut postea quoque faciliùs acie[d] cedĕret, ratus victōres fugientĭbus non usque ad perniciem instatūros esse.

64. Metellus Pius, in Hispaniâ bellum gerens interrogātus, quid postĕro die factūrus esset?[e] *Tunĭcam meam*, inquit, *si id elŏqui posset,*[f] *comburĕrem.*[g]

65. L. Mummius, qui, Corintho captâ, totam Italiam tabŭlis[h] statuisque exornāvit, ex tantis manubiis nihil in suum usum convertit, ita ut, eo defuncto, non esset[i] unde ejus filia dotem accipĕret.[j] Quare senātus ei ex publico dotem decrēvit.

66. Scipio Africānus major Ennii poëtæ imagĭnem in sepulcro gentis Corneliæ collocāri jussit, quòd Scipiōnum res gestas carminĭbus[h] suis illustravĕrat.

67. M. Cato, Catōnis Censorii filius, in acie cadente equo prolapsus, quum se recollegisset,[k] animadvertissetque gladium excidisse[l] vagīnâ,[m] rediit in hostem: acceptisque alĭquot vulnerĭbus,[n] recuperāto[n] demum gladio ad suos reversus est.

68. Q. Metellus Macedonĭcus in Hispaniâ quinque cohortes, quæ hostĭbus[o] cessĕrant, testamentum facĕre jussas ad locum[p] recuperandum misit; minātus[q] eos nonnĭsi post victoriam receptum iri.[r]

---

[a] Gr. 399, R. IV.
[b] Id. 113, 8.
[c] Gr. 627, 6.
[d] Gr. 611.
[e] Gr. 627, 5.
[f] Gr. 627, 2.
[g] Id. 78, 8, & Gr. 142, 2d.
[h] Gr. 542, R. XXXV.
[i] Gr. 627, 1, 1st.
[j] Gr. 656.
[k] Id. 74, 8, & Gr. 631.
[l] Id. 98, 3.
[m] Gr. 613, R. LII.
[n] Id. 104, 1.
[o] Gr. 405, 5th.
[p] Id. 112, 7.
[q] Id. 106, 1.
[r] Id. 94, 1, 2d, & 100, 8.

69. Publius Decius consul, quum in bello contra Latīnos, Romanōrum aciem cedentem vidēret, capĭte pro reipublĭcæ salūte devōto,[a] in medium hostium agmen irruit, et magnâ strage edĭtâ[a] plurĭmis telis obrŭtus cecĭdit. Hæc ejus mors Romanōrum aciem restituit, iisque victoriam parāvit.

70. L. Junius Brutus, qui Romam a regĭbus liberāvit, filios suos, qui Tarquinium regem expulsum restituĕre conāti erant, ipse[b] capĭtis[c] damnāvit, eosque virgis cæsos secūri[d] percŭti[e] jussit.

71. Q. Marcius Rex consul, quum filium unĭcum, juvĕnem summæ pietātis[f] et magnæ spei, morte[g] amisisset, dolōrem suum ita coërcuit, ut a rogo adolescentis protĕnus curiam petĕret,[h] ibique munĕris sui negotia strenuè obīret.

72. In bello Romanōrum cum Perseo, ultĭmo Macedoniæ rege, accĭdit,[i] ut serēnâ nocte[j] subĭtò luna deficeret. Hæc res ingentem apud milĭtes terrōrem excitāvit, qui existimābant hoc omĭne[g] futūram cladem portendi.[k] Tum verò Sulpicius Gallus, qui erat in eo exercĭtu, in conciōne milĭtum causam hujus rei tam disertè exposuit, ut postĕro die[j] omnes intrepĭdo anĭmo[g] pugnam committĕrent.[h]

73. L. Siccius Dentātus ob insignem fortitudĭnem appellātus est Achilles Romānus. Pugnâsse[l] is dicĭtur centum et viginti prœliis;[m] cicatrīcem aversam nullam, adversas quinque et quadraginta tulisse; corōnis[n] esse

[a] Id. 104, 1.
[b] Id. 32, 4.
[c] Gr. 489, R. XXVII.
[d] Gr. 90, 6, *Note* 3.
[e] Id. 90, 4, or 94, 3.
[f] Gr. 339, R. VII.
[g] Gr. 542, R. XXXV.
[h] Gr. 627, 1, 1st.
[i] Id. 51, 3.
[j] Id. 6, 7; Gr. 565, R. XL.
[k] Id. 96, 5.
[l] Gr. 676.
[m] Gr. 611, (in.)
[n] Gr. 505, and Gr. 519, R. XXXII.

donātus aureis duodeviginti, obsidionāli unâ, muralĭbus tribus, civĭcis quatuordĕcim, torquĭbus tribus et octoginta, armillis plùs centum sexaginta, hastis duodeviginti. Phalĕris idem donātus est quinquies viciesque. Triumphāvit cum imperatorĭbus suis triumphos[a] novem.

74. Hannibălem in Italiam proficiscentem tria millia[b] Carpetanōrum reliquērunt. Quorum[c] exemplum ne cetĕri quoque barbări sequerentur,[d] edixit eos a se esse dimissos,[e] et insŭper in fidem ejus rei alios etiam, quorum fides ipsi[f] suspecta erat, domum[g] remīsit.

75. Hannĭbal quum elephantos compellĕre non posset,[h] ut præaltum flumen transīrent,[i] neque rates habēret,[h] quibus eos trajicĕret,[i] jussit ferocissĭmum elephantōrum sub aure vulnerāri, et eum, qui vulnerâsset,[j] se in flumen conjicĕre illudque tranāre. Tum elephantus exasperātus ad persequendum dolōris sui auctōrem tranāvit amnem,[k] et relĭqui quoque eum secūti sunt.

---

[a] Gr. 438, R. II.
[b] Gr. 104, 5.
[c] Id. 38.
[d] Gr. 627, 1, 2d.
[e] Id. 98, 6.
[f] Id. 5, 2, and Gr. 528, R. XXXIII.
[g] Gr. 558, R. XXXIX.
[h] Gr. 631.
[i] Gr. 656.
[j] Gr. 650, R. VI.
[k] Gr. 613, R. LII.

AN EPITOME OF ROMAN HISTORY,

FROM THE EARLIEST TIMES TO THE EMPERORS.

LIBER PRIMUS.

1. ANTIQUISSĬMIS temporĭbus Saturnus in Italiam venisse dicĭtur. Ibi haud procul a Janicŭlo arcem condĭdit, eamque Saturniam[a] appellāvit. Hic Itălos primus[b] agricultūram docuit.[c]

2. Postea Latīnus in illis regionĭbus imperāvit. Sub hoc rege Troja in Asiâ eversa est. Hinc Ænēas, Anchīsæ filius, cum multis Trojānis, quibus[d] ferrum Græcōrum pepercĕrat, aufŭgit, et in Italiam pervēnit. Ibi Latīnus rex ei benignè recepto[e] filiam Laviniam in matrimonium dedit. Ænēas urbem condĭdit, quam in honōrem conjŭgis Lavinium[a] appellāvit.

3. Post Ænēæ mortem Ascanius, Ænēæ filius, regnum accēpit. Hic sedem regni in alium locum transtŭlit, urbemque condĭdit in monte Albāno, eamque Albam[a] Longam nuncupāvit. Eum secūtus est Silvius, qui post Ænēæ mortem a Laviniâ genĭtus erat.

---

[a] Gr. 440.
[b] Gr. 274.
[c] Gr. 508, R. XXX.
[d] Id. 7, 2, and Gr. 403, R. V.
[e] Id. 104, 3.

Ejus postĕri omnes usque ad Romam condĭtam[a] Albæ[b] regnavērunt.

4. Unus horum regum, Romŭlus Silvius, se Jove[c] majōrem esse dicēbat,[d] et, quum tonāret, militĭbus imperāvit, ut clypeos hastis percutĕrent,[e] dicebatque hunc sonum multò clariōrem esse quàm tonitru. Fulmĭne ictus,[f] et in Albānum lacum præcipitātus est.

5. Silvius Procas, rex Albanōrum, duos filios relīquit Numitōrem[g] et Amulium. Horum minor[h] natu,[i] Amulius, fratri optiōnem dedit, utrùm regnum habēre vellet,[j] an bona, quæ pater reliquisset.[k] Numĭtor paterna bona prætŭlit; Amulius regnum obtinuit.

6. Amulius, ut regnum firmissĭmè possidēret,[l] Numitōris filium per insidias interēmit, et filiam fratris Rheam Silviam Vestālem virgĭnem[m] fecit. Nam his Vestæ sacerdotĭbus non licet viro[n] nubĕre. Sed hæc a Marte gemĭnos filios, Romŭlum et Remum pepĕrit. Hoc quum Amulius comperisset,[e] matrem in vincŭla conjēcit, puĕros autem in Tibĕrim abjĭci jussit.

7. Fortè Tibĕris aqua ultra ripam se effudĕrat, et, quum puĕri in vado essent posĭti,[o] aqua refluens eos in sicco relīquit. Ad eōrum vagītum lupa accurrit, eosque uberĭbus suis aluit. Quod[p] videns Faustŭlus quidam, pastor illius regiōnis, puĕros sustŭlit, et uxōri Accæ Laurentiæ nutriendos[q] dedit.

8. Sic Romŭlus et Remus pueritiam inter pastōres transegērunt. Quum adolevissent, et fortè comperissent,

[a] Gr. 684.
[b] Id. 4, 1.
[c] Id. 6, 3.
[d] Gr. 160, 1.
[e] Gr. 627, 1, 3d.
[f] Id. 115, 1.
[g] Gr. 257.
[h] Gr. 358.
[i] Gr. 535, R. XXXIV.
[j] Gr. 627, 5.
[k] Gr. 656.
[l] Gr. 627, 1, 2d.
[m] Gr. 440.
[n] Gr. 403, R. V.
[o] Id. 74, 8, & Gr. 631.
[p] Id. 38, & Gr. 285.
[q] Id. 107, 2.

quis ipsōrum avus, quæ mater fuisset,[a] Amulium interfecērunt, et Numitōri avo regnum restituērunt. Tum urbem condidērunt in monte Aventīno, quam Romŭlus a suo nomĭne Romam [b] vocāvit. Hæc quum mœnĭbus circumdarētur, Remus occīsus est, dum fratrem irrīdens mœnia [c] transiliēbat.

Ante Christum, 754.

9. Romŭlus, ut civium numĕrum augēret, asȳlum patefēcit, ad quod multi ex civitatĭbus suis pulsi accurrērunt. Sed novæ urbis civĭbus [d] conjŭges deĕrant. Festum ităque Neptūni et ludos instituit. Ad hos quum multi ex finitĭmis popŭlis cum mulierĭbus et libĕris venissent,[a] Romāni inter ipsos ludos spectantes virgĭnes rapuērunt.

10. Popŭli illi, quorum virgĭnes raptæ erant, bellum adversùs raptōres susceperunt. Quum Romæ [e] appropinquārent,[f] fortè in Tarpēiam virgĭnem incidērunt, quæ in arce sacra procurābat. Hanc rogābant, ut viam in arcem monstrāret,[g] eīque permisērunt, ut munus sibi poscĕret.[g] Illa petiit, ut sibi darent, quod in sinistris manĭbus gerĕrent,[h] annŭlos aureos et armillas signifĭcans. At hostes in arcem ab eâ perducti scutis Tarpēiam obruērunt; nam et ea in sinistris manĭbus gerēbant.

11. Tum Romŭlus cum hoste, qui montem Tarpēium tenēbat, pugnam conseruit in eo loco, ubi nunc forum Romānum est. In mediâ [i] cæde raptæ [j] processērunt, et hinc patres hinc conjŭges et socĕros complectebantur, et rogābant, ut cædis finem facĕrent.[g] Utrīque his precĭbus commōti sunt. Romŭlus fœdus icit, et Sabīnos in urbem recēpit.

---

[a] Id. 74, 8, & 627, 5.
[b] Gr. 440.
[c] Gr. 613, R. LII.
[d] Id. 118, 8, & Gr. 396.
[e] Gr. 399, R. IV.
[f] In. 74, 3, & Gr. 631.
[g] Gr. 627, 1, 3d.
[h] Gr. 656.
[i] Id. 17, 1.
[j] —— Sup. *muliĕres.*

12. Postea civitātem descripsit. Centum senatōres legit, eosque cùm[a] ob ætātem, tum ob reverentiam iis[b] debĭtam patres appellāvit. Plebem in triginta curias dis-
A. U. C. tribuit, easque raptārum[c] nominĭbus nuncu-
37. pāvit. Anno regni tricessĭmo septĭmo, quum
exercĭtum lustrāret, inter tempestātem ortam[d] repentè ocŭlis[e] homĭnum subductus est. Hinc alii eum a senatorĭbus interfectum,[f] alii ad deos sublātum esse[f] existimavērunt.

13. Post Romŭli mortem unius anni interregnum fuit. Quo[g] elapso, Numa Pompilius Curĭbus,[h] urbe in agro Sabinōrum natus, rex creātus est. Hic vir bellum quidem nullum gessit; nec minùs tamen civitāti profuit. Nam et leges dedit, et sacra plurĭma instituit, ut popŭli barbări et bellicōsi mores mollīret.[i] Omnia autem, quæ faciēbat,[j] se nymphæ Egeriæ, conjŭgis suæ, jussu facĕre[k] dicēbat.[j] Morbo decessit, quadragesĭmo tertio imperii anno.

A. U. 14. Numæ[l] successit Tullus Hostilius, cujus
81. avus se in bello adversùs Sabīnos fortem et
strenuum virum[m] præstitĕrat. Rex creātus bellum Albānis indixit, idque trigeminōrum Horatiōrum et Curiatiōrum certamĭne finīvit. Albam propter perfidiam Metii Suffetii diruit. Quum triginta duōbus annis[n] regnâsset, fulmĭne ictus cum domo suâ arsit.

A. U. 15. Post hunc, Ancus Marcius, Numæ ex
114. filiâ nepos, suscēpit imperium. Hĭc vir æqui-
tāte[o] et religiōne avo[p] simĭlis, Latīnos bello domuit, ur-

[a] Id. 124, 8.
[b] Gr. 522, & I. 64, 6.
[c] Gr. 269.
[d] Gr. 688.
[e] Id. 5, 1, & Gr. 522.
[f] Id. 97, 5.
[g] Id. 38, 5.
[h] Gr. 549, & Id. 6, 2.
[i] Gr. 627, 1, 2d.
[j] Gr. 160, 1.
[k] Id. 96, 1.
[l] Gr. 399, R. IV.
[m] Gr. 440.
[n] Gr. 565, R. XLI., & Gr. 566.
[o] Gr. 535, R. XXXIV.
[p] Id. 7, 6, & Gr. 382, R.

bem ampliāvit, et nova ei[a] mœnia circumdĕdit. Carcĕrem primus ædificāvit. Ad Tibĕris ostia urbem condĭdit, Ostiamque vocāvit. Vicesĭmo quarto anno imperii morbo obiit.

16. Deinde regnum Lucius Tarquinius Pris- A. U.
cus accēpit, Demarāti filius, qui tyrannos pa- 137.
triæ Corinthi fugiens in Etruriam venĕrat. Ipse[b] Tarquinius, qui nomen ab urbe Tarquiniis accēpit, aliquando Romam[c] profectus erat. Advenienti[d] aquĭla pileum abstŭlit, et, postquam altè evolavĕrat, reposuit. Hinc Tanăquil conjux, mulier auguriōrum[e] perīta, regnum ei portendi intellexit.

17. Quum Romæ commorarētur, Anci regis familiaritātem consecūtus est, qui eum filiōrum suōrum tutōrem[f] relīquit. Sed is pupillis[d] regnum intercēpit. Senatorĭbus, quos Romŭlus creavĕrat, centum alios addĭdit, qui minōrum gentium[g] sunt appellāti. Plura bella felicĭter gessit, nec paucos agros hostĭbus[h] ademptos urbis territorio adjunxit. Primus triumphans urbem intrāvit. Cloācas fecit; Capitolium inchoāvit. Tricesĭmo octāvo imperii anno per Anci filios, quibus[d] regnum eripuĕrat, occīsus est.

18. Post hunc Servius Tullius suscēpit impe- A. U.
rium, genĭtus ex nobĭli femĭnâ, captīvâ tamen 176.
et famŭlâ. Quum in domo Tarquinii Prisci educarētur,[i] flamma in ejus capĭte visa est. Hoc prodigio Tanăquil ei summam dignitātem portendi[j] intellexit, et conjŭgi[k] persuāsit, ut eum sicŭti libĕros suos educāret.[l] Quum adolevisset, rex ei filiam in matrimonium dedit.

[a] Gr. 501, R. XXIX., and 505.
[b] Id. 32, 4.
[c] Gr. 553, R.
[d] Gr. 501, R., and Id. 5, 1. (Sup. *ei*.)
[e] Gr. 349, R. IX.
[f] Gr. 440.
[g] Gr. 332. Sup. *Senatores*.
[h] Gr. 522, R. III.
[i] Gr. 631, & 159.
[j] Id. 96, 6.
[k] Gr. 403, R. V.
[l] Gr. 627, 1, 3d.

19. Quum Priscus Tarquinius occīsus esset, Tanăquil de superiōre parte domûs popŭlum[a] allocūta est, dicens, *regem grave quidem sed non letāle vulnus accepisse;*[b] *eum petĕre,*[c] *ut popŭlus, dum convaluĭsset,*[d] *Servio Tullio obedīret.* Sic Servius regnāre cœpit, sed benè imperium administrāvit. Montes tres urbi adjunxit. Primus omnium censum ordināvit. Sub eo Roma habuĭt capĭtum octoginta tria millia civium Romanōrum, cum his qui in agris erant.

A. U. 220. 20. Hic rex interfectus est scelĕre filiæ Tulliæ et Tarquinii Superbi, filii ejus regis, cui[e] Servius successĕrat. Nam ab ipso Tarquinio de gradĭbus curiæ dejectus, quum domum[f] fugĕret, interfectus est. Tullia in forum properāvit, et prima conjŭgem regem[g] salutāvit. Quum domum redīret, aurīgam super patris corpus in viâ jacens carpentum agĕre jussit.

21. Tarquinius Superbus cognōmen morĭbus meruĭt. Bello tamen strenuus plures finitimōrum pepulōrum[h] vicit. Templum Jovis in Capitolio ædificāvit. Postea, dum Ardeam[a] oppugnābat, urbem Latii, imperium perdĭdit. Nam quum filius ejus Lucretiæ,[i] nobilissĭmæ femĭnæ, conjŭgi Tarquinii Collatīni, vim fecisset, hæc se ipsam[j] occīdit in conspectu marīti, patris, et amicōrum, postquam eos obtestāta fuĕrat, ut hanc injuriam ulciscerentur.[k]

A. U. 243. 22. Hanc ob causam L. Brutus, Collatīnus, aliīque nonnulli in exitium[l] regis conjurârunt populōque[i] persuasērunt, ut ei portas urbis claudĕret.[k] Exercĭtus quoque, qui civitātem Ardeam cum rege oppugnābat, eum relīquit. Fugit ităque cum uxōre

[a] Gr. 613, R. LII.
[b] Id. 94, 1, 2d, & 98, 2.
[c] Id. 96, 2.
[d] Id. 80, 3, & 627, 4.
[e] Gr. 399, R. IV.
[f] Gr. 558, R. XXXIX.
[g] Gr. 440.
[h] Gr. 355, R. X.
[i] Gr. 501, R. XXIX.
[j] Id. 32.
[k] Gr. 627, 1, 3d.
[l] Id. 123, 1, & Gr. 607, R.

et libĕris suis. Ita Romæ[a] regnātum[b] est per septem reges annos[c] ducentos quadraginta tres.

23. Hinc consŭles cœpēre pro uno rege duo creāri, ut, si unus malus esset,[d] alter eum coërcēret.[e] Annuum iis imperium tribūtum est, ne per diuturnitātem potestātis insolentiōres redderentur.[e] Fuērunt igĭtur anno primo, expulsis regĭbus,[f] consŭles L. Junius Brutus, acerrĭmus libertātis vindex, et Tarquinius Collatīnus, marītus Lucretiæ. Sed Collatīno[g] paulò pòst dignĭtas sublāta est. Placuĕrat enim, ne quis ex Tarquiniōrum familiâ Romæ[a] manēret.[e] Ergo cum omni patrimonio suo ex urbe migrāvit, et in ejus locum Valerius Publicŏla consul factus est.

24. Commōvit bellum urbi rex Tarquinius. In primâ pugnâ Brutus consul, et Aruns, Tarquinii filius, sese invĭcem[h] occidērunt. Romāni tamen ex eâ pugnâ victōres recessērunt. Brutum Romānæ matrōnæ quasi commūnem patrem per annum luxērunt. Valerius Publicŏla Sp. Lucretium, Lucretiæ patrem, collēgam sibi fecit; qui quum morbo exstinctus esset,[i] Horatium Pulvillum sibi collēgam[j] sumpsit. Ita primus annus quinque consŭles habuit.

25. Secundo quoque anno itĕrum Tarquinius bellum Romānis intŭlit, Porsĕna,[f] rege Etruscōrum, auxilium ei ferente. In illo bello Horatius Cocles solus pontem ligneum defendit, et hostes cohibuit, donec pons a tergo ruptus esset.[k] Tum se cum armis in Tibĕrim conjēcit, et ad suos transnāvit. A. U. 245.

26. Dum Porsĕna urbem obsidēbat, Qu. Mucius Scævŏla, juvĕnis fortis anĭmi,[l] in castra hostis se contŭlit eo

[a] Id. 4, 1.
[b] Gr. 223, 3.
[c] Gr. 565, R. XLI.
[d] Gr. 627, 2.
[e] Gr. 627, 1, 2d.
[f] Id. 9, 1.
[g] Gr. 522, R. III.; Id. 5, 1.
[h] Gr. 118, 5.
[i] Gr. 631.
[j] Gr. 440.
[k] Gr. 627, 4.
[l] Gr. 339, R. VII.

consilio, ut regem occidĕret. At ibi scribam regis pro ipso rege interfēcit. Tum a regiis[a] satellitĭbus comprehensus et ad regem deductus, quum Porsĕna eum ignĭbus allātis terrēret,[b] dextram aræ[c] accensæ imposuit, donec flammis consumpta esset.[d] Hoc facĭnus rex mirātus[e] juvĕnem dimīsit incolŭmem. Tum hic quasi beneficium refĕrens ait,[f] trecentos alios juvĕnes in eum conjurâsse.[g] Hac re terrĭtus Porsĕna pacem cum Romānis fecit, Tarquinius autem Tuscŭlum se contŭlit, ibique privātus cum uxōre consenuit.

A. U. 259. 27. Sexto decĭmo anno post reges exactos,[h] popŭlus Romæ seditiōnem fecit, questus quòd tribūtis et militiâ a senātu exhaurirētur.[i] Magna pars plebis urbem relīquit, et in montem trans Aniēnem amnem secessit. Tum patres turbāti Menenium Agrippam misērunt ad plebem, qui[j] eam senatui conciliāret. Hic iis inter alia fabŭlam narrāvit de ventre et membris humāni corpŏris; quâ popŭlus commotus est, ut in urbem redīret. Tum primùm tribūni plebis creāti sunt, qui[j] plebem adversùm nobilitātis superbiam defendĕrent.

A. U. 261. 28. Octāvo decĭmo anno post exactos reges,[h] Qu. Marcius, Coriolānus[k] dictus ab urbe Volscōrum Coriŏlis,[l] quam[m] bello cepĕrat, plebi[n] invīsus fiĕri cœpit. Quare urbe[o] expulsus ad Volscos, acerrĭmos Romanōrum hostes, contendit, et ab iis dux[k] exercĭtûs factus Romānos sæpe vicit. Jam usque ad quintum milliarium urbis accessĕrat, nec ullis civium suōrum le-

[a] Gr. 337.
[b] Gr. 160, 2, & 141.
[c] Gr. 501, R. XXIX.
[d] Gr. 627, 4.
[e] Id. 106, 1, & Gr. 688.
[f] Gr. 157, 3.
[g] Id. 98, 2, & 94, 1, 2d.
[h] Gr. 684.
[i] Gr. 655.
[j] Id. 40, 4, & Gr. 643, 4th.
[k] Gr. 319, R. V., & 440.
[l] Gr. 251, R. I.
[m] Gr. 288.
[n] Gr. 382, R. XVI.
[o] Gr. 613, R. LII.

gationĭbus flecti potĕrat, ut patriæ parcĕret.[a] Denĭque Veturia mater et Volumnia uxor ex urbe ad eum venērunt; quarum fletu et precĭbus commotus est, ut exercĭtum removēret.[a] Quo[b] facto a Volscis ut prodĭtor[c] occīsus esse dicĭtur.

29. Romāni quum adversùm Veientes bellum gerĕrent familia Fabiōrum sola hoc bellum suscēpit. Profecti sunt trecenti sex nobilissĭmi homĭnes, duce[d] A. U.
Fabio consŭle. Quum sæpe hostes vicissent, apud 274.
Cremĕram fluvium castra posuērunt. Ibi Veientes dolo[e] usi eos in insidias pellexērunt. In prœlio ibi exorto[f] omnes periērunt. Unus superfuit ex tantâ familiâ, qui propter ætātem puerīlem duci non potuĕrat ad pugnam. Hic genus propagāvit ad Qu. Fabium Maxĭmum illum,[g] qui Hannibălem prudenti cunctatiōne debilitāvit.

30. Anno trecentesĭmo et altĕro[h] ab urbe A. U.
condĭtâ[i] decemvĭri creāti sunt, qui[j] civitāti 302.
leges scribĕrent. Hi primo anno benè egērunt; secundo autem dominatiōnem exercēre cœpērunt. Sed quum unus eōrum[k] Appius Claudius virgĭnem ingenuam, Virginiam, Virginii centuriōnis filiam, corrumpĕre vellet, pater eam occīdit. Tum ad milĭtes profūgit, eosque ad seditiōnem commōvit. Sublāta est decemvĭris[l] potestas, ipsīque omnes aut[m] morte aut exilio punīti sunt.

31. In bello contra Veientānos Furius Ca- A. U.
millus urbem Falerios obsidēbat. In quâ ob- 358.
sidiōne quum ludi literarii magister principum filios ex urbe in castra hostium duxisset,[o] Camillus hoc donum

a Gr. 627, 1, 2d.
b Id. 38, 5.
c Gr. 722.
d Id. 110, 1.
e Gr. 484, R. XXVI., & Id. 7, 4.
f Gr. 688.
g Id. 27, 1st.
h Gr. 106, 7.
i Gr. 684.
j Gr. 643, 4th.
k Gr. 355, R. X.
l Gr. 522, R., & Id. 5, 1.
m Id. 124, 3.
n Id. 38, 8.
o Gr. 631.

non accēpit, sed scelestum homĭnem, manĭbus post tergum vinctis, puĕris Falerios[a] reducendum[b] tradĭdit; virgasque iis dedit, quibus proditōrem in urbem agĕrent.[c]

32. Hâc tantâ anĭmi nobilitāte commōti Falisci urbem Romānis tradidērunt. Camillo[d] autem apud Romānos crimĭni datum[d] est, quòd albis equis triumphâs-
A. U. set,[e] et prædam inīquè divisisset; damnatus-
364. que[f] ob eam causam, et civitāte expulsus est. Paulò pòst Galli Senŏnes ad urbem venērunt, Romānos apud flumen Alliam vicērunt, et urbem etiam occupârunt.[g] Jam nihil præter Capitolium defendi[h] potuit. Et jam præsidium fame laborābat, et in eo[i] erant,[j] ut pacem a Gallis auro emĕrent,[k] quum Camillus cum manu milĭtum superveniens hostes magno prœlio superāret.

LIBER SECUNDUS.

A. U. 1. ANNO trecentesĭmo nonagesĭmo quarto
394. post urbem condĭtam Galli itĕrum ad urbem accessĕrant, et quarto milliario[l] trans Aniēnem fluvium consedĕrant. Contra eos missus est T. Quinctius. Ibi Gallus quidam eximiâ corpŏris magnitudĭne[m] fortissĭmum Romanōrum ad certāmen singulāre provocāvit. T. Manlius, nobilissĭmus juvĕnis, provocatiōnem accēpit, Gallum occīdit, eumque torque[n] aureo spoliāvit, quo[o] ornātus erat. Hinc et ipse et postĕri ejus Torquāti appellāti sunt. Galli fugam capessivērunt.

---

[a] Gr. 553, R. XXXVII.
[b] Id. 107, 1.
[c] Id. 83, 3, and Gr. 643 & 644.
[d] Gr. 427, R. XIX.
[e] Gr. 655.
[f] Id. 115, 1.
[g] Gr. 214, 1, 1st.
[h] Id. 87, 6.
[i] Id. 19, 6, & Gr. 123, 2.
[j] Gr. 316, R. II.
[k] Gr. 627, 1, 1st.
[l] Gr. 573, R. & 577.
[m] Id. 6, 1, and Gr. 339, R. VII.
[n] Id. 6, 8, & Gr. 514, R.
[o] Gr. 542, R. XXXV.

2. Novo bello cum Gallis exorto, anno urbis A. U.
quadringentesĭmo sexto, itĕrum Gallus proces- 406.
sit robŏre[a] atque armis insignis, et provocāvit unum ex Romānis, ut secum armis decernĕret.[b] Tum se M. Valerius, tribūnus milĭtum, obtŭlit; et, quum processisset armātus, corvus ei[c] supra dextrum brachium sedit. Mox, commissâ pugnâ, hic corvus alis[d] et unguibus Galli ocŭlos verberāvit. Ita factum est, ut Gallus nullo negotio a Valerio interficerētur,[e] qui hinc Corvīni nomen accēpit.

3. Postea Romāni bellum gessērunt cum A. U.
Samnitĭbus, ad quod L. Papirius Cursor cum 430.
honōre dictatōris profectus est. Qui[f] quum negotii cujusdam causâ Romam ivisset, præcēpit Q. Fabio[g] Rulliāno, magistro equĭtum, quem apud exercĭtum relīquit, ne pugnam cum hoste committĕret.[h] Sed ille occasiōnem nactus felicissĭmè dimicāvit, et Samnītes delēvit. Ob hanc rem a dictatōre capĭtis[h] damnātus est. At ille in urbem confūgit, et ingenti favōre milĭtum et popŭli liberātus est; in Papirium autem tanta exorta est seditio, ut pæne ipse[i] interficerētur.[n]

4. Duōbus annis pòst[j] T. Veturius et Spurius Postumius consŭles bellum adversùm Samnītes gerēbant. Hi a Pontio Thelesīno, duce hostium, in insidias inducti sunt.
Nam ad Furcŭlas Caudīnas Romānos pellexit A. U.
in angustias, unde sese expedīre non potĕrant. 433.
Ibi Pontius patrem suum Herennĭum rogāvit, quid[k] faciendum putāret. Ille respondit, aut omnes occidendos[m]

[a] Gr 535, R. XXXIV.
[b] Gr. 627, 1, 3d.
[c] Gr. 380, R.
[d] Gr. 542, R. XXXV.
[e] Gr. 627, 1, 4th.
[f] Id. 39, 1.
[g] Gr. 403, R. V.
[h] Gr. 520, I.
[i] Id. 32, 3.
[j] Gr. 236, 4, & Gr. 612.
[k] Id. 91, 5.
[l] Gr. 627, 5.
[m] Id. 108, 4.
[n] Gr. 627, 1, 1st.

esse, ut Romanōrum vires frangerentur,[a] aut omnes dimittendos, ut beneficio obligarentur.[a] Pontius utrumque consilium improbāvit, omnesque sub jugum misit Samnītes denĭque post bellum undequinquaginta annōrum superāti sunt.

A. U. 472. 5. Devictis Samnitĭbus, Tarentīnis[b] bellum indictum est, quia legātis Romanōrum injuriam fecissent.[c] Hi Pyrrhum,[d] Epīri regem, contra Romānos auxilium[d] poposcērunt. Is mox in Italiam venit, tumque primùm Romāni cum transmarīno hoste pugnavērunt. Missus est contra eum consul P. Valerius Lævīnus. Hic, quum exploratōres Pyrrhi cepisset, jussit eos per castra duci,[e] tumque dimitti, ut renuntiārent[a] Pyrrho, quæcunque a Romānis agerentur.[f]

6. Pugnâ commissâ, Pyrrhus auxilio elephantōrum vicit. Nox prœlio finem dedit. Lævīnus tamen per noctem fugit. Pyrrhus Romānos mille[g] octingentos cepit, eosque summo honōre tractāvit. Quum eos, qui in prœlio interfecti fuĕrant, omnes adversis vulnerĭbus et truci vultu etiam mortuos jacēre vidēret, tulisse ad cœlum manus dicĭtur cum hac voce: *Ego cum talĭbus viris brevi orbem terrārum subigĕrem.*[h]

7. Postea Pyrrhus Romam perrexit; omnia ferro ignĕque vastāvit. Campaniam depopulātus est, atque ad Præneste venit, milliario ab urbe octāvo decĭmo. Mox terrōre exercĭtûs, qui cum consŭle sequebātur, in Campaniam se recēpit. Legāti ad Pyrrhum de captīvis redimendis[i] missi honorifĭcè ab eo suscepti sunt; captīvos sine pretio reddĭdit. Unum ex legātis, Fabricium, sic

[a] Gr. 627, 1, 2d.
[b] Gr. 522, R. III.
[c] Gr. 629.
[d] Gr. 508, R., & Id. 62, 5.
[e] Id. 94, 3.
[f] Gr. 656.
[g] Gr. 104, 5, & Id. 7.
[h] Gr. 142, 2d.
[i] Id. 112, 8.

admirātus est, ut ei quartam partem regni sui promittĕret, si ad se transīret,[a] sed a Fabricio contemptus est.

8. Quum jam Pyrrhus ingenti Romanōrum admiratiōne tenerētur, legātum misit Cineam, præstantissĭmum virum, qui[b] pacem petĕret eâ conditiōne,[c] ut Pyrrhus eam partem Italiæ, quam armis occupavĕrat, obtinēret. Romāni respondērunt, eum cum Romānis pacem habēre non posse, nisi ex Italiâ recessisset.[d] Cineas quum rediisset, Pyrrho eum[e] interroganti, qualis ipsi Roma visa esset,[f] respondit, se regum patriam vidisse.[g]

9. In altĕro[h] prœlio cum rege Epīri commisso Pyrrhus vulnerātus est, elephanti interfecti, viginti millia hostium cæsa sunt. Pyrrhus Tarentum[i] fugit. Interjecto anno, Fabricius contra eum missus est. Ad hunc medĭcus Pyrrhi nocte venit promittens, se Pyrrhum venēno occisūrum,[j] si munus sibi darētur. Hunc Fabricius vinctum redūci jussit ad domĭnum. Tunc rex admirātus illum dixisse fertur: *Ille*[k] *est Fabricius, qui difficiliùs ab honestāte, quàm sol a cursu suo averti potest.*
Paulò pòst Pyrrhus tertio etiam prœlio fusus a A. U.
Tarento recessit, et, quum in Græciam rediis- 481.
set, apud Argos, Peloponnēsi urbem, interfectus est.

10. Anno quadringentesĭmo nonagesĭmo post A. U.
urbem condĭtam[l] Romanōrum exercĭtus pri- 490.
mùm in Siciliam trajecērunt, regemque Syracusārum
Hierōnem, Pœnosque, qui multas civitātes in A. U.
eâ insŭlâ occupavĕrant, superavērunt. Quinto 495.
anno hujus belli, quod contra Pœnos gerebātur, pri-

[a] Gr. 627, 2.
[b] Gr. 641, R. II., and Id. 40, 4.
[c] Gr. 542, R. XXXV.
[d] Gr. 627, 6.
[e] Id. 63, 3.
[f] Gr. 627, 5.
[g] Id. 98, 2.
[h] Gr. 106, 7.
[i] Gr. 553, R. XXXVII.
[j] Id. 100, 2, & 94, 1, 2d.
[k] Gr. 319, R. V.
[l] Gr. 684.

mùm Romāni, C. Duillio et Cn. Cornelio Asĭnâ consulĭbus,[a] in mari dimicavērunt. Duillius Carthaginienses vicit, triginta naves occupāvit, quatuordĕcim mersit, septem millia hostium[b] cepit, tria millia occīdit. Nulla victoria Romānis[c] gratior fuit. Duillio concessum est, ut quum a cœnâ redīret, puĕri funalia gestantes, et tibīcen eum comitarentur.[d]

A. U. 499. 11. Paucis annis interjectis, bellum in Afrĭcam translātum est. Hamilcar, Carthaginiensium dux, pugnâ navāli superātur; nam perdĭtis sexaginta quatuor navĭbus se recēpit; Romāni viginti duas amisērunt. Quum in Afrĭcam venissent, Pœnos in plurĭbus prœliis vicērunt, magnam vim homĭnum cepērunt, septuaginta quatuor civitātes in fidem accepērunt. Tum victi Carthaginienses pacem a Romānis[e] petiērunt. Quam[f] quum M. Atilius Regŭlus, Romanōrum dux, dare nollet nisi durissĭmis conditionĭbus, Carthaginienses auxilium petiērunt a Lacedæmoniis.[e] Hi Xanthippum misērunt, qui Romānum exercĭtum magno prœlio vicit. Regŭlus ipse captus et in vincŭla conjectus est.

12. Non tamen ubīque fortūna Carthaginiensĭbus[g] favit. Quum alĭquot prœliis victi essent, Regŭlum rogavērunt, ut Romam proficiscerētur, et pacem captivorumque permutatiōnem a Romānis obtinēret. Ille quum Romam venisset, inductus in Senātum dixit, se desiisse Romānum esse ex illâ die, quâ[h] in potestātem Pœnōrum venisset.[i] Tum Romānis[j] suasit, ne pacem cum Carthaginiensĭbus facĕrent:[k] illos[l] enim tot casĭbus fractos spem nullam nisi in pace habēre:[m] tanti[n] non esse, ut

[a] Id. 110, 2.
[b] Gr. 332, R. VI.
[c] Gr. 382, R. XVI.
[d] Gr. 627, 1, 4th.
[e] Gr. 511.
[f] Id. 39, 3.
[g] Gr. 403, R. V.
[h] Gr. 565, R. XL.
[i] Gr. 650, R. VI.
[j] Gr. 501, R. XXIX.
[k] Gr. 627, 1, 3d.
[l] Id. 94, 4.
[m] Id. 96, 2, & 94, 1, 2d.
[n] Gr. 496.

tot millia[a] captivōrum propter se unum et paucos, qui ex Romānis capti essent, redderentur. Hæc sententia obtinuit. Regressus igĭtur in Afrĭcam crudelissĭmis suppliciis exstinctus est.

13. Tandem, C. Lutatio Catŭlo, A. Postumio consulĭbus, anno belli Punĭci vicesĭmo tertio magnum prœlium navāle commissum est contra Lilybæum, promontorium Siciliæ. In eo prœlio septuaginta tres Carthaginiensium naves captæ,[b] centum viginti quinque demersæ, triginta duo millia hostium capta, tredĕcim millia occīsa sunt. Statim Carthaginienses pacem petiērunt, eisque pax tribūta est. Captīvi Romanōrum,[c] qui tenebantur a Carthaginiensĭbus reddĭti sunt. Pœni Siciliâ,[d] Sardiniâ, et cetĕris insŭlis, quæ inter Italiam Africamque jacent, decessērunt, omnemque Hispaniam quæ citra Ibērum est, Romānis permisērunt.

A. U. 513.

LIBER TERTIUS.

1. Anno quingentessĭmo undetricesĭmo ingentes Gallōrum copiæ Alpes transiērunt. Sed pro Romānis tota Italia consensit: traditumque est,[e] octingenta millia[a] homĭnum[c] ad id bellum parāta fuisse.[f] Res prospĕrè gesta est apud Clusium: quadraginta millia homĭnum interfecta sunt. Alĭquot annis[g] pòst[h] pugnātum est[i] contra Gallos in agro Insŭbrum, finitumque est bellum M. Claudio Marcello, Cn. Cornelio Scipiōne consulĭbus. Tum Marcellus regem Gal-

A. U. 529.

---

[a] Gr. 104, 5.
[b] Id. 115, 2.
[c] Gr. 355, R. X.
[d] Gr. 613, R. LII.
[e] Gr. 158, & 164, 5, & Id. 51, 2.
[f] Id. 94, 1, 2d, & 98, 9.
[g] Gr. 565, R. XL.
[h] Gr. 612.
[i] Gr. 223, 3.

lōrum, Viridomărum, manu suâ occīdit, et triumphans spolia Galli stipĭti[a] imposĭta humeris suis vexit.

2. Paulo pòst Punĭcum bellum renovātum est per Hannibălem, Carthaginiensium ducem, quem pater Hamilcar novem annos[b] natum aris admovĕrat, ut odium perenne in Romānos jurāret.[c] Hic annum agens vicesĭmum ætā-
A. U. tis Saguntum, Hispaniæ civitātem, Romānis am-
536. ĭcam, oppugnāre[d] aggressus est. Huic Romāni per legātos denuntiavērunt, ut bello abstinēret.[e]. Qui[f] quum legātos admittĕre nollet, Romāni Carthagĭnem misērunt, ut mandarētur[g] Hannibăli,[a] ne bellum contra socios popŭli Romāni gerĕret.[e] Dura responsa a Carthaginiensĭbus reddĭta. Saguntīnis interea fame victis, Romāni Carthaginiensĭbus bellum indixērunt.

3. Hannĭbal, fratre Hasdrubăle in Hispaniâ relicto, Pyrenæum et Alpes transiit. Tradĭtur† in Italiam octoginta millia pedĭtum, et viginti millia equĭtum, septem et triginta elephantos abduxisse. Interea multi Ligŭres et Galli Hannibăli se conjunxērunt. Primus ei occurrit P. Cornelius Scipio, qui, prœlio ad Ticīnum commisso,[h] superātus est, et, vulnĕre accepto,[h] in castra rediit. Tum Sempronius Gracchus conflixit ad Trebiam amnem. Is quoque vincĭtur. Multi popŭli se Hannibăli dedidērunt. Inde in Tusciam progressus, Flaminium consŭlem ad Trasimēnum lacum supĕrat. Ipse Flaminius interemptus,[i] Romanōrum viginti quinque millia cæsa sunt.

A. U. 4. Quingentesĭmo et quadragesĭmo anno post
540. urbem condĭtam L. Æmilius Paullus et P. Terentius Varro contra Hannibălem mittuntur. Quam-

† Supply *is* with *traditur*, or *eum* with *abduxisse*. Gr. 676.

[a] Gr. 522, R. III. [d] Gr. 665. [g] Id. 51, & Gr. 662

[b] Gr. 565, R. XLI. [e] Gr. 627, 1, 3d [h] Id. 104, 2.

[c] Gr. 627, 1, 2d. [f] Id. 39, 1. [i] Id. 115, 2

quam intellectum erat,[a] Hannibălem non alĭter vinci posse quàm morâ, Varro tamen moræ[b] impatiens apud vicum, qui Cannæ[c] appellātur, in Apuliâ pugnāvit; ambo consŭles victi, Paullus interemptus est. In eâ pugnâ, consulāres aut prætorii viginti, senatōres triginta capti aut occīsi; milĭtum quadraginta millia; equĭtum tria millia et quingenti periērunt. In his tantis malis nemo tamen pacis mentiōnem facĕre dignātus est. Servi, quod[d] nunquam antè factum, manumissi et milĭtes facti sunt.

5. Post eam pugnam multæ Italiæ civitātes, quæ Romānis[e] paruĕrant, se ad Hannibălem transtulērunt. Hannĭbal Romānis obtŭlit,[f] ut captīvos redimĕrent; responsumque est[a] a senātu, eos cives non esse necessarios, qui armāti capti potuissent.[g] Hos omnes ille postea variis suppliciis interfēcit, et tres modios aureōrum annulōrum Carthagĭnem misit, quos manĭbus[h] equĭtum Romanōrum, senatōrum, et milĭtum detraxĕrat. Interea in Hispaniâ frater Hannibălis, Hasdrŭbal, qui ibi remansĕrat cum magno exercĭtu, a duōbus Scipionĭbus vincĭtur, perditque in pugnâ triginta quinque millia homĭnum.

6. Anno quarto postquàm Hannĭbal in Italiam venĕrat, M. Claudius Marcellus consul apud Nolam, civitātem Campaniæ, contra Hannibălem benè pugnāvit. Illo tempŏre Philippus, Demetrii filius, rex Macedoniæ, ad Hannibălem legātos mittit, eīque auxilia contra Romānos pollicētur. Qui legāti[i] quum a Romānis capti essent,[j] M. Valerius Lævīnus cum navĭbus missus est, qui regem impedīret,[k] quò minùs copias in Italiam trajicĕret.[l] Idem in Macedoniam penetrans regem Philippum vicit.

---

[a] Id. 51, 2, & Gr. 662.
[b] Gr. 349, R. IX.
[c] Gr. 321.
[d] Id. 37, 9.
[e] Gr. 403, R. V.
[f] Id. 60, 4.
[g] Gr. 627, 6.
[h] Gr. 501, R. XXIX.
[i] Id. 38, 1.
[j] Gr. 631.
[k] Gr. 643, 4th, & Id. 83, 2.
[l] Id. 78, 7.

7. In Siciliâ quoque res prospĕrè gesta est. Marcellus magnam hujus insŭlæ partem cepit, quam Pœni occupavĕrant; Syracūsas, nobilissĭmam urbem, expugnāvit, et ingentem inde prædam Romam[a] misit. Lævīnus in Macedoniâ cum Philippo et multis Græciæ popŭlis amicitiam fecit; et in Siciliam profectus Hannōnem, Pœnōrum ducem, apud Agrigentum cepit; quadraginta civitātes in deditiōnem accēpit, viginti sex expugnāvit. Ita omni Siciliâ receptâ, cum ingenti gloriâ Romam[a] regressus est.

8. Interea in Hispaniam, ubi duo Scipiōnes ab Hasdrubăle interfecti erant, missus est P. Cornelius Scipio, vir Romanōrum[b] omnium ferè primus. Hic,[c] puer,[d] duodeviginti annōrum,[e] in pugnâ ad Ticīnum, patrem singulāri virtūte servāvit. Deinde post cladem Cannensem[f] multos[g] nobilissimōrum juvĕnum Italiam deserĕre[h] cupientium, auctoritāte suâ ab hoc consilio deterruit. Viginti quatuor annōrum[c] juvĕnis in Hispaniam missus, die quâ venit, Carthagĭnem Novam cēpit, in quâ omne aurum et argentum et belli apparātum Pœni habēbant, nobilissĭmos quoque obsĭdes, quos ab Hispānis accepĕrant. Hos obsĭdes parentĭbus suis[i] reddĭdit. Quare omnes ferè Hispaniæ civitātes ad eum uno anĭmo transiērunt.

9. Ab eo inde tempŏre res Romanōrum in dies lætiōres factæ sunt. Hasdrŭbal a fratre ex Hispaniâ in Italiam evocātus, apud Senam, Picēni civitātem, in insidias incĭdit, et strenuè pugnans occīsus est. Plurĭmæ autem civitātes, quæ in Brutiis ab Hannibăle tenebantur, Romānis se tradidērunt.

a Gr. 553, R.
b Gr. 355, R. X.
c Id. 27, 4.
d Id. 13, 2.
e Gr. 339, R. VII.
f Gr. 337.
g Id. 21, 3.
h Gr. 659, 4, & 665.
i Gr. 118, 3, 1st, *Exc.*

10. Anno decĭmo quarto postquam in Italiam Hannĭbal venĕrat, Scipio consul creātus,[a] et in Afrĭcam missus est. Ibi contra Hannōnem, ducem Carthaginiensium, prospĕrè pugnat, totumque ejus exercĭtum delet. Secundo prœlio undĕcim millia homĭnum occīdit, et castra cepit cum quatuor millĭbus et quingentis milităbus. Syphācem, Numidiæ regem, qui se cum Pœnis conjunxĕrat, cepit, eumque cum nobilissĭmis Numĭdis et infinītis spoliis Romam misit. Quâ[b] re audĭtâ, omnis ferè Italia Hannibălem desĕrit. Ipse[c] a Carthaginiensĭbus in Afrĭcam redīre jubētur. Ita anno decĭmo septĭmo Italia ab Hannibăle liberāta est. A. U. 550. A. U. 553.

11. Post plures pugnas et pacem plùs[d] semel frustrà tentātam, pugna ad Zamam committĭtur, in quâ peritissĭmi duces copias suas ad bellum educēbant. Scipio victor recēdit; Hannĭbal cum paucis equitĭbus evādit. Post hoc prœlium pax cum Carthaginiensĭbus facta est. Scipio, quum Romam rediisset, ingenti gloriâ triumphāvit, atque Afrĭcānus appellātus est. Sic finem accepit secundum Punĭcum bellum pòst[e] annum undevicesĭmum quàm cœpĕrat.

LIBER QUARTUS.

1. Finīto Punĭco bello, secūtum est Macedonĭcum contra Philippum regem. Superātus est rex a T. Quinctio Flaminio apud Cynocephălas, paxque ei data est his legĭbus: *ne Græciæ civitatĭbus, quas Romāni contra eum defendĕrant, bellum inferret*[f] *ut captīvos* A. U. 556.

---

[a] Id. 115, 1.
[b] Id. 38, 3.
[c] Id. 32, 3.
[d] Gr. 471.
[e] Gr. 569.
[f] Gr. 627, 1, 2d.

et transfŭgas reddĕret; quinquaginta solùm naves habē ret; relĭquas Romānis daret; mille talenta præstāret, et obsĭdem[a] *daret filium Demetrium.* T. Quinctius etiam Lacedæmoniis intŭlit bellum, et ducem eōrum Nabĭdem vicit.

A. U. 563. 2. Finīto bello Macedonĭco, secūtum est bellum Syriăcum contra Antiŏchum regem, cum quo Hannĭbal se junxĕrat. Missus est contra eum L. Cornelius Scipio consul, cui[b] frater ejus Scipio Africānus legātus est addĭtus. Hannĭbal navāli prœlio victus,[c] Antiŏchus autem ad Magnesiam, Asiæ civitātem, a Cornelio Scipiōne consŭle ingenti prœlio fusus est. Tum rex Antiŏchus pacem petit. Data est ei[b] hâc lege, *ut ex Eurōpâ et Asiâ recedĕret, atque intra Taurum se contineret, decem millia talentōrum et viginti obsĭdes præbēret, Hannibălem, concitōrem belli, dedĕret.* Scipio Romam rediit, et ingenti gloriâ triumphāvit. Nomen et ipse, ad imitatiōnem fratris, Asiatĭci accēpit.

3. Philippo, rege Macedoniæ, mortuo, filius ejus Perseus rebellāvit, ingentĭbus copiis parātis.[d] Dux Romanōrum, P. Licinius consul, contra eum missus, gravi prœlio a rege victus est. Rex tamen pacem petēbat. Cui Romāni eam præstāre noluērunt, nisi his conditionĭbus,[e] ut se et suos Romānis dedĕret. Mox Æmilius Paullus con-

A. U. 586. sul regem ad Pydnam superāvit, et viginti millia pedĭtum ejus occīdit. Equitātus cum rege fugit. Urbes Macedoniæ omnes, quas rex tenuĕrat, Romānis se dedidērunt. Ipse Perseus ab amīcis desertus in Paulli potestātem venit. Hic, multis etiam aliis rebus gestis,[d] cum ingenti pompâ,[f] Romam rediit in nave Persei,

[a] Id. 13, 1.
[b] Gr. 522, R. III.
[c] Id. 115, 2.
[d] Id. 104, 1.
[e] Gr. 542, R. XXXV.
[f] Gr. 545.

inusitātæ magnitudĭnis;[a] nam sedĕcim remōrum ordĭnes habuisse dicĭtur. Triumphāvit magnificentissĭmè in curru aureo, duōbus filiis utrōque latĕre[b] adstantĭbus. Ante currum inter captīvos duo regis filii et ipse Perseus ducti sunt.

4. Tertium deinde bellum contra Carthagi- A. U.
nem susceptum est sexcentesĭmo et altĕro[c] anno 602.
ab urbe condĭtâ,[d] anno quinquagesĭmo primo postquàm secundum bellum Punĭcum transactum erat. L. Manlius Censorīnus et M. Manlius consŭles in Afrĭcam trajecērunt,[e] et oppugnavērunt Carthagĭnem. Multa ibi præclarè gesta sunt per Scipiōnem, Scipiōnis Africāni nepōtem, qui tribūnus[f] in Afrĭcâ militābat. Hujus apud omnes ingens metus et reverentia erat, neque quidquam magis Carthaginiensium duces vitābant, quàm contra eum prœlium committĕre.

5. Quum jam magnum esset Scipiōnis nomen, tertio anno postquàm Romāni in Afrĭcam trajecĕrant,[e] consul est creātus, et contra Carthagĭnem missus. Is A. U.
hanc urbem a civĭbus acerrĭmè defensam[g] ce- 608.
pit ac diruit. Ingens ibi præda facta, plurimăque inventa sunt, quæ multārum civitātum excidiis Carthāgo collegĕrat. Hæc omnia Scipio civitatĭbus[h] Italiæ, Siciliæ, Afrĭcæ reddĭdit, quæ[i] sua[j] recognoscēbant. Ita Carthāgo septingentesĭmo anno, postquam condĭta erat, delēta est. Scipio nomen Africāni juniōris accēpit.

6. Intĕrim in Macedoniâ quidam Pseudophilippus arma movit, et P. Juvencium, Romanōrum ducem, ad interneciōnem vicit. Post eum Q. Cæcilius Metellus dux a Romānis contra Pseudophilippum missus est, et,

---

[a] Gr. 339, R. VII.
[b] Gr. 612, (*in.*)
[c] Gr. 106, 7.
[d] Gr. 684.
[e] Gr. 444.
[f] Id. 13, 1.
[g] Gr. 688.
[h] Id. 63
[i] Id. 34.
[j] Id. 31, 5, Note.

viginti quinque millĭbus ex milităbus[a] ejus occīsis, Macedoniam recēpit; ipsum etiam Pseudophilippum in potestātem suam redēgit. Corinthiis quoque bellum indictum est, nobilissĭmæ Græciæ civitāti,[b] propter injuriam Romānis legātis illātam. Hanc Mummius con-
A. U. sul cepit ac diruit. Tres igĭtur Romæ simul
608. celeberrĭmi triumphi fuērunt; Scipiōnis[d] ex Afrĭcâ, ante cujus currum ductus est Hasdrŭbal; Metelli[d] ex Macedoniâ, cujus currum præcessit Andriscus, qui et Pseudophilippus dicĭtur; Mummii[d] ex Corintho, ante quem signa ænea et pictæ tabŭlæ et alia urbis clarissĭmæ ornamenta prælāta sunt.

A. U. 7. Anno sexcentesĭmo decĭmo post urbem con-
610. dĭtam Viriāthus in Lusitaniâ bellum contra Romānos excitāvit. Pastor primò fuit, mox latrōnum dux; postrēmò tantos ad bellum popŭlos concitāvit, ut vindex[e] libertātis Hispaniæ existimarētur.[f] Denĭque a suis[g] interfectus est. Quum interfectōres ejus præmium a Cæpiōne consŭle petĕrent, responsum est, nunquam Romānis placuisse[h] imperatōrem a milităbus suis interfĭci.

8. Deinde bellum exortum est cum Numantīnis, civitāte[b] Hispaniæ. Victus ab his Qu. Pompēius, et post eum C. Hostilius Mancīnus consul, qui pacem cum iis fecit infāmem, quam popŭlus et senātus jussit infringi,[i] atque ipsum Mancīnum hostĭbus tradi.[i] Tum P. Scipio Africānus in Hispaniam missus est. Is primùm milĭtem ignāvum et corruptum correxit; tum multas Hispaniæ
A. U. civitātes partim bello cepit, partim in deditiō-
621. nem accēpit. Postrēmò ipsam Numantiam fame ad deditiōnem coēgit, urbemque evertit; relĭquam provinciam in fidem accēpit.

a Gr. 360.
b Gr. 253.
c Gr. 522, R. III.
d — Sup. *triumphus*.
e Gr. 319, R. V., & 320.
f Gr. 627, 1, 1st.
g Id. 19, 2.
h Id. 51, 5.
i Id. 90, 4.

9. P. Scipiōne Nascīcâ[a] et L. Calpurnio Bestiâ consulĭbus, Jugurthæ, Numidārum regi, bellum illātum est, quòd Adherbălem et Hiempsălem, Micipsæ filios, patruēles suos, interemisset.[b] Missus adversùs eum consul Calpurnius Bestia corruptus regis pecuniâ pacem cum eo flagitiosissĭmam fecit, quæ a senātu improbāta est. Denĭque Qu. Cæcilius Metellus consul Jugurtham variis prœliis vicit, elephantos ejus occīdit vel cepit, multas civitātes ipsius in deditiōnem accēpit. Ei successit C. Marius, qui bello termĭnum posuit, ipsumque Jugurtham cepit. Ante currum triumphantis Marii A. U.
Jugurtha cum duōbus filiis ductus est vinctus, 648.
et mox jussu consŭlis in carcĕre strangulātus.

LIBER QUINTUS.

1. Dum bellum in Numidiâ contra Jugurtham gerĭtur, Cimbri et Teutŏnes aliæque Germanōrum et Gallōrum gentes Italiæ[c] minabantur, aliæque Romanōrum exercĭtus fudērunt. Ingens fuit Romæ[d] timor, ne[e] itĕrum Galli urbem occupārent. Ergo Marius consul[f] creātus, eīque bellum contra Cimbros et Teutŏnes decrētum est; bellōque protracto, tertius ei et quartus consulātus delātus est. In duōbus prœliis cum Cimbris ducenta millia hostium cecīdit, octoginta millia cepit, eorumque regem Theutobŏchum; propter quod merĭtum absens quintò Consul creātus est. Interea Cimbri et Teutŏnes, quo- A. U
rum copia adhuc infinīta erat, in Italiam trans- 653.
iērunt. Itĕrum a C. Mario et Qu. Catŭlo contra eos

[a] Id. 110, 2
[b] Gr. 655.
[c] Gr. 403, R. V.
[d] Id. 4, 1.
[e] Id. 121, 6, & Gr. 634.
[f] Gr. 319, R. V.

dimicātum est[a] ad Verōnam. Centum et quadraginta millia aut in pugnâ aut in fugâ cæsa sunt; sexaginta millia capta. Tria et triginta Cimbris[b] signa sublāta sunt.

A. U. 659. 2. Sexcentesĭmo quinquagesĭmo nono anno ab urbe condĭtâ in Italiâ gravissĭmum bellum exarsit. Nam Picentes, Marsi, Pelignīque, qui multos annos popŭlo Romāno obediĕrant, æqua cum illis jura sibi[b] dari postulābant. Perniciōsum admŏdum hoc bellum fuit. P. Rutilius consul in eo occīsus est; plures exercĭtus fusi fugatīque. Tandem L. Cornelius Sulla cùm[c] alia egregiè gessit, tum Cluentium, hostium ducem, cum magnis copiis, fudit. Per quadriennium cum gravi utriusque partis calamitāte hoc bellum tractum est. Quinto demum anno L. Cornelius Sulla ei imposuit finem. Romāni tamen, id[d] quod priùs negavĕrant, jus civitātis, bello finīto, sociis tribuērunt.

A. U. 666. 3. Anno urbis condĭtæ sexcentesĭmo sexagesĭmo sexto primum Romæ bellum civīle exortum est; eōdem anno etiam Mithridatĭcum. Causam bello civīli C. Marius dedit. Nam quum Sullæ bellum adversùs Mithridātem regem Ponti decrētum esset, Marius ei[e] hunc honōrem eripĕre conātus est. Sed Sulla, qui adhuc cum legionĭbus suis in Italia morabātur, cum exercĭtu Romam venit, et adversarios cùm[c] interfēcit, tum fugāvit. Tum rebus Romæ utcunque composĭtis, in Asiam profectus est, pluribusque prœliis Mithridātem coëgit, ut pacem a Romānis petĕret,[f] et Asiâ, quam invasĕrat, relictâ, regni sui finĭbus contentus esset.

4. Sed dum Sulla in Græciâ et Asiâ Mithridātem vincit, Marius, qui fugātus fuĕrat, et Cornelius Cinna, unus

[a] Gr. 223, 3. [c] Id. 124, 8. [e] Gr. 501, R., & Id. 5, 1.
[b] Gr. 522, R. III. [d] Id. 37, 9. [f] Gr. 627, 1, 3d.

ex consulĭbus, bellum in Italiâ reparârunt, et ingressi Romam nobilissĭmos ex senātu et consulāres viros interfecērunt; multos proscripsērunt; ipsius Sullæ domo eversâ, filios et uxōrem ad fugam compulērunt. Universus relĭquus senātus ex urbe fugiens ad Sullam in Græciam venit, orans ut patriæ subvenīret.[a] Sulla in Italiam trajēcit,[b] hostium exercĭtus vicit, mox etiam urbem ingressus est, quam cæde[c] et sanguĭne civiûm replēvit. Quatuor millia inermium, qui se dedidĕrant, interfĭci[d] jussit; duo millia equĭtum et senatōrum proscripsit. Tum de Mithridāte triumphāvit. Duo hæc bella funestissĭma, Italĭcum, quod et sociāle dictum est, et civīle, consumpsērunt ultra centum et quinquaginta millia homĭnum, viros consulāres viginti quatuor, prætorios septem, ædilitios sexaginta, senatōres ferè ducentos.

LIBER SEXTUS.

1. Anno urbis condĭtæ sexcentesĭmo septua- A. U.
gesĭmo sexto, L. Licinio Lucullo[g] et M. Aurelio 676.
Cottâ consulĭbus, mortuus est Nicomēdes, rex Bithyniæ, et testamento popŭlum Romānum fecit herēdem.[e] Mithridātes, pace ruptâ,[f] Asiam rursus voluit invadĕre. Adversùs eum ambo consŭles missi variam habuêre fortūnam. Cotta apud Chalcedŏnem victus prœlio, a rege etiam intra oppĭdum obsessus est. Sed quum se inde Mithridātes Cyzĭcum[h] transtulisset, ut, hac urbe captâ,[i]

---

[a] Gr. 627, 1, 3d.
[b] Gr. 444.
[c] Gr. 515, R. XXXI.
[d] Id. 90, 4.
[e] Gr. 440.
[f] Id. 104, 1.
[g] Id. 110, 2, & Gr. 695.
[h] Gr. 553, R. XXXVII.

totam Asiam invadĕret, Lucullus ei,[a] alter consul, occurrit, ac dum Mithridātes in obsidiōne Cyzĭci commorātur, ipse[b] eum a tergo obsēdit, famēque consumptum multis prœliis vicit. Postrēmò Byzantium[c] fugāvit; navāli quoque prœlio ejus duces oppressit. Ita unâ hiĕme[d] et æstāte a Lucullo centum ferè millia[e] milĭtum regis exstincta sunt.

A. U. 678. 2. Anno urbis sexcentesĭmo[f] septuagesĭmo octāvo novum in Italiâ bellum commōtum est. Septuaginta enim quatuor gladiatōres, ducĭbus[g] Spartăco, Crixo, et Œnomao, e ludo gladiatorio, qui Capuæ[h] erat, effugērunt, et per Italiam vagantes pæne non levius bellum, quàm Hannĭbal,[i] movērunt. Nam contraxērunt exercĭtum ferè sexaginta millium[e] armatōrum, multosque duces et duos Romānos consŭles vicērunt. Ipsi victi sunt in Apuliâ a M. Licinio Crasso proconsŭle, et, post multas calamitātes Italiæ,[j] tertio anno huic bello finis est imposĭtus.

3. Intĕrim L. Lucullus bellum Mithridatĭcum persecūtus regnum Mithridātis invāsit, ipsumque regem apud Cabīra civitātem, quò ingentes copias ex omni regno adduxĕrat Mithridātes, ingenti prœlio superātum fugāvit, et castra ejus diripuit. Armenia quoque Minor, quam tenēbat, eīdem[k] erepta est. Susceptus est Mithridātes a Tigrāne, Armeniæ rege, qui tum ingenti gloriâ imperābat; sed hujus quoque regnum[l] Lucullus est ingressus. Tigranocerta, nobilissĭmam Armeniæ civitātem, cepit, ipsum regem, cum magno exercĭtu venientem, ita vicit,

[a] Gr. 399, R. IV.
[b] Id. 32, 3.
[c] Gr. 553, R. XXXVII.
[d] Gr. 565, R. XLI.
[e] Gr. 104, 5.
[f] Gr. 106, 7.
[g] Id. 110, 2.
[h] Gr. 548, R. XXXVI.
[i] Gr. 470, 1st.
[j] Gr. 334.
[k] Id. 5, 1, & Gr. 522, R.
[l] Gr. 613, R. LII.

[III.

ut robur milĭtum Armeniōrum delēret.[a] Sed quum Lucullus finem bello imponĕre parāret, successor ei[b] missus est.

4. Per illa tempŏră piratæ omnia maria infestābant ita, ut Romānis, toto orbe[c] terrārum victorĭbus, sola navigatio tuta non esset.[a] Quare id bellum Cn. Pompēio[d] decrētum est, quod intra paucos menses incredibĭli felicitāte et celeritāte confēcit. Mox ei[d] delātum bellum contra regem Mithridātem et Tigrānem. Quo[e] suscepto, Mithridātem in Armeniâ Minōre nocturno prœlio vicit, castra diripuit, et quadraginta millĭbus ejus occīsis,[f] viginti tantùm de exercĭtu suo perdidit et duos centuriōnes. Mithridātes fugit cum uxōre et duōbus comitĭbus, neque multò pòst, Pharnăcis filii sui seditiōne coactus, venēnum hausit. Hunc vitæ finem habuit Mithridātes, vir ingentis industriæ[g] atque consilii. Regnāvit annis[h] sexaginta, vixit septuaginta duōbus: contra Romānos bellum habuit annis quadraginta.

A. U. 687.

5. Tigrāni deinde Pompēius bellum intŭlit. Ille[i] se[j] ei* dedĭdit, et in castra Pompēii venit, ac diadēma suum[j] in ejus* manĭbus collocāvit, quod ei† Pompēius reposuit. Parte[k] regni eum multāvit et grandi pecuniâ. Tum alios etiam reges et popŭlos superāvit. Armeniam Minōrem Deiotăro, Galatiæ regi, donāvit, quia auxilium contra Mithridātem tulĕrat. Seleuciam, vicīnam Antiochīæ civitātem, libertāte[l] donāvit, quòd regem Tigrānem non recepisset.[m] Inde in Judæam transgressus, Hierosolўmam, caput gentis, tertio mense cepit, duodĕcim mil-

* i. e. Pompey.
† i. e. Tigranes.
[a] Gr. 627, 1, 1st.
[b] Gr. 378, R. XV.
[c] Gr. 611, (*in.*)
[d] Gr. 522, R. III.
[e] Id. 38, 5.
[f] Id. 104, 1.
[g] Gr. 339, R. VII.
[h] Gr. 565, R. XLI.
[i] Gr. 118, 3, 3d.
[j] Gr. 118, 3, 1st.
[k] Gr. 514, R. XXXI.
[l] Gr. 505.
[m] Gr. 655.

lĭbus Judæōrum occīsis, cetĕris in fidem receptis. His gestis finem antiquissĭmo bello imposuit. Ante triumphantis [a] currum ducti sunt filii Mithridātis, filius Tigrānis, et Aristobūlus, rex Judæōrum. Prelāta ingens pecunia, auri atque argenti infinītum.[b] Hoc tempŏre nullum per orbem terrārum grave bellum erat.

A. U. 689. 6. M. Tullio Cicerōne oratōre et C. Antonio consulĭbus, anno ab urbe condĭtâ sexcentesĭmo undenonagesĭmo L. Sergius Catilīna, nobilissĭmi genĕris [c] vir, sed ingenii pravissĭmi, ad delendam [d] patriam conjurāvit cum quibusdam claris quidem sed audacĭbus viris. A Cicerōne urbe [e] expulsus est, socii ejus deprehensi et in carcĕre strangulāti sunt. Ab Antonio, altĕro consŭle, Catilīna ipse prœlio victus est et interfectus.

A. U. 693. 7. Anno urbis condĭtæ sexcentesĭmo nonagesĭmo tertio C. Julius Cæsar cum L. Bibŭlo consul est factus. Quum ei Gallia decrēta esset, semper vincendo [f] usque ad Oceănum Britannĭcum processit. Domuit autem annis [g] novem ferè omnem Galliam, quæ inter Alpes, flumen Rhodănum, Rhenum et Oceănum est. Britannis mox bellum intŭlit, quibus [h] ante eum ne nomen quidem Romanōrum cognĭtum erat; Germānos quoque trans Rhenum aggressus, ingentĭbus prœliis vicit.

8. Circa eădem tempŏra M. Licinius Crassus contra Parthos missus est. Et quum circa Carras contra omĭna
A. U. 700. et auspicia prœlium commisisset, a Surēnâ Orōdis regis duce, victus et interfectus est cum filio, clarissĭmo et præstantissĭmo juvĕne. Reliquiæ exercĭtûs per C. Cassium quæstōrem servātæ sunt.

---

[a] — Sup. *Pompeii.*
[b] — Sup. *pondus.*
[c] Gr. 339, R. V.
[d] Id. 112, 7.
[e] Gr. 613, R. LII.
[f] Gr. 705.
[g] Gr. 565, R. XLI.
[h] Gr. 528, R. XXXIII.

9. Hinc jam bellum civīle successit, quo Ro- A. U.
māni nomĭnis fortūna mutāta est. Cæsar enim 705.
victor e Galliâ rediens, absens cœpit poscĕre altĕrum[a] consulātum; quem quum alĭqui sine dubitatiōne deferrent,[b] contradictum est[c] a Pompēio et aliis, jussusque est, dimissis exercitĭbus, in urbem redīre. Propter hanc injuriam ab Arimĭno, ubi milĭtes congregātos habēbat, infesto exercĭtu Romam[d] contendit. Consŭles cum Pompēio, senatùsque omnis atque universa nobilĭtas ex urbe fugit, et in Græciam transiit; et, dum senātus bellum contra Cæsărem parābat, hic vacuam urbem ingressus dictatōrem se fecit.

10. Inde Hispanias[e] petit, ibique Pompēii legiōnes superāvit; tum in Græciâ adversùm Pompēium ipsum dimicāvit. Primo prœlio victus est et fugātus; evāsit tamen, quia nocte interveniente Pompēius sequi noluit; dixitque Cæsar, nec* Pompēium scire vincĕre, et illo tantùm die se potuisse superāri. Deinde in Thessaliâ apud Pharsālum ingentĭbus utrinque copiis commissis dimicavērunt. Nunquam† adhuc Romānæ copiæ majōres neque meliorĭbus ducĭbus[f] convenĕrant. Pugnātum est[c] ingenti contentiōne, victusque ad Postrēmum Pompēius, et castra ejus direpta sunt. Ipse fugātus Alexandrīam[e] petiit, ut a rege Ægypti, cui tutor a senātu datus fuĕrat, accipĕret[g] auxilia. At hic fortūnam magis quàm amicitiam[h] secūtus, occīdit Pompēium, caput ejus et annŭlum Cæsări misit. Quo[i] conspectu, Cæsar lacrȳmas fudisse dicĭtur, tanti viri intuens caput, et genĕri quondam sui.

* *Nec*, i. e. *et non*, Id. 124, 1. † *Nunquam*, i. e. *neque unquam*, Id. 124, 5.
[a] Gr. 106, 7. [d] Gr. 553, R. XXXVII. [g] Gr. 627, 1, 2d.
[b] Gr. 631, & Gr 159, II. [c] Gr. 562. [h] Gr. 470, 1st.
[e] Gr. 223, 3. [f] Gr. 611, (*cum.*) [i] Id. 38, 5, & Gr. 684.

11. Quum ad Alexandrīam venisset Cæsar, Ptolemæus ei insidias parāre voluit, quâ de causâ regi bellum illātum est. Rex victus in Nilo periit, inventumque est corpus ejus cum lorīcâ aureâ. Cæsar, Alexandrīâ[a] potītus, regnum Cleopatræ dedit. Tum inde profectus Pompeianārum[b] partium reliquias est persecūtus, bellisque civilĭbus toto terrārum orbe composĭtis, Romam rediit. Ubi quum insolentiùs agĕre cœpisset,[c] conjurātum[d] est in eum a sexaginta vel ampliùs senatorĭbus, equitibusque Romānis. Præcipui fuērunt inter conjurātos Bruti duo ex genĕre illius Bruti, qui, regĭbus expulsis,[e] primus Romæ consul fuĕrat, C. Cassius et Ser-
A. U. vilius Casca. Ergo Cæsar, quum in Curiam ve-
709. nisset,[c] viginti tribus vulnerĭbus confossus est.

12. Interfecto Cæsāre, anno urbis septingentesĭmo nono bella civilia reparāta sunt. Senātus favēbat Cæsăris percussorĭbus,[f] Antonius consul a Cæsăris partĭbus stabat. Ergo turbātâ republĭcâ, Antonius, multis scelerĭbus commissis,[e] a senātu hostis judicātus est. Fusus fugatusque Antonius, amisso exercĭtu,[e] confūgit ad Lepĭdum, qui Cæsări[g] magister equĭtum fuĕrat, et tum grandes copias milĭtum habēbat: a quo susceptus est. Mox Octaviānus cum Antonio pacem fecit, et quasi vindicatūrus[h] patris[i] sui mortem, a quo per testamentum fuĕrat adoptātus, Romam cum exercĭtu profectus extorsit, ut sibi[j] juvĕni viginti annōrum[k] consulātus darētur.[l] Tum junctus cum Antonio et Lepĭdo rempublĭcam armis tenēre cœpit, senatumque proscripsit. Per hos etiam Cicĕro orātor occīsus est, multīque alii nobĭles.

[a] Id. 7, 5, & Gr. 484, R. [XXVI.
[b] Gr. 337.
[c] Gr. 631.
[d] Gr. 223, 3.
[e] Id. 104, 1.
[f] Gr. 403, R. V.
[g] Gr. 380, R. I.
[h] Id. 102, 1.
[i] — viz. *Julii Cæsaris.*
[j] Gr. 522, R. III.
[k] Gr. 339, R. VII.
[l] Gr. 627, 1, 3d.

13. Interea Brutus et Cassius, interfectōres Cæsăris, ingens bellum movērunt. Profecti contra eos Cæsar Octaviānus, qui postea Augustus est appellātus, et M. Antonius, apud Philippos, Macedoniæ urbem, con- A. U.
tra eos pugnavērunt. Primo prœlio victi sunt 712.
Antonius et Cæsar; periit tamen dux nobilitātis Cassius; secundo Brutum et infinītam nobilitātem, quæ cum illis bellum suscepĕrat, victam[a] interfecērunt. Tum victōres rempublĭcam ita inter se divisērunt, ut Octaviānus Cæsar Hispanias, Gallias, Italiam tenēret; Antonius Orientem, Lepĭdus Afrĭcam accipĕret.

14. Paulò pòst Antonius, repudiātâ[b] sorōre Cæsăris Octaviāni, Cleopatram regīnam Ægypti, uxōrem duxit. Ab hâc incitātus ĭngens bellum commōvit, dum Cleopatra cupiditāte[c] muliebri optat Romæ regnāre. Victus est ab Augusto navāli pugnâ clarâ et illustri A. U.
apud Actium, qui[d] locus in Epīro est. Hinc 723.
fugit in Ægyptum, et, desperātis rebus, quum omnes ad Augustum transīrent, se ipse[e] interēmit. Cleopatra quoque aspĭdem sibi admīsit, et venēno ejus exstincta est. Ita bellis toto orbe confectis, Octaviānus Augustus Romam rediit anno duodecĭmo[f] quàm consul fuĕrat. Ex eo inde tempŏre rempublĭcam per quadraginta et quatuor annos solus obtinuit. Antè enim* duodĕcim annis cum Antonio et Lepĭdo tenuĕrat.† Ita ab initio principātûs ejus usque ad finem quinquaginta sex anni fuēre.

* "*Enim*," &c., assigning a reason for "*Solus*."

† Sup. *eam*, i. e. *rempublicam*.

[a] Id. 104, 3, & Gr. 268. [c] Gr. 542, R. XXXV. [e] Id. 33, 1.

[b] Id. 104, 1. [d] Id. 37, 5. [f] Gr. 569 & 570.

THE GEOGRAPHY AND THE NATIONS OF ANTIQUITY.

1. Universus terrārum orbis in tres partes dividĭtur, Eurōpam,[a] Asiam, Afrĭcam. Eurōpa ab Afrĭcâ sejungĭtur freto Gaditāno, in cujus utrâque parte montes sunt altissĭmi, Abȳla[a] in Afrĭcâ, in Eurōpâ Calpe, qui[b] montes Hercŭlis columnæ[c] appellantur. Per idem fretum mare internum, quod littorĭbus Eurōpæ, Asiæ, et Afrĭcæ includĭtur, jungĭtur cum Oceăno.

2. Eurōpa termĭnos[d] habet ab oriente Tanaim fluvium, pontum Euxīnum, et palūdem Mæotĭda;[e] a meridie,[f] mare internum; ab occidente, mare Atlantĭcum sive Oceănum; a septentriōne,[f] mare Britannĭcum. Mare internum tres maxĭmos sinus habet. Quorum[g] is, qui Asiam a Græciâ sejungit, Ægæum mare vocātur; secundus, qui est inter Græciam et Italiam, Ionium; tertius denĭque, qui occidentāles Italiæ oras alluit, a Romānis Tuscum, a Græcis Tyrrhēnum mare appellātur.

3. In eâ Eurōpæ parte, quæ ad occāsum vergit, prima terrārum[g] est Hispania, quæ a tribus laterĭbus mari circumdăta per Pyrenæos montes cum Galliâ cohæret.

---

[a] Gr. 257.
[b] Id. 37, 6, Note.
[c] Gr. 319, R. V.
[d] Gr. 440.
[e] Gr. 90, 4.
[f] Gr. 236, 6.
[g] Gr. 355, R. X. & Id. 38.

Quum universa Hispania dives sit[a] et fœcunda, ea tamen regio, quæ a flumĭne Bæti[b] Bætĭca vocātur, cetĕras fertilitāte[c] antecellit. Ibi Gades sitæ, insŭla cum urbe a Tyriis condĭtâ, quæ freto Gaditāno nomen dedit. Tota illa regio viris,[d] equis, ferro, plumbo, ære, argento, aurōque abundat, et ubi penuriâ aquārum minùs est fertĭlis, linum tamen aut spartum alit. Marmŏris quoque lapicidīnas habet. In Bætĭcâ minium reperītur.

4. Gallia posĭta est inter Pyrenæos montes et Rhenum, orientālem oram Tuscum mare alluit, occidentālem Oceănus. Ejus pars illa, quæ Italiæ[e] est opposĭta, et Narbonensis vocātur, omnium[f] est lætissĭma. In eâ orâ sita est Massilia, urbs a Phocæis condĭta, qui, patriâ a Persis devictâ, quum servitūtem ferre non possent,[g] Asiâ relictâ,[h] novas in Eurōpâ sedes quæsivĕrant. Ibīdem est campus lapideus, ubi Hercŭles dicĭtur contra Neptūni libĕros dimicâsse. Quum tela defecissent,[g] Jupĭter filium imbre lapĭdum adjūvit. Credas[i] plusisse;[j] adeò multi passim jacent.

5. Rhodănus, fluvius, haud longè a Rheni fontĭbus ortus, lacu Lemāno excipĭtur, servatque impĕtum, ita ut per medium lacum intĕger fluat,[k] tantusque, quantus[l] venit, egrediātur. Inde ad occāsum versus, Gallias aliquandiu dirĭmit; donec, cursu in meridiem flexo, aliōrum amnium accessu auctus in mare effundĭtur.

6. Ea pars Galliæ, quæ ad Rhenum porrigĭtur, frumenti pabulīque[m] feracissĭma est, cœlum salūbre; noxia animalium genĕra pauca alit. Incŏlæ superbi et superstitiōsi, ita ut deos humānis victĭmis[n] gaudēre existĭment.[k]

a Gr. 630.
b Gr. 90, 5.
c Gr. 535, R. XXXIV.
d Gr. 480, R. XXV.
e Gr. 522, R. III.
f Id. 19, & Gr. 355, R. X.
g Gr. 631.
h Id. 104, 1.
i Gr. 171, 3, last Ex., & Gr. 627, 1, 1st.
j Id. 94, 1, 2d, & 98, 2.
k Gr. 627, 1, 1st.
l Id. 44, 3.
m Gr. 361, R. XI.
n Gr. 485.

Magistri religiōnum et sapientiæ sunt Druĭdæ, qui, quæ[a] se scire profitentur, in antris abditisque silvis docent. Anĭmas æternas esse[b] credunt, vitamque altĕram post mŏrtem incipĕre.[b] Hanc ob causam cum defunctis[c] arma cremant aut defodiunt, eamque doctrīnam homĭnes ad bellum[d] alacriōres facĕre existĭmant.

7. Universa Gallia divīsa est inter tres magnos popŭlos, qui fluviis terminantur. A Pyrenæo monte usque ad Garumnam Aquitāni habĭtant; inde ad Sequănam Celtæ; Belgæ denĭque usque ad Rhenum pertĭnent.

8. Garumna amnis, ex Pyrenæo monte delapsus, diu vadōsus est et vix navigabĭlis. Quanto[e] magis procēdit, tanto fit latior; ad postrēmum magni freti[f] simĭlis, non solùm majōra navigia tolĕrat, verùm etiam more maris exsurgit, navigantesque[c] atrocĭter jactat.

9. Sequăna ex Alpĭbus ortus in septentriōnem pergit. Postquàm se haud procul Lutetiâ[g] cum Matrŏnâ conjunxit, Oceăno[h] infundĭtur. Hæc flumĭna opportunissĭma sunt mercĭbus[i] permutandis[j] et ex mari interno in Oceănum transvehendis.[j]

10. Rhenus itĭdem ex Alpĭbus ortus haud procul ab origĭne lacum effĭcit Venĕtum, qui etiam Brigantīnus appellātur. Deinde longo spatio[k] per fines Helvetiōrum, Mediomatricōrum, et Trevirōrum continuo alveo fertur, aut modĭcas insŭlas[l] circumfluens; in agro Batăvo autem, ubi Oceăno appropinquāvit, in plures amnes dividĭtur; nec jam amnis, sed ripis longè recedentĭbus, ingens lacus,

[a] Id. 37, 2.
[b] Id. 95, 1.
[c] Id. 19, 1.
[d] Gr. 353, 2d.
[c] Gr. 579, R. XLIII., & 578.
[f] Gr. 385.
[g] Gr. 611, (a).
[h] Gr. 522, R. III.
[i] Gr. 382, R. XVI.
[j] Id. 112, 6.
[k] Gr. 573, R. XLII.
[l] Gr. 613, R. LII.

Flevo appellātur, ejusdemque nomĭnis insŭlam amplexus, fit itĕrum arctior et fluvius[a] itĕrum in mare emittĭtur.

11. Trans Rhenum Germāni habĭtant usque ad Vistŭlam, quæ finis est Germaniæ ad orientem. Ad meridiem terminātur Alpĭbus, ad septentriōnem mari Britannĭco et Baltĭco. Incŏlæ corpŏrum proceritāte[b] excellunt. Anĭmos bellando,[c] corpŏra laborĭbus exercent. Hanc ob causam crebrò bella gerunt cum finitĭmis, non tam finium prolatandōrum[d] causâ, aut imperii cupiditāte, sed ob belli amōrem. Mites[e] tamen sunt erga supplĭces,[e] et boni hospitĭbus. Urbes mœnĭbus cinctas aut fossis aggeribusque munītas non habent. Ipsas domos ad breve tempus struunt non lapidĭbus aut laterĭbus coctis sed lignis, quæ frondĭbus tegunt. Nam diu eōdem in loco morāri[f] periculōsum[g] arbitrantur libertāti.

12. Agricultūræ[h] Germāni non admŏdùm student, nec quisquam agri modum certum aut fines proprios habet. Lacte vescuntur et caseo et carne. Ubi fons, campus, nemusve iis[h] placuĕrit,[i] ibi domos figunt, mox aliò transitūri cum conjugĭbus et libĕris. Interdum etiam hiĕmem in subterraneis specŭbus dicuntur transigĕre.

13. Germania altis montĭbus, silvis, paludibusque invia reddĭtur. Inter silvas[j] maxĭma est Hercynia, cujus latitudĭnem[k] Cæsar novem diērum iter[l] patēre narrat. Insequenti tempŏre magna pars ejus excīsa est. Flumĭna sunt in Germaniâ multa et magna. Inter hæc clarissĭmum nomen Rheni, de quo suprà dixĭmus, et Danubii. Clari quoque amnes, Mœnus, Visurgis, Albis. Danubius,

[a] Id. 13, 1, & Gr. 252. [e] Id. 19, 1. [i] Gr. 627, 5
[b] Gr. 535, R. XXXIV. [f] Id. 89, 5. [j] Gr. 360.
[c] Gr. 705, & Id. 111, 6. [g] Gr. 270 [k] Gr. 671, R. LVIII.
[d] Id. 112, 5. [h] Gr. 403, R. V. [l] Gr. 573, R. XLII.

omnium Europæ flumĭnum[a] maxĭmus, apud Rhætos orĭtur, flexōque ad ortum solis cursu, receptisque sexaginta amnĭbus, in Pontum Euxīnum sex vastis ostiis effundĭtur.

14. Britaniam insŭlam Phœnicĭbus innotuisse, eosque stannum inde et plumbum pellesque petivisse, probabĭle est. Romānis eam Julius Cæsar primus aperuit; neque tamen priùs cognĭta esse cœpit quàm Claudio[b] imperante. Hadriānus eam, muro ab oceăno Germanĭco ad Hibernĭcum mare ducto, in duas partes divīsit, ut inferiōrem insŭlæ partem, quæ Romānis parēbat, a barbarōrum populōrum, qui in Scotiâ habitābant, incursionĭbus tuerētur.[c]

15. Maxĭma insŭlæ pars campestris, collĭbus passim silvisque distincta. Incŏlæ Gallos proceritāte[d] corpŏrum vincunt, cetĕrùm ingenio[d] Gallis simĭles, simpliciōres tamen illis[e] magisque barbări. Nemŏra habĭtant pro urbĭbus. Ibi tuguria exstruunt et stabŭla pecŏri, sed plerùmque ad breve tempus. Humanitāte[d] cetĕris præstant ii, qui Cantium incŏlunt. Tota hæc regio est maritĭma. Qui interiōrem insŭlæ partem habĭtant, frumenta non serunt; lacte[f] et carne vivunt. Pro vestĭbus indūti sunt pellĭbus.[g]

16. Italia ab Alpĭbus usque ad fretum Sicŭlum porrigĭtur inter mare Tuscum et Adriatĭcum. Multo[h] longior est quàm latior.[i] In medio se attollit Appennīnus mons, qui, postquàm continenti jugo progressus est usque ad Apuliam, in duos quasi ramos dividĭtur. Nobilissĭma regio ob fertilitātem soli cœlīque salubritātem. Quum longè in mare procurrat,[j] plurĭmos habet portus populōrum inter se[k] patentes commercio.[l] Neque ulla facĭlè[m] est

[a] Gr. 355, R. X.
[b] Gr. 694.
[c] Gr. 627, 1, 2d.
[d] Gr. 535, R. XXXIV.
[e] Id. 6, 3, & Gr. 467, R.
[f] Gr. 485.
[g] Gr. 524, R. V.
[h] Gr. 579, R. XLIII.
[i] Gr. 474.
[j] Gr. 630, & Id. 74, 1.
[k] Gr. 118, 5.
[l] Gr. 391, R. XVII.
[m] Gr. 591, 3d.

regĭo, quæ tot tamque pulchras urbes habeat,[a] inter quas Roma et magnitudĭne[b] et nomĭnis famâ emĭnet.

17. Hæc urbs, orbis terrārum caput, septem montes complectĭtur. Initio quatuor portas habēbat; Augusti ævo triginta septem. Urbis magnificentiam augēbant fora, templa, portĭcus, aquæductus, theātra, arcus triumphāles, horti denĭque, et id genus[c] alia, ad quæ vel lecta[d] anĭmus stupet. Quare rectè de eâ prædicāre videntur, qui nullius urbis in toto orbe terrārum magnificentiam ei[e] comparāri posse dixērunt.

18. Felicissĭma in Italiâ regio est Campania. Multi ibi vitifĕri colles, ubi nobilissĭma vina gignuntur, Setīnum, Cæcŭbum, Falernum, Massĭcum. Calĭdi ibīdem fontes[f] saluberrĭmi. Nusquam generosior olea. Conchylio[g] quoque et pisce nobĭli maria vicīna scatent.

19. Clarissĭmi amnes Italiæ sunt Padus et Tibĕris. Et Padus quidem in superiōre parte, quæ Gallia Cisalpīna vocātur, ab imis radicĭbus Vesŭli montis exorĭtur; primùm exīlis, deinde aliis amnĭbus ita alĭtur, ut se per septem ostia in mare effundat.[h] Tibĕris, qui antiquissĭmis temporĭbus Albŭlæ nomen habēbat, ex Appennīno orĭtur; deinde duōbus et quadraginta fluminĭbus auctus fit navigabĭlis. Plurĭmas in utrâque ripâ villas adspĭcit, præcipuè autem urbis Romānæ magnificentiam. Placidissĭmus amnium rarò ripas[i] egredĭtur.

20. In inferiōre parte Italiæ clara quondam urbs Tarentum, quæ maris sinui, cui adjăcet, nomen dedit. Soli fertilĭtas cœlīque jucunda temperies in causâ fuisse vidētur, ut incŏlæ luxuriâ et deliciis enervarentur. Quum-

[a] Gr. 636, R. I.
[b] Gr. 535, R. XXXIV.
[c] Gr. 611, (ad).
[d] Id. 101, 4, & Gr. 688.
[e] Gr. 522, R. III.
[f] Gr. 308.
[g] Gr. 480, R. XXV
[h] Gr. 627, 1, 1st.
[i] Gr. 611, (ultra.)

que aliquandiu potentiâ[a] florērent,[b] copiasque haud contemnendas alĕrent, peregrīnis tamen plerùmque ducĭbus in bellis utebantur, ut Pyrrho,[c] rege Epīri, quo superāto, urbs in Romanōrum potestātem venit.

21. Proxĭma Italiæ est Sicilia, insŭla omnium[d] maris interni maxĭma. Antiquissĭmis temporĭbus eam cum Italiâ cohæsisse,[e] marisque impĕtu, aut terræ motu inde divulsam esse,[e] verisimĭle est. Forma triangulāris, ita ut littĕræ, quam Græci Delta vocant, imagĭnem refĕrat. A tribus promontoriis vocātur Trinacria. Nobilissĭmus ibi mons Ætnæ[f] qui urbi Catănæ immĭnet, tum[g] ob altitudĭnem, tum etiam ob ignes, quos effundit; quare Cyclōpum in illo monte officīnam esse poëtæ dicunt. Cinĕres e craterĭbus egesti agrum circumjacentem fœcundum et ferācem reddĕre existimantur. Sunt ibi Piōrum campi, qui nomen habent a duōbus juvenĭbus Catanensĭbus, qui, flammis quondam repentè ingruentĭbus, parentes senectūte confectos, humĕris sublātos, flammæ[h] eripuisse feruntur. Nomĭna fratrum Amphinŏmus et Anāpus fuērunt.

22. Inter urbes Siciliæ nulla est illustrior Syracūsis, Corinthiōrum coloniâ, ex quinque urbĭbus conflātâ. Ab Atheniensĭbus bello petīta, maxĭmas hostium copias delēvit: Carthaginienses etiam magnis interdum cladĭbus affēcit. Secundo bello Punĭco per triennium oppugnāta, Archimēdis potissĭmùm ingenio et arte defensa, a M. Marcello capta est. Vicīnus huic urbi fons Arethūsæ Nymphæ[i] sacer, ad quam Alphēus amnis ex Peloponnēso per mare Ionium lapsus* commissāri† dicĭtur. Nam si quid ad Olympiam in illum amnem jactum fuĕrit, id in

* Sup. *esse*, Gr. 179, 6. † *Commissari*, "in order to enjoy a banquet." Gr. 665.

[a] Gr. 535. R. XXXIV. [b] Gr. 630. [c] Gr. 720, R. (*ut*, *as*). [d] Id. 19, & Gr. 355, R. X. [e] Id. 97, 1, & 4. [f] Gr. 260. [g] Id. 124, 7. [h] Gr. 501, R. XXIX. [i] Gr. 382, R. XVI.

Arethusæ fonte reddi.[a] De illâ fabŭlâ quid statuendum sit,[b] sponte appāret.

23. In mari Ligustĭco insŭla est Corsĭca, quam Græci Cyrnum vocant. Terra aspĕra multisque locis[c] invia, cœlum grave, mare circà[d] importūnum. Incŏlæ, latrociniis dedĭti, feri sunt et horrĭdi. Mella quoque illius insŭlæ amāra esse dicuntur corporibusque[e] nocēre. Proxĭma ei est Sardinia, quæ a Græcis mercatorĭbus Ichnūsa vocātur, quia formam humāni vestigii habet. Solum[f] quàm cœlum melius. Illud[k] fertĭle, hoc[k] grave ac noxium. Noxia quoque animalia herbasque venenātas gignit. Multum inde frumenti[g] Romam mittĭtur; unde hæc insŭla et Sicilia nutrīces urbis vocantur.

24. Græcia nomĭnis celebritāte omnes ferè alias orbis terrārum regiōnes superāvit. Nulla enim magnōrum ingeniōrum[h] fuit feracior; neque ulla belli pacisque artes majōre studio[i] excoluit. Plurĭmas eădem colonias in omnes terræ partes deduxit. Multùm ităque terrâ marīque valuit, et gravissĭma bella magnâ cum gloriâ gessit.

25. Græcia inter Ionium et Ægæum mare porrigĭtur. In plurĭmas regiōnes divīsa est, quarum[j] amplissĭmæ sunt Macedonia et Epīrus—quamquam hæ a nonnullis a Græciâ sejunguntur—tum Thessalia. Macedoniam Philippi et Alexandri regnum illustrāvit; quorum ille[k] Græciam subēgit, hic[k] Asiam latissĭmè domuit, ereptumque Persis[l] imperium in Macedŏnes transtŭlit. Centum ejus regiōnis et quinquaginta urbes numerantur; quarum[j] septuaginta

[a] — Sup. *dicitur*.
[b] Gr. 627, 5, & Id. 108, 9.
[c] Gr. 611, (*in*).
[d] Gr. 236, 4.
[e] Gr. 403, R. V.
[f] Gr. 308.
[g] Gr. 343, R. VIII.
[h] Gr. 351, 1st.
[i] Gr. 542, R. XXXV.
[j] Gr. 355, R. X.
[k] Gr. 118, 3, 3d.
[l] Id. 5, 1, & Gr. 522, R. III.

duas, Perseo, ultĭmo Macedoniæ rege, superāto, Paullus Æmilius diripuit.

26. Epīrus, quæ ab Acrocerauniis incĭpit montĭbus, desĭnit in Achelōo flumĭne. Plures eam popŭli incŏlunt. Illustris ibi Dodōna[a] in Molossōrum finĭbus, vetustissĭmo Jovis oracŭlo inclȳta. Columbæ ibi ex arborĭbus oracŭla dedisse narrantur; quercusque ipsas et lebētes æneos inde suspensos deōrum voluntātem tinnītu significâsse[b] fama est.

27. Achelōi fluvii ostiis[c] insŭlæ alĭquot objăcent, quarum maxĭma est Cephallenia. Multæ præterea insŭlæ littŏri[c] Epīri adjăcent, interque eas Corcȳra, quam Homērus Scheriam appellâsse existimātur.[d] In hâc Phæācas posuit ille et hortos Alcinoi. Coloniam huc deduxērunt Corinthii, quo[e] tempŏre Numa Pompilius Romæ regnāvit. Vicīna ei Ithăca, Ulyssis patria, aspĕra montĭbus, sed Homēri carminĭbus adeò nobilitāta, ut ne fertilissĭmis quidem regionĭbus cedat.[f]

28. Thessalia latè patet inter Macedoniam et Epīrum, fœcunda regio, generōsis præcipuè equis excellens, unde Thessalōrum equitātus celeberrĭmus. Montes ibi memorabĭles Olympus, in quo deōrum sedes esse existimātur,[d] Pelion et Ossa, per quos gigantes cœlum petivisse dicuntur;[d] Œta denĭque, in cujus vertĭce Hercŭles, rogo conscenso[g] se ipsum cremāvit. Inter[h] Ossam et Olympum Penēus, limpidissĭmus amnis, delabĭtur, vallem amœnissĭmam, Tempe vocātam, irrĭgans.

29. Inter[h] relĭquas Græciæ regiōnes nomĭnis claritāte[i] emĭnet Attĭca, quæ etiam Atthis vocātur. Ibi Athēnæ,

[a] Gr. 308. [b] Id. 97, 1. [c] Gr. 399, R. IV. [d] Gr. 676. [e] Id. 37, 2d, & Note. [f] Gr. 627, 1, 1st. [g] Id. 104, 1. [h] Id. 123, 3. [i] Gr. 535, R. XXXIV.

de quâ urbe deos inter se certâsse fama est. Certius est[a] nullam unquam urbem tot poëtas tulisse, tot oratōres, tot philosŏphos, totque in omni virtūtis genĕre claros viros. Res autem bello eas[b] gessit, ut huic soli[c] gloriæ[d] studēre viderētur; pacisque artes ita excoluit, ut hac laude magis etiam quàm belli gloriâ splendēret. Arx ibi sive Acropŏlis[e] urbi immĭnens, unde latus in mare prospectus patet. Per propylæa ad eam adscendĭtur,[f] splendĭdum Periclis opus. Cum ipsâ urbe per longos muros conjunctus est portus Piræeus, post bellum Persĭcum secundum a Themistŏcle munītus. Tutissĭma ibi statio[e] navium.

30. Attĭcam attingit Bœotia, fertilissĭma regio. Incŏlæ magis corporĭbus[g] valent quàm ingeniis. Urbs celeberrĭma Thebæ,[e] quas Amphīon musĭces[h] ope mœnĭbus cinxisse dicĭtur. Illustrāvit eam Pindări poëtæ ingenium, Epaminondæ virtus. Mons[e] ibi Helĭcon, Musārum sedes, et Cithæron plurĭmis poëtārum fabŭlis celebrātus.

31. Bœotiæ Phōcis finitĭma,[e] ubi Delphi urbs clarissĭma. In quâ urbe oracŭlum Apollĭnis quantam[i] apud omnes gentes auctoritātem habuĕrit, quot[i] quàmque præclāra munĕra ex omni ferè terrārum orbe Delphos[j] missa fuĕrint, nemo ignōrat. Immĭnet urbi Parnassus mons, in cujus verticĭbus Musæ habitāre dicuntur,[k] unde aqua fontis Castalii poëtārum ingenia inflammāre existimātur.[k]

32. Cum eâ parte Græciæ, quam hactĕnus descripsĭmus, cohæret ingens peninsŭla, quæ Peloponnēsus vocātur, platăni folio[l] simillĭma. Augustus ille trames inter

---

[a] Id. 51, 2.
[b] Id. 28, 1.
[c] Id. 16, 4.
[d] Gr. 403, R. V.
[e] Gr. 308.
[f] — Sup. *a hominibus*, & Id. 67, 2.
[g] Gr. 535, R. XXXIV.
[h] Gr. 62.
[i] Gr. 627, 5.
[j] Gr. 553, R. XXXVII.
[k] Gr. 676.
[l] Gr. 382, R. XVI.

Ægæum mare et Ionium, per quem cum Megarĭde cohæret, Isthmus appellātur. In eo templum Neptūni est, ad quod ludi celebrantur Isthmĭci. Ibīdem in ipso Peloponnēsi adĭtu, Corinthus sita est, urbs antiquissĭma, ex cujus summâ[a] arce, (Acrocorinthon[b] appellant,) utrumque mare conspicĭtur. Quum opĭbus florēret,[c] maritimisque valēret copiis, gravia bella gessit. In bello Achaĭco, quod Romāni cum Græcis gessērunt, pulcherrĭma urbs, quam Cicĕro Græciæ lumen appellat, a L. Mummio expugnāta[d] funditusque delēta est. Restituit eam Julius Cæsar, colonosque[e] eò milĭtes veterānos misit.

33. Nobĭlis est in Peloponnēso urbs Olympia templo Jovis Olympii ac statuâ illustris. Statua[f] ex ebŏre facta, Phidiæ summi artifĭcis opus præstantissĭmum. Prope[g] illud templum ad Alphēi flumĭnis ripas ludi celebrantur Olympĭci, ad quos videndos[h] ex totâ Græciâ concurrĭtur.[i] Ab his ludis Græca gens res gestas suas numĕrat.

34. Nec Sparta prætereunda[j] est, urbs nobilissĭma, quam Lycurgi leges, civiumque virtus et patientia illustrāvit.[k] Nulla ferè gens bellĭcâ laude[l] magis floruit, pluresque viros fortes constantesque genuit. Urbi immĭnet mons Taygĕtus, qui[m] usque ad Arcadiam procurrit. Proxĭmè urbem[g] Eurōtas fluvius delabĭtur, ad cujus ripas Spartāni se exercēre solēbant. In sinum Laconĭcum effundĭtur. Haud procul inde abest promontorium Tænărum, ubi altissĭmi specus, per quos Orpheum ad infĕros descendisse[n] narrant.

35. Mare Ægæum, inter[o] Græciam Asiamque patens,

[a] Id. 17, 2.
[b] Gr. 74.
[c] Gr. 631.
[d] Id. 115, 1.
[e] Gr. 440.
[f] Gr. 308.
[g] Gr. 611, (ad).
[h] Id. 112, 7.
[i] — Sup. *ab hominibus*, Id. 67, 2.
[j] Id. 108, 1.
[k] Gr. 313.
[l] Gr. 535, R. XXXIV.
[m] Id. 35, 1.
[n] Id. 97, 1.
[o] Id. 123, 3.

plurĭmis insŭlis distinguĭtur. Illustres inter eas sunt Cyclădes, sic appellātæ, quia in orbem jacent. Media eārum[a] est Delus, quæ repentè e mari enāta esse dicĭtur. In eâ insŭlâ Latōna Apollĭnem et Diānam pepĕrit, quæ numĭna ibi unà cum matre summâ religiōne coluntur. Urbi immĭnet Cynthus, mons excelsus et arduus. Inōpus amnis parĭter cum Nilo decrescĕre et augēri dicĭtur. Mercātus in Delo celeberrĭmus, quòd ob portûs commoditātem templīque religiōnem mercatōres ex toto orbe terrārum eò confluēbant. Eandem ob causam civitātes Græciæ, post secundum Persĭcum bellum, tribūta ad belli usum in eam insŭlam, tanquam in commūne totius Græciæ ærarium, conferēbant; quam pecuniam insequenti tempŏre Athenienses in suam urbem transtulērunt.

36. Eubœa insŭla littŏri[b] Bœotiæ et Attĭcæ prætendĭtur, angusto freto a continenti distans. Terræ motu a Bœotiâ avulsa esse credĭtur; sæpiùs eam concussam esse[c] constat. Fretum, quo a Græciâ sejungĭtur, vocātur Eurīpus, sævum et æstuōsum mare, quod continuo motu agitātur. Nonnulli dicunt septies quovis die statis tempori̅bus fluctus alterno motu agitāri; alii hoc negant, dicentes, mare temĕrè in venti modum huc illuc movēri. Sunt, qui narrent,[d] Aristotĕlem philosŏphum, quia hujus miracŭli causas investigāre non posset,[e] ægritudĭne confectum esse.

37. Jam ad Boreāles regiōnes pergāmus.[f] Supra Macedoniam Thracia porrigĭtur a Ponto Euxīno usque ad Illyriam. Regio frigĭda et in iis tantùm partĭbus fœcundior, quæ propriōres sunt mari. Pomifĕræ arbŏres raræ; frequentiōres vites; sed uvæ non maturescunt, nisi frigus studiōsè arcētur. Sola Thasus, insŭla littŏri Thraciæ

[a] Gr. 355, R. X.
[b] Gr. 522, R. III.
[c] Id. 97, 1.
[d] Gr. 636, R. I.
[e] Gr. 656.
[f] Gr. 171, 1, & Id. 77, 7.

adjăcens, vino excellit. Amnes sunt celeberrĭmi Hebrus, ad quem Orpheus a Mænadĭbus discerptus esse dicĭtur, Nestus et Strymon. Montes altissĭmi, Hæmus, ex cujus vertĭce Pontus et Adria conspicĭtur; Rhodŏpe et Orbēlus.

38. Plures Thraciam gentes incŏlunt nominĭbus diversæ et morĭbus. Inter has Getæ omnium sunt ferocissĭmi et ad mortem paratissĭmi.[a] Anĭmas enim post mortem reditūras existĭmant. Recens nati apud eos deflentur; funĕra autem cantu lusūque celebrantur. Plures singŭli[b] uxōres habent. Hæ omnes, viro defuncto, mactāri simulque cum eo sepelīri cupiunt, magnōque id certamĭne a judicĭbus[c] contendunt. Virgĭnes non a parentĭbus traduntur viris, sed aut publĭcè ducendæ[d] locantur, aut veneunt. Formōsæ in pretio sunt; cetĕræ marītos mercēde datâ inveniunt.

39. Inter urbes Thraciæ memorabĭle est Byzantium, ad Bospŏrum Thracium, urbs natūrâ munīta et arte, quæ, cùm[e] ob soli fertilitātem, tum ob vicinitātem maris, omnium rerum, quas vita requīrit, copiâ abundat. Nec Sestos prætereunda est silentio, urbs ad Hellespontum posĭta, quam amor Herûs et Leandri memorabĭlem reddĭdit; nec Cynossēma, tumŭlus Hecŭbæ, ubi illa, post Trojam dirŭtam,[f] in canem mutāta et sepulta esse dicĭtur. Nomen etiam habet in iisdem regionĭbus urbs Ænos, ab Ænēâ e patriâ profŭgo condĭta; Zone, ubi nemŏra Orpheum canentem secūta esse narrantur; Abdēra denĭque, ubi Diomēdes rex advĕnas equis suis devorandos[d] objiciēbat, donec ipse ab Hercŭle iisdem objectus est. Quæ[g] urbs quum ranārum muriumque multitudĭne infestarētur, incŏlæ, relicto[h] patriæ solo,

[a] Gr. 386.
[b] Id. 26, 6.
[c] Gr. 511.
[d] Id. 107, 1.
[e] Id. 124, 8.
[f] Gr. 684.
[g] Id. 38, 1.
[h] Id. 104, 1.

novas sedes quæsivērunt. Hos Cassander, rex Macedoniæ, in societātem accepisse, agrosque in extrēmâ[a] Macedoniâ assignâsse dicĭtur.

40. Jam de Scythis pauca dicenda sunt. Terminātur Scythia ab uno latĕre Ponto Euxīno, ab altĕro montĭbus Rhipæis, a tergo Asiâ et Phasĭde flumĭne. Vasta regio nullis ferè intus finĭbus dividĭtur. Scythæ enim nec agrum exercent, nec certas sedes habent, sed armenta et pecŏra pascentes per incultas solitudĭnes errāre solent. Uxōres liberosque secum in plaustris vehunt. Lacte et melle vescuntur; aurum et argentum, cujus nullus apud eos usus est, aspernantur. Corpŏra pellĭbus[b] vestiunt.

41. Diversæ sunt Scythārum gentes, diversīque mores. Sunt, qui funĕra parentum festis sacrificiis celebrent,[c] eorumque capitĭbus[d] affabrè expolītis aurōque vinctis pro pocŭlis utantur. Agathyrsi ora et corpŏra pingunt, idque[e] tanto* magis, quanto quis illustriorĭbus gaudet majorĭbus. Ii, qui Taurĭcam Chersonēsum incŏlunt, antiquissĭmis temporĭbus advĕnas Diānæ mactābant. Interiùs habitantes cetĕris[f] rudiōres sunt. Bella amant, et quò[g] quis plures hostes interemĕrit, eò[g] majōre existimatiōne apud suos[h] habētur. Ne fœdĕra quidem incruenta sunt. Sauciant se qui paciscuntur, sanguinemque permistum degustant. Id fidei pignus certissĭmum esse putant.

42. Maxĭma flumĭnum Scythicōrum sunt Ister, qui et Danubius vocātur, et Borysthĕnes. De Istro suprà dictum est.[i] Borysthĕnes, ex ignōtis fontĭbus ortus, liqui-

---

* *Tanto magis quanto quis;* literally, "more by so much as any one," (Gr. 580,) i. e., "in proportion as," &c.

[a] Id. 17, 1.
[b] Gr. 514, R. XXXI.
[c] Gr. 631, R. I.
[d] Gr. 484, R. XXVI, & Id. 7, 4.
[e] — Sup. *faciunt.*
[f] Id. 6, 3.
[g] Id. 22, 4, & 44, 7.
[h] Id. 19, 3.
[i] Gr. 223, 3.

dissĭmas aquas trahit et potātu[a] jucundas. Placĭdus idem lætissĭma pabŭla alit. Magno spatio navigabĭlis juxta urbem Borysthenĭda[b] in Pontum effundĭtur.

43. Ultra Rhipæos montes et Aquilōnem gens habitāre existimātur felicissĭma, Hyperborēos[c] appellant. Regio aprīca, felix cœli temperies omnīque afflātu[d] noxio carens. Semel in anno sol iis orĭtur solstitio,[e] brumâ semel occĭdit. Incŏlæ in nemorĭbus et lucis habĭtant; sine omni discordiâ et ægritudĭne vivunt. Quum vitæ[f] eos tædet, epŭlis sumptis[g] ex rupe se in mare præcipĭtant. Hoc enim sepultūræ genus beatissĭmum esse existĭmant.

44. Asia cetĕris terræ partĭbus[h] est amplior. Oceănus eam alluit, ut locis ita nominĭbus diffĕrens; Eōus ab oriente, a meridie Indĭcus, a septentriōne Scythĭcus. Asiæ nomĭne appellātur etiam peninsŭla, quæ a mari Ægæo usque ad Armeniam patet. In hac parte est Bithynia ad Propontĭdem sita, ubi Granīcus in mare effundĭtur, ad quem amnem Alexander, rex Macedoniæ, primam victoriam de Persis reportāvit. Trans illum amnem sita est Cyzĭcus in cervīce peninsŭlæ, urbs nobilissĭma, a Cyzĭco appellāta, qui in illis regionĭbus ab Argonautis pugnâ occīsus est. Haud procul ab illâ urbe Rhyndăcus in mare effundĭtur, circa quem angues nascuntur, non solùm ob magnitudĭnem mirabĭles, sed etiam ob id, quòd, quum ex aquâ emergunt et hiant, supervolantes aves absorbent.

45. Propontis cum Ponto jungĭtur per Bospŏrum,[i] quod fretum quinque stadia[j] latum Eurōpum ab Asiâ sepărat. Ipsis[k] in faucĭbus Bospŏri oppĭdum est Chalcēdon,[l]

[a] Gr. 716, R. LXIV, & Id. 114, 2.
[b] Gr. 90, 4.
[c] — Sup. *quam*, & Gr. 440.
[d] Gr. 480, R. XXV.
[e] Gr. 565, R. XL.
[f] Gr. 419, & Id. 66, 5.
[g] Id. 104, 1.
[h] Id. 6, 3.
[i] Gr. 545.
[j] Gr. 573, R. XLII.
[k] Id. 32, 6.
[l] — Sup. *condita*.

ab Argiâ, Megarensium princĭpe, et templum Jovis, ab Jasŏne condĭtum. Pontus ipse ingens est maris sinus, non molli[a] neque arenōso circumdătus littŏre, tempestatĭbus[b] obnoxius, raris stationĭbus.[c] Olim ob sævitātem populōrum, qui circà habĭtant, Axĕnus appellātus fuisse dicĭtur; postea, mollītis illōrum morĭbus, dictus est Euxīnus.

46. In littŏre Ponti, in Mariandynōrum agro, urbs est Heraclēa, ab Hercŭle, ut fertur, condĭta. Juxta eam spelunca est Acherusia, quam ad Manes perviam esse existĭmant.[d] Hinc Cerbĕrus ab Hercŭle extractus fuisse dicĭtur. Ultra fluvium Thermodonta Mossȳni habĭtant. Hi totum corpus distinguunt notis. Reges suffragio elĭgunt; eosdem in turre ligneâ inclūsos arctissĭmè custodiunt, et, si quid perpĕram imperitavĕrint,[e] inediâ totius diēi afficiunt. Extrēmum Ponti angŭlum Colchi tenent ad Phasĭdem; quæ[f] loca fabŭla de vellĕre aureo et Argonautārum expeditio illustrāvit.

47. Inter provincias Asiæ propriè dictæ illustris est Ionia, in duodĕcim civitātes divīsa. Inter eas est Milētus, belli pacisque artĭbus inclȳta; eīque vicīnum Panionium, sacra regio, quò omnes Iōnum civitātes statis temporĭbus legātos solēbant mittĕre. Nulla facĭlè[g] urbs plures colonias misit, quàm Milētus. Ephĕsi, quam[f] urbem Amazŏnes condidisse traduntur, templum est Diānæ, quod septem mundi miracŭlis annumerāri solet. Totius templi longitūdo est quadringentōrum viginti quinque pedum,[e] latitūdo ducentōrum viginti; columnæ centumviginti septem numĕro, sexaginta pedum altitudĭne;[h] ex iis triginta sex cælātæ. Opĕri[i] præfuit Chersĭphron architectus.

[a] Id. 16, 6.
[b] Gr. 382, R. XVI.
[c] Gr. 339, R. VII.
[d] Gr. 305.
[e] Id. 74, 6, & Gr. 305.
[f] Id. 37, 4
[g] Gr. 591, 3d.
[h] Gr. 535, R. XXXIV.
[i] Gr. 393, R. I.

48. Æŏlis olim Mysia appellāta,[a] et, ubi Hellespontum attingit, Troas. Ibi Ilium fuit situm ad radīces montis Idæ, urbs bello, quod per decem annos cum universâ Græciâ gessit, clarissĭma. Ab Idæo monte Scamander defluit et Simŏis, amnes famâ quàm natūrâ majōres. Ipsum montem certāmen deārum Paridisque judicium illustrem reddĭdit. In littŏre claræ sunt urbes Rhœtēum et Dardania; sed sepulcrum Ajācis, qui ibi post certāmen cum Ulysse gladio incubuit, utrâque[b] clarius.

49. Ionĭbus[c] Cares sunt finitĭmi, popŭlus armōrum[d] bellīque adeò amans, ut aliēna etiam bella mercēde acceptâ gerĕret.[e] Princeps Cariæ urbs[a] Halicarnassus, Argivōrum colonia, regum sedes olim. Unus eōrum Mausōlus fuit. Qui[f] quum vitâ[g] defunctus esset, Artemisia conjux desiderio marīti flagrans, ossa ejus cineresque contūsa cum aquâ miscuit ebibitque, splendidumque præterea sepulcrum exstruxit, quod inter septem orbis terrārum miracŭla censētur.

50. Cilicia sita est in intĭmo recessu maris, ubi Asia propriè sic dicta cum Syriâ conjungĭtur. Sinus ille ab urbe Isso Issĭci nomen habet. Fluvius ibi Cydnus aquâ[h] limpidissĭmâ et frigidissĭmâ, in quo Alexander Macĕdo quum lavāret,[i] parum abfuit, quin frigŏre enecarētur.[j] Antrum Corycium in iisdem regionĭbus ob singulārem natūram memorabĭle est. Ingenti illud hiātu patet in monte arduo, altēque demissum undĭque viret lucis pendentĭbus. Ubi ad ima[k] perventum est,[l] rursus aliud antrum aperĭtur. Ibi sonĭtus cymbalōrum ingredientes[k]

[a] Gr. 308.
[b] — Sup. *urbe.*
[c] Gr. 382, R. XVI.
[d] Gr. 349, R. IX.
[e] Gr. 627, 1, 1st.
[f] Id. 39, 1.
[g] Gr. 484, R. XXVI.
[h] Gr. 339, R. VII.
[i] Gr. 631.
[j] Gr. 627, 3.
[k] Id. 19, 6, & 19, 1.
[l] Id. 67, 5.

terrēre dicĭtur. Totus hic specus augustus est et verè sacer, et a diis habĭtāri existimātur.

51. E Ciliciâ egressos[a] Syria excĭpit, cujus pars est Phœnīce in littŏre maris interni posĭta. Hanc regiōnem sollers homĭnum genus colit. Phœnīces enim litterārum formas a se inventas aliis popŭlis tradidērunt; alias etiam artes, quæ ad navigatiōnem et mercatūram spectant, studiōsè coluērunt. Cetĕrùm fertĭlis regio[b] crebrisque fluminĭbus rigāta, quorum ope terræ marisque opes facĭli negotio inter se[c] permutantur. Nobilissĭmæ Phœnīces urbes Sidon, antĕquam a Persis caperētur, maritimārum urbium maxĭma; et Tyrus, aggĕre cum terrâ conjuncta. Purpŭra[b] hujus urbis omnium pretiosissĭma. Conficĭtur ille color ex succo in conchis, quæ etiam purpŭræ vocantur, latente.

52. Ex Syriâ descendĭtur[d] in Arabiam, peninsŭlam inter duo maria, Rubrum et Persĭcum, porrectam. Hujus ea pars, quæ ab urbe Petrâ Petrææ nomen accēpit, planè est sterĭlis; hanc excĭpit ea, quæ ob vastas solitudĭnes Deserta vocātur. His partĭbus adhæret Arabia Felix, regio angusta, sed cinnămi,[e] thuris, aliorumque odōrum feracissĭma. Multæ ibi gentes sunt, quæ fixas sedes non habeant,[f] Nomădes a Græcis appellātæ. Lacte[g] et carne ferīnâ vescuntur. Multi etiam Arăbum popŭli latrociniis[g] vivunt. Primus e Romānis Ælius Gallus in hanc terram cum exercĭtu penetrāvit.

53. Camēlos inter armenta pascit Oriens. Duo harum sunt genĕra, Bactriānæ et Arabiæ. Illæ[h] bina habent in dorso tubĕra, hæ[h] singŭla; unum autem sub pectŏre, cui incumbant. Dentium ordĭne[i] superiōre carent. Sitim

[a] Id. 19, 1.
[b] Gr. 308.
[c] Gr. 118, 5.
[d] Id. 67, 6.
[e] Gr. 349, R. IX.
[f] Gr. 644.
[g] Gr. 484, R. XXVI, & Gr. 485.
[h] Gr. 118, 3, 3d.
[i] Gr. 480, R. XXV.

quatriduo tolĕrant; aquam, antĕquam bibant,[a] pedĭbus turbant. Vivunt quinquagēnis annis;[b] quædam etiam centēnis.

54. Ex Arabiâ pervenītur in Babyloniam, cui Babȳlon nomen dedit, Chaldaicārum gentium caput, urbs et magnitudĭne et divitiis clara. Semirămis eam condidĕrat, vel, ut multi credidērunt, Belus, cujus regia ostendĭtur. Murus exstructus latercŭlo[c] coctĭli, triginta et duos pedes[d] est latus, ita ut quadrīgæ inter se[e] occurentes sine pericŭlo commeāre dicantur; altitūdo ducentōrum pedum; turres autem denis[d] pedĭbus[f] quàm murus altiōres sunt. Totius opĕris ambĭtus sexaginta millia passuum complectĭtur. Mediam urbem[g] permeat Euphrātes. Arcem habet viginti stadiōrum[h] ambĭtu;[i] super eâ pensĭles horti conspiciuntur, tantæque sunt moles tamque firmæ, ut onĕra nemŏrum sine detrimento ferant.

55. Amplissĭma Asiæ regio[j] India primùm patefacta est armis Alexandri Magni, regis Macedoniæ, cujus exemplum successōres secūti in interiōra[k] Indiæ penetravērunt. In eo tractu, quem Alexander subēgit, quinque millia oppidōrum fuisse,[l] gentesque novem, Indiamque tertiam partem esse[m] terrārum omnium, ejus comĭtes scripsērunt. Ingentes ibi sunt amnes, Indus et Indo[n] major Ganges. Indus in Paropamĭso ortus undeviginti amnes recĭpit, totĭdem Ganges interque eos plures navigabĭles.

56. Maxĭma in Indiâ gignuntur animalia. Canes ibi grandiōres cetĕris.[n] Arbŏres tantæ proceritātis[h] esse traduntur, ut sagittis superjăci nequeant. Hoc effĭcit uber-

[a] Gr. 627, 4.
[b] Gr. 565, R. XLI, and Gr. 107, 11.
[c] Gr. 541.
[d] Gr. 573, R. XLII.
[e] Gr. 118, 5.
[f] Gr. 579, R. XLIII.
[g] Gr. 613, R. LII.
[h] Gr. 339, R. VII.
[i] Gr. 535, R. XXXIV.
[j] Gr. 251, R. I.
[k] Id. 19, 6.
[l] Id. 98, 2.
[m] Id. 96, 2.
[n] Id. 6, 3.

tas soli, temperies cœli, aquārum abundantia. Immānes quoque serpentes alit, qui elephantos morsu et ambĭtu corpŏris conficiunt. Solum tam pingue et ferax, ut mella frondĭbus[a] defluant,[b] sylvæ lanas ferant,[b] arundĭnum internodia fissa cymbārum usum præbeant, binosque, quædam etiam ternos[c] homĭnes, vehant.

57. Incolārum habĭtus moresque diversi. Lino[d] alii vestiuntur et lanis arbŏrum, alii ferārum aviumque pellĭbus, pars nudi[e] incēdunt.[f] Quidam animalia occidĕre eorumque carnĭbus vesci nefas[g] putant; alii piscĭbus tantùm aluntur. Quidam parentes et propinquos, priùs quàm annis et macie conficiantur,[h] velut hostias cædunt eorumque viscerĭbus[i] epulantur; ubi senectus eos morbusve invādit, mortem in solitudĭne æquo anĭmo exspectant. Ii, qui sapientiam profitentur, ab ortu solis ad occāsum stare solent, solem immobilĭbus ocŭlis intuentes; ferventĭbus arēnis[j] toto die[k] alternis pedĭbus[l] insistunt. Mortem non exspectant, sed sponte arcessunt in rogos incensos se præcipitantes.

58. Maxĭmos India elephantos gignit, adeōque ferōces, ut Afri elephanti illos paveant, nec contuēri audeant.[b] Hoc anĭmal cetĕra omnia docilitāte superat. Discunt arma jacĕre, gladiatōrum more congrĕdi, saltāre et per funes incedĕre. Plinius narrat, Romæ unum segniōris ingenii[m] sæpius castigātum esse verberĭbus, quia tardiùs[n] accipiēbat, quæ tradebantur; eundem repertum esse noctu eădem meditantem. Elephanti gregātim semper ingrediuntur. Ducit agmen maxĭmus natu,[o] cogit is, qui ætāte ei est

[a] Gr. 613, R. LII.
[b] Gr. 627, 1, 1st.
[c] Id. 26, 1.
[d] Gr 524, R.
[e] Gr. 279.
[f] Gr. 316, R. II.
[g] Id. 51, 5, sup. *esse*.
[h] Gr. 627, 4.
[i] Gr. 485.
[j] Gr. 611, (in.)
[k] Gr. 565, R. XLI.
[l] Gr. 542, R. XXXV.
[m] Gr. 339, R. VII.
[n] Id. 22, 3.
[o] Gr. 113, 6, *Note*, & Gr. 535, R. XXXIV.

proxĭmus. Amnem transitūri minĭmos præmittunt. Capiuntur foveis. In has ubi elĕphas decidĕrit,[a] cetĕri ramos congĕrunt, aggĕres construunt, omnĭque vi conantur extrahĕre. Domantur fame et verberĭbus. Domĭti milĭtant et turres[b] armatōrum in hostes ferunt, magnâque ex parte Orientis bella conficiunt. Totas acies prosternunt, armātos protĕrunt. Ingens dentĭbus[c] pretium. In Græciâ ebur ad deōrum simulācra tanquam pretiosissĭma materia adhibētur; in extrēmis[d] Afrĭcæ postium vicem in domiciliis præbet, sepesque in pecŏrum stabŭlis elephantōrum dentĭbus[e] fiunt. Inter omnia animalia[f] maxĭmè odērunt[g] murem. Infestus elephanto etiam rhinocĕros, qui nomen habet a cornu, quod in naso gerit. In pugnâ maxĭmè adversarii alvum petit, quam scit esse molliōrem. Longitudĭne elephantum ferè exæquat; crura multo breviōra; color buxeus.

59. Etiam Psittăcos India mittit. Hæc avis humānas voces optĭmè reddit. Quum loqui discit, ferreo radio verberātur, alĭter enim non sentit ictus. Capĭti[h] ejus eădem est duritia, quæ rostro.[h] Quum devŏlat, rostro se excĭpit, eĭque innitĭtur.

60. Testudĭnes tantæ magnitudĭnis Indĭcum mare emittit, ut singulārum testis[i] casas intĕgant.[j] Insŭlas[k] rubri præcipuè maris his navĭgant cymbis. Capiuntur obdormiscentes in summâ aquâ, id[l] quod prodĭtur stertentium sonĭtu. Tum terni adnătant, a duōbus in dorsum vertĭtur, a tertio laqueus injicĭtur, atque ita a plurĭbus in littŏre stantĭbus trahĭtur. In mari testudĭnes conchyliis vivunt; tanta enim oris est duritia, ut lapĭdes comminuant;[j]

---

[a] Gr. 627, 5, & Id. 74, 6.
[b] — Sup, *plenas*, full, & Gr. 361, [R. XI.
[c] Gr. 378, R. XV.
[d] Id. 19, (*partibus.*)
[e] Gr. 541.
[f] Gr. 360.
[g] Gr. 222, Obs. 2.
[h] Gr. 394, R .II.
[i] Gr. 514, R. XXXI.
[j] Gr. 627, 1, 1st.
[k] Gr. 553, R., & 562.
[l] Id. 37, 9, Note 3.

in terram egressæ, herbis.[a] Pariunt ova ovis avium simĭlia, ad centēna[b] numĕro; eăque extra aquam defossâ terrâ cooperiunt.

61. Margarītæ Indĭci oceăni omnium[c] maxĭmè laudantur. Inveniuntur in conchis scopŭlis adhærentĭbus. Maxĭma laus est in candōre, magnitudĭne, lævōre, pondĕre. Raró duæ inveniuntur, quæ sibi ex omni parte sint simĭles. Has aurĭbus[d] suspendĕre,[e] feminārum est gloria. Duos maxĭmos uniōnes Cleopatra, Ægypti regīna, habuisse dicĭtur. Horum unum, ut Antonium magnificentiâ superāret,[f] in cœnâ acēto solvit, solūtum hausit.

62. Ægyptus, inter Catabathmum et Arăbas posĭta, a plurĭmis ad Asiam refertur; alii Asiam Arabĭco sinu terminări existĭmant. Hæc regio, quanquam expers[g] est imbrium, mirè tamen est fertĭlis. Hoc Nilus effĭcit, omnium fluviōrum, qui in mare internum effunduntur, maxĭmus. Hic in desertis Afrĭcæ orĭtur, tum Æthiopiâ descendit in Ægyptum, ubi de altis rupĭbus præcipitātus usque ad Elephantĭdem urbem fervens adhuc decurrit. Tum demum fit placidior. Juxta Cercasōrum oppĭdum in plures amnes dividĭtur, et tandem per septem ora effundĭtur in mare.

63. Nilus, nivĭbus in Æthiopiæ montĭbus solūtis, crescĕre incĭpit Lunâ novâ post solstitium per quinquaginta ferè dies; totĭdem diēbus minuĭtur. Justum incrementum est cubitōrum[h] sedĕcim. Si minōres sunt aquæ, non omnia rigant. Maxĭmum incrementum fuit cubitōrum[h] duodeviginti; minĭmum quinque. Quum stetēre aquæ, aggĕres aperiuntur, et arte aqua in agros immittĭtur. Quum omnis recessĕrit,[i] agri irrigāti et limo obducti seruntur.

[a] Gr. 485, (*vivunt*).
[b] Gr. 107, 11.
[c] Gr. 600, R. XLVII.
[d] Gr. 501, R. XXIX.
[e] Gr. 660, R. LVI.
[f] Gr. 627, 1, 2d.
[g] Gr. 361, R. XI.
[h] Gr. 339, R. VII.
[i] Id. 74, 6.

64. Nilus crocodīlum alit, belluam quadrupĕdem, in terrâ non minùs quàm in flumĭne hominĭbus infestam. Unum hoc anĭmal terrestre linguæ usu[a] caret; dentium plures habet ordĭnes; maxilla inferior est immobĭlis. Magnitudĭne excēdit plerùmque duodeviginti cubĭta. Parit ōva anserīnis[b] non majōra. Unguĭbus etiam armātus est, et cute contra omnes ictus invictâ. Dies in terrâ agit, noctes in aquâ. Quum satur est, et in littŏre somnum capit ore hiante, trochĭlus, parva avis, dentes ei[c] faucesque purgat. Sed hiantem conspicātus ichneumon, per easdem fauces ut telum alĭquod immissus, erōdit alvum. Hebĕtes ocŭlos dicĭtur habēre in aquâ, extra aquam acerrĭmos. Tentyrĭtæ in insŭlâ Nili habitantes, diræ huic belluæ[d] obviàm ire audent, eamque incredibĭli audaciâ expugnant.

65. Aliam etiam belluam Nilus alit, hippopotămum; ungŭlis[e] binis, dorso[e] equi et jubâ et hinnītu; rostro resīmo, caudâ et dentĭbus aprōrum. Cutis impenetrabĭlis, præterquam si humōre madeat.[f] Primus hippopotămum et quinque crocodīlos M. Scaurus ædilitātis suæ ludis[g] Romæ ostendit.

66. Multa in Ægypto mira sunt et artis et natūræ opĕra. Inter ea, quæ manĭbus homĭnum facta sunt, emĭnent pyramĭdes, quarum maxĭmæ sunt et celeberrĭmæ in monte sterĭli inter Memphin oppĭdum et eam partem Ægypti, quæ Delta vocātur. Amplissĭmam eārum trecenta sexaginta sex homĭnum[h] millia annis viginti extruxisse traduntur. Hæc octo jugĕra soli occŭpat; unumquodque latus octingentos octoginta tres pedes[i] longum est; alti-

[a] Gr. 480, R. XXV.
[b] Gr. 337, & Id. 19, (*ovis*, [6,3.])
[c] Gr. 380, *Rule*.
[d] Gr. 600, R. XLVII.
[e] Gr. 339, R. VII.
[f] Gr. 627, 1, 2d, & Id. 74, 2.
[g] Gr. 565, R. XL.
[h] Gr. 355, R. X.
[i] Gr. 573, R. XLII.

tūdo a cacumĭne pedum[a] quindĕcim millium. Intus in eâ est puteus octoginta sex cubitōrum.[a] Ante has pyramĭdes Sphinx est posĭta miræ magnitudĭnis.[a] Capĭtis ambĭtus centum duos pedes habet; longitūdo est pedum centum quadraginta trium; altitūdo a ventre usque ad summum capĭtis apĭcem sexaginta duōrum.

67. Inter miracŭla Ægypti commemorātur etiam Mœris lacus, quingenta millia[b] passuum in circuĭtu patens; Labyrinthus ter mille domos et regias duodĕcim uno pariĕte amplexus, totus marmŏre[c] exstructus tectusque; turris denĭque in insŭlâ Pharo, a Ptolemæo, Lagi filio, condĭta. Usus[d] ejus navĭbus[e] noctu ignes ostendĕre ad prænuntianda[f] vada portûsque introĭtum.

68. In palustrĭbus Ægypti regionĭbus papȳrum nascĭtur. Radicĭbus incōlæ pro ligno utuntur; ex ipso autem papȳro navigia texunt, e libro vela, tegĕtes, vestem ac funes. Succi causâ etiam mandunt modò crudum modò decoctum. Præparantur ex eo etiam chartæ. Chartæ ex papȳro usus post Alexandri demum victorias repertus est. Primò enim scriptum[g] in palmārum foliis, deinde in libris quarundam arbŏrum; postea publĭca monimenta plumbeis tabŭlis[h] confĭci, aut marmorĭbus[i] mandāri cœpta sunt. Tandem æmulatio regum Ptolemæi et Eumĕnis in bibliothēcis condendis occasiōnem dedit membrānas Pergămi inveniendi. Ab eo inde tempŏre libri modò[j] in chartâ ex papȳro factâ, modò in membrānis scripti sunt.

69. Mores incolārum Ægypti ab aliōrum populōrum morĭbus vehementer discrĕpant. Mortuos nec cremant, nec sepeliunt; verùm arte medicātos intra penetralia col-

---

[a] Gr. 339, R. VII.
[b] Gr. 573, R. XLII, &
[c] Gr. 104, 5.
[c] Gr. 541.
[d] Gr. 308.
[e] Gr. 501, R. XXIX.
[f] Id. 112, 7.
[g] Id. 67, 6, sup. *est.*
[h] Gr. 611, (*in*).
[i] Gr. 522, R. III.
[j] Id. 124, 12.

lŏcant. Negotia extra domos femĭnæ, viri domos et res domestĭcas curant; onĕra illæ humĕris, hi capitĭbus gerunt. Colunt effigies multōrum animalium et ipsa animalia. Hæc interfecisse[a] capitāle est; mòrbo exstincta lugent et sepeliunt.

70. Apis omnium Ægypti populōrum numen est; bos niger cum candĭdâ in dextro latĕre macŭlâ; nodus sub linguâ, quem canthărum appellant. Non fas est eum certos vitæ annos excedĕre. Ad hunc vitæ termĭnum quum pervenĕrit, mersum in fonte enĕcant. Necātum lugent, aliumque quærunt, quem ei substituant;[b] nec tamen unquam diu quærĭtur. Delūbra ei sunt gemĭna, quæ thalămos vocant, ubi popŭlus auguria captat. Altĕrum[c] intrâsse[a]* lætum est; in altĕro dira portendit. Pro bono etiam habētur signo, si e manĭbus consulentium cibum capit. In publĭcum procedentem grex puerōrum comitātur, carmenque in ejus honōrem canunt,[d] idque vidētur intelligĕre.

71. Ultra Ægyptum Æthiŏpes habĭtant. Horum popŭli quidam Macrobii vocantur, quia paulò quàm nos diutiùs vivunt. Plus auri[e] apud eos reperītur, quàm æris; hanc ob causam æs illis vidētur pretiosius. Ære se exornant, vincŭla auro[f] fabrĭcant. Lacus est apud eos, cujus aqua tam est liquĭda atque levis, ut nihil eōrum, quæ immittuntur, sustinēre queat; quare arbŏrum quoque folia non innătant aquæ, sed pessum aguntur.

72. Afrĭca ab oriente termĭnātur Nilo; a cetĕris partĭbus mari. Regiōnes ad mare posĭtæ eximiè sunt fertĭles; interiōres incultæ et arēnis sterilĭbus tectæ, et ob nimium

* *(Apim,) intrasse alterum,* "for Apis to have entered the one," *lætum est.*
[a] Gr. 660, R. LVI, & 661. [c] Id. 19, *(thalamum).* [e] Gr. 343, R. VIII.
[b] Gr. 630. [d] Gr. 317. [f] Gr. 541.

calōrem desertæ. Prima pars ab occidente est Mauritania. Ibi mons præaltus Abӯla, Calpæ monti in Hispaniâ oppositus. Hi montes columnæ Hercŭlis appellantur. Fama est, ante Hercŭlem mare internum terris inclūsum fuisse, nec exĭtum habuisse in Oceănum; Hercŭlem autem junctos montes diremisse et mare junxisse cum Oceăno. Cetĕrùm regio illa est ignobĭlis et parvis tantùm oppĭdis habitātur. Solum melius quàm incŏlæ.

73. Numidia magìs culta et opulentior. Ibi satìs longo a littŏre intervallo saxa cernuntur attrīta fluctĭbus, spinæ piscium, ostreorumque fragmenta, ancŏræ etiam cautĭbus infixæ, et alia ejusmŏdi signa maris olim usque ad ea loca effūsi. Finitĭma regio, a promontorio Metagonio ad aras Philænōrum, propriè vocātur Afrĭca. Urbes in eâ celeberrĭmæ Utĭca et Carthāgo, ambæ a Phœnicĭbus condĭtæ. Carthagĭnem divitiæ, mercatūrâ imprīmis comparātæ, tum bella cum Romānis gesta, excidium denĭque illustrāvit.[a]

74. De aris Philænōrum hæc narrantur. Pertinacissĭma fuĕrat contentio inter Carthagĭnem et Cyrēnas de finĭbus. Tandem placuit,[b] utrinque eōdem tempŏre juvĕnes mitti, et locum, quò convenissent, pro finĭbus habēri. Carthaginiensium legāti, Philæni fratres, paulò ante tempus constitūtum egressi esse dicuntur. Quod quum Cyrenensium legāti intellexissent, magnăque exorta esset contentio, tandem Cyrenenses dixērunt, se tum demum hunc locum pro finĭbus habitūros esse, si Philæni se ibi vivos obrui passi essent. Illi conditiōnem accepērunt. Carthaginienses autem animōsis juvenĭbus in illis ipsis locis, ubi vivi sepulti sunt, aras consecravērunt, eorumque virtūtem æternis honorĭbus prosecūti sunt.

---

[a] Gr. 313. [b] Id. 51, 5. Sup. *illis*, 80, 2.

75. Inde ad Catabathmum Cyrenaĭca porrigĭtur, ubi Ammōnis oracŭlum et fons quidam, quem Solis esse [a] dicunt. Hic fons mediâ nocte fervet,[b] tum paulātim tepescit; sole oriente fit frigĭdus; per meridiem maxĭmè riget. Catabathmus vallis est devexa versùs Ægyptum. Ibi finītur Afrĭca. Proxĭmi his popŭli urbes non habent, sed in tuguriis vivunt, quæ mapalia vocantur. Vulgus pecŭdum vestītur pellĭbus.[c] Potus est lac succusque baccārum; cibus caro. Interiōres etiam incultiùs vivunt. Sequuntur greges suos, utque hi pabŭlo ducuntur, ita illi tuguria sua promŏvent. Leges nullas habent, nec in commūne consultant. Inter hos Troglodȳtæ in specŭbus habĭtant, serpentibusque aluntur.

76. Ferārum Afrĭca feracissĭma. Pardos, panthĕras, leōnes gignit, quod belluārum genus Eurōpa ignōrat. Leōni [d] præcipua generosĭtas. Prostrātis parcĕre dicĭtur; in infantes nonnĭsi summâ fame sævit. Anĭmi ejus index [e] cauda, quam, dum placĭdus est, immōtam servat; dum irascĭtur, terram et se ipsum [f] eâ flagellat. Vis [e] summa in pectŏre. Si fugĕre cogĭtur, contemptim cedit, quàm diu spectāri potest; in silvis acerrĭmo cursu fertur.[g] Vulnerātus percussōrem novit,[h] et in quantâlĭbet multitudĭne appĕtit. Hoc tam sævum anĭmal gallinacei cantus terret. Domātur etiam ab homĭnĭbus. Hanno Pœnus primus leōnem mansuefactum ostendisse dicĭtur. Marcus autem Antonius triumvir primus, post pugnam in campis Philippĭcis, Romæ leōnes ad currum junxit.

77. Struthiocamēli Afrĭci altitudĭnem equĭtis equo [i]

[a] Gr. 319, R. Sup. *fontem*.
[b] Gr. 157, 1.
[c] Gr. 524, R. V.
[d] Gr. 394, R. II.
[e] Gr. 308.
[f] Id. 33, 1.
[g] Id. 116, 3.
[h] Id. 84, 3.
[i] Gr. 399, R. IV.

insidentis exæquant, celeritātem vincunt. Pennæ ad hoc demum videntur datæ, ut currentes adjŭvent; nam a terrâ tolli non possunt. Ungŭlæ cervīnis[a] sunt simĭles. His in fugâ comprehendunt lapĭdes, eosque contra sequentes jaculantur. Omnia concŏquunt. Cetĕrùm magna iis[b] stolidĭtas, ita ut, quum caput et collum frutĭce occultavĕrint, se latēre existĭment.[c] Pennæ eōrum quæruntur ad ornātum.

78. Afrĭca serpentes genĕrat vicēnûm[d] cubitōrum;[e] nec minōres India. Certè Megasthĕnes scribit, serpentes ibi in tantam magnitudĭnem adolescĕre, ut solĭdos hauriant cervos taurosque. In primo Punĭco bello ad flumen Bagrădum serpens centum viginti pedum[e] a Regŭlo, imperatōre Romāno, ballistis et tormentis expugnāta esse fertur. Pellis ejus et maxillæ diu Romæ in templo quodam asservātæ sunt. In Indiâ serpentes perpetuum bellum cum elephantis gerunt. Ex arborĭbus se in prætereuntes[f] præcipĭtant gressusque ligant nodis. Hos nodos elephanti manu resolvunt. At dracōnes in ipsas[g] elephantōrum nares caput condunt spiritumque præclūdunt; plerùmque in illâ dimicatiōne utrīque commoriuntur, dum victus elĕphas corruens[h] serpentem pondĕre suo elīdit.

[a] Id. 18, (*ungulis*), & Gr. 337.
[b] Gr. 394, R. II.
[c] Gr. 627, 1, 1st.
[d] Id. 26, 1.
[e] Gr. 339, R. VII.
[f] Id. 19, (illos).
[g] Id. 32, 6.
[h] Gr. 688.

DICTIONARY.

EXPLANATION OF ABBREVIATIONS.

adj.	adjective.	*fr.*	from.	*obsol.*	obsolete.
adv	adverb.	*freq.*	frequentative.	*ord.*	ordinal.
app.	appendix.	*inc.*	inceptive.	*part.*	participle.
c.	common gender.	*ind.*	indeclinable.	*pass.*	passive.
conj.	conjunction.	*imp.*	impersonal.	*pl.*	plural.
compar.	comparative.	*int.*	interjection.	*prep.*	preposition.
d.	doubtful gender.	*intr.*	intransitive.	*pret.*	preteritive.
def.	defective.	*irr.*	irregular.	*pro.*	pronoun.
dep.	deponent.	*m.*	masculine.	*rel.*	relative.
dim.	diminutive.	*n.*	neuter.	*subs.*	substantive.
dis.	distributive.	*neut. pass.*	neuter passive.	*sup.*	superlative.
f.	feminine	*num.*	numeral.	*tr.*	transitive.

comp. compared regularly as directed, § 25.
id. derived from the same word as the preceding.
§ Refers to the sections in Bullions' Latin Grammar.
Id. (Idioms,) Refers to the Introduction, in this work, concerning Latin idioms.

*** Words marked m. f. n. c. d. denoting gender, are *nouns*, and their declension is known by the ending of the genitive, placed next after the word, according to § 8.

Words conjugated, are *verbs*, and their conjugation is known by the vowel before *re*, in the infinitive, according to 184, 3.

A., *an abbreviation of* Aulus.

A, ab, abs, prep. *from, by,* (abl.) ab oriente, *on the east:* a meridie, *on the south.*

Abdēra, æ, f. *a maritime town of Thrace.*

Abdĭtus, a, um, part. & adj. *removed; hidden; concealed; secret;* from

Abdo, abdĕre, abdĭdi, abdĭtum, tr. (ab & do,) *to remove from view; to hide; to conceal.*

Abdūco, abducĕre, abduxi, abductum, tr. (ab & duco,) *to lead away.*

Abductus, a, um, part. (abdūco)

Abeo, abīre, abii, abĭtum, intr. irr. (ab & eo,) *to go away; to depart.*

Aberro, āre, āvi, ātum, intr. (ab & erro,) *to stray; to wander; to lose the way.*

Abjectus, a, um, part. from

Abjicio, abjicĕre, abjēci, abjectum, tr. (ab & jacio,) *to cast from; to cast away; to throw aside.*

Abluo, ĕre, i, tum, tr. (ab & luo,) *to wash from,* or *away; to wash; to purify.*

Abrumpo, abrumpĕre, abrūpi, abruptum, tr. (ab & rumpo,) *to break off; to break.*

Abscindo, abscindĕre, abscĭdi, abscissum, tr. (ab & scindo,) *to cut off.*

Absens, tis, part. (absum § 54, *Obs.* 3,) *absent.*

Absolvo, absolvĕre, absolvi, absolūtum, tr. (ab & solvo,) *to loose from; to loose; to release.*

Absorbeo, absorbēre, absorbui & absorpsi, tr. (ab & sorbeo,) *to suck in from,* (viz: an object;) *to absorb,* or *suck in; to swallow.*

Absterreo, ēre, ui, ĭtum, tr. (abs & terreo,) *to frighten away; to deter.*

Abstinentia, æ, f. *abstinence; disinterestedness; freedom from avarice;* from

Abstineo, abstinēre, abstinui, tr. (abs & teneo, § 81,) *to keep from; to abstain.*

Absum, abesse, abfui, intr. irr. (ab & sum,) (*to be from,* viz: a place, i. e.) *to be absent,* or *distant; to be gone;* parum abesse, *to want but little; to be near.*

Absūmo, absumĕre, absumpsi, absumptum, tr. (ab & sumo,) *to take away; to consume; to destroy; to waste.*

Absumptus, a, um, part. (absūmo.)

Absurdus, a, um, adj. (ab & surdus, *deaf; senseless;*) *harsh; grating;* hence *senseless; absurd.*

Abundantia, æ, f. *plenty; abundance;* from

Abundo, āre, āvi, ātum, intr. (ab & undo, *to rise in waves, to boil,* and hence) *to overflow; to abound.*

Abȳla, æ, f. *Abyla; a mountain in Africa, at the entrance of the Mediterranean sea, opposite to mount Calpe in Spain. These mountains were anciently called the Pillars of Hercules.*

Ac, atque, conj. *and; as; than.*

Acca, æ, f. *Acca Laurentia, the wife of Faustulus, and nurse of Romulus and Remus.*

Accēdo, accedĕre, accessi, accessum, intr. (ad & cedo,) *to move near to; to draw near; to approach; to advance; to engage in; to undertake.*

Accendo, accendĕre, accendi, accensum, tr. (ad & candeo,) *to set on fire.*

Accensus, a, um, part. (accendo,) *set on fire; kindled; lighted; inflamed; burning.*

Acceptus, a, um, part. (accipio.)

Accessus, ûs, m. (accēdo,) *approach: access; accession.*

Accĭdo, accidĕre, accĭdi, intr. (ad & cado,) *to fall down at,* or *before:* accĭdit, imp. *it happens,* or *it happened.*

Accipio, accipĕre, accēpi, acceptum, tr. (ad & capio, Gr. 215, 5, 2d.) *to take; to receive; to learn; to hear; to understand; to accept:*

accipĕre finem, *to come to an end; to terminate.*

Accipiter, tris, m. *a hawk.*

Accumbo, accumbĕre, accubui, intr. (ad & cubo, § 81,) *to sit* or *recline at table.*

Accurātè, adv. (iùs, issĭmè) (accurātus, ad & curo,) *accurately; carefully.*

Accurro, accurrĕre, accurri *or* accucurri, intr. (ad & curro,) *to run to.*

Accūso, āre, āvi, ātum, tr. (ad & causor, *to allege,* from causa,) *to accuse; to blame; to find fault with.*

Acer, cris, cre, adj. (acrior; acerrĭmus,) *sharp; sour; eager; vehement; rapid; courageous; fierce; violent; acute; keen; piercing.*

Acerbus, a, um, adj. comp. *sour; unripe; vexatious; harsh; morose; disagreeble;* from acer.

Acerrĭmè, adv. sup. *See* Acrĭter.

Acervus, i, m. *a heap.*

Acētum, i, n. *vinegar.*

Achaïcus, a, um, adj. *Achæan, Grecian.*

Achelōus, i, m. *a river of Epirus.*

Acherusia, æ, f. *a lake in Campania;* also, *a cave in Bithynia.*

Achilles, is & eos, m. (§ 15, 13,) *the son of Peleus and Thetis, and the bravest of the Grecian chiefs, at the siege of Troy.*

Acĭdus, a, um, adj. comp, *sour; sharp; acid.*

Acies, ēi, f. *an edge; a line of soldiers; an army in battle array; a squadron; a rank; an army; a battle.*

Acĭnus, i, m. *a berry; a grapestone.*

Acrĭter, acrius, accerrĭmè, adv. (from acer) *sharply; ardently; fiercely; courageously.*

Acroceraunia, ōrum, n. pl. (§ 18, 19,) *lofty mountains between Albania and Epirus.*

Acrocorinthos, i, f. (Gr. 74,) *the citadel of Corinth.*

Acropŏlis, is, f. *the citadel of Athens.*

Actio, ōnis, f. (from ago,) *an action; operation; a process.*

Actium, i, n. *a promontory of Epirus, famous for a naval victory of Augustus over Anthony and Cleopatra.*

Actus, a, um, part. (ago,) *driven; led.*

Aculeus, i, m. (acuo) *a sting; a thorn; a prickle; a porcupine's quill.*

Acūmen, ĭnis, n, (from acuo,) *acuteness; perspicacity.*

Acus, ûs, f. (acuo) *a needle.*

Ad, prep. *to; near; at; towards:* with a numeral, *about.* In composition, see Gr. 237, & 239.

Adămas, antis, m. *adamant; a diamond.*

Adămo, āre, āvi, ātum, tr. (ad & amo,) *to love greatly,* or *desperately.*

Addīco, dicĕre, dixi, dictum, tr. (ad & dico,) *to adjudge; assign; make over.*

Addĭtus, a, um, part. from

Addo, addĕre, addĭdi, addĭtum, tr. (ad & do,) *to put a thing close to another;* i. e. *to add; to annex; to appoint; to give.*

Addūco, adducĕre, adduxi, adductum, tr. (ad & duco,) *to lead; to bring:* in dubitatiōnem, *to bring into question.*

Ademptus, a, um, part. (adímo.)

Adeò, adv. *so; therefore; so much; to such a degree; so very.*

Adeo, adīre, adii, adĭtum, intr. irr. (ad & eo,) *to go to.* § 83, 3.

Adhærens, tis, part. from

Adhæreo, hærēre, hæsi, hæsum, (ad & hæreo,) *to stick to; to adhere; to adjoin; to lie contiguous.*

Adherbal, ălis, m. *a king of Numidia, put to death by his cousin Jugurtha.*

Adhibeo, adhibēre, adhibui, adhibĭtum, tr. (ad & habeo,) *to hold forth; to admit; to apply; to use; to employ.*

Adhuc, adv. (ad & huc) *hitherto; yet; as yet; still.*

Adĭmo, adimĕre, adēmi, ademptum, tr. (ad & emo,) *to take away.*

Adipiscor, adipisci, adeptus sum, dep. (ad & apiscor) *to reach; to attain; to overtake; to get.*

Adĭtus, ûs, m. (adeo,) *a going to; entrance; access; approach.*

Adjaceo, ēre, ui, ĭtum, intr. (ad & jaceo,) *to lie near; to adjoin; to border upon.*

Adjungo, adjungĕre, adjunxi, adjunctum, tr. (ad & jungo,) *to join to; to unite with.*

Adjūtus, a, um, part. from

Adjŭvo, adjuvāre, adjūvi, adjūtum, tr. (ad & juvo,) *to assist; to help; to aid.*

Admētus, i, m. *a king of Thessaly.*

Administer, tri, m. *a servant; an assistant.*

Administro, āre, āvi, ātum, tr. (ad & ministro,) *to administer; to manage.*

Admiratio, ōnis, f. (admīror,) *admiration.*

Admirātus, a, um, part. from

Admīror, āri, ātus sum, tr. dep. *to admire.*

Admissus, a, um, part. from

Admitto, admittĕre, admīsi, admissum, tr. (ad & mitto,) *to admit; to allow; to receive.*

Admŏdum, adv. (ad & modus,) *very; much; greatly.*

Admoneo, ēre, ui, ĭtum, tr. (ad & moneo,) *to put in mind; to admonish; to warn.*

Admonĭtus, a, um, part, (admoneo.)

Admoveo, admovēre, admōvi, admōtum, tr. (ad & moveo) *to move to; to bring to.*

Adnăto, āre, āvi, ātum, intr. freq. (ad & nato, from no,) *to swim to.*

Adolescens, tis, adj. (adolesco,) (compar. ior, § 26, 6,) *young:* subs. *a young man or woman; a youth.*

Adolescentia, æ, f. (*the state or time of youth;*) *youth; a youth;* from

Adolesco, adolescĕre, adolēvi, adultum, intr. inc. (227, 2) *to grow, to increase; to grow up.*

Adopto, āre, āvi, ātum, tr. (ad & opto,) *to choose to* or *for one's self;* i. e. *to adopt; to take for a son; to assume.*

Adorior, orīri, ortus sum, tr. dep. (ad & orior,) *to rise* or *go to;* (hence,) *to attack; to accost; to address, to undertake.*

Adria, æ, m. *the Adriatic sea.*

Adriatĭcus, a, um, adj. *Adriatic:* mare Adriaticum, *the Adriatic sea;* now, *the gulf of Venice.*

Adscendo, *see* Ascendo.

Adsĕquor, *see* Assĕquor.

Adservo, *see* Asservo.

Adsigno, *see* Assigno.

Adsisto, or assisto, sistĕre, stĭti, intr. (ad & sisto,) *to stand by; to assist; to help.*

Adspectūrus, a, um, part. (aspicio.)

Adspergo, *or* aspergo, gĕre, si, sum, tr. (ad & spargo,) *to sprinkle.*

Adspicio, *or* aspicio, spicĕre, spexi, spectum, tr. (ad & specio,) *to look at; see; regard; behold.*

Adstans, tis, part.; from

Adsto, *or* asto, stāre, stĭti, intr. (ad & sto,) *to stand by; to be near.*

Adsum, adesse, adfui, intr. irr. (ad & sum,) *to be present; to aid; to assist.*

Adulātor, ōris, m. (adūlor,) *a flatterer.*

Aduncus, a, um, adj. (ad & uncus,) *bent; crooked.*

Advectus, a, um, part. from

Advĕho, advehĕre, advexi, advectum, tr (ad & veho,) *to carry; to convey.*

Advĕna, æ, c. (advenio,) *a stranger.*

Adveniens, tis, part. from

Advenio, advenīre, advēni, adventum, intr. (ad & venio,) *to arrive; to come.*

Adventus, ûs, m. (from advenio,) *an arrival; a coming.*

Adversarius, i, m. (adversor, *to oppose,*) *an adversary; an enemy.*

Adversus, a, um, adj. (adverto, *to turn to,*) *turned towards; adverse; opposite; unfavorable; bad; fronting;* adversa cicātrix, *a scar in front:* adverso corpŏre, *on the breast.*

Adversùs & adversùm, prep. (id.) *against; toward.*

Advŏco, āre, āvi, ātum, tr. (ad & voco,) *to call for*, or *to; to call; to summon.*

Advŏlo, āre, āvi, ātum, intr. (ad & volo,) *to fly to.*

Ædifĭco, āre, āvi, ātum, tr. (ædes, *a house;* & facio,) *to build.*

Ædīlis, is, m. (ædes) *an ædile; a magistrate who had charge of the public buildings.*

Ædilĭtas, ātis, f. (ædīlis,) *the office of an ædile; ædileship.*

Ædilitius, (vir,) i, m. *one who has been an ædile.*

Ægæus, a, um, adj. *Ægæan;* Ægæum mare, *the Ægæan sea, lying between Greece and Asia Minor; now called the Archipelago.*

Æger, ra, rum, adj. (ægrior,) ægerrĭmus,) *sick, weak, infirm; diseased.*

Ægrè, adv. (æger,) *grievously; with difficulty.*

Ægritūdo, ĭnis, f. (æger,) *sorrow; grief.*

Ægyptus, i, f. (45, 2;) *Ægypt.*

Ælius, i, m. *the name of a Roman family.*

Æmilius, i, m. *the name of several noble Romans of the* gens Æmilia, or *Æmilian tribe.*

Æmulatio, ōnis, f. (æmŭlor,) *emulation; rivalry; competition.*

Æmŭlus, a, um, adj. *emulous.*

Æmŭlus, i, m. *a rival; a competitor.*

Ænēas, æ, m. *a Trojan prince, the son of Venus and Anchises.*

Æneus, a, um, adj. (æs,) *brazen.*

Ænos, i, f. (74,) *a town in Thrace, at the mouth of the Hebrus, named after its founder, Æneas.*

Æŏlis, ĭdis, f. *a country on the western coast of Asia Minor, between Troas and Ionia.*

Æquālis, e, adj. (æquus,) *equal.*

Æqualĭter, adv. (æquālis,) *equally.*

Æquĭtas, ātis, f. *equity; justice; moderation;* from

Æquus, a, um, adj. (comp.) *equal:* æquus anĭmus, *or* æqua mens, *equanimity.*

Aër, is, m. *the air; the atmosphere.*

Ærarium, i, n. *the treasury;* from

Æs, æris, n. *brass; money.*

Æschȳlus, i, m. *a celebrated Greek tragic poet.*

Æsculapius, i, m. *the son of Apollo, and god of medicine.*

Æstas, ātis, f. (æstus,) *summer.*

Æstimandus, a, um, part. *to be esteemed, prized;* or *regarded;* from

Æstĭmo, āre, āvi, ātum, tr. *to esteem; to value; to regard; to judge of, to estimate.*

Æstuo, āre, āvi, ātum, intr. (æstus,) *to be very hot; to boil.*

Æstuōsus, a, um, adj. (comp.)

undulating; rising in surges; boiling; stormy; turbulent.

Æstus, ûs, m. *heat.*

Ætas, ātis, f. (scil. ævĭtas, from ævum,) *age.*

Æternus, a, um, adj. (scil. æviternus, id.) *eternal; immortal.*

Æthiopia, æ. f. *Ethiopia, a country in Africa, lying on both sides of the equator.*

Æthiops, ŏpis, m. *an Ethiopian.*

Ætna, æ, f. *a volcanic mountain in Sicily.*

Ævum, i, n. *time; an age.*

Afer, ra, rum, adj. *of Africa.*

Affăbrè, adv. (ad & faber, *an artist,*) *artfully; ingeniously; curiously; in a workmanlike manner.*

Affectus, a, um, part. *affected; afflicted.*

Affero, afferre, attŭli, allātum, tr. irr. (ad & fero,) *to bring; to carry.*

Afficio, icĕre, ēci, ectum, tr. (ad & facio,) *to affect:* inediâ, *to affect with hunger; i. e. to deprive of food:* cladĭbus, *to overthrow:* pass. *to be affected:* gaudio, *to be affected with joy; to rejoice;* febri, *to be attacked with a fever.*

Affīgo, affigĕre, affixi, affixum, tr. (ad & figo,) *to affix; to fasten;* affigĕre cruci, *to crucify.*

Affīnis, e, adj. (ad & finis,) *neighboring; contiguous:* hence,

Affīnis, is, c. *a relation.*

Affirmo, āre, āvi, ātum, tr. (ad & firmo,) *to affirm; to confirm.*

Affixus, a, um, part. (affīgo.)

Afflātus, ûs, m. (afflo, *to blow against:*) *a blast; a breeze; a gale; inspiration.*

Afrĭca, æ, f. *Africa; also a part of the African continent, lying east of Numidia, and west of Cyrene.*

Africānus, i, m. *the agnomen of two of the Scipios, derived from their conquest of Africa.* (887, 4.)

Afrĭcus, a, um, adj. *belonging to Africa; African.* Afrĭcus ventus, *the southwest wind.*

Agamemnon, ŏnis, m. *a king of Mycenæ, the commander-in-chief of the Grecian forces at the siege of Troy.*

Agathyrsi, ōrum, m. pl. *a barbarous tribe living near the* palus Mæōtis.

Agellus, i, m. dim. (ager,) *a small farm.*

Agēnor, ŏris, m. *a king of Phœnicia.*

Agens, tis, part. (ago.)

Ager, gri, m. *a field; land; a farm; an estate; ground; a territory; the country.*

Agger, ĕris, m. (aggĕro, ad & gero, *to carry to:*) *a heap; a pile; a mound; a bulwark; a bank; a rampart; a dam.*

Aggredior, ĕdi, essus sum, tr. & intr. dep. (ad & gradior,) *to go to; to attack.*

Agressus, a, um, part. *having attacked.*

Agitātor, ōris, m. *a driver;* from

Agĭto, āre, āvi, ātum, tr. freq. (ago,) 227, Obs. 2, *to drive; to agitate; to revolve.*

Aglāus, i, m. *a poor Arcadian.*

Agmen, ĭnis, n. (ago,) *a train; a troop upon the march; a band; an army.*

Agnĭtus, a, um, part. from

Agnosco, agnoscĕre, agnōvi, agnĭtum, tr. (ad & nosco,) *to recognize; to know.*

Agnus, i, m. *a lamb.*

Ago, agĕre, ēgi, actum, tr. *to set in motion; to drive; to lead; to act; to do; to reside; to live:* funus, *to perform funeral rites:* annum vigesĭmum, *to be spending,* or *to be in his twentieth year:* bene, *to behave well:* agĕre gratias, *to thank.*

Agor, agi, actus sum, pass. *to be led:* agĭtur, *it is debated:* res de quâ agĭtur, *the point in debate:* pessum agi, *to sink.*

Agricŏla, æ, m. (ager & colo,) *a husbandman; a farmer.*

Agricultūra, æ, (id.) f. *agriculture.*

Agrigentum, i, n. *a town upon the southern coast of Sicily,* now *Girgenti.*

Agrippa, æ, m. *the name of several distinguished Romans.*

Ahēnum, i, n. (*scil.* vas aeneum,) *a brazen vessel; a kettle; a caldron.*

Aio, ais, ait, def. verb, (§84, 5,) *I say.*

Ajax, ācis, m. *the name of two distinguished Grecian warriors at the siege of Troy.*

Ala, æ, f. *a wing; an armpit; an arm.*

Alăcer, or ăcris, ăcre, adj. (comp.) *lively; courageous; ready; fierce; spirited.*

Alba, æ, f. Alba Longa; *a city of Latium, built by Ascanius.*

Albānus, i, m. *an inhabitant of Alba; an Alban.*

Albānus, a, um, adj. *Alban:* mons Albānus, *mount Albanus, at the foot of which Alba Longa was built,* 16 *miles from Rome.*

Albis, is, m. *a large river of Germany,* now *the Elbe.*

Albŭla, æ, m. *an ancient name of the Tiber.*

Albus, a, um, adj. *white;* (*a pale white; see* candĭdus.)

Alcestis, ĭdis, f. *the daughter of Pelias, and wife of Admētus.*

Alcibiădes, is, m. *an eminent Athenian, the pupil of Socrates.*

Alcinoüs, i, m. *a king of Phœa-*

cia, or *Corcyra, whose gardens were very celebrated.*

Alcyŏne, ės, f. *the daughter of Æŏlus, and wife of Ceyx: she and her husband were changed into sea-birds, called* Alcyŏnes, *kingfishers.*

Alcyon, is, m. *kingfisher.*

Alcyonēus, a, um, adj. *halcyon.*

Alexander, dri, m. *Alexander surnamed the Great, the son of Philip, king of Macedon.*

Alexandria, æ, f. *the capital of Egypt; founded by Alexander the Great.*

Algeo, algēre, alsi, intr. *to be cold.*

Alicunde, adv. (alĭquis & unde,) *from some place.*

Alĭenātus, a, um, part. *alienated; estranged;* from

Aliēno, āre, āvi, ātum, tr. *to alienate; to estrange;* from

Aliēnus, a, um, adj. *of or belonging to another; foreign; another man's; another's;* m. *a stranger.*

Aliò, adv. *to another place; elsewhere.*

Aliquandiu, adv. (aliquis & diu,) *for some time.*

Aliquando, adv. (alius & quando,) *once; formerly; at some time; at length; sometimes.*

Aliquantum, n. adj. *something; somewhat; a little.*

Alĭquis, alĭqua, alĭquod & alĭquid, indef. pron. (§ 37, 3,) *some; some one; a certain one.*

Alĭquot, ind. adj. *some.*

Alĭter, adv. (alius,) *otherwise;* alĭter—alĭter, *in one way—in another.*

Alius, a, ud, adj. § 20, Note 2; *another; other:* alii—alii, *some—others.*

Allātus, a, um, part. (affĕro,) *brought.*

Allectus, a, um, part. (allicio.)

Allĕvo, āre, āvi, ātum, tr. (ad & levo,) *to raise up; to alleviate; to lighten.*

Allia, æ, f. *a small river of Italy, flowing into the Tiber.*

Allicio, licĕre, lexi, lectum, (ad & lacio, *to draw,*) tr. *to allure; to entice.*

Alligātus, a, um, part. *bound; confined;* from

Allĭgo, āre, āvi, ātum, tr. (ad & ligo,) *to bind to; to fasten; to bind or tie.*

Allocūtus, a, um, part. *speaking,* or *having spoken to;* from

Allŏquor, -lŏqui, -locūtus sum, tr. dep. (ad & loquor,) *to speak to; to address; to accost.*

Alluo, -luĕre, -lui, tr. (ad & luo,) *to flow near; to wash; to lave.*

Alo, alĕre, alui, alĭtum or altum, tr. *to nourish; to feed; to support; to increase; to maintain; to strengthen.*

Alōeus, i, m. *a giant, son of Titan and Terra.*

Alpes, ium, f. pl. *the Alps.*

Alpheus, i, m. *a river of Peloponnesus.*

Alpīnus, a, um, adj. *of* or *belonging to the Alps; Alpine:* Alpīni mures, *marmots.*

Altè, (iùs, issĭmè,) adv. *on high; highly; loudly; deeply; low.*

Alter, ĕra, ĕrum, adj. § 20, 4, *the one (of two;) the other; the second.* 106, 7.

Alternus, a, um, adj. (alter,) *alternate; by turns.*

Althæa, æ, f. *the wife of Œneus, and mother of Meleager.*

Altitūdo, ĭnis, f. *height;* from

Altus, a, um, adj. (ior, issĭmus,) *high; lofty; deep; loud.*

Alumnus, i, m. (alo,) *a pupil; a foster-son.*

Alveus, i, m. *a channel;* from

Alvus, i, f. *the belly.*

Am, insep. prep. 239, 2.

Amans, tis, part. and adj. (ior, issĭmus,) *loving; fond of.*

Amărus, a, um, adj. (comp.) *bitter.*

Amātus, a, um, part. (amo.)

Amăzon, ŏnis; pl. Amazŏnes, um, f. *Amazons, a nation of female warriors, who lived near the river Don, and afterwards passed over into Asia Minor.*

Ambitio, ōnis, f. (ambio,) *ambition.*

Ambĭtus, ûs, m. (id.) *a going round* or *about; compass; extent; circuit; circumference.*

Ambo, æ, o, adj. pl. 104, 3; *both; (taken together; see* uterque.)

Ambŭlo, āre, āvi, ātum, intr. (dim. f. ambio,) *to walk.*

Amīcè, adv. -ciùs, -cissĭmè, (amīcus,) *in a friendly manner; kindly.*

Amicitia, æ, f. *friendship;* from

Amīcus, a, um, adj. comp. (amo,) *friendly.*

Amīcus, i, m. (amo,) *a friend.*

Amissus, a, um, part. from

Amitto, amittĕre, amīsi, amissum, tr. (a & mitto,) *to send away; to lose; to relinquish.*

Ammon, ōnis, m. *a surname of Jupiter, who was worshiped under this name, in the deserts of Lybia, under the form of a ram.*

Amnis, is, d. *a river.*

Amo, āre, āvi, ātum, tr. *to love; (viz., cordially, from the impulse of natural affection; see* dilĭgo.)

Amœnus, a, um, adj. (ior, issĭmus,) *pleasant; agreeable; delightful;* from amo.

Amor, ōris, m. (amo,) *love.*

Amoveo, vēre, vi, tum, tr. (a & moveo,) *to move away* or *from; to remove.*

Amphinŏmus, i, m. *a Catanean distinguished for his filial affection.*

Amphīon, ŏnis, m. *a son of Jupiter and Antiope, and the husband of Niobe. He is said to have built Thebes by the sound of his lyre.*

Amplè, adv. (iùs, issĭmè,) *amply; from* amplus.

Amplector, ecti, exus sum, tr. dep. (am & plector,) *to embrace.*

Amplexus, a, um, part. *having embraced; embracing.*

Amplio, āre, āvi, ātum, tr. (amplus,) *to enlarge.*

Ampliùs, adv. (amplè,) *more.*

Amplus, a, um, adj. (comp.) *great; abundant; large; spacious.*

Amulius, i, m. *the son of Silvius Procas, and brother of Numitor.*

Amȳclæ, ārum, f. pl. *a town on the western coast of Italy.*

Amȳcus, i, m. *a son of Neptune, and king of Bebrycia.*

An, adv. *whether; or.*

Anacreon, tis, m. *a celebrated lyric poet of Teos, in Ionia.*

Anāpus, i, m. *a Catanean, the brother of Amphinomus.*

Anaxagŏras, æ, m. *a philosopher of Clazomene, in Ionia.*

Anceps, cipĭtis, adj. (ancipitior,) (am and caput,) *uncertain; doubtful.*

Anchīses, æ, m. *a Trojan, the father of Æneas.*

Anchŏra, *or* Ancŏra, æ, f. *an anchor.*

Ancilla, æ, f. *a female servant; a maid.*

Ancus, i, m. (Martius,) *the fourth king of Rome.*

Andriscus, i, m. *a person of mean birth, called also Pseudophilippus, on account of his pretending to be Philip, the son of Persis, king of Macedon.*

Andromĕda, æ, f. *the daughter of Cephus and Cassiope, and wife of Perseus.*

Ango, angĕre, anxi, tr. (*to press close* or *tight; to strangle;* hence,) *to trouble; to disquiet; to torment; to vex.*

Anguis, is, c. (ango,) *a snake; a serpent.*

Angŭlus, i. m. *a corner.*

Angustiæ, ārum, f. pl. *narrowness; a narrow pass; a defile;* from

Angustus, a, um, adj. comp. (ango,) *narrow; limited; straitened; pinching.*

Anĭma, æ, f. (anĭmus,) *breath; life; the soul.*

Animadverto, vertĕre, verti, versum, tr. (animus ad & verto, *to turn the mind to;*) *to attend to; to observe; to notice; to punish.*

Anĭmal, ālis, n. (anĭma,) *an animal.*

Animōsus, a, um, adj. *full of wind or breath; spirited; courageous; bold;* from

Anĭmus, i, m. *wind; breath; spirit; the soul* or *mind; disposition; spirit* or *courage; a design;* uno anĭmo, *unanimously;* mihi est anĭmus, *I have a mind; I intend. See* mens.

Anio, ēnis, m. *a branch of the*

Tiber, which enters it three miles above Rome. It is now called *the Teverone*,

Annecto,-nectĕre, -nexui, -nexum, tr. (ad & necto,) *to annex; to tie* or *fasten to.*

Annōna, æ, f. (annus,) *yearly; produce; corn; provisions.*

Annŭlus, i, m. (dim, from annus,) *a small circle; a ring.*

Annumĕro, āre, āvi, ātum, tr. (ad & numĕro,) *to reckon among; to number; to reckon.*

Annuo, -nuĕre, -nui, intr. (ad & nuo, *to nod,*) *to assent; to agree.*

Annus, i, m. *a circle; a year;* hence

Annuus, a, um, adj. *annual; yearly; lasting a year.*

Anser, ĕris, m. *a goose;* hence

Anserīnus, a, um, adj. *of* or *belonging to a goose:* ova, *goose-eggs.*

Antè, adv. *before; sooner.*

Ante, prep. *before.*

Antea, adv. (ante & ea acc. pl. n. of is,) *before; heretofore.*

Antecello,-cellĕre, tr. (ante & cello, obsol, *to drive,*) *to drive or move before;* hence *to excel; to surpass; to exceed; to be superior to.*

Antepōno,-ponĕre, -posui, -posĭtum, tr. (ante & pono,) *to set before; to prefer.*

Antepositus, a, um, part. (antepōno.)

Antĕquam, adv. *before that; before.*

Antigŏnus, i, m. *a king of Macedonia.*

Antiochīa, æ, f. *the capital of Syria.*

Antiŏchus, i, m. *a king of Syria.*

Antiōpe, es, f. *the wife of Lycus, king of Thebes, and the mother of Amphion.*

Antīquus, a, um, adj. (ior, issĭmus,) *ancient; old; of long continuance;* fr. ante.

Antipăter, tris, m. *a Sidonian poet.*

Antium, i, n. *a maritime town of Italy.*

Antonius, i, m. *Antony, the name of a Roman family.*

Antrum, i, n. *a cave.*

Apelles, is, m. *a celebrated painter of the island of Cos.*

Apennīnus, i, m. *the Appenines.*

Aper, apri, m. *a boar; a wild boar.*

Aperio,-perīre, -perui, -pertum, tr. (ad & pario,) *to open; to discover; to disclose; to make known.*

Apertus, a, um, part. (aperio.)

Apex, ĭcis, m. *a point; the top; the summit.*

Apis, is, f. *a bee.*

Apis, is, m. *an ox worshipped as a deity among the Egyptians.*

Apollo, ĭnis, m. *the son of Jupiter and Latona, and the god of music and poetry.*

Apparātus, ûs, m. (appăro, *to prepare;*) *a preparation; apparatus; equipment; habiliment.*

Appareo, ēre, ui, intr. (ad & pareo,) *to appear; to be manifest* or *clear.*

Appellandus, a, um, part. from

Appello, āre, āvi, ātum, tr. (ad & pello,) *to name* or *call; to address; to call upon.*

Appendo, -pendĕre, -pendi, -pensum, tr. (ad & pendo,) *to hang upon* or *to; to weigh out; to pay.*

Appĕtens, tis, part. *seeking after;* from

Appĕto, -petĕre, -petīvi, -petītum, tr. (ad & peto,) *to seek to;* hence, *to desire; strive for; to aim at; to attack.*

Appius, i, m. *a Roman* prænōmen *belonging to the Claudian gens or tribe.*

Appōno, -ponĕre, -posui, -posĭtum, tr. (ad & pono,) *to set* or *place before; to put to; to join.*

Apposĭtus, a, um, part. (appōno.)

Appropinquo, āre, āvi, ātum, intr. (ad & propinquo,) *to approach; to draw near.*

Aprīcus. a, um, adj. (comp.) *sunny; serene; warm: (as if* apericus *from* aperio.)

Apto, āre, āvi, ātum, tr. *to fit; to adjust.*

Apud, prep. *at; in; among; before; to; in the house of; in the writings of.*

Apulia, æ, f. *a country in the eastern part of Italy, near the Adriatic.*

Aqua, æ, f. *water.*

Aquæductus, ûs, m. (aqua & duco, *to lead:*) *an aqueduct; a conduit.*

Aquĭla, æ, f. *an eagle.*

Aquĭlo, ōnis, m. *the north wind.*

Aquitania, æ, f. *a country of Gaul.*

Aquitāni, ōrum, m. pl. *the inhabitants of Aquitania.*

Ara, æ, f. *an altar.*

Arabia, æ, f. *Arabia;* hence,

Arabĭcus, a, um, adj. *Arabian; of* or *belonging to Arabia.* Arabĭcus sinus, *the Red Sea.*

Arabius, a, um, adj. *Arabian.*

Arabs, ăbis, m. *an Arabian.*

Arbitrātus, a, um, part. *having thought;* from

Arbitror, āri, ātus sum, tr. dep. (arbiter,) *to believe; to think.*

Arbor, & Arbos, ŏris, f. *a tree.*

Arca, æ, f. *a chest.*

Arcadia, æ, f. *Arcadia, a country in the interior of Peloponnesus.*

Arcas, ădis, m. an Arcadian; also, *a son of Jupiter and Calisto.*

Arceo, ēre, ui, tr. *to ward off; to keep from; to restrain.*

Arcessītus, a, um, part. from

Arcesso, ĕre, īvi, ītum, tr. (arcio, i. e. adcio, ad *and* cio,) *to call; to send for; to invite; to summon.*

Archimēdes, is, m. *a famous mathematician and mechanician of Syracuse.*

Architectus, i, m. *an architect; a builder.*

Archytas, æ, m. *a Pythagorean philosopher of Tarentum.*

Arctè, adv. (iùs, issĭmè,) *straitly; closely;* from

Arctus, a, um, adj. (ior, issĭmus,) *narrow; close;* from arceo.

Arcus, ûs, m. *a bow; an arch.*

Ardea, æ, f. *a city of Latium, the capital of the Rutuli.*

Ardens, tis, part. & adj. *burning; hot;* from

Ardeo, ardēre, arsi, arsum, intr. *to glow; to be on fire; to burn; to sparkle; to shine; to dazzle.*

Arduus, a, um, adj. *high; lofty; steep; arduous; difficult.*

Arēna, æ, f. (areo, *to be dry;*) *sand;* hence

Arenōsus, a, um, adj. *sandy.*

Arethūsa, æ, f. *the name of a nymph of Elis, who was changed into a fountain in Sicily.*

Argentum, i, n. *silver.*

Argias, æ, m. *a chief of the Megarensians.*

Argīvus, a, um, adj. (Argos,) *of Argos; Argive.*

Argīvi, ōrum, m. pl. (id.) *Argives; inhabitants of Argos.*

Argonautæ, ārum, m. pl. (Argo & nautæ,) *the Argonauts; the crew of the ship Argo.*

Argos, i, n. sing., & Argi, ōrum, m. pl. *a city in Greece, the capital of Argolis.*

Arguo, uĕre, ui, ūtum, *to speak in loud or shrill tones:* hence, *to argue; to accuse; to prove; to show; to convict.*

Arimĭnum, i, n. *a city of Italy, on the coast of the Adriatic.*

Aristobūlus, i, m. *a name of several of the high priests and kings of Judea.*

Aristotĕles, is, m. *Aristotle, a Greek philosopher, born at Stagīra, a city of Macedonia.*

Arma, ōrum. n. pl. *arms.*

Armātus, a, um, part. of armo, *armed:* pl. armāti, ōrum, *armed men; soldiers.*

Armenia, æ, f. (Major,) *a country of Asia, lying between Taurus and the Caucasus.*

Armenia, æ, f. (Minor,) *a small country lying between Cappadocia and the Euphrates.*

Armenius, a, um, adj. *Armenian.*

Armentum, i, n. (*for* aramentum, *from* aro,) *a herd.*

Armilla, æ, f. (dim. fr. armus, *the arm,*) *a bracelet or ring worn on the left arm by soldiers who had been distinguished in battle.*

Armo, āre, āvi, ātum, tr. (arma, *to arm.*

Aro, -āre, -āvi, ātum, tr. *to plough; to cover with the plough.*

Arreptus, a, um, part. from

Arripio, -ripĕre, -ripui, -reptum, tr. (ad & rapio,) § 80, 5,) *to seize upon.*

Arrŏgo, āre, āvi, ātum, tr. (ad & rogo) *to demand for one's self; to arrogate; to claim.*

Ars, tis, f. *art; contrivance; skill; employment; occupation; pursuit.*

Arsi. *See* Ardeo.

Artemisia, æ, f. *the wife of Mausōlus, king of Caria.*

Artĭfex, ĭcis, c. (ars & facio,) *an artist.*

Arundo, ĭnis, f. *a reed; a cane.*

Aruns, tis, m. *the eldest son of Tarquin the Proud.*

Arx, cis, f. (arceo,) *a citadel; a fortress.*

Ascanius, i, m. *the son of Æneas and Creūsa.*

Ascendo, (*or* adscendo,) dĕre, di, sum, tr. & intr. (ad & scando, *to climb to,*) *to ascend; to rise:* ascendĭtur, imp *it is ascended,*or *they ascend;* 223, 6. & Id, 67, note.

Asia, æ, f. *Asia; Asia Minor;* also, *proconsular Asia,* or *the Roman province.*

Asiatĭcus, i, m. *an* agnŏmen *of L. Cornelius Scipio, on account of his victories in Asia.* 887, 4,

Asĭna, æ, m. *a* cognōmen *or surname of a part of the Cornelian family.*

Asĭnus, i, m. *an ass.*

Aspectūrus, a, um, pārt. (aspicio.)

Asper, ĕra, ĕrum, adj. (erior, errĭmus,) *rough; rugged.*

Aspergo. *See* Adspergo.

As- or ad- spernor, āri, ātus sum, tr. dep. *to spurn; to despise; to reject.*

Aspicio. *See* Adspicio.

Aspis, ĭdis, f. *an asp.*

Assecūtus, a, um, part. from

Assĕquor, -sĕqui, -secūtus sum, tr. dep. (ad & sequor,) *to come up to; to overtake; to obtain.*

Asservo, āre, āvi, ātum, tr. (ad & servo,) *to take care of; to preserve; to keep.*

Assigno, āre, āvi, ātum, tr. (ad & signo,) *to mark with a seal:* hence, *to appoint; to allot; to distribute.*

Assisto. *See* Adsisto.

Assuesco, -suescĕre, -suēvi, -suētum, intr. inc. (ad & suesco,) *to be accustomed; to be wont.*

Assurgo, -surgĕre, -surrexi, -surrectum, intr. (ad & surgo,) *to rise up; to arise.*

Astronomia, æ, f. *astronomy.*

Astūtus, a, um, adj. (ior, issĭmus,) (*from* astu, *the city,* viz.; *of Athens,) knowing; shrewd; cunning; crafty.*

Asy̆lum, i, n. *an asylum.*

At, conj. *but.*

Atalanta, æ, f. *the daughter of Schœneus, king of Arcadia, celebrated for her swiftness, in running.*

Athēnæ, ārum, f. pl. *Athens, the capital of Attica;* hence,

Atheniensis, is, m. *an Athenian.*

Atilius, i, m. *a Roman proper name.*

Atlantĭcus, a, um, adj. *Atlantic; relating to Atlas:* mare Atlantĭcum, *the Atlantic ocean.*

Atque, conj. *and; as; than.*

Atrocĭter, adv. (iùs, issĭmè,) (atrox,) *fiercely; violently; severely.*

Attălus, i, m. *a king of Pergămus.*

Attĕro, -terĕre, -trīvi, -trītum, (ad & tero,) tr. *to rub close; to rub off; to wear.*

Atthis, ĭdis, f. *the same as Attica.*

Attĭca, æ, f. *Attica, a country in the southern part of Greece proper.*

Attingo, -tingĕre, -tĭgi, -tactum, tr. (ad & tango,) *to touch; to border upon; to attain; to reach.*

Attollo, ĕre, tr. (ad & tollo,) *to raise up.*

Attrītus, a, um, part. (attĕro,) *rubbed away; worn off.*

Auctor, ōris, c. (augeo,) *one who increases or enlarges;* hence, *an author.*

Auctorĭtas, ātis, f. *authority; influence; reputation;* fr. auctor.

Auctus, a, um, part. (augeo,) *increased; enlarged; augmented.*

Audacia, æ, f. *audacity; boldness;* from

Audax, ācis, adj. (comp.) *bold; daring; audacious; desperate;* from

Audeo, audēre, ausus sum, neut. pass. *to dare; to attempt.* § 78.

Audio, īre, īvi, ītum, tr. *to hear.*

Audītus, a, um, part.

Audĭtus, ûs, m. *the hearing.*

Aufĕro, auferre, abstŭli, ablātum, tr. irr. (ab & fero,) *to take away; to remove.*

Aufugio, -fugĕre, -fūgi, -fugĭtum, intr. (ab & fugio,) *to fly away; to run off; to escape; to flee.*

Augendus, a, um, part. from

Augeo, augēre, auxi, auctum, tr. *to cause to grow; to increase; to augment; to enlarge;* intr. *to grow; to increase; to rise.*

Augurium, i, n. (avis, *a bird,* & garrio, *to chirp,*) *a foretelling of future events from the singing of birds;* hence, *augury; divination.*

Augustè, adv. (iùs, issĭmè,) *nobly;* from

Augustus, a, um, adj. (comp.)

august; grand; venerable; (from augeo.)

Augustus, i, m. *an honorary appellation bestowed by the senate upon Cæsar Octavianus; succeeding emperors took the same name.*

Aulis, ĭdis, f. *a seaport town in Bœotia.*

Aulus, i, m. *a common* prænōmen *among the Romans.* 887, 1.

Aurelius, i, m. *the name of several Romans.*

Aureus, a, um, adj. (aurum,) *golden.*

Aurīga, æ, m. (aurea, Obsol. *a rein,* and ago, *to hold,* or *drive,*) *a charioteer.*

Auris, is, f. *the ear.*

Aurum, i, n. *gold.*

Auspicicum, i, n. (avis *a bird,* and specio, *to look:*) *a species of divination, from the flight, &c., of birds; an auspice; the guidance,* or *protection of another.*

Ausus, a, um, part. (audeo,) *daring; having dared.*

Aut, conj. *or;* aut—aut, *either —or.*

Autem, conj. *but; yet.*

Autumnus, i, m. (augeo,) *autumn.*

Auxi. *See* Augeo.

Auxilium, i, n. (augeo,) *help; aid; assistance.*

Avaritia, æ. f. *avarice;* from

Avārus, a, um, adj. (comp.) *avaricious; covetous:* (fr. aveo, *to long for.*)

Avĕho, -vehĕre, -vexi, -vectum, tr. (a & veho,) *to carry off,* or *away.*

Avello, -vellĕre, -velli *or* -vulsi, -vulsum, tr. (a & vello,) *to pull off,* or *away; to pluck; to take away* (forcibly).

Aventīnus, i, m. *mount Aventine, one of the seven hills on which Rome was built.*

Aversus, a, um, part. *turned away:* cicātrix averso, *a scar in the back:* from

Averto, -vertĕre, -verti, -versum, tr. (a & verto,) *to turn away; to avert; to turn.*

Avicŭla, æ, f. dim. (avis,) *a small bird.*

Avĭdus, a, um, adj. (aveo,) (ior, issĭmus,) *desirous; ravenous; greedy; eager.*

Avis, is, f. *a bird.*

Avŏco, āre, āvi, ātum, tr. (a & voco,) *to call away; to divert; to withdraw.*

Avolatūrus, a, um, part. from

Avŏlo, āre, āvi, ātum, intr. (a & volo,) *to fly away,* or *off.*

Avulsus, part. (avello.)

Avuncŭlus, i, m. (dim. of avus,) *a mother's brother; an uncle.*

Avus. i, m. *a grandfather.*

Axĕnus, i, m. (from a Greek word signifying *inhospitable:*) *the Euxine sea; anciently so called, on account of the cruelty of the neighboring tribes.*

B.

Babўlon, ōnis, f, *the metropolis of Chaldea, lying upon the Euphrates.*

Babylonia, æ, f. *the country about Babylon.*

Bacca, æ, f. *a berry.*

Bacchus, i, m. *the son of Jupiter and Semĕle, and the god of wine.*

Bactra, ōrum, n. *the capital of Bactriana, situated upon the sources of the Oxus.*

Bactriāni, ōrum, m. pl. *the inhabitants of Bactriana.*

Bactriānus, a, um, adj. *Bactrian, pertaining to Bactra* or *Bactriana.*

Bacŭlus, i, m. and Bacŭlum, i, n. *a staff.*

Bætĭca, æ, f. *a country in the southern part of Spain, watered by the river Bætis.*

Bætis, is, m. *a river in the southern part of Spain,* now *the Gaudalquiver.*

Bagrăda, æ, m. *a river of Africa, between Utica and Carthage.*

Ballista, æ, f. *an engine for throwing stones.*

Baltĭcus, a, um, adj. *Baltic:* mare Balticum, *the Baltic sea.*

Barbărus, a, um, adj. *speaking a strange language; (not Greek or Roman;) foreign;* hence, *barbarous; rude; uncivilized; savage:* subs. barbări, *barbarians.*

Batăvus, a, um, adj. *Batavian; belonging to Batavia,* now *Holland.*

Beatitūdo, ĭnis, f. *blessedness; happiness;* from

Beātus, a, um, adj. (ior, issĭmus,) *happy; blessed;* (fr. beo, *to make happy.*)

Bebrycia, æ, f. *a country of Asia.*

Belgæ, ārum, m. pl. *the inhabitants of the north-east part of Gaul; the Belgians.*

Belgĭcus, a, um, adj. *of* or *pertaining to the Belgæ.*

Bellerŏphon, tis, m. *the son of Glaucus, king of Ephyra.*

Bellicōsus, a, um, adj. (ior, issĭmus, (bellum,) *of a warlike spirit; given to war.*

Bellĭcus, a, um, adj. (bellum,) *relating to war; warlike.*

Belligĕro, āre, āvi, ātum, intr. (bellum & gero,) *to wage war; to carry on war.*

Bello, āre, āvi, ātum, tr. *to war; to wage war; to contend; to fight.*

Bellua, æ, f. *a large beast; a monster.*

Bellum, i, n. (duellum,) *war.*

Belus, i, m. *the founder of the Babylonish empire.*

Benè, adv. (meliùs, optĭmè,) *well; finely; very:* benè pugnāre, *to fight successfully;* (fr. benus *obsol. for* bonus.)

Beneficium, i, n. (benè & facio,) *a benefit; a kindness.*

Benevolentia, æ, f. (benè & volo,) *benevolence; good will.*

Benignè, adv. (iùs, issĭmè,) *kindly;* from

Benignus, a, um, adj. (comp.) *kind; benign:* (benigenus fr. benus for bonus, & genus.)

Bestia, æ, f. *a beast; a wild beast.*

Bestia, æ, m. *the surname of a Roman consul.*

Bias, antis, m. *a philosopher born at Priēne, and one of the seven wise men of Greece.*

Bibliothēca, æ, f. *a library.*

Bibo, bibĕre, bibi, bibĭtum, tr. *to drink,* (in order to quench thirst:) *to imbibe: See* poto.

Bibŭlus, i, m. *a colleague of Julius Cæsar in the consulship.*

Bini, æ, a, num. adj. § 24. III; *two by two; two, two each.*

Bipes, ĕdis, adj. (bis & pes,) *two footed; with two feet.*

Bis, num. adv. *twice.*

Bithynia, æ, f. *a country of Asia Minor, east of the Propontis.*

Blanditia, æ, f. *complimenting;* blanditiæ, pl. *blandishments; caresses; flattery:* from

Blandus, a, um, adj. (ior, issĭmus,) *courteous; agreeable; flattering; enticing; inviting; tempting.*

Bœotia, æ, f. *a country of Greece, north of Attica.*

Bonĭtas, ātis, f. *goodness; excellence.* from

Bonus, a, um, adj. (melior, optĭmus,) *good; happy; kind.*

Bonum, i, n. *a good thing; an endowment; an advantage; profit:* bona, n. pl. *an estate; goods:* (fr. bonus.)

Boreālis, e, adj. *northern;* from

Boreas, æ, m. *the north wind.*

Borysthĕnes, æ, m. *a large river of Scythia, flowing into the Euxine; it is now called the Dneiper.*

Borysthĕnis, ĭdis, f. *the name of a town at the mouth of the Borysthenes.*

Bos, bovis, c. *an ox; a cow:* § 15. 12.

Bosphŏrus, *or* Bospŏrus, i, m. *the name of two straits between Europe and Asia; one the Thracian Bosphorus,* now *the straits of Constantinople; the other the Cimmerian Bosphorus,* now *the straits of Caffa.*

Brachium, i, n. *the arm;* (viz. from the hand to the elbow.)

Brevì, adv. *shortly; briefly; in short time;* from

Brevis, e, adj. (comp.) *short; brief;* hence,

Brevĭtas, ātis, f. *shortness; brevity.*

Brigantīnus, a, um, adj. *belonging to Brigantium, a town of the Vindelici;* Brigantīnus lacus, *the lake of Constance.*

Britannia, æ, f. *Great Britain.*
Britannĭcus, a, um, adj. *belonging to Britain; British.*
Britannus, a, um, adj. *British:* Britanni, *the Britons.*
Bruma, æ, f. *the winter solstice; the shortest day.*
Bruttium, i, n. *a promontory of Italy.*
Bruttii, ōrum, m. pl. *a people in the southern part of Italy.*
Brutus, i, m. *the name of an illustrious noble family.*
Bucephălus, i, f. *the name of Alexander's war-horse.*
Bucephălos, i, f. *a city of India, near the Hydaspes, built by Alexander, in memory of his horse.*
Buxeus, a, um, adj. (buxus, *the box-tree:*) *of box; of a pale yellow color, like box-wood.*
Byzantium, i, n. *now Constantinople, a city of Thrace, situated upon the Bosphŏrus.*

C.

C., *an abbreviation of Caius.*
Cabīra, ind. *a town of Pontus.*
Cacūmen, ĭnis, n. *the top; the peak; the summit.*
Cadens, tis, part. (cado.)
Cadmus, i, m. *the son of Agēnor, king of Phœnicia.*
Cado, cadĕre, cecĭdi, casum, intr. *to fall.*
Cæcilius, i, m. *a Roman name.*
Cæcŭbum. i, n. *a town of Campania, famous for its wine.*
Cæcŭbus, a, um, adj. *Cæcuban; of Cæcubum.*
Cædes, is, f. *slaughter; carnage; homicide; murder;* from
Cædo, cædĕre, cecīdi, cæsum, tr. *to cut; to kill; to slay; to beat.*
Cælātus, a, um, part. from
Cælo, āre, āvi, ātum, tr. *to carve; to engrave; to sculpture; to emboss.*
Cæpe, *or* Cepe, n. indec. *an onion.*
Cæpio, ōnis, m. *a Roman consul who commanded in Spain.*
Cæsar, ăris, m. *a* cognōmen *or surname given to the Julian family.*
Cæstus, ûs, m. (cædo,) *a gauntlet; a boxing-glove.*
Cæsus, a, um, part. (cædo,) *cut; slain; beaten.*
Caius, i, m. *a Roman* prænōmen.
Calais, is, m. *a son of Boreas.*
Calamĭtas, ātis, f. (*a storm which breaks the reeds or stalks of corn,* hence,) *a calamity; a misfortune;* fr.
Calămus, i, m. *a reed.*
Călăthiscus, i, m. (dim. calathus,) *a small basket.*
Calefacio, calefacĕre, calefēci, calefactum, tr. (caleo & facio,) *to warm; to heat.*
Calefīo, fiĕri, factus sum, intr. irr. § 83, Obs. 3; *to be warmed.*

Calefactus, a, um, part. (calefīo,) *warmed.*
Calĭdus, a, um, adj. (comp. fr. caleo,) *warm.*
Callĭdus, a, um. adj. (calleo, *from* callus, *hardness*, viz: *of skin occasioned by hard labor;* hence,) *practiced; experienced; shrewd; cunning.*
Calor, ōris, m. *warmth; heat.*
Calpe, es, f. *a hill* or *mountain in Spain, opposite to Abyla in Africa.*
Calpurnius, i, m. *the name of a Roman family.*
Calydonius, a, um, adj. *of* or *belonging to Calydon, a city of Ætolia; Calydonian.*
Camēlus, i, c. *a camel.*
Camillus, i, m. (M. Furius,) *a Roman general.*
Campania, æ, f. *a pleasant country of Italy, between Latium and Lucania.*
Campester, tris, tre, adj. *even; plain; level; champaign; flat;* from
Campus, i, m. *a plain; a field; the Campus Martius.*
Cancer, cri, m. *a crab.*
Candĭdus, a, um, adj. (comp.) *white;* (*a bright* or *shining white;* see albus.)
Candor, ōris, m. (id.) *brightness; whiteness; clearness.*
Canens, tis, part. of cano, *singing.*
Canis, is, c. *a dog.*
Cannæ, ārum, f. pl. *a village in Apulia, famous for the defeat of the Romans by Hannibal.*
Cannensis, e, adj. *belonging to Cannæ.*
Cano, canĕre, cecĭni, cantum, tr. *to sing; to sound* or *play upon an instrument.*
Cantans, tis, part. (canto.)
Canthărus, i, m. *a beetle; a knot under the tongue of the god Apis.*
Cantium, i, n. *now the county of Kent, England.*
Canto, āre, āvi, ātum, tr. freq. (cano,) *to sing; to repeat often.*
Cantus, ûs, m. (id.) *singing; a song:* cantus galli, *the crowing of the cock.*
Caper, pri, m. *a he-goat.*
Capesso, ĕre, īvi, ītum, tr. (capio,) § 88, 5, *to take; to take the management of:* fugam capessĕre, *to flee.*
Capiens, tis, part. from
Capio, capĕre, cepi, captum, tr. (properly, *to hold; to contain;* commonly,) *to take; to capture, to take captive; to enjoy; to derive.*
Capitālis, e, adj. (caput,) *relating to the head* or *life; capital; mortal; deadly; pernicious:* capitāle, (sc. crimen,) *a capital crime.*
Capitolium, i, n. (id.) *the capitol; the Roman citadel on the Capitoline hill.*
Capra, æ, f. *a she-goat.*
Captīvus, a, um, adj. (capio,) *captive.*

Capto, āre, āvi, ātum, tr. freq. 227, 1, (capio,) *to catch at; to seek for; to hunt for.*

Captus, a, um, part. (capio,) *taken; taken captive;*

Capua, æ, f. *the principal city of Campania.*

Caput, ĭtis, n. *a head; life; the skull; a capital city;* capĭtis damnāre, *to condemn to death.*

Carbonarius, i, m. (carbo, *a coal;*) *a collier; a maker of charcoal.*

Carcer, ĕris, m. *a prison.*

Careo, ēre, ui, ĭtum, intr. *to be without; to be free from; to be destitute; not to have; to want.*

Cares, ium, m. pl. *Carians; the inhabitants of Caria.*

Caria, æ, f. *a country in the southeastern part of Asia Minor.*

Carĭca, æ, f. *a fig;* (properly, carĭca ficus.)

Carmen, ĭnis, n. *a song; a poem.*

Carneădes, is, m. *a philosopher of Cyrene.*

Caro, carnis, f. *flesh.*

Carpentum, i, n. *a chariot; a wagon.*

Carpetāni, ōrum, m. pl. *a people of Spain, on the borders of the Tagus.*

Carpo, carpĕre, carpsi, carptum, tr. *to pluck; to gather; to tear.*

Carræ, ārum, f. pl. *a city of Mesopotamia, near the Euphrates.*

Carthaginiensis, e, adj. *of* or *belonging to Carthage; Carthaginian:* subs. *a Carthaginian.*

Carthāgo, ĭnis, f. *Carthage, a maritime city in Africa:* Carthāgo Nova, *Carthagena, a town of Spain.*

Carus, a, um, adj. (ior, issĭmus,) *dear; precious; costly.*

Casa, æ, f. *a cottage; a hut.*

Casca, æ, m. *the surname of P. Servilius, one of the conspirators against Cæsar.*

Caseus, i, m. *cheese.*

Cassander, dri, m. *the name of a Macedonian.*

Cassiŏpe, es, f. *the wife of Cepheus, king of Ethiopia, and mother of Andromeda.*

Cassius, i, m. *the name of several Romans.*

Castalius, a, um, adj. *Castalian; of Castalia, a fountain of Phocis, at the foot of mount Parnassus.*

Castigātus, a, um, part. from

Castĭgo, āre, āvi, ātum, tr. *to chastise; to punish; to correct.*

Castor, ŏris, m. *the brother of Pollux and Helen.*

Castrum, i, n. (casa,) *a castle:* castra, ōrum, pl. *a camp:* castra ponĕre, *to pitch a camp; to encamp.*

Casus, ûs, m. (cado,) *a fall; accident; chance; an event.*

a misfortune: a disaster; a calamity.

Catabathmus, i, m. *a declivity; a gradual descent; a valley between Egypt and Africa proper.*

Catăna, æ, f. *now Catania, a city of Sicily, near mount Ætna.*

Catanensis, e, adj. *belonging to Catana; Catanean.*

Catiēnus, i, m. Catiēnus Plotīnus, *a Roman distinguished for his attachment to his patron.*

Catilīna, æ, m. *a conspirator against the Roman government, whose plot was detected and defeated by Cicero.*

Cato, ōnis, m. *the name of a Roman family.*

Catŭlus, i, m. *the name of a Roman family.*

Catŭlus, i, m. (dim. canis,) *a little dog; a whelp; the young of beasts.*

Caucăsus, i, m. *a mountain of Asia, between the Black and Caspian seas.*

Cauda, æ, f. *a tail.*

Caudīnus, a, um, adj. *Caudine; of* or *belonging to Caudium, a town of Italy.*

Caula, æ, f. *a fold; a sheepcote.*

Causa, æ, f. *a cause; a reason; a lawsuit:* in causâ est, *or* causa est, *is the reason:* causâ, *for the sake of.*

Cautes, is, f. *a sharp rock; a crag; a cliff:* from

Caveo, cavēre, cavi, cautum, intr. & tr. *to beware; to avoid; to shun:* cavēre sibi ab, *to secure themselves from; to guard against.*

Caverna, æ, f. (cavus,) *a cave; a cavern.*

Cavus, a, um, adj. *hollow.*

Cecīdi. *See* Cædo.

Cecĭdi. *See* Cado.

Cecĭni. *See* Cano.

Cecropia, æ, f. *an ancient name of Athens;* from

Cecrops, ŏpis, m. *the first king of Athens.*

Cedo cedĕre, cessi, cessum, intr. *to yield; to give place; to retire; to retreat; to submit.*

Celĕber, bris, bre, adj. (celebrior, celeberrĭmus,) *crowded; much visited; renowned; famous; distinguished.*

Celebrātus, a, um, part. (celĕbro.)

Celebrĭtas, ātis, f. (celĕber,) *a great crowd; fame; glory; celebrity; renown.*

Celĕbro, āre, āvi, ātum, tr. *to visit; to celebrate; to make famous; to perform.*

Celerĭtas, ātis, f. (celer, *swift,*) *speed; swiftness; quickness.*

Celerĭter, adv. (iùs, rĭmè,) *swiftly.*

Celeus, i, m. *a king of Eleusis.*

Celo, āre, āvi, ātum, tr. *to hide; to conceal.*

Celtæ, ārum, m. pl. *the Celts; a people of Gaul.*

Censeo, ēre, ui, um, tr. *to estimate; to judge; to believe; to count; to reckon.*

Censor, is, m. (censeo,) *a censor; a censurer; a critic.*

Censorīnus, i, m. (L. Manlius,) *a Roman consul in the third Punic war.*

Censorius, i, m. (censor,) *one who has been a censor; a surname of Cato the elder.*

Census, ûs, m. (censeo,) *a census; an enumeration of the people; a registering of the people, their ages, &c.*

Centēni, æ, a, num, adj. pl. distrib. (centum,) *every hundred; a hundred.*

Centesĭmus, a, um, num, adj. ord. (id.) *the hundredth.*

Centies, num, adv. *a hundred times;* from

Centum, num, adj. pl. ind. *a hundred.*

Centurio, ōnis, m. (centuria,) *a centurion; a captain of a hundred men.*

Cephallenia, æ, f. *an island in the Ionian sea,* now *Cephalonia.*

Cepe. *See* Cæpe.

Cepi. *See* Capio.

Çera, æ, f. *wax.*

Cerbĕrus, i, m. *the name of the three-headed dog which guarded the entrance of the infernal regions.*

Cercasōrum, i, n. *a town of Egypt.*

Ceres, ĕris, f. *Ceres, the goddess of corn.*

Cerno, cernĕre, crevi, cretum, tr. properly, *to sift; to distinguish:* hence, *to see; to perceive.*

Certāmen, ĭnis, n. (certo,) *a contest; a battle; zeal; eagerness; strife; contention; debate; a game* or *exercise:* Olympĭcum certāmen, *the Olympic games.*

Certè, adv. iùs, issĭmè, (certus,) *certainly, at least.*

Certo, āre, āvi, ātum, tr. & intr. (certus,) *to determine,* or *make sure; to contend; to strive; to fight.*

Certus, a, um, adj. (cerno,) (ior, issĭmus,) *certain; fixed:* certiōrem facĕre, *to inform.*

Cerva, æ, f. *a female deer; a hind;* hence,

Cervīnus, a, um, adj. *belonging to a stag or deer.*

Cervix, īcis, f. (*the hinder part of*) *the neck; an isthmus.*

Cervus, i, m. *a male deer; a stag.*

Cessātor, is, m. *a loiterer; a lingerer; an idler;* from

Cesso, āre, āvi, ātum, intr. freq. (cedo,) *to cease; to loiter.*

Cetĕrus, (*and* ceter, *seldom used,*) cetĕra, cetĕrum, adj. *other; the other; the rest;* hence,

Cetĕrùm, adv. *but; however; as for the rest.*

Cetus, i, m. (& cete, is, n.) *a whale; any large sea fish.*

Ceyx, ȳcis, m. *the son of Hesperus, and husband of Alcyone.*

Chalcēdon, ŏnis, f. *a city of Bithynia, opposite Byzantium.*

Chaldaĭcus, a, um, adj. (Chaldæa,) *Chaldean.*

Charta, æ, f. *paper.*

Chersĭphron, ōnis, m. *a distinguished architect, under whose direction the temple of Ephesus was built.*

Chersonēsus, i, f. *a peninsula.*

Chilo, ōnis, m. *a Lacedæmonian philosopher, and one of the seven wise men of Greece.*

Christus, i, m. *Christ.*

Cibus, i, m. *food; nourishment.*

Cicātrix, īcis, f. *a wound; a scar; a cicatrice.*

Cicĕro, ōnis, m. *a celebrated Roman orator.*

Ciconia, æ, f. *a stork.*

Cilicia, æ, f. *a country in the southeast part of Asia Minor.*

Cimbri, ōrum, m. pl. *a nation formerly inhabiting the northern part of Germany.*

Cinctus, a, um, part. (cingo.)

Cineas, æ, m. *a Thessalian, the favorite minister of Pyrrhus.*

Cingo, cingĕre, cinxi, cinctum, tr. *to surround; to encompass; to encircle; to gird.*

Cinis, ĕris, d. *ashes; cinders.*

Cinna, æ, m. (L. Cornelius,) *a consul at Rome, in the time of the civil war.*

Cinnămum, i, n. *cinnamon.*

Circa & Circum, prep. & adv. *about; around; in the neighborhood of.*

Circuĭtus, ûs, m. (circumeo,) *a circuit; a circumference.*

Circumdătus, a, um, part. from

Circumdo, dăre, dĕdi, dătum, tr. (circum & do,) *to put around; to surround; to environ; to invest.*

Circumeo, īre, ii, ĭtum, intr. irr. (circum & eo, § 83, 3,) *to go round; to visit.*

Circumfluo, -fluĕre, -fluxi,-fluxum, intr. (circum & fluo,) *to flow round.*

Circumiens, euntis, part. (circumeo.)

Circumjaceo, ēre, ui, intr. (circum & jaceo,) *to lie around; to border upon.*

Circumsto, stāre, stĕti, intr. (circum & sto,) *to stand round.*

Circumvenio, -venīre, -vēni -ventum, tr. (circum & venio,) *to go round; to surround; to circumvent.*

Circumventus, a, um, part.

Ciris, is, f. *the name of the fish into which Scylla was changed.*

Cisalpīnus, a, um, adj. (cis & Alpes,) *Cisalpine; on this side of the Alps; that is, on the side nearest to Rome.*

Cithæron. ōnis, m. *a moun-*

tain of Bœotia, near Thebes, sacred to Bacchus.

Citò, adv. (iùs, issĭmè,) *quickly;* from

Citus, a, um, adj. (citus, part. cieo,) (ior, issĭmus,) *quick.*

Citra, prep. & adv. *on this side.*

Civĭcus, a, ŭm, adj, (civis,) *civic:* corōna civĭca, *a civic crown given to him who had saved the life of a citizen by killing an enemy.*

Civīlis, e, adj. (comp,) *of* or *belonging to a citizen; civil; courteous;* from

Civis, is, c. (cio, *or* cieo,) *a citizen.*

Civĭtas, ātis, f. (civis,) *a city; a state; the inhabitants of a city; the body of citizens; a constitution; citizenship; freedom of the city.*

Clades, is, f. *loss; damage; defeat; disaster; slaughter.*

Clam, prep. *without the knowledge of:*—adv. *privately; secretly.*

Clamo, āre, āvi, ātum, intr. & tr. *to cry out; to call on;* hence,

Clamor, ōris, m. *a clamor; a cry.*

Clandestīnus, a, um, adj. (clam,) *secret; clandestine.*

Clarĭtas, ātis, f. *celebrity; fame;* from

Clarus, a, um, adj. (ior, issĭmus,) *clear; famous; renowned; celebrated; loud.*

Classis, is, f. *a class; a fleet.*

Claudius, i, m. *the name of several Romans, belonging to the tribe hence called Claudian.*

Claudo, claudĕre, clausi, clausum, tr. *to close; to shut.*

Claudus, a, um, adj. *lame.*

Clausus, a, um, part. (claudo,) *shut up.*

Clavus, i, m. *a nail; a spike.*

Clemens, tis, adj. (ior, issĭmus,) *merciful;* hence,

Clementer, adv. (iùs, issĭmè,) *gently; kindly.*

Clementia, æ, f. (id.) *clemency; mildness.*

Cleopatra, æ, f. *an Egyptian queen celebrated for beauty.*

Cloāca, æ, f. *a drain; a common sewer.*

Clodius, i, m. *a Roman of illustrious family, remarkable for his licentiousness.*

Cluentius, i, m. *the name of several Romans.*

Clusium, i, n. *a city of Etruria.*

Clypeus, i, m. *a shield.*

Cneius, i, m. *a Roman* prænōmen; abbreviated Cn.

Coactus, a, um, part. (cogo,) *collected; assembled; compelled.*

Coccyx, ȳgis, m. *a cuckoo.*

Cocles, ĭtis, m. *a Roman distinguished for his bravery.*

Coctĭlis, e, adj. (coquo,) *baked; dried; burnt.*

Coctus, a, um, part. (coquo,) *baked; burnt; boiled.*

Cœlum, i, n. sing. m. pl. 96,

4, *heaven; the climate; the sky; the air; the atmosphere.*

Cœna, æ, f. *a supper.*

Cœpi, isse, def. § 84, Obs. 2, *I begin*, or *I began.*

Cœptus, a, um, part. *begun.*

Coërceo, ēre, ui, ĭtum, tr. (con & arceo,) *to surround; to restrain; to check; to control.*

Cogitatio, ōnis, f. (cogĭto,) *a thought; a reflection.*

Cogitātum, i, n. *a thought;* from

Cogĭto, āre, āvi, ātum, tr. (for coagĭto, con & agĭto,) *to revolve in the mind; to think; to consider; to meditate.*

Cognĭtus, a, um, part. (cognosco.)

Cognōmen, ĭnis, n. (con & nomen,) *a surname.* 887, 3.

Cognosco, -noscĕre, -nōvi, -nĭtum, tr. (con & nosco,) *to investigate;* hence, *to know; to learn:* de causâ, *to try or decide a suit at law.*

Cogo, cogĕre, coēgi, coactum, tr. (coĭgo, con & ago,) *to drive together; to drive; to compel; to force; to urge; to collect;* agmen, *to bring up the rear.*

Cohæreo, -hærēre, -hæsi, hæsum, intr. (con & hæreo,) *to stick together; to adhere; to be united; to be joined to.*

Cohibeo, -hibēre, -hibui, -hibĭtum, tr. (con & habeo,) *to hold together; to hold back; to restrain.*

Cohors, tis, f. *a cohort; the tenth part of a legion.*

Colchi, ōrum, m. *the people of Colchis.*

Colchis, ĭdis, f. *a country of Asia, east of the Euxine.*

Collābor, -lābi, -lapsus sum, intr. dep, (con & labor,) *to fall down; to fall together; to fall.*

Collāre, is, n. (collum,) *a collar; a necklace.*

Collatīnus, i, m. *a surname of Tarquinius, the husband of Lucretia.*

Collectus, a, um, part. (collĭgo.)

Collēga, æ, m. (con & lego, -āre,) *one who has charge along with another,* i. e. *a colleague.*

Collegium, i, n. (collēga,) *a college; a company.*

Collĭgo, -ligĕre, -lēgi, -lectum, tr. (con & lego,) *to collect.*

Collis, is, m. *a hill.*

Collocātus, a, um, part. from

Collōco, āre, āvi, ātum, tr. (con & loco,) *to place:* statuam, *to erect: to set up.*

Colloquium, i, n. *conversation; an interview;* from

Collōquor, -lōqui, -locūtus sum, intr. dep. (con & loquor,) *to speak together; to converse.*

Collum, i, n. *the neck.*

Colo, colĕre, colui, cultum, tr. *to care for; to cultivate; to exercise; to pursue; to practise; to respect; to re-*

gard; to venerate; to worship; to inhabit.

Colonia, æ, f. *a colony:* from

Colōnus, i, m. (colo,) *a colonist.*

Color, & Colos, ōris, m. *a color.*

Columba, æ, f. *a dove; a pigeon.*

Columbāre, is, n. *a dovecote.*

Columna, æ, f. (colŭmen, *a prop,*) *a pillar; a column.*

Combūro, -urĕre, -ussi, -ustum, tr. (con & uro, 80, 5,) *to burn up; to consume.*

Comedendus, a, um, part. from

Comĕdo, edĕre, ēdi, ēsum & estum, tr. (con & edo,) *to eat up; to devour.*

Comes, ĭtis, c. (con & eo,) *one who gives with another; a companion.*

Comētes, æ, m. *a comet;* 62.

Comissor, or Commissor, āri, ātus sum, intr. dep. *to revel as Bacchanalians; to riot; to banquet; to carouse.*

Comĭtans, tis, part. (comĭtor.)

Comitātus, a, um, part. from

Comĭtor, āri, ātus sum, tr. dep. (comes,) *to accompany; to attend; to follow.*

Commemŏro, āre, āvi, ātum, tr. (con & memŏro,) *to commemorate; to mention.*

Commendo, āre, āvi, ātum, tr. (con & mando,) *to commit to one's care; to commend; to recommend.*

Commeo, āre, āvi, ātum, intr. (con & meo,) *to go to and fro; to go and come; to pass.*

Commercium, i, n. (con & merx,) *commerce; exchange; traffic; intercourse.*

Commĭgro, āre, āvi, ātum, intr. (con & migro,) *to emigrate; to remove.*

Comminuo, -minuĕre, -minui, -minūtum, tr. (con & minuo,) *to dash or break in pieces; to crush; bruise.*

Comminūtus, a, um, part. *broken in pieces; diminished.*

Committo, -mittĕre, -mīsi, -missum, tr. (con & mitto,) *to bring* or *put together; to commit; to entrust; to begin:* pugnam, *to join battle; to commence* or *to fight a battle.*

Commissus, a, um, part. *intrusted; perpetrated; committed; commenced:* prœlium commissum, *a battle begun* or *fought:* copiis commissis, *forces being engaged.*

Commodĭtas, ātis, f. (commŏdus,) *aptness; fitness; a convenience; commodiousness.*

Commŏdum, i, n. (id.) *an advantage; gain.*

Commorior, -mŏri & -morīri, -mortuus sum, intr. dep. (con & morior,) *to die together.*

Commŏror, āri, ātus sum, intr. dep. (con & moror,)

to reside with; to stay at; to remain; to continue.

Commōtus, a, um, part. from

Commoveo, -movēre, -mōvi, -mōtum, tr. (con & moveo,) *to move together* or *wholly; to move; to excite; to stir up; to influence; to induce.*

Communĭco, āre, āvi, ātum, tr. *to communicate; to impart; to tell;* from

Commūnis, e, adj. (comp.) *common:* in commūne consulĕre, *to consult for the common good.*

Commūto, āre, āvi, ātum, tr. (con & muto,) *to change; to alter; to exchange.*

Comœdia, æ, f. *a comedy.*

Compăro, āre, āvi, ātum, tr. (con & paro,) *to prepare; to get together; to gain; to procure; to compare.*

Compello, -pellĕre, -pŭli, -pulsum, tr. (con & pello,) *to drive; to compel; to force;* in fugam, *to put to flight.*

Compenso, āre, āvi, ātum, tr. (con & penso,) *to weigh together; to compensate; to make amends for.*

Comperio, -perīre, -pĕri, -pertum, tr. (con & pario,) *to find out; to learn; to discover.*

Complector, -plecti, -plexus sum, tr. dep. (con & plector,) *to embrace; to comprise; to comprehend; to reach; to extend:* complecti amōre, *to love.*

Compōno, -ponĕre, -posui, -posĭtum, tr. (con & pono,) *to put together; to compose; to arrange; to construct; to finish; to compare;* hence,

Composĭtus, a, um, part. *finished; composed; quieted.*

Comprehendendus, a, um, fr.

Comprehendo, -prehendĕre, -prehendi, -prehensum, tr. (con & prehendo,) *to grasp* or *hold together; to comprehend; to seize; to apprehend.*

Comprehensus, a, um, part.

Compulsus, a, um, part. (compello.)

Conātus, a, um, part. (conor,) *having endeavored.*

Concēdo, -cedĕre, -cessi, -cessum, intr. & tr. (con & cedo,) *to step aside; to yield; to permit; to grant.*

Conceptus, a, um, part, (concipio,) *conceived; couched; expressed.*

Concessus, a, um, part. (concēdo.)

Concha, æ, f. *a shell fish.*

Conchyliŭm, i, n. *a shell-fish.*

Concilio, āre, āvi, ātum, tr. *to join together; to conciliate; to reconcile; to acquire for one's self; to gain; to obtain;* from

Concilium, i, n. *a council.*

Concio, ōnis, f. (concieo,) *an assembly; an assembly of the people.*

Concipio,-cipĕre,-cēpi,-ceptum, tr. (con & capio,) *to take together; to conceive; to imagine; to form; to draw up; to comprehend.*

Concīto, āre, āvi, ātum, tr. freq. (con & cito,) *to set in motion; to excite; to raise.*

Concītor, ōris, m. *one who excites; an exciter; a mover; a disturber.*

Concŏquo,-coquĕre, -coxi, -coctum, tr. (con & coquo,) *to boil; to digest.*

Concordia, æ, f. (concors,) *concord; agreement; harmony.*

Concrēdo, -credĕre, -credĭdi, -credĭtum, tr. (con & credo,) *to consign; to trust; to intrust.*

Concrĕmo, āre, āvi, ātum, tr. (con & cremo,) *to burn with; to burn; to consume.*

Concurro, -currĕre, -curri, -cursum, intr. (con & curro,) *to run together:* concurrĭtur, pass. imp. *a crowd assemble.* Id. 67, Note.

Concussus, a, um, part. *shaken; moved;* from

Concutio, cutĕre, cussi, cussum, tr. (con & quatio,) *to shake; to agitate; to tremble.*

Conditio, -ōnis, f. (condo,) *condition; situation; a proposal; terms.*

Condĭtus, a, um, part. from

Condo, -dĕre, -dĭdi, -dĭtum, tr. (con & do,) *to put together; to lay up; to found; to build; to make; to form; to hide; to bury; to conceal.*

Condūco, -ducĕre, -duxi, -ductum, tr. (con & duco,) *to lead together; to conduct; to hire.*

Confectus, a, um, part. (conficio.)

Confĕro, conferre, contŭli, collātum, tr. irr. (con & fero,) *to bring together; to heap up; to bestow; to give:* se conferre, *to betake one's self; to go.*

Conficio, -ficĕre, -fēci, -fectum, (con & facio, *to do thoroughly;*) *to make; to finish; to waste; to wear out; to terminate; to consume; to ruin; to destroy; to kill.*

Conflīgo, -fligĕre, -flixi,-flictum, (con & fligo,) *to strike or dash together; to contend; to engage; to fight;* (viz.: *in close combat.*) See dimĭco.

Conflo, āre, āvi, ātum, tr. (con & flo,) *to blow together; to melt; to unite; to compose.*

Confluo, -fluĕre, -fluxi, -fluxum, intr. (con & fluo,) *to flow together; to flock; to assemble.*

Confodio,-fodĕre, -fōdi, -fossum, tr. (con & fodio,) *to dig through and through; to pierce; to stab.*

Confossus, a, um, part. (confodio.)

Confugio, -fugĕre, -fūgi, -fugĭtum, intr. (con & fugio,) *to flee to; to flee for refuge; to flee.*

Congĕro, -gerĕre, -gessi, -gestum, tr. (con & gero,) *to*

bring together; to collect; to heap up.

Congredior, -grĕdi, -gressus sum, intr. dep. (con & gradior,) *to meet; to encounter; to engage; to fight.*

Congrĕgo, āre, āvi, ātum, tr. (con & grex,) *to assemble in flocks; to assemble.*

Conjectus, a, um, part. from

Conjicio, -jicĕre, -jēci, -jectum, tr. (con & jacio,) *to cast; to throw forcibly; to conjecture.*

Conjugium, i, n. (con & jugo,) *marriage.*

Conjungo, -jungĕre, -junxi, -junctum, tr. (con & jungo,) *to unite; to bind; to join.*

Conjurātus, a, um, part *conspired:* conjurāti, subs. *conspirators;* from

Conjūro, āre, āvi, ātum, tr. (con & juro,) *to swear together; to combine; to conspire:* conjurātum est, *a conspiracy was formed.*

Conjux, ŭgis, c. (con & jugo,) *a spouse; a husband* or *wife.*

Conor, āri, ātus sum, intr. dep. *to attempt; to venture; to endeavor; to strive.*

Conquĕror, quĕri, questus sum, intr. dep. (con & queror,) *to complain; to lament.*

Conscendo, -scendĕre, -scendi, -scensum, tr. (con & scando,) *to climb up; to ascend.*

Conscensus, a, um, part. (conscendo.)

Conscisco, -sciscĕre, -scīvi, -scītum, tr. (con & scisco,) *to investigate; to vote together; to agree; to decree; to execute;* sibi mortem consciscĕre, *to lay violent hands on one's self; to commit suicide.*

Consecro, āre, āvi, ātum, tr. (con & sacro,) *to consecrate; to dedicate; to devote.*

Consēdi. *See* Consīdo.

Consenesco, senescĕre, senui, intr. inc. (con & senesco,) *to grow old.*

Consentio, -sentīre, -sensi, -sensum, intr. (con & sentio,) *to think together; to agree; to consent; to unite.*

Consĕquor, -sĕqui, -secūtus sum, tr. dep. (con & sequor,) *to follow closely; to gain; to obtain.*

Consecūtus, a, um, part. *having obtained.*

Consĕro, -serĕre, -serui, -sertum, tr. (con & sero,) *to join; to put together:* pugnam, *to join battle; to fight.*

Conservandus, a, um, part. from

Conservo, āre, āvi, ātum, tr. (con & servo,) *to preserve; to maintain; to perpetuate.*

Consīdens, tis, part. from

Consīdo, -sidĕre, -sēdi, -sessum, intr. (con & sido,) *to sit down; to encamp; to take one's seat; to perch; to light.*

Consilium, i, n. (consŭlo,) *counsel; design; intention; a council; deliberation; ad-*

vice; a plan; judgment; discretion; prudence; wisdom.

Consisto, -sistĕre, -stĭti, intr. (con & sisto,) *to stand together; to stand; to consist.*

Consōlor, āri, ātus sum, tr. dep. (con & solor,) *to console; to comfort.*

Conspectus, a, um, part. (conspicio.)

Conspectus, ûs, m. (id.) *a seeing; a sight; a view.*

Conspicātus, a, um, part. (conspĭcor.)

Conspicio, -spicĕre, -spexi, -spectum, tr. (con & specio,) *to behold; to see.*

Conspĭcor, āri, ātus sum, tr. dep. (id.) *to behold; to see.*

Conspicuus, a, um, adj. (id.) *conspicuous; distinguished.*

Constans, tis, part. & adj. (comp.) *firm; constant; steady.*

Constituo, -stituĕre, -stitui, -stitūtum, tr. (con & statuo,) *to cause to stand,* i. e., *to place; to establish; to appoint; to resolve.*

Consto, -stāre, -stĭti, intr. (con & sto,) *to stand together; to consist of:* constat, imp. *it is certain; it is evident.*

Construo, -struĕre, -struxi, structum, tr. (con & struo,) *to pile together; to construct; to build; to compose; to form.*

Consuesco, -suescĕre, -suēvi, -suētum, intr. (con & suesco,) *to be accustomed:* hence,

Consuetūdo, ĭnis, f. *habit; custom.*

Consul, ŭlis, m. *a consul;* hence,

Consulāris, e, adj. *of* or *pertaining to the consul; consular:* vir consulāris, *one who has been a consul; a man of consular dignity.*

Consulātus, ûs, m. (consul,) *the consulship.*

Consŭlo, -sulĕre, -sului, -sultum, tr. *to advise; to consult.*

Consulto, āre, āvi, ātum, tr. & intr. freq. (consŭlo,) *to advise together; to consult.*

Consūmo, -sumĕre, -sumsi, -sumptum, tr. (con & sumo,) *to take together,* or *at once;* hence, *to consume; to wear out; to exhaust; to waste; to destroy; hence,*

Consumptus, a, um, part.

Contagiōsus, a, um, adj. comp. (contingo,) *contagious.*

Contemnendus, a, um, part. from

Contemno, -temnĕre, -tempsi, -temptum, tr. (con & temno,) *to despise; to reject with scorn.*

Contemplātus, a, um, part. *observing; regarding; considering;* from

Contemplor, āri, ātus sum, tr. dep. (con & templum, *a quarter in the heavens,*) *to look attentively at the heavens;* (said originally of the augurs; hence,) *to contemplate; to regard; to consider; to look at; to gaze upon.*

Contemptim, adv. *with contempt; contemptuously; scornfully;* from

Contemptus, a, um, part. (contemno.)

Contemptus, ûs, m. (id.) *contempt.*

Contendo, dĕre, di, tum, tr. & intr. (con & tendo, *to stretch,* or *draw,* or *strive together,* hence,) *to dispute; to fight; to contend; to go to; to direct one's course; to request;* hence,

Contentio, ōnis, f. *contention; a debate; a controversy; exertion; an effort; a strife.*

Contentus, a, um, adj, (comp.) *content; satisfied:* fr. contineo.

Contĕro, -terĕre, -trīvi, -trītum, tr. (con & tero,) *to break; to pound; to waste.*

Contĭnens, tis, part. & adj. (comp.) *holding together;* hence, *joining; continued; uninterrupted; temperate;* subs. f. *the continent,* or *main land:* from

Contineo, -tinēre, -tinui, -tentum, tr. (con & teneo,) *to hold together,* or *in; to contain.*

Contingo, -tingĕre, -tĭgi, -tactum, tr. (con & tango,) *to touch;* contĭgit, imp. *it happens:* mihi, *it happens to me; I have the fortune.*

Continuò, adv. *immediately; forthwith; in succession;* from

Continuus, a, um, adj. (contineo,) *continued; adjoining; incessant; uninterrupted; continual; without intermission; in close succession:* continuo alveo, *in one entire* or *undivided channel.*

Contra. prep. *against; opposite to:* adv. *on the other hand.*

Contractus, a, um, part. (contrăho.

Contradīco, -dicĕre, -dixi, -dictum, tr. (contra & dico,) *to speak against; to contradict; to oppose.*

Contradictus, a, um, part. *contradicted; opposed.*

Contrăho,-trahĕre, -traxi, -tractum, tr. (con & traho,) *to draw together; to contract; to assemble; to collect.*

Contrarius, a, um, adj, (contra,) *contrary; opposite.*

Contueor, -tuēri, -tuĭtus sum, tr. dep. (con & tueor,) *to regard; to behold; to view; to gaze upon; to survey.*

Contundo, -tundĕre, -tŭdi, -tūsum, tr. (con & tundo,) *to beat together; to beat; to bruise; to crush; to pulverize.*

Contūsus, a, um, part.

Convalesco, -valescĕre, -valui, intr. inc. (con & valesco, from valeo,) *to grow well; to recover.*

Convenio, -venīre, -vēni, -ventum, intr. (con & venio,) *to come together; to meet; to assemble.*

Converto, -vertĕre, -verti, -versum, tr. (con & verto,) *to turn; to resort to; to appropriate; to convert into; to change;* se in preces, *to turn one's self to entreating.*

Convicium, i, n. (con & vox,) *loud noise; scolding; reproach; abuse.*

Convivium, i, n. (con & vivo,) *a feast; a banquet; an entertainment.*

Convŏco, āre, āvi, ātum, tr. (con & voco,) *to call together; to assemble.*

Convolvo, -volvĕre, -volvi, -volūtum, tr. (con & volvo,) *to roll together;* pass. *to be rolled together:* se, *to roll one's self up.*

Coöperio, -perīre, -perui, -pertum, tr. (con & operio,) *to cover.*

Copia, æ, f. *an abundance; a multitude; a swarm:* copiæ, pl. *forces, troops.*

Copiōsè, adv. (iûs, issĭmè,) *copiously; abundantly:* from copiōsus, from copia.

Coquo, coquĕre, coxi, coctum, tr. *to cook; to bake; to boil; to roast;* hence,

Coquus, i, m. *a cook.*

Cor, cordis, n. *the heart.*

Coram, prep. *in the presence of; before:* adv. *openly.*

Corcy̆ra, æ, f. *an island on the coast of Epirus,* now *Corfu.*

Corinthius, a, um, adj. *Corinthian; belonging to Corinth.*

Corinthius, i, m. *a Corinthian.*

Corinthus, i, f. Corinth, *a city of Achaia, in Greece.*

Coriŏli, ōrum, m. pl. *a town of Latium.*

Coriolānus, i, m. *a distinguished Roman general.*

Corium, i, n. *the skin; the skin* or *hide of a beast; leather.*

Cornelia, æ, f. *a noble Roman lady.*

Cornelius, i, m. *the name of an illustrious tribe,* or *clan, at Rome,* adj. *Cornelian.*

Cornix, īcis, f. *a crow.*

Cornu, n. ind. in Sing. (91); *a horn.*

Corōna, æ, f. *a crown.*

Corpus, ŏris, n. *a body; a corpse.*

Correptus, a, um, part. (corripio.)

Corrĭgo, -rigĕre, -rexi, -rectum, tr. (con & rego,) *to set right; to straighten; to make better; to correct.*

Corripio, -ripĕre, -ripui, -reptum, tr. (con & rapio,) *to seize.*

Corrōdo, rodĕre, rōsi, rōsum, tr. (con & rodo,) *to gnaw; to corrode.*

Corrōsus, a, um, part. (corrōdo,)

Corrumpo, -rumpĕre, -rūpi, -ruptum, tr. (con & rumpo,) *to break up*, (or *thoroughly;*) *to corrupt; to bribe; to hurt; to violate; to seduce; to impair; to destroy.*

Corruo, -ruĕre, -rui, intr. (con & ruo,) *to fall down; to decay.*

Corruptus, a, um, part. & adj. (corrumpo,) *bribed; vitiated; foul; corrupt.*

Çorsĭca, æ, f. *an island in the Mediterranean sea, north of Sardinia.*

Corvīnus, i, m. *a surname given to M. Valerius, from an incident in his life;* from

Corvus, i, m. *a raven.*

Corycius, a, um, adj. *Corycian; of Corycus.*

Corȳcus, i, m. *the name of a city and mountain of Cilicia.*

Cos., *an abbreviation of* consul; Coss., *of* consŭles; Gr. 891.

Cotta, æ, m. *a Roman* cognōmen, *belonging to the Aurelian tribe.*

Crater, ēris, m. *a goblet; a crater; the mouth of a volcano.*

Crates, ētis, m. *a Theban philosopher.*

Crassus, i, m. *the name of a Roman family of the Lucinian tribe.*

Creātus, a, um, part. (creo.)

Creber, crebra, crebrum, adj. (crebrior, creberrĭmus,) *frequent.*

Crebrò, adv. (crebriùs, creberrĭmè,) (creber,) *frequently.*

Credo, -dĕre, -dĭdi, -dĭtum, tr. *to believe; to trust.*

Credŭlus, a, um, adj. (credo,) *easy of belief; credulous.*

Cremĕra, æ, f. *a river of Etruria, near which the Fabian family were defeated and destroyed.*

Cremo, āre, āvi, ātum, tr. *to burn; to consume.*

Creo, āre, āvi, ātum, tr. *to make; to choose; to elect.*

Cresco, crescĕre, crevi, cretum, intr. (creo,) *to spring up; to increase; to grow.*

Creta, æ, f. *Crete*, now *Candia, an island in the Mediterranean sea, south of the Cyclădes.*

Cretensis, e, adj. *belonging to Crete; Cretan.*

Crevi. *See* Cresco.

Crimen, ĭnis, n. *a crime; a fault; an accusation:* alĭcui crimĭni dare, *to charge as a crime against one.*

Crinis, is, m. *the hair.*

Crixus, i, m. *the name of a celebrated gladiator.*

Crocodīlus, i, m. *a crocodile.*

Cruciātus, a, um, part. (crucio.)

Cruciātus, ûs, m. (id.) *torture; distress; trouble; affliction.*

Crucio, āre, āvi, ātum, tr. (crux,) *to crucify; to torment; to torture.*

Crudēlis, e, adj. (ior, issĭmus,) *cruel;* (fr. crudus,) hence,

Crudelĭter, adv. (iùs, issĭmè,) *cruelly*.

Crudus, a, um, adj. (cruor,) properly, *full of blood; crude; raw; unripe*.

Cruor, ōris, m. *blood; gore*.

Crus, cruris, n. *the leg; (from the knee to the ankle.)*

Crux, crucis, f. *a cross*.

Cubĭtus, i, m., & Cubĭtum, i, n. (cubo, *to recline*,) *the arm, from the elbow to the wrist; a cubit*.

Cucurri. *See* Curro.

Cui, & Cujus. *See* Qui, & Quis.

Culex, ĭcis, m. *a gnat*.

Culpa, æ. f. *a fault; guilt; blame;* hence,

Culpo, āre, āvi, ātum, tr. *to blame*.

Cultellus, i, m. (dim. from culter,) *a little knife; a knife*.

Cultus, a, um, part. (colo,) *cultivated; improved; dressed*.

Cum, prep. *with:* adv. the same as quum, *when:* cùm—tum, *not only—but also; as well—as also*.

Cunctatio, ōnis, f. (cunctor,) *delaying; a delaying; hesitation*.

Cunctus, a, um, adj. *all; the whole*.

Cunicŭlus, i, m. *a rabbit; a cony*.

Cupidĭtas, ātis, f. (cupio,) *a wish; a desire; cupidity;* (with moderation.)

Cupīdo, ĭnis, f. *desire;* (with eagerness.)

Cupĭdus, a, um, adj. comp. (id.) *desirous*.

Cupiens, tis, part. from

Cupio, ĕre, īvi, ītum, tr. *to desire; to wish; to long for*.

Cur., adv. (abbreviated for quare,) *why; wherefore*.

Cura, æ, f. *care; anxiety*.

Cures, ium, f. pl. *a city of the Sabines*.

Curia, æ, f. *a curia* or *ward; one of thirty parts into which the Roman people were divided; the senate house*.

Curiatii, ōrum, m. pl. *the name of an Alban tribe. Three brothers belonging to this tribe fought with the Horatii*.

Curo, āre, āvi, ātum, tr. (cura,) *to take care of; to care; to be concerned; to cure* or *heal*.

Curro, currĕre, cucurri, cursum, intr. *to run;* hence,

Currus, ûs, m. *a chariot:* and

Cursor, ōris, m. (curro,) *a runner;* also *a surname given to L. Papirius*.

Cursus, ûs, (id.) *a running; a course*.

Curvus, a, um, adj. *crooked*.

Custodia, æ, f. (custos,) *a watch; a guard; a prison*.

Custodio, īre, īvi, ītum, tr. (id.) *to guard; to watch; to preserve; to keep safely*.

Custos, ōdis, c. *a guard; a keeper*.

Cutis, is, f. *the skin*.

Cyaneus, a. um, adj. *dark blue*.

Cyclădes, um, f. pl. *a cluster of islands in the Archipela-*

go, which derive their name from lying in a circle.

Cyclōpes, um, m. pl. *the Cyclops, giants of Sicily, living near Ætna.*

Cydnus, i, m. *a river of Cilicia.*

Cyllēne, es, f. *a mountain in Arcadia.*

Cymba, æ, f. *a boat; a skiff; a canoe.*

Cymbălum, i, n. *a cymbal.*

Cynĭcus, i. m. *a Cynic. The Cynics were a sect of philosophers founded by Antisthĕnes.*

Cynocephălæ, ārum, f. pl. *small hills near Scotussa in Thessaly.*

Cynocephăli, ōrum, m. pl. *a people of India with heads like dogs.*

Cynocephălus, i, m. *an Egyptian deity.*

Cynossēma, ătis, n. *a promontory of Thrace, near Sestos, where queen Hecŭba was buried.*

Cynthus, i, m. *a hill near the town of Delos.*

Cyrēnæ, ārum, f. pl. *Cyrene, a city of Africa, the capital of Cyrenaica.*

Cyrenaĭca, æ, f. *a country in the northern part of Africa, so called from its capital, Cyrēnæ.*

Cyrenæus, a, um, adj. *Cyrenean; belonging to Cyrēnæ.*

Cyrenensis, e, adj. *Cyrenean; of Cyrēnæ.*

Cyrnus, i. f. *a Greek name of the island of Corsica.*

Cyrus, i, m. *Cyrus, the name of a Persian king.*

Cyzĭcus, i, f. *the name of an island near Mysia, containing a town of the same name.*

D.

Dædălus, i, m. *an ingenious Athenian artist, the son of Euphēmus.*

Damno, āre, āvi, ātum, tr. (damnum, *loss,*) *to adjudge to loss of any kind; to condemn.*

Damnōsus, a, um, adj. *injurious; hurtful.*

Danăus, i, m. *an ancient king of Argos, and brother of Ægyptus.*

Dandus, a, um, part. (do.)

Dans, tis, part. (do.)

Danubius, i, m. *the Danube, a large river of Germany, called also the Ister, after its entrance into Illyricum.*

Daps, dapis, f. *a feast; a meal.*

Dardania, æ, f. *a country and city of Asia Minor, near the Hellespont.*

Datūrus, a, um, part. (do.)

Datus, a, um, part. (do.)

De, prep. *from; of; concerning; on account of.*

Dea, æ, f. 61, 4, *a goddess.*

Debello, āre, āvi, ātum, tr. (de

& bello,) *to put down by war;* hence, *to conquer; to subdue.*

Debeo, ēre, ui, ĭtum, tr. (de & habeo,) *to owe; to be obliged;* with an infinitive, *ought,* or *should.*

Debeor, ēri, ĭtus sum, pass. *to be due.*

Debilĭto, āre, āvi, ātum, tr. (debĭlis,) *to weaken; to enfeeble.*

Debĭtus, a, um, part. (debeo,) *due; deserved; owing.*

Decēdo, -cedĕre, -cessi, -cessum, intr. (de & cedo,) *to depart; to retire; to withdraw; to yield; to die.*

Decem, num. adj. *ten.*

Decemvĭri, ōrum, m. pl. *decemvirs, ten men appointed to prepare a code of laws for the Romans, and by whom the laws of the twelve tables were formed.*

Decerno, -cernĕre, -crēvi, crētum, tr. (de & cerno,) *to separate one thing from another; to judge; to decide; to fight; to contend; to discern; to decree:* bellum decrētum est, *the management of the war was decreed.*

Decerpo,-cerpĕre,-cerpsi,-cerptum, tr. (de & carpo,) *to pluck off; to pick; to gather.*

Decĭdo, -cidĕre, -cĭdi, intr. (de & cado,) *to fall,* (viz: *from* or *down:*) dentes decĭdunt, *the teeth fail,* or *come out.*

Decĭmus, a, um, num. adj. ord. (decem,) *the tenth.*

Decius, i, m. *the name of several Romans distinguished for their patriotism.*

Declāro, āre, āvi, ātum, tr. (de & claro, *to make clear;*) *to declare; to show.*

Decoctus, a, um, part. from

Decŏquo, -coquĕre, -coxi, -coctum, tr. (de & coquo,) *to boil down; to boil.*

Decōrus, a, um, adj. (decor,) *becoming; handsome; adorned; decorous; beautiful.*

Decrētus, a, um, part. (decerno.)

Decresco, -crescĕre, -crēvi, intr. (de & cresco,) *to sink down,* or *subside; to decrease; to diminish; to fall to decay.*

Decumbo, -cumbĕre, -cubui, intr. (de & cubo) *to lie down.*

Decurro, -currĕre, -curri, -cursum, intr. (de & curro,) *to run down; to flow down.*

Decus, ŏris, n. (deceo,) *an ornament.*

Dedi. *See* Do.

Dedĭdi. *See* Dedo.

Deditio, ōnis, f. (dedo,) *a giving up; a surrender.*

Dedĭtus, a, um, part. (dedo.)

Dedo, dedĕre, dedĭdi, dedĭtum, tr. (de & do,) *to give up; to surrender; to deliver up; to addict* or *devote one's self.*

Dedūco, -ducĕre, -duxi, -ductum, tr. (de & duco,) *to lead* or *draw downwards; to lead forth; to bring; to lead.*

Defatīgo, āre, āvi, ātum, tr. (de & fatīgo,) *to weary out; to fatigue.*

Defendo, -fendĕre, -fendi, -fensum, tr. (de & fendo, obsol, *to hit;*) *to defend; to protect.*

Defensus, a, um, part. (defendo.)

Defĕro, -ferre, -tŭli, -lātum, tr. irr. (de & fero,) *to bring,* (viz: *down,* or *along;*) *to convey; to proffer; to confer; to give.*

Deficiens, tis, part. from

Deficio, -ficĕre, -fēci, -fectum, tr. & intr. (de & facio,) *to fail; to abandon; to be wanting; to decrease; to be eclipsed; to revolt.*

Defleo, ēre, ēvi, ētum, (de & fleo,) *to deplore; to bewail; to lament; to weep for.*

Defluo, -fluĕre, -fluxi, -fluxum, intr. (de & fluo,) *to flow down.*

Defodio, -fodĕre, -fōdi, -fossum, tr. (de & fodio, *to dig down;*) *to bury; to inter.*

Deformĭtas, ātis, f. (deformis,) *deformity; ugliness.*

Defossus, a, um, part. (defodio.)

Defunctus, a, um, part. *finished:* defunctus *or* defunctus vitâ, *dead;* from

Defungor, -fungi, -functus sum, intr. dep. (de & fungor,) *to execute; to perform; to be free from; to finish.*

Degens, tis, part. from

Dego, degĕre, degi, tr. & intr. (de & ago,) *to lead; to live; to dwell:* degĕre ætātem, *to live.*

Degusto, āre, āvi, ātum, tr. (de & gusto,) *to taste.*

Deinde, adv. (de & inde,) *then; further; after that; next.*

Deiotărus, i, m. *a man who was made king of Galatia, by the Roman senate, by the favor of Pompey.*

Dejectus, a, um, part. from

Dejicio, -jicĕre, -jēci, -jectum, tr. (de & jacio,) *to throw,* or *cast down.*

Delābor, -lābi, lapsus sum, intr. dep. (de & labor,) *to fall; to glide down; to flow.*

Delātus, a, um, part. (defĕro,) *carried down; conferred.*

Delecto, āre, āvi, ātum, tr. (de & lacto,) *to allure; to delight; to please.*

Delectus, a, um, part. (delĭgo.)

Delendus, a, um, part. *to be destroyed;* from

Deleo, ēre, ēvi, ētum, tr. (de & leo, *to daub;*) *to extinguish; to destroy.*

Deliciæ, ārum, f. pl. (delicio,) *delights; diversions; pleasures.*

Delictum, i, n. (delinquo,) *a neglect of duty; a fault; crime.*

Delĭgo, -ligĕre, -lēgi, -lectum, tr. (de & lego,) *to select; to choose.*

Delinquo, -linquĕre, -līqui, -lictum, tr. (de & linquo,) *to fail in duty; to offend; to do wrong.*

Delphĭcus, a, um, adj. *Delphic, belonging to Delphi.*

Delphi, ōrum, m. pl. *a town of Phocis, famous for the temple and oracle of Apollo.*

Delphīnus, i, m. *a dolphin.*

Delta, æ, f. *a part of Egypt, so called from its resemblance to the Greek letter delta, Δ.*

Delūbrum, i, n. (deluo, *to purify;*) *a temple; a shrine.*

Delus *or* os, i, f. *an island in the Ægean sea; the birth place of Apollo and Diana.*

Demarātus, i, m. *a Corinthian, father of the elder Tarquin.*

Demergo, -mergĕre; -mersi, -mersum, tr. (de & mergo,) *to plunge; to sink.*

Demersus, a, um, part.

Demetrius, i, m. *a Greek proper name.*

Demissus, a, um, part. *cast down; descending;* from

Demitto,- mittĕre, -mīsi, -missum, tr. (de & mitto,) *to send down; to let down; to drop.*

Democrĭtus, i, m. *a Grecian philosopher, born at Abdēra.*

Demonstro, āre, āvi, ātum, tr. (de & monstro,) *to point out; to show; to demonstrate; to prove.*

Demosthĕnes, is, m. *the most celebrated of the Athenian orators.*

Demum, adv. *at length; not till then; at last; only; in fine.*

Deni, æ, a, dis. num. adj. pl. *every ten; ten; by tens.*

Denĭque, adv. *finally; at last.*

Dens, tis, m. *a tooth.*

Densus, a, um, adj. (comp.) *thick.*

Dentātus, i, m. (Siccius,) *a brave Roman soldier.*

Denuntio *or* -cio, āre, āvi, ātum, tr. (de & nuntio,) prop. *to make known; to foreshow; to proclaim; to declare; to denounce.*

Depascor, -pasci, -pastus sum, tr. dep. (de & pascor,) *to feed upon; to eat up; to feed.*

Depingo, -pingĕre, -pinxi, -pictum, tr. (de & pingo,) *to paint; to depict; to describe; to exhibit.*

Deplōro, āre, āvi, ātum, tr. (de & ploro,) *to deplore; to weep for; to mourn.*

Depōno, -ponĕre, -posui, -posĭtum, tr. (de & pono,) *to lay down* or *aside.*

Depopulātus, a, um, part. from

Depopŭlor, āri, ātus sum, tr. dep. (de & popŭlus,) *to lay waste.*

Deporto, āre, āvi, ātum, tr. (de & porto,) *to carry down.*

Deprehendo, -prehendĕre,-prehendi, -prehensum, tr. (de & prehendo,) *to seize; to catch; to detect.*

Deprehensus, a, um, part.

Depulso, āre, āvi, ātum, tr.

freq. (de & pulso,) *to push away; to keep off; to repel.*

Descendo, -scendĕre, -scendi, -scensum, intr. (de & scando,) *to descend:* in certāmen descendĕre, *to engage in a contest:* descendĭtur imp. *one descends; we descend;* Id. 76, Note.

Descrībo, -scribĕre, -scripsi, scriptum, tr. (de & scribo,) prop. *to write down; to describe; to divide; to order.*

Desĕro, -serĕre, -serui, -sertum, tr. (de & sero,) *to desert; to forsake; to abandon:* (opposite of sero, 238, 3.)

Desertum, i, n. *a desert;* from

Desertus, a, um, part. & adj. (comp.) *deserted; waste; desolate; desert.*

Desiderium, i, n. (desidĕro, *to desire:*) *a longing for; a desire; love; affection; regret; grief.*

Desĭno, sinĕre, sĭvi, and sii sĭtum, intr. (de & sino,) *to leave off; to terminate; to cease; to end; to renounce.* *Note*—An acc. after this verb is governed by an infinitive understood.

Desperātus, a, um, part. & adj. comp. *despaired of; past hope; desperate; hopeless:* from

Despēro, āre, āvi, ātum, tr. (de & spero,) *to despair:* Gr. 238, 3.

Desponsātus, a, um, part. from

Desponso, āre, āvi, ātum, tr. freq. (despondeo,) *to promise in marriage; to betroth; to affiance.*

Destĭno, āre, āvi, ātum, tr. prop. *to fix; to destine; to appoint; to resolve; to aim at.*

Desum, -esse, -fui, -intr. irr. (de & sum,) *to be wanting;* 238, 3.

Deterior, adj. compar. (sup. deterrĭmus, § 26, 4,) *worse.*

Deterreo, ēre, ui, ĭtum, tr. (de & terreo,) *to frighten from; to deter.*

Detestor, āri, ātus sum, tr. dep. (de & testor,) *to call to witness; to wish (as a curse): to deprecate; to detest.*

Detractus, a, um, part. from

Detrăho, -trahĕre, -traxi, -tractum, tr. (de & traho,) *to draw down* or *away; to draw off; to take from.*

Detrimentum, i, n. (detĕro,) *detriment; damage; harm; loss.*

Deus, i, m. *God; a god.*

Devĕho, -vehĕre, -vexi, -vectum, tr. (de & veho,) *to carry down,* or *away.*

Devexus, a, um, adj. *sloping; inclining.*

Devictus, a, um, part. from

Devinco, -vincĕre, -vīci, -victum, tr. (de & vinco,) *to conquer; to subdue; to overcome.*

Devŏlo, āre, āvi, ātum, intr. (de & volo,) *to fly down; to fly away.*

Devŏro, āre, āvi, ātum, tr. (de & voro,) *to devour; to eat up.*

Devōtus, a, um, part. from

Devoveo, -vovēre, -vōvi, -vōtum, tr. (de & voveo,) *to vow; to devote; to consecrate.*

Dexter, ĕra, ĕrum, *or* ra, rum, § 20, 3, adj. *right; on the right hand.* See §26, 2.

Dextra, æ, f. *the right hand.*

Diadēma, ătis, n. *a diadem; a white fillet worn upon the heads of kings.*

Diagŏras, æ, m. *a Rhodian who died of excessive joy, because his three sons were victorious at the Olympic games.*

Diāna, æ, f. *the daughter of Jupiter and Latōna, and sister of Apollo.*

Dĭco, āre, āvi, ātum, tr. *to consecrate; to dedicate;* from

Dīco, dicĕre, dixi, dictum, tr. *to say; to name; to call.*

Dictātor, ōris, m. *a dictator; a chief magistrate, elected on special occasions, and vested with absolute authority;* from

Dicto, āre, āvi, ātum, freq. *to say often; to dictate.*

Dictum, i, n, (dico,) *a word; an expression.*

Dictus, a, um, part. (dico.)

Dies, ēi, m. *or* f. in sing., m. in pl., *a day;* in dies, *daily; every day.*

Diffĕrens, tis, adj. *different; differing;* from

Diffĕro, differre, distŭli, dilātum, tr. & intr. irr. (dis & fero,) *to carry apart,* or *in different directions; to carry up and down; to scatter; to disperse; to spread abroad; to publish; to defer; to be different.*

Difficĭlè, adv. (iùs, lĭmè,) *difficultly; with difficulty;* from

Difficĭlis, e, adj. comp. (dis & facĭlis,) *difficult;* 239, Obs. 1, hence,

Difficultas, ātis, f. *difficulty; trouble; poverty.*

Digĭtus, i, m. *a finger; a finger's breadth.*

Dignātus, a, um, part. (dignor,) *vouchsafing; thought worthy.*

Dignĭtas, ātis, f. (dignus,) *dignity; office; honor.*

Dignor, āri, ātus sum, tr. dep. *to think worthy; to vouchsafe; to deign;* from

Dignus, a, um, adj. (ior, issĭmus,) *worthy.*

Dilanio, āre, āvi, ātum, tr. (dis & lanio,) *to tear* or *rend in pieces.*

Diligenter, adv. (iùs issĭmè,) *diligently; carefully;* fr. diligens.

Dilĭgo, -ligĕre, -lexi, -lectum, tr. (dis & lego,) *to select carefully; to esteem a thing for its value;* hence, *to love.* *See* amo.

Dimicatio, ōnis, f. *a fight; a contest; a battle;* from

Dimĭco, āre, āvi, (*or* ui,) ātum, intr. (dis & mico, *to glitter,*) *to fight:* viz., with swords gleaming: dimicātum est, *a battle was fought.*

Dimissus, a, um, part. from

Dimitto, -mittĕre, -mīsi, -missum, tr. (dis & mitto,) *to send away; to dismiss; to let go.*

Diogĕnes, is, m. *an eminent Cynic philosopher, born at Sinōpe, a city of Asia Minor.*

Diomēdes, is, m. *a Grecian warrior;* also, *a cruel king of Thrace.*

Dionysius, i, m. *the name of two tyrants of Syracuse.*

Diremptūrus, a, um, part. (dirĭmo,) *about to decide.*

Direptus, a, um, part. (diripio.)

Dirĭmo, -imĕre, -ēmi, -emptum, tr. (dis & emo,) properly, *to take one thing from another; to divide; to part; to separate; to decide.*

Diripio, -ripĕre, -ripui, -reptum, tr. (dis & rapio,) *to tear asunder; to rob; to plunder; to pillage; to destroy.*

Diruo, -ruĕre, -rui, -rŭtum, tr. (dis & ruo,) *to pull down; to overthrow; to raze; to destroy.*

Dirus, a, um, adj. *frightful; terrible; direful; ominous.*

Dirŭtus, a, um, part. (diruo.)

Discēdo, -cedĕre, -cessi, -cessum, intr. (dis & cedo,) *to go away; to depart.*

Discerpo, -cerpĕre, -cerpsi, cerptum, tr. (dis & carpo,) *to tear asunder,* or *in pieces.*

Discerptus, a, um, part. (discerpo.)

Discipŭlus, i, m. (disco,) *a pupil; a scholar.*

Disco, discĕre, didĭci, tr. *to learn.*

Discordia, æ, f. (discors, dis & cor,) *discord; disagreement; the Goddess Discord.*

Discordo, āre, āvi, ātum, intr. (id,) *to differ in feeling; to be at variance; to differ.*

Discrĕpo, āre, āvi, *or* ui, ĭtum, intr. (dis & crepo,) *to differ in sound; to differ; to disagree.*

Disertè, adv. (iùs, issĭmè,) *clearly; eloquently.*

Disputatio, ōnis, f. *a dispute; a discourse; a discussion;* from

Dispūto, āre, āvi, ātum, tr. (dis & puto,) *to be of opposite sentiments;* hence, *to dispute; to discuss; to discourse.*

Dissemĭno, āre, āvi, ātum, tr. (dis & semĭno,) *to spread abroad; to scatter; to promulgate.*

Dissĕro, -serĕre, -serui, -sertum, tr. (dis & sero, *to plait;*) *to unplait;* 239, *to disentangle;* hence, *to explain; to discourse; to reason; to debate; to say.*

Dissidium, i, n. (dissideo,) *a disagreement; a dissension.*

Dissimĭlis, e, adj. (comp. § 26, 1,) *unlike; dissimilar;* fr. dis & similis.

Distans, tis, part. (disto,) *standing asunder; differing; distant; being divided.*

Distinguo, -stinguĕre, -stinxi, stinctum, tr. (di & stinguo,) *to distinguish,* (viz: *by marks;*) *to mark; to adorn; to variegate; to spot; to sprinkle.*

Disto, stāre, intr. (di & sto,) intr. *to stand apart; to be distant; to be divided; to differ.*

Distribuo,-tribuĕre, -tribui, -tribūtum, (dis & trĭbuo,) *to distribute; to divide.*

Ditis, e, adj. (ior, issĭmus,) *rich.*

Diu, adv. (utiùs, utissĭmè,) (dies,) *long; for a long time.*

Diurnus, a, um, adj. (id.) *daily.*

Diutĭnus, a, um, adj. (diu,) *continual; long continued.*

Diuturnĭtas, ātis, f. *long continuance; duration;* from

Diuturnus; a, um, adj. (diu,) *long; lasting;* ior, §26, 6.

Divello, -vellĕre, -velli, *or* vulsi,-vulsum, tr. (di & vello,) *to pull asunder; to separate; to disjoin; to tear off.*

Diversus, a, um, adj. part. (fr. diverto,) *turned different ways; different.*

Dives, ĭtis, adj. *rich; wealthly; fertile; fruitful.*

Divĭdo, dividĕre, divīsi, divīsum, tr. (di & ĭduo, obsol. *to divide;*) *to divide; to separate; to distribute.*

Divīnus, a, um. adj. (comp.) *divine; heavenly;* fr. divus.

Divīsus, a, um, part. (divĭdo.)

Divitiæ, ārum, f. pl. (divès,) *riches; wealth.*

Divulsus, a, um, part. (divello.)

Do, dăre, dĕdi, dătum, tr. *to give; to grant; to surrender:* pœnas, *to suffer punishment:* crimĭni, *to impute as a crime; to accuse:* finem, *to terminate:* nomen, *to give name.*

Doceo, ēre, ui, tum, tr. *to teach.*

Docilĭtas, ātis, f. (doceo,) *docility; teachableness.*

Doctrīna, æ, f. (doceo,) *instruction; education; doctrine.*

Doctus, a, um, part. & adj. comp. (doceo,) *taught; learned.*

Dodōna, æ, f. *a town and forest of Epīrus, where were a temple and oracle of Jupiter.*

Doleo, ēre, ui, intr. *to grieve; to sorrow; to be in pain.*

Dolor, ōris, m. (doleo,) *pain; sorrow; grief.*

Dolus, i, m. *a device; a trick; a stratagem; guile; artifice.*

Domestĭcus, a, um, adj. (domus,) *domestic.*

Domicilium, i, n. (id.) *a habitation; a house; an abode.*

Domĭna, æ, f. (domĭnus,) *a mistress.*

Dominatio, ōnis, f. *government, absolute power; dominion; usurpation; despotism:* from

Domĭnus, i, m. (domus,) *master; owner; lord.*

Domĭtus, a, um, part. from

Domo, āre, ui, ĭtum, tr. *to subdue; to tame; to overpower; to conquer; to vanquish.*

Domus, ûs, & i, f. 93, 5, *a house:* domi, *at home:* domo, *from home:* domum, *home.*

Donec, adv. *until; as long as.*

Dono, āre, āvi, ātum, tr. (donum,) *to give freely; to present.*

Donum, i, n. (do,) *a free gift; an offering; a present.*

Dormio, īre, īvi, ītum, intr. *to sleep.*

Dorsum, i, n. *the back.*

Dos, dotis, f. *a portion; a dowry.*

Draco, ōnis, m. *a dragon; a species of serpent.*

Druĭdæ, ārum, m. pl. *Druids, priests of the ancient Britons and Gauls.*

Dubitatio, ōnis, f. *a doubt; hesitation; question:* from

Dubĭto, āre, āvi, ātum, intr. (dubius,) *to hesitate; to doubt.*

Ducenti, æ, a, num. adj. pl *two hundred.*

Duco, cĕre, xi, ctum, tr. *to lead; to conduct:* uxōrem, *to take a wife; to marry:* exequias, *to perform funeral rites:* murum, *to build a wall.*

Ductus, a, um, part. *led.*

Duillius, i, m. (Caius,) *a Roman commander, who first conquered the Carthaginians in a naval engagement.*

Dulcis, e, adj. (ior, issĭmus,) *sweet; pleasant.*

Dum, adv. & conj. *while; whilst; as long as; until.*

Duo, æ, o. num. adj. pl. 104, 3, *two.*

Duodĕcim, num. adj. ind. pl. (duo & decem,) *twelve;* hence,

Duodecĭmus, a, um, num. adj. ord. *the twelfth.*

Duodeviginti, num. adj. ind. pl. (duo, de & viginti, 104, 1,) *eighteen.*

Duritia, æ, & Durities, ēi, f. *hardness;* from

Durus, a, um, adj. (ior, issĭmus,) *hard; severe; harsh; unfavorable.*

Dux, cis, c (duco,) *a leader; a guide; a commander.*

E.

E, ex, prep. *out of; from; of; among.*

Ea. *See* Is.

Ebĭbo, -bibĕre, -bĭbi, -bibĭtum, tr. (e & bibo,) *to drink up.*

Ebriĕtas, ātis, f. (ebrius,) *drunkenness.*

Ebur, ŏris, n. *ivory.*

Ecce, int. *See! lo! behold!*

Edīco, -dicĕre, -dixi, -dictum, tr. (e & dico,) *to proclaim; to announce; to publish; to order.*

Edīdi. *See* Edo.

Edītus, a, um, part. *published; uttered; produced;* from

Edo, -dĕre, -dīdi, -dĭtum, tr. (e & do,) *to give out; to publish; to cause; to occasion; to produce; to make:* spectacŭlum edĕre, *to give an exhibition.*

Edo, edĕre *or* esse, edi, esum, tr. irr. § 83, 9, *to eat; to consume.*

Educātus, a, um, part. from

Edŭco, āre, āvi, ātum, tr. (e & duco,) *to bring up; to educate; to instruct.*

Edūco, -ducĕre, -duxi, -ductum, tr. (e & duco,) *to lead forth; to bring forth; to produce; to draw out.*

Efficio, -ficĕre, -fēci, -fectum, tr. (e & facio,) *to effect; to make; to form; to cause; to accomplish.*

Effigies, iēi, f. (effingo,) *an image; an effigy.*

Efflo, āre, āvi, ātum, tr. (e & flo,) *to breathe out:* anĭmam, *to die; to expire.*

Effugio, -fugĕre, -fūgi, -fugĭtum, tr. & intr. (e & fugio,) *to fly from; to escape; to flee.*

Effundo, -fundĕre, -fūdi, -fūsum, tr. (e & fundo,) *to pour out; to spill; to discharge; to waste; to overflow; to extend* or *spread.*

Effūsus, a, um, part. *poured out; wasted.*

Egeria, æ, f. *a nymph of the Aricinian grove, and from whom Numa professed to receive instructions respecting religious rites.*

Egĕro, -gerĕre, -gessi, -gestum, tr. (e & gero,) *to carry out; to cast forth; to throw out.*

Egestus, a, um, part.

Egi. *See* Ago.

Ego, mei, subs. pro. *I;* 117.

Egredior, -grĕdi, -gressus sum, intr. dep. (e & gradior,) *to go out; to overflow; to go beyond.*

Egregiè, adv. *in a distinguished manner; excellently; famously;* from

Egregius, a, um, adj. (e & grex,) properly, *chosen from the flock;* hence, *distinguished; eminent; choice.*

Egressus, a, um, part. (egredior.)

Ejusmŏdi, pro. (genitive of is & modus,) *such; such like; of the same sort.*

Elābor, -lābi, -lapsus sum, intr. dep. (e & labor,) *to glide away; to escape.*

Elapsus, a, um, part. *having passed.*

Elephantis, ĭdis, f. *an island and city in the southern part of Egypt.*

Elephantus, i, & Elĕphas, antis, m. *an elephant.*

Eleusinii, ōrum, m. pl. *the Eleusinians; the inhabitants of Eleusis.*

Eleusis & -in, īnis, f. *a town of Attĭca, sacred to Ceres.*

Elīdo, -lidĕre, -līsi, -līsum, tr. (e & lædo,) *to strike out; to dash in pieces; to crush.*

Elĭgo, -ligĕre, -lēgi, -lectum, tr. (e & lego,) *to pick out; to choose; to select.*

Elŏquens, tis, adj. (ior, issĭmus,) (elŏquor,) *eloquent.*

Eloquentia, æ, f. (id.) *eloquence.*

Elŏquor, -lŏqui, -locūtus sum, tr. dep. (e & loquor,) *to speak out; to say; to declare; to tell.*

Eluceo, -lucēre, -luxi, intr. (e & luceo,) *to shine forth.*

Emergo,-mergĕre,-mersi,-mersum, intr. (e & mergo,) *to emerge; to come out; to rise up.*

Emineo, ēre, ui, intr. (e & mineo, obsol. *to stand,* or *appear above;* hence,) *to be eminent; to rise above; to be conspicuous; to be distinguished; to appear.*

Emitto, -mittĕre, -mīsi, -missum, tr. (e & mitto,) *to send forth; to discharge.*

Emo, emĕre, emi, emptum, tr. primarily, *to take:* commonly, *to buy; to purchase.*

Emorior, -mŏri, *or* morīri,-mortuus sum, intr. dep. *to die.*

Emptus, a, um, part. (emo.)

Enascor,-nasci,-nātus sum, intr. dep. *to spring from,* or *up; to be born; to arise.*

Enātus, a, um, part. *born of.*

Enĕco,-necāre,-necāvi *or* -necui,-necātum, tr. (e & neco,) *to kill* (*outright.*)

Enervo, āre, āvi, ātum, tr. *to unnerve,* or *enervate; to enfeeble; to weaken.*

Enim, conj. *for; but; truly; indeed.*

Enna, æ, f. *a town of Sicily.*

Ennius, i, m. *a very ancient Roman poet.*

Enuntio, *or* -cio, āre, āvi, ātum, tr. (e & nuntio, *or* -cio,) *to say,* or *tell out; to proclaim; to disclose; to divulge.*

Eo, īre, īvi, ītum, intr. irr. § 83, 3, *to go.*

Eò, adv. (i. e. eo loco,) *thither; to that degree; to that pitch; to that degree of eminence.*

Eōus, i, m. *the morning star.*

Eōus, a, um, adj. *eastern; the eastern.*

Epaminondas, æ, m. *a distinguished Theban general.*

Ephĕsus, i, m. *a city on the western coast of Ionia, near the river Caÿster.*

Ephialtes, is, *a giant, the son of Neptune,* or *of Alōeus, and brother of Otos.*

Epimenĭdes, is, m. *a poet of Gnossus, in Crete.*

Epīrus, i, f. *a country in the western part of Greece.*

Epistŏla, æ, f. *an epistle; a letter.*

Epŭlor, āri, ātus sum, intr. dep. *to feast; to feast upon; to eat;* from

Epŭlum, i, n. sing., & Epŭlæ, ārum, f. pl. *a solemn feast; a banquet; a feast.* § 18,6.

Eques, ĭtis, m. (equus,) *a knight; a horseman:* equĭtes, pl. *knights; horsemen; cavalry.*

Equĭdem, conj. (ego & quidem,) *indeed; I for my part;* (joined mostly with verbs of the first person.)

Equitātus, ûs, m. (equĭto,) *cavalry.*

Equus, i, m. *a horse.*

Eram, Ero, &c. *See* Sum, § 54.

Ereptus, a, um, part. (eripio.)

Erga, prep. *towards.*

Ergo, conj. *therefore.*

Erinaceus, i, m. *a hedgehog.*

Eripio, -ripĕre, -ripui, -reptum, tr. (e & rapio,) *to tear from; to take from; to rescue; to take away; to deliver.*

Erro, āre, āvi, ātum, intr. *to wander; to err; to stray; to roam.*

Erōdo, -rodĕre, -rōsi, -rōsum, tr. (e & rodo,) *to gnaw away; to consume; to eat into.*

Erudio, īre, īvi, ītum, tr. (e & rudis,) *to free from a rude state;* hence, *to instruct; to form;* hence,

Eruditio, ōnis, f. *instruction; learning.*

Erudītus, a, um, part. (erudio.)

Esse, Essem, &c. *See* Sum.

Esuriens, tis, part. *hungry; being hungry;* from

Esurio, īre, īvi, ītum, intr. *to be hungry.*

Et, conj. *and; also; even:* et —et, *both—and.*

Etiam, conj. (et & jam,) *also; especially;* with an adjective or adverb in the comparative degree, *even.*

Etruria, æ, f. *a country of Italy, north and west of the Tiber; Tuscany.*

Etrusci, ōrum, m. pl. *the people of Etruria; the Tuscans* or *Etrurians.*

Etruscus, a, um. adj. *belonging to Etruria; Tuscan* or *Etrurian.*

Eubœa, æ, f. *a large island in the Ægean sea, near Bœotia.*

Eumĕnes, is, m. *a general in Alexander's army;* also, *the name of several kings of Pergamus.*

Euns, for iens, part. of eo.

Euphēmus, i, m. *the father of Dædălus.*

Euphrātes, is, m. *a large river which forms the western boundary of Mesopotamia.*

Euripĭdes, is, m. *a celebrated Athenian tragic poet.*

Eurīpus, i, m. *a narrow strait between Bœotia and Eubœa.*

Eurōpa, æ, f. *Europe, one of the quarters of the earth, supposed to have been named from Europa, the daughter of Agēnor, king of Phœnicia.*

Eurōtas, æ, m. *a river of Laconia, near Sparta.*

Euxīnus, i, m. from Εὔξεινος, (*hospitable,*) (pontus,) *the Euxine,* now *the Black Sea.*

Evādo, -vadĕre, -vāsi, -vāsum, tr. & intr. (e & vado,) *to go out; to escape; to become.*

Everto, -vertĕre, -verti, -versum, tr. (e & verto,) *to overturn; to destroy.*

Eversus, a, um, part. *overturned; destroyed.*

Evŏco, āre, āvi, ātum, tr. (e & voco,) *to call out; to summon; to implore.*

Evŏlo, āre, āvi, ātum, intr. (e & volo,) *to fly out* or *away.*

Evŏmo, -vomĕre, -vomui, -vomĭtum, tr. (e & vomo,) *to vomit forth; to discharge.*

Ex, prep. (before a vowel.) *See* E.

Exactus, a, um, part. (exĭgo,) *banished; driven away.*

Exæquo, āre, āvi, ātum, tr. (ex & æquo,) *to make equal; to equal.*

Exanĭmo, āre, āvi, ātum, tr. (ex & anĭma,) *to deprive of life; to kill; to render lifeless.*

Exardesco, -ardescĕre, -arsi, intr. inc. *to burn; to become inflamed; to kindle; to become excited; to be enraged:* bellum exarsit, *a war broke out.*

Exaspĕro, āre, āvi, ātum, tr. (ex and aspĕro, *to make rough;* fr. asper,) *to exasperate; to incense.*

Excæco, āre, āvi, ātum, tr. (ex & cæcus,) *to make blind; to blind.*

Excēdo, -cedĕre, -cessi, -cessum, intr. (ex & cedo,) *to go forth* or *out; to depart;* tr. *to exceed; to surpass; to go beyond.*

Excello, -cellĕre, -cellui, -celsum, intr. (ex & cello, obsol. *to move;*) *to be high;— to excel; to be eminent.*

Excelsus, a, um, adj. (comp. excelsior,) *high; lofty.*

Excidium, i, n. *destruction; ruin;* from

Excĭdo, -cidĕre, -cĭdi, intr. (ex & cado,) *to fall out* or *from; to fall; to drop; to perish.*

Excīdo, -cidĕre, -cīdi, -cīsum, tr. (ex & cædo,) *to cut out; to cut down; to hew out.*

Excīsus, a, um, part.

Excipio, -cipĕre, -cēpi, -ceptum, tr. (ex & capio,) *to take out; to except; to receive; to support; to follow; to succeed; to sustain.*

Excitandus, a, um, part. from

Excĭto, āre, āvi, ātum, tr. freq. (excieo,) *to excite; to awaken; to arouse; to stir up.*

Exclāmo, āre, āvi, ātum, tr. (ex & clamo,) *to cry out; to exclaim.*

Exclūdo, -cludĕre, -clūsi, -clūsum, tr. (ex & claudo,) *to shut out; to exclude; to hatch.*

Excŏlo, -colĕre, -colui, -cultum,

tr. (ex & colo,) *to cultivate: to exercise.*

Excrucio, āre, āvi, ātum, tr. (ex & crucio,) *to torture; to torment; to trouble;* § 91, 4.

Excubiæ, ārum, f. pl. (excŭbo,) *a guard; a watch; a sentinel;* (*generally by night.*) See vigilia & statio.

Excusatio, ōnis, f. (excūso,) *an excusing; an excuse; an apology.*

Exĕdo, -edĕre & esse, -ēdi, -ēsum, tr. irr. (ex & ĕdo, § 83, 9,) *to eat; to eat up; to devour.*

Exemplum, i, n. *an example; an instance.*

Exequiæ. *See* Exsequiæ.

Exerceo, ēre, ui, ĭtum, tr. (ex & arceo,) *to exercise; to train; to discipline; to practice:* agrum, *to cultivate the earth.*

Exercĭtus, ûs, m. *an army;* (*a body of disciplined troops.*)

Exhaurio, -haurīre, -hausi, -haustum, tr. (ex & haurio,) *to draw out; to exhaust; to drain; to wear out; to impoverish.*

Exĭgo, -igĕre, -ēgi, -actum, tr. (ex & ago,) *to drive away; to banish.*

Exiguus, a, um, adj. (comp.) *little; small; scanty;* see parvus.

Exīlis, e, adj. (exilior, § 26, 1,) *slender; small; thin.*

Exilium, and Exsilium, i, n. (ex & solum,) *exile; banishment.*

Eximiè, adv. *remarkably; very;* from

Eximius, a, um, adj. (exĭmo,) *extraordinary; remarkable.*

Existimatio, ōnis, f. *opinion; reputation; respect;* from

Existĭmo, āre, āvi, ātum, tr. (ex & æstĭmo,) *to judge,* or *think; to imagine; to suppose.*

Exitium, i, n. (exeo,) properly *issue; end:* usually *destruction; ruin.*

Exĭtus, ûs, m. (id.) *an exit; the event; the issue; an outlet.*

Exorātus, a, um, part. (exōro,) *entreated; influenced; induced.*

Exorior, -orīri, -ortus sum, intr. dep. (ex & orior,) *to rise up,* or *out of; to arise; to appear.*

Exorno, āre, āvi, ātum, tr. (ex & orno,) *to adorn; to deck.*

Exōro, āre, āvi, ātum, tr. (ex & oro,) *to entreat* or *beseech earnestly.* 238, 4.

Exortus, a, um, part. (exorior,) *risen; having arisen.*

Expecto, or -specto, āre, āvi, ātum, tr. (ex & specto,) *to look for; to wait for.*

Expedio, īre, īvi, ītum, tr. (ex & pes,) properly *to take the foot out of confinement;* hence, *to free; to extricate; to expedite:* expĕdit, imp.

it is fit; it is expedient; hence,

Expeditio, ōnis, f. *an expedition.*

Expello, -pellĕre, -pŭli, -pulsum, tr. (ex & pello,) *to drive out; to expel; to banish.*

Expers, tis, adj. (ex & pars,) *having no part in;* hence, *without; devoid; void of; destitute of.*

Expĕto, ĕre, īvi, ītum, tr. (ex & peto,) *to ask; to demand; to strive after; to seek earnestly.*

Expio, āre, āvi, ātum, tr. (ex & pio,) *to free from the pollution of some crime or offence; to expiate; to appease.*

Expleo, ēre, ēvi, ētum, tr. (ex & pleo,) *to fill up; to fill full.*

Explĭco, āre, āvi, & ui, ātum, & ĭtum, tr. (ex & plico,) *to unfold; to spread; to explain.*

Explorātor, ōris, m. (explōro,) *a spy; a scout.*

Expolio, īre, īvi, ītum, tr. (ex & polio,) *to polish; to adorn; to improve; to finish.* 238, 4.

Expōno, ponĕre, -posui, -posĭtum, tr. (ex & pono,) *to set forth; to expose; to explain.*

Exprobro, āre, āvi, ātum, tr. (ex & probrum,) *to upbraid; to blame; to reproach; to cast in one's teeth.*

Expugno, āre, āvi, ātum, tr. (ex & pugno,) *to take by assault; to conquer; to vanquish; to subdue; to take by storm.* 238, 4.

Expulsus, a, um, part. (expello.)

Exsequiæ, ārum, f. pl. (exsĕquor,) *funeral rites.*

Exsilio, *or* Exilio, īre, ii & ui, intr. (ex & salio,) *to spring up* or *out; to leap forth.*

Exspīro, *or* Expīro, āre, āvi, ātum, tr. (ex & spiro,) *to breathe forth; to expire; to die.*

Exstinctus, *or* Extinctus, a, um, part. *dead;* from

Exstinguo, -stinguĕre, -stinxi, -stinctum, tr. (ex & stinguo,) *to extinguish; to kill; to put to death; to destroy.*

Exstructus, *or* Extructus, a, um, part. from

Exstruo, *or* Extruo, -struĕre, -struxi, -structum, tr. (ex & struo,) *to build,* or *pile up; to construct.*

Exsurgo, -surgĕre, -surrexi, -surrectum, intr. (ex & surgo,) *to rise up; to arise; to swell; to surge.*

Exter, *or* Extĕrus, a, um, adj. (exterior, extĭmus or extrēmus, § 26, 2,) *foreign; strange; outward.*

Exto, extāre, extĭti, intr. (ex & sto,) *to stand out* or *forth;* usually, *to be; to remain; to be extant.*

Extorqueo, -torquēre, -torsi, -tortum, tr. (ex & torqueo,) *to extort; to wrest from; to obtain by force.*

Extra, prep. (for extĕra, scil. parte,) *beyond; without; except.*

Extractus, a, um, part. from

Extrăho, -trahĕre, -traxi, -tractum, tr. (ex & traho,) *to draw out; to extract; to extricate; to free; to rescue; to liberate.*

Extrēmus, a, um, adj. (sup. of extĕrus,) *extreme; the last; the farthest.*

F.

Faba, æ, f. *a bean.*

Fabius, i, m. *the name of an illustrious Roman family.*

Fabricius, i, m. *a Roman, distinguished for his integrity.*

Fabrĭco. āre, āvi, ātum, tr. (faber,) *to make; to forge; to manufacture.*

Fabŭla, æ, f. (fari,) *a story; a fable; a tradition; a play.*

Fabulōsus, a, um, adj. comp. (fabŭla,) *fabulous.*

Faciendus, a, um, part. (facio.

Faciens, tis, part. (facio.)

Facies, iēi, f. (facio,) *a face; appearance.*

Facĭlè, adv. (iùs, lĭmè,) *easily; willingly; clearly; undoubtedly;* from

Facĭlis, e, adj. (facio,) (comp. § 26, 1,) *easy.*

Facĭnus, ŏris, n. *any action; a bold deed; a crime; an exploit;* from

Facio, facĕre, feci, factum, tr. *to do; to make; to value: (spoken of individual things:)* facĕre iter, *to travel:* malè facĕre, *to injure; to hurt:* sacra facĕre, *to offer sacrifice:* facĕre pluris, *to value higher:* certiōrem, *to inform:* fac, *take care; cause;* hence,

Factum, i, n. *an action; a deed.*

Factūrus, a, um, part. (facio.)

Factus, a, um, part. (facio,) *made; done:* facta obviàm, *meeting:* prædâ factâ, *booty having been taken.*

Facundus, a, um, adj. (ior, issĭmus,) *eloquent; from* fari.

Falerii, ōrum, m. pl. *a town of Etruria.*

Falernus, i, m. *a mountain of Campania, famous for its wine.*

Falernus, a, um, adj. *belonging to Falernus; Falernian.*

Falisci, ōrum, m. pl. *the inhabitants of Falerii.*

Fama, æ, f. *fame; reputation; report.*

Famelĭcus, a, um, adj. *hungry; famished;* from

Fames, is, f. *hunger; famine.*

Familia, æ, f. (famŭlus,) *a family; servants;* hence,

Familiāris, e, adj. (comp.) *of the same family; familiar;* hence,

Familiarĭtas, ātis, f. *friendship; intimacy; confidence.*

Familiarĭter, adv. (iùs, issĭmè,) (id.) *familiarly; on terms of intimacy.*

Famŭla, æ, f. (famŭlus, *a servant;*) *a maid; a female servant or slave.*

Fas, n. ind. (for,) *right;* (by the laws of religion or of God:) *a lawful thing.*

Fascis, is, m. *a bundle; a fagot:* fasces, pl. *bundles of birchen rods, carried before the Roman magistrates, with an axe bound up in the middle of them.*

Fatālis, e, adj. (fatum,) *fatal; ordained by fate.*

Fateor, fatēri, fassus sum, tr. dep. *to confess.*

Fatidĭcus, a, um, adj. (fatum & dico,) *prophetic.*

Fatigātus, a, um, part. from

Fatĭgo, āre, āvi, ātum, tr. *to weary.*

Fatum, i, n. (for; i. e. *a thing declared or determined;*) *fate; destiny:* fata, pl. *the fates.*

Fauce, f. (in the abl. only, in the sing. § 18, 10,) *the throat:* pl. fauces, *the throat; the jaws; the straits.*

Faustŭlus, i, m. *the shepherd by whom Romŭlus and Remus were brought up.*

Faveo, favēre, favi, fautum, intr. *to favor;* hence,

Favor, ōris, m. *favor; good will; partiality; applause.*

Febris, is, f. (for ferbis, from ferveo,) *a fever.*

Feci. *See* Facio.

Felicĭtas, ātis, f. (felix,) *felicity; good fortune; happiness.*

Felicĭter, adv. (iùs, issĭmè,) *fortunately; successfully; happily.*

Felis, is, f. *a cat.*

Felix, īcis, adj. (ior, issĭmus,) *happy; fortunate; fruitful; fertile; opulent; auspicious; favorable.*

Femĭna, æ, f. *a female; a woman.*

Femineus, a, um, adj. (femĭna,) *female; feminine; pertaining to females.*

Fera, æ, f. *a wild beast.*

Ferax, ācis, adj. (ior, issĭmus,) (fero,) *fruitful; productive; fertile; abounding in.*

Ferè, adv. *almost; nearly; about:* ferè nullus, *scarcely any one.*

Ferens, tis, part. (fero.)

Ferīnus, a, um, adj. (fera,) *of wild beasts.*

Ferio, īre, tr. *to strike,* or *beat.*

Fero, ferre, tuli, latum, tr. irr. *to bear; to carry; to relate; to bring; to produce:* ferre manum, *to stretch forth; to extend:* ferunt, *they say.*

Feror, ferri, latus sum, pass. *to be carried; to flow; to move rapidly; to fly:* fertur, imp. *it is said;* hence,

Ferox, ōcis, adj. (ior, issĭmus,) *wild; fierce; savage; ferocious.*

Ferreus, a, um, adj. *iron; obdurate;* from

Ferrum, i, n. *iron; a sword; a knife.*

Fertĭlis, e, adj. (ior, issĭmus, (fero,) *fertile; fruitful;* hence,

Fertilĭtas, ātis, f. *fertility; richness; fruitfulness.*

Ferŭla, æ, f. (ferio,) *a staff; a reed.*

Ferus, a, um, adj. *wild; rude; uncultivated; uncivilized; savage.*

Ferveo, fervēre, ferbui, intr. *to boil; to seethe; to foam; to be hot; to glow.*

Fessus, a, um, adj. (fatiscor,) *weary; tired; fatigued.*

Festum, i, n. *a feast;* from

Festus, a, um, adj. *festive; joyful; merry.*

Ficus, i & ûs, f. *a fig-tree; a fig.*

Fidēlis, e, adj. (comp.) *faithful;* from

Fides, ĕi, f. *fidelity; faith:* in fidem, *in confirmation:* in fidem accipĕre, *to receive under one's protection.*

Figo, figĕre, fixi, fixum, tr. *to fix; to fasten.*

Filia, æ, f. 61, 4; *a daughter.*

Filius, i, m. § 10, Exc. 5; *a son.*

Filum, i, n. *a thread.*

Findo, findĕre, fidi, fissum, tr. *to split; to cleave.*

Fingens, tis, part. *feigning; pretending;* from

Fingo, fingĕre, finxi, fictum, tr. *to form; to make; to devise; to pretend; to feign.*

Finio, īre, īvi, ītum, tr. *to end; to finish; to terminate;* from

Finis, is, d. *the end; a boundary; a limit:* fines, m. pl. *the limits of a country,* &c.

Finītus, a, um, part. (finio.)

Finitĭmus, a, um, adj. (finis,) *neighboring.*

Fio, fĭeri, factus sum, irr. pass. § 83, 8; (facio,) *to be made; to become; to happen:* fit, *it happens:* factum est, *it happened; it came to pass.*

Firmātus, a, um, part. (firmo.)

Firmĭter, adv. (iùs, issĭmè,) (firmus,) *firmly; securely.*

Firmo, āre, āvi, ātum, tr. *to make firm; to confirm; to establish;* from

Firmus, a, um, adj. (comp.) *firm; strong; secure.*

Fissus, a, um, part. (findo.)

Fixus, a, um, part. (figo,) *fixed; permanent.*

Flagello, āre, āvi, ātum, tr. *to whip; to scourge; to lash.*

Flagitiōsus, a, um, adj. (ior, issĭmus,) *shameful; infamous; outrageous;* from

Flagitium, i, n. *a shameful action; an outrage; a crime; a dishonor; villainy.*

Flagro, āre, āvi, ātum, intr. *to burn; to be on fire; to suffer; to be oppressed: to be violent.*

Flaminius, i. m. *a Roman.*
Flavus, a, um, adj. *yellow.*
Flamma, æ, f. *a flame.*
Flecto, flectĕre, flexi, flexum, tr. *to bend; to bow; to turn; to move; to prevail upon.*
Flĕo, ēre, ēvi, ētum, tr. & intr. *to weep; to lament.*
Fletus, ûs, m. *weeping; tears.*
Flevo, ōnis, m. *a lake near the mouth of the Rhine,* now *the Zuyder Zee.*
Flexus, a, um, part. (flecto,) *bent; changed; turned.*
Floreo, ēre, ui, intr. (flos,) *to bloom; to blossom; to flourish; to be distinguished.*
Flos, flōris, m. *a flower; a blossom.*
Fluctus, ûs, m. (fluo,) *a wave.*
Fluo, fluĕre, fluxi, fluxum, intr. *to flow;* hence,
Fluvius, i, m. properly, *a river.*
Flumen, ĭnis, n. (fluo,) *an abundant flowing;* viz., of waters, or of any thing else; as, flumen verbōrum oratiōnis. Cic. Usually, *a river.*
Fodio, fodĕre, fodi, fossum, tr. *to dig; to pierce; to bore.*
Fœcundĭtas, ātis, f. *fruitfulness;* from
Fœcundus, a, um, adj. (ior, issĭmus,) *fruitful; fertile.*
Fœdus, ĕris, n. *a league; a treaty.*
Folium, i, n. *a leaf.*
Fons, tis, m. *a fountain; a source; a spring.*
Forem, def. verb, § 84, 5; *would* or *should be;* fore, *to be about to be; it would* or *will come to pass.*
Foris, adv. *abroad.*
Forma, æ, f. *a form; shape; figure; beauty.*
Formīca, æ, f. *an ant.*
Formīdo, ĭnis, f. *fear; dread; terror;* hence,
Formidolōsus, a, um, adj. (comp.) *fearful; timorous.*
Formosĭtas, ātis, f. *beauty; elegance;* from
Formōsus, a, um, adj. (ior, issĭmus,) *beautiful; handsome;* from forma.
Fors, tis, f. (fero,) *chance; fortune.*
Fortasse, adv. (fors,) *perhaps;* (applied to what *may* happen.)
Fortè, adv. (abl fr. fors,) *accidentally; by chance;* (applied to what *did* happen.)
Fortis, e, adj. (ior, issĭmus,) *bold; brave; courageous.*
Fortĭter, adv. (iùs, issĭmè,) *bravely;* from fortis.
Fortitūdo, ĭnis, f. (fortis,) *boldness; bravery.*
Fortūna, æ, f. (fors,) *fortune; chance.*
Forum, i, n. *the market-place; the forum; the court of justice.*
Fossa, æ, f. (fodio,) *a ditch; a trench; a moat.*

Fovea, æ, f. *a pit.*
Foveo, fovēre, fovi, fotum, tr. *to keep warm; to cherish.*
Fractus, a, um, part. (frango.)
Fragĭlis, e, adj. (frango,) *frail; perishable.*
Fragilĭtas, ātis, f. (fragĭlis,) *frailty; weakness.*
Fragmentum, i, n. (frango,) *a fragment; a piece.*
Frango, frangĕre, fregi, fractum, tr. *to break; to break in pieces; to weaken; to destroy.*
Frater, tris, m. *a brother.*
Fraudulentus, a, um, adj. comp. (fraus,) *fraudulent; deceitful; treacherous.*
Frequens, tis, adj. (ior, issĭmus,) *frequent; numerous.*
Fretum, i, n. *a strait; a sea.*
Frico, fricāre, fricui, frictum & fricātum, tr. *to rub.*
Frigĭdus, a, um, adj. (ior, issĭmus,) *cold;* from
Frigus, ŏris, n. *cold.*
Frons, frondis, f. *a leaf of a tree; a branch with leaves.*
Fructus, ûs, m. (fruor,) *use; enjoyment:* hence, *fruit; produce; advantage.*
Frugis, gen. f. (frux, nom. scarcely used,) properly *all that the earth produces for our subsistence; corn;* fruges, um, pl. *fruits; the various kinds of corn.*
Frumentum, i, n. (fruor,) *corn; wheat.*
Fruor, frui, fruĭtus & fructus, intr. dep. *to enjoy.*
Frustrà, adv. (frudo, id. ac fraudo,) *in vain; to no purpose.*
Frustrātus, a, um, part. from
Frustror, āri, ātus sum, dep. (frustrà,) *to frustrate; to deceive.*
Frutex, ĭcis, m. *a shrub; a bush.*
Fuga, æ, f. *a flight.*
Fugax, ācis, adj. (acior, acissĭmus,) *swift; fleeting;* from fugio.
Fugiens, tis, part. from
Fugio, fugĕre, fugi, fugĭtum, intr. & tr. *to fly; to escape; to avoid; to flee; to flee from.*
Fugo, āre, āvi, ātum, tr. *to put to flight; to drive off; to chase.*
Fui, Fuĕram, &c. *See* Sum.
Fulgeo, fulgēre, fulsi, intr. *to shine.*
Fulīgo, ĭnis, f. (fumus,) *soot.*
Fullo, ōnis, m. *a fuller.*
Fulmen, ĭnis, n. (i. e. fulgĭmen, fr. fulgeo,) *thunder; a thunderbolt; lightning.*
Funāle, is, n. (funis,) *a torch.*
Fundĭtus, adv. (fundus,) *from the foundation; utterly.*
Fundo, fundĕre, fudi, fusum, tr. *to pour out:* lacrȳmas, *to shed tears:* hostes, *to scatter; to rout; to discomfit.*
Fundus, i, m. *the bottom of any thing:* also *a farm; a field;* imus fundus, *the very bottom.*
Funestus, a, um, adj. (ior, issĭmus,) (funus,) *polluted by*

a dead body; fatal; destructive.

Fungor, fungi, functus, sum, intr. dep. *to perform* or *discharge an office; to do; to execute:* fato, *to die.*

Funis, is, d. *a rope; a cable.*

Funus, ĕris, n. *a funeral; funeral obsequies.*

Fur, furis, c. *a thief.*

Furcŭla, æ, f. dim. (furca,) *a little fork:* Furcŭlæ Caudinæ, *the name of a narrow defile in the country of the Hirpīni, in Italy, where the Romans were defeated by the Samnites.*

Furiōsus, a, um, adj. (comp.) *furious; mad;* from furo.

Furius, i, m. *the name of several Romans.*

Fusus, a, um, part. (fundo.)

Futūrus, a, um, part. (sum,) *about to be; future.*

G.

Gades, ium, f. pl. *the name of an island and town in Spain, near the straits of Gibraltar,* now *Cadiz.*

Gaditānus, a, um, adj. *of Gades* or *Cadiz:* fretum Gaditānum, *the straits of Gibraltar.*

Galatia, æ, f. *a country in the interior of Asia Minor.*

Gallia, æ, f. *Gaul,* now *France.*

Galliæ, pl. *the divisions of Gaul.*

Gallĭcus, a, um, adj. *belonging to Gaul; Gallic.*

Gallīna, æ, f. *a hen.*

Gallinaceus, i, m. *a cock.*

Gallus, i, m. *a cock.*

Gallus, i, m. *an inhabitant of Gallia; a Gaul;* also a cognōmen *of several Romans.*

Ganges, is, m. *the name of a large river in India.*

Garumna, æ, f. *the Garonne, a river of Aquitania.*

Gaudeo, gaudēre, gavīsus sum, n. pass. §78; *to rejoice; to delight; to be pleased with.*

Gaudium, i, n. *joy; gladness.*

Gavīsus, a, um, part. (gaudeo,) *rejoicing; having rejoiced.*

Gemĭnus, a, um, adj. *double;* gemĭni filii, *twin sons.*

Gemĭtus, ûs, m. (gemo,) *a groan; a sigh.*

Gemmātus, a, um, part. *adorned with gems; gemmed; glittering;* from

Gemmo, āre, āvi, ātum, tr. (gemma,) *to adorn with gems.*

Gener, genĕri, m. *a son-in-law.*

Genĕro, āre, āvi, ātum, tr. (genus,) *to beget; to produce.*

Generosĭtas, ātis, *nobleness of mind; magnanimity;* from

Generōsus, a, um, adj. (ior, issĭmus,) (genus,) *noble; spirited; brave; generous; fruitful; fertile.*

Genĭtus, a, um, part. (gigno,) *born; produced.*

Gens, tis, f. *a nation; a tribe; a family; a clan.*
Genui. *See* Gigno.
Genus, ĕris, n. *a race; a family; a sort or kind.*
Geometria, æ, f. *geometry.*
Gerens, tis, part. (gero,) *bearing; conducting.*
Germānus, i, m. *a German; an inhabitant of Germany.*
Germania, æ, f. *Germany.*
Germanĭcus, a, um, adj. *German; of Germany.*
Gero, gerĕre, gessi, gestum, tr. *to bear; to carry;* (viz: *a load* or *burden;*) *to do; to conduct* or *manage;* (spoken of one who has the charge; *see* ago *and* facio;) res eas gessit, *performed such exploits:* odium, *to hate:* onus, *to bear a burden:* bellum, *to wage or carry on war.*
Gerўon, is, m. *a giant who was slain by Hercules, and whose oxen were driven into Greece*
Gestans, tis, part. from
Gesto, āre, āvi, ātum, tr. freq. (gero,) *to bear; to carry about.*
Gestus, a, um, part. *borne; performed:* res gestæ, *see* Res.
Getæ, ārum, m. pl. *a savage people of Dacia, north of the Danube.*
Gigas, antis, m. *a giant.*
Gigno, gignĕre, genui, genĭtum, tr. *to beget; to bring forth; to bear; to produce.*
Glaber, bra, brum, adj. (brior, berrĭmus,) *bald; bare; smooth.*
Glaciālis, e, adj. *icy; freezing;* from
Glacies, ēi, f. *ice.*
Gladiātor, ōris, m. (gladius,) *a gladiator.*
Gladiatorius, a, um, adj. *belonging to a gladiator; gladiatorial;* from
Gladius, i, m. *a sword.*
Glans, dis, f. *mast; an acorn.*
Glisco, ĕre, intr. *to increase.*
Gloria, æ, f. *glory; fame.*
Glorior, āri, ātus sum, intr. dep. *to boast.*
Gnavus, a, um, adj. (comp.) *active; industrious.*
Gorgias, æ, m. *a celebrated sophist and orator.*
Gracĭlis, e, adj. (ior, lĭmus, § 26, 1,) *slender; lean; delicate.*
Gracchus, i, m. *the name of an illustrious Roman family.*
Gradior, gradi, gressus sum, intr. dep. *to go; to walk;* fr.
Gradus, ûs, m. *a step; a stair.*
Græcia, æ, f. *Greece.*
Græcus, a, um, adj. *Grecian; Greek:*—subs. *a Greek.*
Grandis, e, adj. (ior, issĭmus,) *large; great;* (*in a higher sense than* magnus.)
Granĭcus, i, m. *a river of Mysia, emptying into the Propontis.*
Grassor, āri, ātus sum, intr. dep. freq. (gradior,) *to advance; to march; to proceed; to make an attack.*

Grates, def. f. pl. (gratus,) *thanks:* agĕre grates, *to thank.* § 18, 12.

Gratia, æ, f. (gratus,) *grace; favor; thanks; return; requital; gratitude:* habēre, *to feel indebted* or *obliged; to be grateful:* in gratiam, *in favor of:* gratiâ, *for the sake.*

Gratulātus, a, um, part. *having congratulated;* from

Gratŭlor, āri, ātus sum, intr. dep. *to congratulate;* from

Gratus, a, um, adj. (ior, issĭmus,) *acceptable; pleasing; grateful.*

Gravis, e, adj. (ior, issĭmus,) *heavy; severe; great; grave; important; violent; noxious; unwholesome:* gravis somnus, *sound sleep;* hence,

Gravĭtas, ātis, f. *heaviness; gravity; weight.*

Gravĭter, adv. (iùs, issĭmè,) *hardly; heavily; grievously; severely;* from gravis.

Gravo, āre, āvi, ātum, tr. (gravis,) *to load; to oppress; to burden.*

Gregātim, adv. (grex,) *in herds.*

Gressus, ûs, m. (gradior,) *a step; a pace; a gait.*

Grex, gis, c. *a flock; a herd; a company.*

Grus, gruis, c. *a crane.*

Gubernātor, ōris, m. (guberno, *to govern;*) *a pilot; a ruler.*

Gyărus, i, f. *one of the Cyclădes.*

Gyges, is, m. *a rich king of Lydia.*

Gymnosophistæ, ārum, m. *Gymnosophists; a sect of Indian philosophers.*

H.

Habens, tis, part. from

Habeo, ēre, ui, ĭtum, tr. *to have; to possess; to hold; to esteem; to suppose; to take:* habēre consilium, *to deliberate.*

Habĭto, āre, āvi, ātum, tr. & intr. *to inhabit; to dwell.*

Habitūrus, a, um, part. (habeo.)

Habĭtus, a, um, part. (habeo.)

Habĭtus, ûs, m. (habeo,) *habit; form; dress; attire; manner.*

Hactĕnus, adv. (hic & tenus,) *hitherto; thus far.*

Hadriānus, i, m. *Adrian, the fifteenth emperor of Rome.*

Hæmus, i, m. *a mountain of Thrace, from whose top, both the Euxine and Adriatic seas can be seen.*

Halcyon, *or* Alcyon, ŏnis, f. *the halcyon* or *kingfisher. See* Alcyone.

Halicarnassus, i, f. *a maritime city of Caria, the birthplace of Herodŏtus.*

Hamilcar, ăris, m. *a Carthaginian general.*

Hannĭbal, ălis, m. *a brave Carthaginian general, the son of Hamilcar.*

Hanno, ōnis, m. *a Carthaginian general.*

Harmonia, æ, f. *the wife of Cadmus, and daughter of Mars and Venus.*

Harpyiæ, ārum, f. pl. *the Harpies; winged monsters, having the faces of women, and the bodies of vultures.*

Haruspex, ĭcis, m. (haruga & specio,) *a soothsayer; a diviner; one who pretended to a knowledge of future events from inspecting the entrails of victims.*

Hasdrŭbal, ălis, m. *a Carthaginian general, the brother of Hannibal.*

Hasta, æ, f. *a spear; a lance.*

Haud, adv. *not.*

Haurio, haurīre, hausi, haustum, tr. *to draw out; to drink; to swallow.*

Haustus, ûs, m. (id.) *a draught.*

Hebes, ĕtis, adj. (comp.) *blunt; obtuse; dim.*

Hebesco, ĕre, intr. inc, (hebeo,) *to grow blunt, dim,* or *dull.*

Hebrus, i, m. *a large river of Thrace.*

Hecŭba, æ, f. *the wife of Priam, king of Troy.*

Hedĕra, æ, f. *ivy.*

Hegesias, æ, m. *an eloquent philosopher of Cyrēne.*

Helĕna, æ, f. *Helen, the daughter of Jupiter and Leda, and wife of Menelāus.*

Helĭcon, ōnis, m. *a mountain of Bœotia, near Parnassus, and sacred to Apollo and the Muses.*

Helvetia, æ, f. *a country in the eastern part of Gaul,* now *Switzerland.*

Helvetii, ōrum, m. pl. *Helvetians; the inhabitants of Helvetia.*

Hellebŏrum. i, n. *or* Hellebŏrus, i, m. *the herb hellebore.*

Hellespontus, i. m. *a strait between Thrace and Asia Minor,* now called *the Dardanelles.*

Heraclēa, æ, f. *the name of several cities in Magna Græcia, in Pontus, in Syria, &c.*

Herba, æ, f. *an herb; grass;* hence,

Herbĭdus, a, um, adj. (comp.) *grassy; full of herbs* or *grass.*

Hercŭles, is, m. *a celebrated hero, son of Jupiter and Alcmēna.*

Hercynius, a, um, adj. *Hercynian:* Hercynia sylva, *a large forest in Germany,* now *the Black Forest.*

Heres *or* Hæres, ēdis, c. *an heir.*

Herennius, i, m. *a general of the Samnites.*

Hero, ûs, (§ 15, 13,) f. *a priestess of Venus, who resided at Sestos, and who was beloved by Leander, a youth of Abydos.*

Hespĕrus, i, m. *a son of Iapĕ-*

tus, who settled in Italy, and from whom that country was called Hesperia; also *the evening star.*

Heu! int. *alas! ah!*

Hians, tis, part. (hio.)

Hiātus, ûs, m. (hio,) *an opening; a chasm; an aperture.*

Hibernĭcus, a, um, adj. *Irish;* (probably from *Hiberna,* the winter quarters of the Roman soldiers.)

Hibernus, a, um, adj. (hiems,) *of winter; wintry.*

Hic, adv. *here; in this place.*

Hĭc, hæc, hoc, pro. § 31, 1, *this; he; she,* &c.

Hiempsal, ălis, m. *a king of Numidia.*

Hiems, ĕmis, f. *winter.*

Hiĕro, ōnis, m. *tyrant of Syracuse.*

Hierosolȳma, æ, f. & Hierosolȳma, ōrum, n. pl. *Jerusalem, the capital of Judea.*

Hinc, adv. *hence; from hence; from this; from this time.*

Hinnio, īre, īvi, ītum, intr. *to neigh;* hence,

Hinnītus, ûs, m. *a neighing.*

Hinnuleus, i, m. (hinnus,) *a fawn.*

Hio, āre, āvi, ātum, intr. *gape; to yawn; to open the mouth; to long for.*

Hipparchus, i, m. *the son of Pisistrătus, a tyrant of Athens.*

Hippolȳtus, i, m. *the son of Theseus.*

Hippomĕnes, is, m. *the son of Megareus, and husband of Atalanta.*

Hippopotămus, i, m. *the hippopotamus* or *river-horse.*

Hispania, æ, f. *Spain.*

Hispānus, a, um, adj. *Spanish.* subs. m. *a Spaniard.*

Hodie, adv. (i. e. hoc die,) *today; at this time; now-a-days.*

Hodiēque, (for hodie quoque,) adv. *to this day; to this time.*

Hœdūs, i, m. *a kid; a young goat.*

Homērus, i, m. *Homer, the most ancient and illustrious of the Greek poets.*

Homo, ĭnis, c. (humus,) *a man; a person; one.*

Honestas, ātis, f. *honor; virtue; dignity;* from

Honestus, a, um, adj. *honorable; noble;* from

Honor & -os, ōris, m. *honor; respect; an honor; an office.*

Honorifĭcè, adv. (centiùs, centissĭmè, from honorifĭcus, § 26, 3,) *honorably:* parum honorifĭce, *slightingly; with little respect.*

Hora, æ, f. *an hour.*

Horatius, i, m. *Horace; the name of several Romans:* Horatii, pl. *three Roman brothers, who fought with the three Curiatii.*

Hortensius, i, m. *the name of several Romans.*

Horrĭdus, a, um, adj. comp. (horreo, *to bristle up;*)

rough; rugged; rude; unpolished; barbarous.

Hortātus, ûs, m. *an exhortation; instigation; advice;* from

Hortor, āri, ātus sum, tr. dep. *to exhort.*

Hortus, i, m. *a garden.*

Hospes, ĭtis, c. *a stranger; a visitor; a guest; a host.*

Hospitium, i, n. (hospes,) *hospitality:* hospitio accipĕre, *to entertain.*

Hostia, æ, f. (hostis,) *a victim.*

Hostilius, i, m. (Tullus,) *the third king of Rome: a cognomen among the Romans.*

Hostis, is, c. *an enemy.*

Huc, adv. (hoc,) *hither:* huc — illuc, *hither — thither; now here — now there.*

Hujusmŏdi, adj. ind. (gen. of hic & modus,) *of this sort* or *kind.*

Humanĭtas, ātis, f. *humanity; kindness; gentleness;* from

Humānus, a, um, adj. comp. (homo,) *human.*

Humĕrus, i, m. *the shoulder.*

Humĭlis, e, adj. (humi,) (ior, lĭmus, § 26, 1,) *humble:* humĭli loco natum esse, *to be born in a humble station,* or *of obscure parents.*

Humor, ōris, m. (humeo,) *moisture:* pl. *liquids; humors.*

Humus, i, f. *the ground:* humi, *on the ground.* 559.

Hyæna, æ, f. *the hyena.*

Hydrus, i, m. *a water snake.*

Hymnus, i, m. *a hymn; a song of praise.*

Hyperboreus, a, um, adj. (ὑπὲρ βόρεας,) properly, *living beyond the source of the north wind; northern:* Hyperborei, ōrum, m. pl. *people inhabiting the northern regions; beyond Scythia.*

Hystrix, ĭcis, f. *a porcupine.*

I.

Iapĕtus, i, m. *the son of Cœlus and Terra.*

Ibērus, i, m. *a river of Spain,* now *the Ebro.*

Ibi, adv. *there; here; then.*

Ibīdem, adv. *in the same place.*

Ibis, ĭdis, f. *the Ibis, the Egyptian stork.*

Icărus, i, m. *the son of Dædălus.*

Icarius, a, um, adj. *of Icărus; Icarian.*

Ichneumon, ŏnis, m. *the ichneumon* or *Egyptian rat.*

Ichnūsa, æ, f. *an ancient Greek name of Sardinia.*

Ico, ĭcĕre, ici, ictum, tr. *to strike;* fœdus, *to make, ratify,* or *conclude a league* or *treaty.*

Ictus, a, um, part.

Ictus, ûs, m. (ico,) *a blow; a stroke.*

Ida, æ, f. *a mountain of Troas, near Troy.*

Idæus, a, um, adj. *belonging to Ida:* mons Idæus, *mount Ida.*

Idem, eădem, ĭdem, pro. § 31, *the same.*

Idoneus, a, um, adj. *fit; suitable.*

Igĭtur, conj. *therefore; then.*

Ignārus, a, um, adj. (in & gnarus,) *ignorant.*

Ignāvus, a, um, adj. comp. (in & gnavus,) *inactive; idle; cowardly.*

Ignis, is, m. *fire; flame.*

Ignobĭlis, e, adj. (in & nobĭlis,) *unknown; ignoble; mean.*

Ignōro, āre, āvi, ātum, tr. (ignārus,) *to be ignorant; not to know.*

Ignōtus, a, um, part. & adj. (in & notus,) *unknown.*

Ilium, i, n. *Ilium* or *Troy, the principal city of Troas.*

Illātus, a, um, part. (from infĕro,) *brought in; inferred.*

Ille, a, ud, pro. § 31, 2; *that; he; she; it; the former;* pl. *they; those.*

Illecebra, æ, f. (illicio,) *an allurement; an enticement.*

Illĭco, adv. (in & loco,) *in that place; immediately; instantly.*

Illuc, adv. (illoc,) *thither:* huc—illuc, *now here—now there.*

Illustris, e, adj. (ior, issĭmus,) *illustrious; famous; celebrated;* from

Illustro, āre, āvi, ātum, tr. (in & lustro,) *to enlighten; to illustrate; to render famous; to celebrate; to make renowned.*

Illyria, æ, f. *a country opposite to Italy, and bordering on the Adriatic.*

Imāgo, ĭnis, f. *an image; a picture; a figure; a resemblance.*

Imbecillis, e, adj. (in & bacŭlus, as if *leaning on a staff:*) (lior, lĭmus, § 26, 1,) *weak; feeble.*

Imber, bris, m. *a shower; a rain.*

Imitatio, ōnis, f. *imitation:* ad imitatiōnem, *in imitation;* from

Imĭtor, āri, ātus sum, tr. dep. *to imitate; to copy.*

Immānis, e, adj. comp. (in & magnus,) *very great; huge; monstrous; cruel; dreadful.*

Immensus, a, um, adj. (in & mensus,) *immeasurable; boundless; immoderate.*

Immerĭtus, a, um, part. (in & merĭtus,) *not deserving; undeserved.*

Immĭnens, tis, part. *hanging over; threatening;* from

Immineo, ēre, ui, intr. (in & mineo,) *to hang over; to impend; to threaten; to be near.*

Immissus, a, um, part. *admitted; sent in; darted in;* from

Immitto, -mittĕre, -mīsi, -missum, tr. (in & mitto,) *to let in; to send to, into, against,* or *upon; to throw at.*

Immobĭlis, e, adj. comp. (in & mobĭlis,) *immovable; steadfast.*

Immŏlo, āre, āvi, ātum, tr. (in & mola,) properly, *to*

sprinkle with the mola or *salted cake;* hence, *to sacrifice; to immolate.*

Immortālis, e, adj. (in & mortālis,) *immortal.*

Immōtus, a. um, part. (in & motus,) *unmoved; still; motionless.*

Immutātus, a, um, part. *altered; changed;* (sometimes, *exchanged;*) from

Immūto, āre, āvi, ātum, tr. (in & muto,) *to change; to alter.*

Impatiens, tis, adj. (in & patiens,) *impatient; not able to endure.*

Impedītus, a, um, part. *impeded; hindered; encumbered; entangled;* from

Impedio, īre, īvi, ītum, tr. (in & pes,) properly, *to fetter;* hence, *to impede; to obstruct; to check; to delay; to prevent; to disturb.*

Impendo, -pendĕre, wants pret. & sup. intr. (in & pendeo,) *to hang over; to impend; to threaten.*

Impenetrabĭlis, e, adj. (in & penetrabĭlis,) *impenetrable.*

Impensè, adv. (iùs, issĭme,) *exceedingly; greatly;* from impensus.

Imperātor, ōris, m. (impĕro,) *a commander; a general.*

Imperĭto, āre, āvi, ātum, tr. freq. (impĕro,) *to command; to rule; to govern.*

Imperītus, a, um, adj. (ior, issĭmus,) (in & perītus,) *inexperienced; unacquainted with.*

Imperium, i, n. *a command; government; reign; supreme authority; power;* (imperium, *military command;* potestas, *civil authority;*) from

Impĕro, āre, āvi, ātum, tr. *to command; to order; to direct; to govern; to rule over.*

Impertiens, tis, part. from

Impertio, īre, īvi, ītum, tr. (in & partio,) *to impart; to share; to give.*

Impĕtro, āre, āvi, ātum, tr. (in & patro,) *to obtain; to finish.*

Impĕtus, ûs, m. (in & peto,) *an attack; onset; force; violence; impetuosity.*

Impius, a, um, adj. (in & pius,) *impious; undutiful.*

Impleo, ēre, ēvi, ētum, tr. (in & pleo,) *to fill; to accomplish; to perform.*

Implicītus, a, um, part. *entangled; attacked;* from

Implĭco, āre, āvi *or* ui, ātum *or* ĭtum, tr. (in & plico,) *to infold; to entangle; to implicate.*

Implĭcor, āri, ātus *or* ĭtus sum, pass. *to be entangled:* morbo, *to be attacked with sickness.*

Implōro, āre, āvi, ātum, tr. (in & ploro,) *to implore; to beseech; to beg.*

Impōno, -ponĕre, -posui, -posĭtum, tr. (in & pono,) *to lay* or *place upon; to impose; to put.*

Importūnus, a, um, adj. comp. *dangerous; perilous; troublesome; cruel; outrageous; restless; ungovernable.*

Imposĭtus, a, um, part. (impōno.

Imprīmis, adv. (in & primis, from primus,) *among the first; especially; eminently.*

Improbātus, a, um, part. (improbo,) *disallowed; disapproved.*

Imprŏbo, āre, āvi, ātum, tr. (in & probo,) *to disapprove; to reject.*

Imprŏbus, a, um, adj. comp. (in & probus,) *not good; wicked; bad.*

Imprūdens, tis, adj. comp. (in & prudens,) *imprudent; inconsiderate.*

Impugnatūrus, a, um, part. fr.

Impugno, āre, āvi, ātum, tr. *to fight against; to attack.*

Impūnè, adv. (in & pœna,) *with impunity; without hurt; without punishment.*

Imus, a, um, adj. (sup. of infĕrus, § 26, 2,) *the lowest; the deepest.*

In, prep. with the accusative, signifies, *into; towards; upon; until; for; against:* with the ablative, *in; upon; among; at:* in dies, *from day to day:* in eo esse, *to be on the point of:* in sublīme, *aloft.*

Inānis, e, adj. (comp.) *empty; vain; ineffectual; foolish.*

Inaresco, -arescĕre, -arui, intr. inc. § 88, 2, *to grow dry.*

Incēdo, -cedĕre, -cessi, -cessum, intr. (in & cedo,) *to go on; to go; to walk; to come.*

Incendo, dĕre, di, sum, tr. (in & candeo,) *to light; to kindle; to set fire to; to inflame.*

Incensus, a, um, part. *lighted; kindled; burning; inflamed.*

Incertus, a, um, adj. (ior, issĭmus,) (in & certus,) *uncertain.*

Inchoo, āre, āvi, ātum, tr. *to begin.*

Incĭdens, tis, part. from

Incĭdo, -cidĕre, -cĭdi, intr. (in & cado,) *to fall into* or *upon; to chance to meet with.*

Incipio, -cipĕre, -cēpi, -ceptum, tr. (in & capio,) *to commence; to begin.*

Incĭto, āre, āvi, ātum, tr. (in & cito,) *to stir up; to instigate; to encourage; to animate.*

Inclūdo, dĕre, si, sum, tr. (in & claudo,) *to shut in; to include; to inclose; to encircle; to encompass.*

Inclūsus, a, um, part. (inclūdo.)

Inclȳtus, a, um, adj. (issĭmus, § 26, 5,) *famous; celebrated; renowned.*

Incŏla, æ, c. *an inhabitant;* fr.

Incŏlo, colĕre, colui, cultum,

tr. (in & colo,) *to dwell in a place; to inhabit.*

Incolŭmis, e, adj. comp. (in & colŭmis,) *unhurt; safe; unpunished.*

Incompertus, a, um, adj. (in & compertus,) *not found out; unknown; uncertain.*

Inconsiderātè, adv. (iùs, issĭmè,) *inconsiderately; rashly.*

Incredibĭlis, e, adj. comp. (in & credibĭlis,) *incredible; wonderful;* hence,

Incredibilĭter, adv. (iùs, issĭmè,) *incredibly.*

Incrementum, i, n. (incresco,) *an increase.*

Incrĕpo, āre, ui, ĭtum, tr. (in & crepo,) *to make a loud noise; to reprove; to chide; to blame.*

Incruentus, a, um, adj. (in & cruor,) *bloodless.*

Incultè, adv. (iùs, issĭmè,) *rudely; plainly;* from

Incultus, a, um, part. & adj. comp. (in & colo,) *uncultivated; uninhabited; desert.*

Incumbo, -cumbĕre, -cubui, -cubĭtum, intr. (in & cubo,) *to lean; to lie; to rest* or *recline upon; to apply to:* gladio, *to fall upon one's sword.*

Incursio, ōnis, f. (incurro,) *a running against; an attack; an incursion; an inroad.*

Inde, adv. *thence; from thence.*

Index, ĭcis, d. (indĭco,) *an index; a mark; a sign.*

India, æ, f. *a country of Asia, named from the river Indus.*

Indĭco, āre, āvi, ātum, tr. (in & dico, āre,) *to show; to discover.*

Indīco, cĕre, xi, ctum. tr. (in & dico,) *to indicate; to announce; to declare; to proclaim; to appoint;* hence,

Indictus, a, um, part.

Indĭcus, a, um, adj. *of India; Indian.*

Indigĕna, æ, c. (in & geno,) *one born in a certain place; a native.*

Indŏles, is, f. (in & oleo, to grow,) *the natural disposition; nature; inherent quality. See* Ingenium.

Indūco, cĕre, xi, ctum, tr. (in & duco,) *to lead in; to induce; to persuade;* hence,

Inductus, a, um, part.

Induo, -duĕre, -dui, -dūtum, tr. *to put on; to dress; to clothe.*

Indus, i, m. *a large river in the western part of India.*

Industria, æ, f. (industrius,) *industry; diligence.*

Indūtus, a, um, part. (induo.)

Inedia, æ, f. (in & edo,) *want of food; fasting; hunger.*

Ineo, īre, ii, ĭtum, tr. & intr. irr. (in & eo,) *to go* or *enter into; to enter upon; to make; to form.*

Inermis, e, adj. (in & arma,) *unarmed; defenceless.*

Inertia, æ, f. (iners,) *want of art; laziness; sloth; idleness.*

Infāmis, e, adj. (in & fama,) *ill spoken of; infamous; disgraceful.*

Infans, tis, c. (in & fans,) *one who can not speak; an infant; a child.*

Infĕri, ōrum, m. pl. *the infernal regions; Hades; Orcus; the infernal gods.*

Inferior, us. adj. *See* Infĕrus.

Infĕro, inferre, intŭli, illātum, tr. irr. (in & fero,) *to bring in* or *against; to bring upon; to inflict upon:* bellum, *to make war upon.*

Infĕrus, a, um, adj. (inferior, infĭmus, *or* imus, § 26, 2,) *low; humble.*

Infesto, āre, āvi, ātum, tr. *to infest; to disturb; to molest; to vex; to plague; to trouble; to annoy;* from

Infestus, a, um, adj. (ior, issĭmus,) (in & festus,) *not pleasant; hostile; inimical.*

Infīgo, gĕre, xi, xum, tr. (in & figo,) *to fix; to fasten; to drive in.*

Infinītus, a, um, adj. (in & finio,) *infinite; unbounded; vast; immense:* infinītum argenti, *an immense quantity of silver:* infinīta nobilītas, *a vast number,* &c.

Infirmus, a, um, adj. ior, issĭmus, (in & firmus,) *weak; infirm.*

Infixus, part. (infīgo.)

Inflammo, āre, āvi, ātum, tr. *to set on fire; to inflame; to excite; to animate.*

Inflātus, a, um, part, (inflo,) *blown up; puffed up.*

Inflīgo, gĕre, xi, ctum, tr. (in & fligo,) properly, *to strike one thing against another;* hence, *to inflict.*

Inflo, āre, āvi, ātum, tr. (in & flo,) *to blow upon.*

Infra, prep. *beneath; below.*

Infrendeo, ēre, ui, intr. (in & frendeo,) *to gnash with the teeth.*

Infringo, -fringĕre, -frēgi, -fractum, tr. (in & frango,) *to break* or *rend in pieces; to disannul; to make void.*

Infundo, -fundĕre, -fūdi, -fūsum, tr. (in & fundo,) *to pour in:* infundĭtur, *it empties;* (said of rivers).

Ingenium, i, n. (in & geno,) *judgment; sagacity; penetration; natural disposition; genius; talents; character.*

Ingens, tis, adj. (ior, § 26, 6,) *great; very great; huge;* (*in a much higher sense than* magnus.)

Ingenuus, a, um, adj. (ingeno,) *natural; free-born; free; noble; ingenuous.*

Ingredior, -grĕdi, -gressus sum, tr. & intr. dep. (in & gradior,) *to go in; to enter; to come in; to walk; to walk upon; to go.*

Ingressus, a, um, part.

Ingruo, -gruĕre, -grui, tr. *to invade; to assail; to pour down; to fall upon suddenly.*

Inhæreo, -hærēre, -hæsi, -hæsum, intr. (in & hæreo,) *to cleave* or *stick to* or *in:* cogitationĭbus, *to be fixed* or *lost in thought.*

Inhio, āre, āvi, ātum, tr. & intr. (in & hio,) *to gape for; to desire.*

Inimīcus, a, um, adj. comp. (in & amīcus,) *inimical; hostile.*

Inimīcus, i, m. subs. *an enemy.*

Inīquè, adv. iùs, issĭmè, (inīquus, in & æquus, *not equal;*) *unequally; unjustly.*

Initium, i, n. (ineo,) *a commencement; a beginning.*

Initūrus, a, um, part. (ineo,) *about to enter upon* or *begin.*

Injicio, -jicĕre, -jēci, -jectum, tr. (in & jacio,) *to throw in* or *upon.*

Injuria, æ, f. (injurius, in & jus,) *an injury; an insult.*

Innāto, āre, āvi, ātum, intr. (in & nato,) *to swim* or *float upon.*

Innītor, -nīti, -nīsus *or* nixus sum, intr. dep. (in & nitor,) *to lean* or *depend upon; to rest upon.*

Innocentia, æ, f. (in & nocens,) *harmlessness; innocence.*

Innotesco, -notescĕre, -notui, intr. inc. (in & notesco,) *to become known; to be known.*

Innoxius, a, um, adj. comp. (in & noxius,) *harmless.*

Innumerabĭlis, e, adj. (in & numerabĭlis,) *innumerable.*

Innumĕrus, a, um, adj. (in & numĕrus,) *without number.*

Inopia, æ, f. (inops,) *want; scarcity.*

Inōpus, i, m. *a fountain or river of Delos, near which Apollo and Diana were said to have been born.*

Inprīmis, *and* in primis, adv. *same as* imprīmis.

Inquam, *or* inquio, def. *I say;* § 84, 2.

Inquĭno, āre, āvi, ātum, tr. *to pollute; to stain; to soil.*

Inquīro, -quirĕre, -quisīvi, -quisītum, tr. (in & quæro,) *to seek for; to inquire; to investigate.*

Insania, æ, f. (insānus,) *madness.*

Insanio, īre, īvi, ītum, intr. (insānus,) *to be mad.*

Inscrībo, -scribĕre, -scripsi, -scriptum, tr. (in & scribo,) *to write upon; to inscribe.*

Inscriptus, a, um, part.

Insectum, i, n. (insĕco,) *an insect.*

Insĕquens, tis, part. *succeeding; subsequent; following;* from

Insĕquor, -sĕqui, -secūtus, sum, tr. dep. (in & sequor,) *to follow after; to follow.*

Insīdens, tis, part. from

Insideo, -sidēre, -sēdi, -sessum, intr. (in & sedeo,) *to sit upon.*

Insidiæ, ārum, f. pl. (insideo,) *an ambush; ambuscade; treachery; deceit:* per insidias, *treacherously.*

Insidians, tis, part. from

Insidior, āri, ātus sum, tr. dep. (insidiæ,) *to lie in wait; to lie in ambush; to deceive.*

Insigne, is, n. *a mark; a token; an ensign;* from

Insignis, e, adj. comp. (in & signum,) *distinguished (by some mark;) eminent.*

Insisto, -sistĕre, -stĭti, -stĭtum, intr. (in & sisto,) *to stand upon; to insist.*

Insolabilĭter, adv. (in & solor,) *inconsolably.*

Insŏlens, tis, adj. (in & solens,) (ior, issĭmus,) *not usual; insolent; haughty.*

Insolenter, adv. (insŏlens,) (iùs, issĭmè,) *haughtily; insolently.*

Inspectans, tis, part. from

Inspecto, āre, āvi, ātum, tr. freq. (in & specto,) *to look upon; to inspect.*

Instatūrus, a, um, part. (insto.)

Instituo, -stituĕre, -stitui, -stitūtum, tr. (in & statuo,) *to set* or *put into; to appoint; to resolve; to make; to order.*

Institūtum, i, n. *an institution; a doctrine;* from

Institūtus, a, um, part. (instituo.)

Insto, -stāre, -stĭti, intr. (in & sto,) *to stand near to; to urge; to persist; to harass; to pursue closely; to beg earnestly.*

Instrumentum, i, n. (instruo,) *an instrument; utensil; implement.*

Instruo, -struĕre, -struxi, -structum, tr. (in & struo,) *to put together,* or *in order; to arrange; to prepare; to supply with; to instruct.*

Insŭbres, um, m. pl. *a people living north of the Po, in Cisalpine Gaul.*

Insuesco, -suescĕre, -suēvi, -suētum, intr. inc. (in & suesco,) *to grow accustomed.*

Insŭla, æ, f. *an island.*

Insŭper, adv. (in & super,) *moreover.*

Intĕger, gra, grum, adj. (in & tago, whence tango,) (rior, errĭmus,) *not touched; whole; entire; unhurt; just; uncorrupted.*

Intĕgo, -tegĕre, -texi, -tectum, tr. (in & tego,) *to cover.*

Integrĭtas, ātis, f. (intĕger,) *integrity; probity; honesty.*

Intellectus, a, um, part. from

Intellĭgo, -ligĕre, -lexi, -lectum, tr. (inter & lego,) *to choose between;* hence, *to understand; to perceive; to discern; to know; to learn.*

Inter, prep. *between; among:* inter se, *mutually:* occurrentes inter se, *meeting each other.*

Intercipio, -cipĕre, -cēpi, -ceptum, tr. (inter & capio,) *to seize by surprise; to inter-*

cept; to usurp; to take away fraudulently.

Interdīco, -dicĕre, -dixi, -dictum, tr. (inter & dico,) *to interpose a command; to forbid; to prohibit.*

Interdictus, a, um, part.

Interdiu, adv. (inter & diu,) *by day; in the day time.*

Interdum, adv. (inter & dum,) *sometimes.*

Interea, adv. (inter & ea,) *in the mean time.*

Interemptus, a, um, part. (interĭmo.)

Intereo, īre, ii, ĭtum, intr. irr. (inter & eo, §83,3,) *to perish.*

Intĕrest, imp. (intersum,) *it concerns:* mea, *it concerns me.*

Interfector, ōris, m. *a murderer; a slayer; a destroyer.*

Interfectus, a, um, part. *killed.*

Interficio, -ficĕre, -fēci, -fectum, tr. (inter & facio,) *to destroy; to kill; to slay.*

Intĕrim, adv. (inter & im, the old acc. of is,) *in the mean time.*

Interĭmo, -imĕre, -ēmi, -emptum, tr. (inter & emo,) *to take from the midst; to kill; to put to death; to slay.*

Interior, us, adj. (sup. intĭmus, § 26, 2,) *inner; the interior.*

Interiùs, adv. (intro,) *farther in the interior.*

Interjectus, a, um, part. *cast between:* anno interjecto, *a year having intervened; a year after;* from

Interjicio, -jicĕre, -jēci, -jectum, tr. (inter & jacio,) *to throw between.*

Internecio, ōnis, f. (internĕco,) *ruin; destruction:* ad internecionem, *with a general massacre.*

Internodium, i, n. (inter & nodus,) *the space between two knots; a joint.*

Internus, a, um, adj. *internal:* mare internum, *the Mediterranean sea.*

Interpres, ĕtis, c. *an interpreter.*

Interregnum, i, n. (inter & regnum,) *an interregnum; a vacancy of the throne.*

Interrŏgo, āre, āvi, ātum, tr. (inter & rogo,) *to ask.*

Intersum, esse, fui, intr. irr. (inter & sum,) *to be present at, between, with,* or *among.*

Intervallum, i, n. (inter & vallus,) *an interval; a space; a distance.*

Interveniens, tis, part. from

Intervenio, venīre, vēni, ventum, intr. (inter & venio,) *to come between; to intervene.*

Intexo, ĕre, ui, tum, tr. (in & texo,) *to interweave.*

Intĭmus, a, um, adj. sup. (intĕrus, interior, § 26, 2,) *innermost; inmost; intimate; familiar; much beloved.*

Intra, prep. *within:*—adv. *inward.*

Intrepĭdus, a, um, adj. (in & trepĭdus,) *fearless; intrepid.*

Intro, āre, āvi, ātum, tr. (intro, & eo,) *to enter.*

Introdūco, -ducĕre, -duxi, -ductum, tr. (intro & duco,) *to lead in; to introduce.*

Introĭtus, ûs, m. (introeo,) *an entrance.*

Intuens, tis, part. from

Intueor, ēri, ĭtus sum, tr. dep. (in & tueor,) *to look upon; to consider; to behold; to gaze at.*

Intus, adv. *within.*

Inusitātus, a, um, adj. comp. (in & usitātus,) *unaccustomed; unusual; extraordinary.*

Inutĭlis, e, adj. comp. (in & utĭlis,) *useless.*

Invādo, -vadĕre, -vāsi, -vāsum, tr. (in & vado,) *to invade; to attack; to assail.*

Invenio, -venīre, -vēni, -ventum, tr. (in & venio,) *to come to,* or *upon; to find; to get; to procure; to obtain; to invent; to discover.*

Inventus, a, um, part.

Investīgo, āre, āvi, ātum, tr. (in & vestīgo,) *to trace* or *find out; to investigate; to discover.*

Invĭcem, adv. (in & vicis,) *mutually; in turn:* se invĭcem occidērunt, *they slew one another.*

Invictus, a, um, part. (in & victus,) *unconquerable; impenetrable; invulnerable.*

Invidia, æ, f. (invĭdus,) *envy; hatred.*

Invīsus, a, um, adj. (invideo,) *envied; hated; hateful; obnoxious:* plebi, *unpopular.*

Invitātus, a, um, part. *invited; entertained:*—subs. *a guest.*

Invīto, āre, āvi, ātum, tr. *to invite.*

Invius, a, um, adj. (in & via,) *impassible; inaccessible; impenetrable.*

Invŏco, āre, āvi, ātum, tr. (in & voco,) *to call upon; to invoke.*

Iōnes, um, m. pl. *Ionians; the inhabitants of Ionia.*

Ionia, æ, f. *Ionia; a country on the western coast of Asia Minor.*

Ionius, a, um, adj. *of Ionia; Ionian:* mare, *that part of the Mediterranean which lies between Greece and the south of Italy.*

Iphicrătes, is, m. *an Athenian general.*

Iphigenīa, æ, f. *the daughter of Agamemnon and Clytemnestra, and priestess of Diana.*

Ipse, a, um, pro. § 32, *he himself; she herself; itself;* or simply *he; she; it:* et ipse, *he also;* before a verb of the first or second person, *I; thou:* ego ipse, *I myself:* tu ipse, *thou thyself,* &c.

Ira, æ, f. *anger; rage;* hence,

Irascor, irasci, intr. dep. *to be angry;* hence,

Irātus, a, um, adj. *angry.*

Ire. *See* Eo.

Irreparabĭlis, e, adj. comp. (in & reparabĭlis,) *irreparable; irrecoverable.*

Irretio, īre, īvi, ītum, tr. (in & rete,) *to enclose in a net; to entangle; to ensnare.*

Irrīdens, tis, part. from

Irrideo, dēre, si, sum, tr. (in & rideo,) *to laugh at; to deride.*

Irrĭgo, āre, āvi, ātum, tr. (in & rigo,) *to water; to bedew; to moisten.*

Irrīto, āre, āvi, ātum, tr. (hirrio, *to snarl like a dog;*) *to irritate; to provoke; to incite.*

Irruens, tis, part. from

Irruo, uĕre, ui, (in & ruo,) intr. *to rush in, into,* or *upon; to rush; to attack.*

Is, ea, id, pro. § 31, 3, *this; he: she; it:* in eo esse, i. e. in eo statu, *to be in that state; to be upon the point.*

Issus, i, f. *a maritime city of Cilicia.*

Issĭcus, a, um, adj. *of* or *belonging to Issus.*

Isocrătes, is, m. *a celebrated Athenian orator.*

Iste, a, ud, pro. § 31, 2, *that; that person* or *thing; he; she; it.* (*The demonstrative of the second person, and used to indicate a thing near, relating to,* or *spoken of, by the person addressed.* 118, 3, 3d.)

Ister, tri, m. *the name of the Danube, after it enters Illyricum.*

Isthmĭcus, a, um, adj. *Isthmian; belonging to the Isthmus of Corinth:* ludi, *games celebrated at that place.*

Isthmus, i, m. *an isthmus.*

Ita, adv. (is,) *so; in such a manner; even so; thus.*

Italia, æ, f. *Italy.*

Itălus, a, um, adj. *Italian.*

Ităli, subs. *the Italians.*

Italĭcus, a, um, adj. *belonging to Italy; Italian.*

Ităque, adv. (ita & que,) *and so; therefore.*

Iter, itinĕris, n. (eo,) *a journey; a road; a march.*

Itĕrum, adv. (iter,) *again; once more; a second time.*

Ithăca, æ, f. *a rocky island in the Ionian sea, with a city of the same name.*

Itĭdem, adv. (ita & idem,) *in like manner; likewise; also.*

Itūrus, a, um, part. (eo.)

Ivi. *See* Eo.

J.

Jacens, tis, part. from

Jaceo, ēre, ui, ĭtum, *to lie:* intr. *to be situated.*

Jacio, jacĕre, jēci, jactum, tr. *to throw; to cast; to fling; to hurl.*

Jacto, āre, āvi, ātum, freq. (jacio,) *to throw often; to toss; to agitate.*

Jactus, a, um, part. (jacio,) *cast; thrown.*

Jacŭlor, āri, ātus sum, tr. dep.

(jacŭlum, from jacio,) *to hurl; to dart; to shoot.*

Jam, adv. (a stronger term than nunc,) *now; already; presently; even:* jam nunc, *even now:* jam tum, *even then:* jam inde, *ever since:* jam primum, *in the first place.*

Jamdūdum, adv. (jam & dudum, *lately;*) *long ago.*

Janicŭlum, i, n. *one of the seven hills of Rome.*

Jason, ŏnis, m. *the son of Æson, king of Thessaly, and leader of the Argonauts;* also, *an inhabitant of Lycia.*

Jejūnus, a, um, adj. comp. *fasting; hungry.*

Jovis. *See* Jupĭter.

Juba, æ, f *the mane.*

Jubeo, jubēre, jussi, jussum, tr. *to command; to bid; to order; to direct.*

Jucundus, a, um, adj. comp. (jocus,) *agreeable; delightful; pleasant; sweet.*

Judæa, æ, f. *Judea.*

Judæus, a, um, adj. *belonging to Judea:*—subs. *a Jew.*

Judex, ĭcis, c. (judĭco,) *a judge.*

Judicium, i, n. (judex,) *a judgment; decision.*

Judĭco, āre, āvi, ātum, tr. (jus & dico,) *to judge; to deem; to determine; to decide.*

Jugĕrum, i, n. 96, 7, (*the quantity ploughed by a yoke of oxen in one day;*) *an acre of land.*

Jugum, i, n. (jungo,) *a yoke; a ridge* or *chain of mountains:* in war, *an instrument consisting of two spears placed erect, and a third laid transversely upon them.*

Jugurtha, æ, m. *a king of Numidia.*

Julius, i, m. *a name of Cæsar, who belonged to the* gens Julia.

Junctus, a, um, part. (jungo.)

Junior, adj. (comparative from juvĕnis,) *younger;* § 26, 6.

Junius, i, m. *the name of a Roman tribe which included the family of Brutus.*

Jungo, jungĕre, junxi, junctum, tr. *to unite; to connect; to join:* currui, *to put in; to harness to.*

Juno, ōnis, f. *the daughter of Saturn and wife of Jupiter.*

Jupĭter, Jovis, m. § 15, 12, *the son of Saturn and king of the gods.*

Jurgiōsus, a, um, adj. (jurgium,) *quarrelsome; brawling.*

Juro, āre, āvi, ātum, tr. *to swear;* from

Jus, juris, n. *right; justice; natural law:* jus civitātis, *the freedom of the city; citizenship:* jure, *with reason; rightly; deservedly.*

Jussi. *See* Jubeo.

Jussus, a, um, part. (jubeo.)

Jussu, abl. m. (jubeo,) *a command.*

Justitia, æ, f. *justice;* from

Justus, a, um, adj. comp. (jus,) *just; right; full; regular; ordinary; exact.*

Juvenca, æ, f. (f. of juvencus, i. e. juvenĭcus, fr. juvĕnis,) *a cow; a heifer.*

Juvencius, i, m. *a Roman general, conquered by Andriscus.*

Juvĕnis, adj. (junior, § 26, 6,) (fr. juvo,) *young; youthful.*

Juvĕnis, is, c. *a young man* or *woman; a youth;* hence,

Juventus, ūtis, f. *youth.*

Juvo, juvāre, juvi, jutum, tr. *to help; to assist.*

Juxta, prep. (jungo,) *near; hard by:*—adv. *alike; even; equally.*

L.

L., *an abbreviation of* Lucius.

Labor, & Labos, ōris, m. *labor; toil.*

Labor, labi, lapsus, intr. dep. *to fall; to glide; to glide away; to flow on.*

Laboriōsus, a, um, adj. comp. (labor,) *laborious.*

Labōro, āre, āvi, ātum, intr. *to work* or *labor; to suffer with; to be distressed.*

Labyrinthus, i, m. *a labyrinth.*

Lac, lactis, n. *milk.*

Lacedæmon, ŏnis, f. *Lacedæmon,* or *Sparta, the capital of Laconia.*

Lacedæmonius, a, um, adj. *belonging to Lacedæmon; Lacedæmonian; Spartan.*

Lacerātus, a, um, part. from

Lacĕro, āre, āvi, ātum, tr. (lacer, *mangled;*) *to tear in pieces.*

Lacessītus, a, um, part. from

Lacesso, ĕre, īvi, ītum, tr. (lacio,) *to provoke; to stir up; to disturb; to trouble.*

Lacrȳma, æ, f. *a tear.*

Lacus, ûs, m. *a lake.*

Laconĭcus, a, um, adj. *Laconic; Spartan; Lacedæmonian.*

Lædo, lædĕre, læsi, læsum, tr. *to injure; to hurt.*

Lætātus, a, um, part. (lætor.)

Lætitia, æ, f. (lætus,) *joy.*

Lætor, āri, ātus sum, intr. dep. *to rejoice; to be glad; to be delighted with.*

Lætus, a, um, adj. (ior, issĭmus,) *glad; joyful; full of joy; fortunate; prosperous; fruitful; abundant.*

Lævīnus, i, m. *the name of a Roman family;* (P. Valerius,) *a Roman consul.*

Lævor, ōris, m. (lævis or levis,) *smoothness.*

Lagus, i, m. *a Macedonian, who adopted as his son that Ptolemy who afterwards became king of Egypt.*

Lana, æ, f. *wool.*

Lanātus, a, um, adj. *bearing wool; woolly.*

Laniātus, a, um, part. from
Lanio, āre, āvi, ātum, tr. *to tear in pieces.*
Lapicidīna, æ, f. (lapis & cædo,) *a quarry.*
Lapideus, a, um, adj. *stony;* from
Lapis, ĭdis, m. *a stone.*
Lapsus, a, um, part. (labor.)
Laqueus, i, m. *a noose; a snare.*
Largitio, ōnis, f. (largior, from largus,) *a present.*
Latè, adv. (iùs, issĭmè,) *widely; extensively;* from latus.
Latebra, æ, f. (lateo,) *a lurking-place; a hiding-place; a retreat.*
Latens, tis, part. from
Lateo, ēre, ui, intr. *to be hidden; to be concealed; to be unknown; to be unknown to.*
Later, ĕris, m. *a brick.*
Latercŭlus, i, m. dim. (later,) *a little brick; a brick.*
Latīnus, i, m. *an ancient king of the Laurentes, a people of Italy.*
Latīnus, a, um, adj. *Latin; of Latium:* Latīni, subs. *the Latins.*
Latitūdo, ĭnis, f. (latus,) *breadth.*
Latium, i, n. *Latium.*
Latmus, i, m. *a mountain in Caria, near the borders of Ionia.*
Latōna, æ, f. *the daughter of the giant Cœus, and mother of Apollo and Diana.*
Latro, āre, āvi, ātum, intr. & tr. *to bark; to bark at.*
Latro, ōnis, m. properly, *a mercenary soldier;* commonly, *a robber.*
Latrocinium, i, n. (latrocinor,) *robbery; piracy.*
Latūrus, a, um, part. (fero.)
Latus, a, um, adj. (ior, issĭmus,) *broad; wide.*
Latus, ĕris, n. *a side.*
Laudātus, a, um, part. from
Laudo, āre, āvi, ātum, tr. *to praise; to extol; to commend.*
Laurentia, æ, f. *See* Acca.
Laus, dis, f. *praise; glory; honor; fame; repute; estimation; value.*
Lautè, adv. iùs, issĭmè, (lautus, fr. lavo,) *sumptuously; magnificently.*
Lavinia, æ, f. *the daughter of Latīnus, and the second wife of Ænēas.*
Lavinium, i, n. *a city in Italy, built by Ænēas.*
Lavo, lavāre & lavĕre, lavi, lotum, lautum, & lavātum, tr. *to wash; to bathe.*
Leæna, æ, f. *a lioness.*
Leander, & Leandrus, dri, m. *a youth of Abydos, distinguished for his attachment to Hero.*
Lebes, ētis, m. *a kettle; a caldron.*
Lectus, a, um, part. (lego,) *read; chosen.*
Leda, æ, f. *the wife of Tyndarus, king of Sparta, and the mother of Helĕna.*
Legatio, ōnis, f. (lego, āre,) *an embassy.*

Legātus, i, m. (lego, āre,) *a deputy; a lieutenant; an ambassador.*

Legio, ōnis, f. (lego, ĕre,) *a legion; ten cohorts of soldiers.*

Legislātor, ōris, m. (lex & fero,) *a legislator; a lawgiver.*

Lego, legĕre, legi, lectum, tr. *to gather; to collect; to choose; to read.*

Lemānus, i, m. *the name of a lake in Gaul, bordering upon the country of the Helvetii,* now *the lake of Geneva.*

Leo, ōnis, m. *a lion.*

Leonĭdas, æ, m. *a brave king of Sparta, who fell in the battle of Thermopylæ.*

Leontīnus, a, um, adj. *belonging to Leontini, a city and a people of the same name, on the eastern coast of Sicily.*

Lepĭdus, i, m. *the name of an illustrious family of the Æmilian clan.*

Lepus, ŏris, m. *a hare.*

Letālis, e, adj. *fatal; deadly;* from.

Letum, & Lethum, i, n. *death.*

Levis, e, adj. (ior, issĭmus,) *light; trivial; inconsiderable; smooth;* hence,

Levĭtas, ātis, f. *lightness.*

Levo, āre, āvi, ātum, tr. (levis,) *to make light; to ease; to relieve; to lighten; to alleviate.*

Lex, gis, f. (lego,) *statute* or *written law; a law; a condition.* Legem ferre, *or* rogāre, *to propose a law. See* jus.

Libens, tis, part. (libet;) *willing.*

Libenter, adv. (iùs, issĭmè, fr. libens,) *willingly.*

Libet, *or* Lubet, libuit, imp. *it pleases.*

Liber, libĕra, libĕrum, adj. *free;* (liberior, liberrĭmus.)

Liber, libri, m. *the inner bark of a tree; a writing on bark; a leaf; a book.*

Liberalĭter, adv. (liberālis,) *liberally; kindly.*

Liberātus, a, um, part. (libĕro,) *liberated; set at liberty.*

Libĕrè, adv. iùs, rĭmè, (liber,) *freely; without restraint.*

Libĕri, ōrum, m. pl. (liber,) *persons free born; children.*

Libĕro, āre, āvi, ātum, tr. *to free; to liberate; to deliver.*

Libertas, ātis, f. (liber,) *liberty.*

Libya, æ, f. properly *Libya, a kingdom of Africa, lying west of Egypt; sometimes it comprehends the whole of Africa.*

Licinius, i, m. *a name common among the Romans.*

Licet, uit, ĭtum est, imp. § 85, 4, *it is lawful; it is permitted:* tibi, *you may; one may.*

Licèt, conj. *although.*

Lienōsus, a, um, adj. (lien, *the spleen;*) *splenetic.*

Ligneus, a, um, adj. *wooden;* fr.

Lignum, i, n. *wood; a log of wood; timber:* ligna, *pieces of wood; sticks.*

Ligo, āre, āvi, ātum, tr. *to bind.*

Liguria, æ, f. *Liguria, a country in the west of Italy.*

Ligus, ūris, m. *a Ligurian.*

Ligustĭcus, a, um, adj. *Ligurian*; mare, *the gulf of Genŏa.*

Lilybæum, i, n. *a promontory on the western coast of Sicily.*

Limpĭdus, a, um, adj. (ior, issĭmus,) (lympha *or* limpa,) *transparent; limpid; clear.*

Limus, i, m. *mud; clay.*

Lingua, æ, f. (lingo,) *the tongue; a language.*

Linum, i, n. *flax; linen.*

Liquĭdus, a, um, adj. (liqueo, *to melt;*) (ior, issĭmus,) *liquid; clear; pure; limpid.*

Lis, litis, f. *a strife; a contention; a controversy.*

Littĕra, *or* Litĕra, æ, f. (lino,) *a letter of the alphabet:* (pl.) *letters; literature; learning; a letter; an epistle;* hence,

Litterarius, a, um, adj. *belonging to letters; literary.*

Littus, *or* Litus, ŏris, n. *the shore.*

Loco, āre, āvi, ātum, tr. *to place, set, dispose,* or *arrange; to give* or *dispose of in marriage;* from

Locus, i, m. in sing.; loci & loca, m. & n. in pl. *a place.*

Locusta, æ, f. *a locust.*

Longè, adv. (iùs, issĭmè,) (longus,) *far; far off.*

Longinquus, a um, adj. (comp. ior,) *far; distant; long; foreign.*

Longitūdo, ĭnis, f. *length;* fr.

Longus, a, um, adj. (ior, issĭmus,) *long:* applied both to time and space; *lasting.*

Locūtus, a, um, part. (loquor,) *having spoken.*

Locutūrus, a, um, part. *about to speak;* from

Loquor, loqui, locūtus sum, intr. dep. *to speak; to converse:* tr. *to say.*

Lorīca, æ. f. *a coat of mail; corselet; breast-plate; cuirass;* (anciently made of thongs;) from

Lorum, i, n. *a thong.*

Lubens, tis, part. (lubet.)

Lubenter, adv. (iùs, issĭmè.) *See* Libenter.

Lubet. *See* Libet.

Lubīdo, *or* Libīdo, ĭnis, f. *lust; desire.*

Lubrĭcus, a, um, adj. (labor,) *to slip; slippery.*

Luceo, lucēre, luxi, intr. *to shine.*

Lucius, i, m. *a Roman* prænōmen.

Lucretia, æ, f. *a Roman matron, the wife of Collatīnus.*

Lucretius, i, m. *the father of Lucretia.*

Luctus, ûs, m. (lugeo,) *mourning; sorrow.*

Lucullus, i, m. *a Roman celebrated for his luxury, his patronage of learned men, and his military talents.*

Lucus, i, m. *a wood, consecrated to some deity; a grove.*

Ludo, ludĕre, lusi, lusum, tr. *to play; to be in sport; to deceive;* from

Ludus, i, m. *a game; a play; a place of exercise; a school:* gladiatorius, *a school for gladiators.*

Lugeo, lugēre, luxi, intr. *to mourn; to lament.*

Lumen, ĭnis, n. (luceo,) *light; an eye.*

Luna, æ, f. *the moon.*

Lupa, æ, f. *a she-wolf.*

Lupus, i, m. *a wolf.*

Luscinia, æ, f. *a nightingale.*

Lusitania, æ, f. *a part of* Hispania, now *Portugal.*

Lustro, āre, āvi, ātum, tr. *to purify; to appease; to expiate:* exercĭtum, *to review; to muster;* from

Lustrum, i, n. (luo *or* lavo,) *purification; a sacrifice of purification offered at the conclusion of the census every five years; a period of five years; a place for bathing;* hence, *the place where swine wallow; a den* or *lair of wild beasts.*

Lusus, ûs, m. (ludo,) *a game: a play:* per lusum, *in sport; sportively.*

Lutatius, i, m. *the name of a Roman tribe:* C. Lutatius Catŭlus, *a Roman consul in the Punic war.*

Lutetia, æ, f. *a city of Gaul,* now *Paris.*

Lutum, i, n. (luo,) *clay.*

Lux, lucis, f. *light.*

Luxuria, æ, f. (luxus, fr. luo,) *that which dissolves or loosens the energies of body and mind;* hence, *luxury; excess; voluptuousness.*

Lycius, a, um, adj. *Lycian; of Lycia, a country of Asia Minor.*

Lycomēdes, is, m. *a king of Scyros.*

Lycurgus, i, m. *the Spartan law-giver.*

Lydia, æ, f. *a country of Asia Minor.*

Lysander, dri, m. *a celebrated Lacedæmonian general.*

Lysimăchus, i, m. *one of Alexander's generals, who was afterwards king of a part of Thrace.*

M.

M., *an abbreviation of* Marcus.

Macĕdo, ŏnis, m. *a Macedonian.*

Macedonia, æ, f. *a country of Europe, lying west of Thrace, and north of Thessaly and Epīrus.*

Macedonĭcus, a, um, adj. *of Macedonia; Macedonian;* also, *an* agnōmen, *or surname of Q. Metellus.*

Macies, ēi, f. (maceo,) *leanness; decay.*

Macrobii, ōrum, m. pl. (*a Greek word signifying* long-lived,) *a name given to certain tribes of Ethiopians.*

who were distinguished for their longevity.

Mactātus, a, um, part. from

Macto, āre, āvi, ātum, tr. (magis aucto, from augeo,) *to increase with honors; to enrich; to honor with sacrifices:* hence, *to sacrifice; to slay.*

Macŭla, æ, f. *a spot; a stain.*

Madeo, ēre, ui, intr. *to be moist; to be wet.*

Mænădes, um, f. pl. *priestesses of Bacchus; bacchants; bacchanals.*

Mæōtis, ĭdis, adj. *Mæotian:* palus Mæōtis, *a lake* or *gulf, lying north of the Euxine,* now called *the sea of Azoph.*

Magis, adv. (sup. maxĭmè, Gr. 234,) *more; rather; better.*

Magister, tri, m. (magis,) *a teacher; a master:* magister equĭtum, *the commander of the cavalry, and the dictator's lieutenant;* hence,

Magistrātus, ûs, m. *a magistracy; a civil office; a magistrate.*

Magnesia, æ, f. *a town of Ionia.*

Magnifĭce, adv. (entiùs, entissĭmè,) (magnifĭcus,) *magnificently; splendidly.*

Magnificentia, æ, f. (id.) *magnificence; splendor; grandeur;* from

Magnifĭcus, a, um, adj. (entior, entissĭmus,) (magnus and facio,) *magnificent; splendid.*

Magnitūdo, ĭnis, f. (magnus,) *greatness; magnitude; size;* (applied chiefly to material objects.)

Magnopĕre, adv. *sometimes* magno opĕre, (magnus & opus,) *greatly; very; earnestly.*

Magnus, a, um, adj. (major, maxĭmus, 113,) *the general term applied to greatness of every kind;) great; large.*

Major, comp. (magnus,) *greater; the elder;* hence,

Majōres, um, m. pl. *forefathers; ancestors.*

Malè, adv. (pejùs, pessĭmè,) (malus,) *badly; ill; hurtfully.*

Maledīco, -dicĕre, -dixi, -dictum, intr. (malè & dico,) *to revile; to rail at; to abuse; to reproach.*

Maledĭcus, a, um, adj. (entior. entissĭmus, 113, 3,) *reviling; railing; scurrilous; abusive.*

Malefĭcus, a, um, adj. (entior, entissĭmus, 113, 3,) (malè & facio,) *wicked; hurtful; mischievous; injurious:*—subs. *an evil doer.*

Malo, malle, malui, tr. irr. (magis & volo,) § 83, 6, *to prefer; to be more willing; to wish.*

Malum, i, n. *an apple.*

Malum, i, n. (malus,) *evil;*

misfortune; calamity; sufferings; evil deeds.

Malus, a, um, adj. (pejor, pessĭmus, § 26,) *bad; wicked:* mali, *bad men.*

Mancīnus, i, m. *a Roman consul who made a disgraceful peace with the Numantians.*

Mando, mandĕre, mandi, mansum, tr. *to chew; to eat.*

Mando, āre, āvi, ātum, tr. (manui & do,) *to give into one's hand;* hence, *to command; to intrust; to commit; to bid; to enjoin:* mandāre marmorĭbus, *to engrave upon marble.*

Mane, ind. n. *the morning;* adv. *early in the morning.*

Maneo, ēre, ·si, sum, intr. *to remain; to continue.*

Manes, ium, m. pl. *the manes; ghosts or shades of the dead.*

Manlius, i, m. *a Roman proper name.*

Mano, āre, āvi, ātum, intr. *to flow.*

Mansuefacio, -facĕre, -fēci, -factum, tr. (mansues & facio,) *to tame; to make tame.*

Mansuefīo, -fiĕri, -factus sum, irr. § 83, Obs. 3, p. 188, *to be made tame.*

Mansuefactus, a, um, part.

Mantinēa, æ, f. *a city of Arcadia.*

Manubiæ, ārum, f. pl. (manus,) *booty; spoils; plunder.*

Manumissus, a, um, part. fr.

Manumitto, -mittĕre, -mīsi, -missum, tr. (manus & mitto,) *to set free; at liberty; to free; to manumit.*

Manus, ûs, f. *a hand; the trunk of an elephant; a band* or *body of soldiers.*

Mapāle, is, n. *a hut* or *cottage of the Numidians.*

Marcellus, i, m. *the name of a Roman family which produced many illustrious men.*

Marcius, i, m. *a Roman name and* cognōmen or *surname.*

Marcus, i, m. *a Roman* prænōmen.

Mare, is, n. *the sea; (a general term:* æquor, *a level surface:* pontus, *the sea, so called from Pontus, an ancient god of the sea:* pelăgus, *the deep sea.)*

Margarīta, æ, f. *a pearl.*

Mariandȳni, ōrum, m. pl. *a people of Bithynia.*

Marīnus, a, um, adj. (mare,) *marine; pertaining to the sea:* aqua marīna, *seawater.*

Maritĭmus, a, um, adj. (id.) *maritime; on the sea-coast:* copiæ, *naval forces.*

Marītus, i, m. (mas,) *a husband.*

Marius, i, m. (C.) *a distinguished Roman general, who was seven times elected consul.*

Marmor, ōris, n. *marble.*

Mars, tis, m. *the son of Jupiter and Juno, and god of war.*

Marsi, ōrum, m. pl. *a people of Latium, upon the borders of Lake Ticīnus.*

Marsÿas, æ, m. *a celebrated Phrygian musician;* also, *a brother of Antigŏnus, the king of Macedonia.*

Massa, æ, f. *a mass; a lump.*

Massĭcus, a, um, adj. *Massic; of Massĭcus, a mountain in Campania, famous for its wine:* vinum, *Massic winè.*

Massilia, æ, f. *a maritime town of* Gallia Narbonensis, now *Marseilles.*

Mater, tris, f. *a mother; a matron;* hence,

Materia, æ, f. *a material; matter; stuff; timber.*

Matrimōnium, i, n. (id.) *matrimony; marriage.*

Matrōna, æ, f. *a river of Gaul.*

Matrōna, æ, f. *a matron.*

Maturesco, maturescĕre, maturui, intr. inc. *to ripen; to grow ripe;* from

Matūrus, a, um, adj. (ior, rĭmus, *or* issĭmus,) *ripe; mature; perfect.*

Mauritania, æ, f. *a country in the western part of Africa, extending from Numidia to the Atlantic ocean.*

Mausōlus, i, m. *a king of Caria.*

Maxilla, æ, f. *a jaw; a jawbone.*

Maxĭmè, adv. (sup. of magìs,) *most of all; especially; greatly.*

Maxĭmus, i, m. *a Roman surname:* Qu. Fabius Maxĭmus, *a distinguished Roman general.*

Maxĭmus, a, um, adj. (sup. of magnus,) *greatest; eldest:* maxĭmus natu, *oldest. See* Natu.

Mecum, (me & cum,) *with me.*

Medeor, ēri, intr. dep. *to cure; to heal.*

Medicīna, æ, f. (medĭcus,) *medicine.*

Medĭco, āre, āvi, ātum, tr. (id.) *to heal; to administer medicine; to medicate; to prepare medically; to embalm.*

Medĭcus, i, m. *a physician.*

Meditātus, a, um, part. *designed; practiced;* from

Medĭtor, āri, ātus sum, tr. dep. *to meditate; to reflect; to practice.*

Mediomatrĭci, ōrum, m. pl. *a people of Belgic Gaul.*

Medius, a, um, adj. *middle; the midst:* medium, *the middle.*

Medūsa, æ, f. *one of the three Gorgons.*

Megăra, æ, f. *the capital of Megaris.*

Megarenses, ium, m. pl. *Megarensians; the inhabitants of Megăra.*

Megăris, ĭdis, f. *a small country of Greece.*

Megasthĕnes, is, m. *a Greek historian, whose works have been lost.*

Mehercŭlè, adv. *by Hercules; truly; certainly.*

Mel, lis, n. *honey.*

Meleāgrus, & -āger, gri, m. *a king of Calydonia.*

Melior, us, adj. (comp of bonus, 113,) *better.*

Meliùs, adv. (comp. of benè, 234,) *better.*

Membrāna, æ, f. *a thin skin; a membrane; parchment.*

Membrum, i, n. *a limb; a member.*

Memĭni, def. pret. 222, 2, *I remember; I relate.*

Memor, ŏris, adj. *mindful.*

Memorabĭlis, e, adj. comp. (memor,) *memorable; remarkable; worthy of being mentioned.*

Memoria, æ, f. (id.) *memory.*

Memŏro, āre, āvi, ātum, tr. *to remember; to call to one's memory; to say; to mention.*

Memphis, is, f. *a large city of Egypt.*

Mendacium, i, n. *a falsehood;* from

Mendax, ācis, adj. (mentior,) *false; lying.*

Menelāus, i, m. *a king of Sparta, the son of Atreus, and husband of Helen.*

Menenius, i, m. (Agrippa,) a *Roman, distinguished for his success in reconciling the plebeians to the patricians.*

Mens, tis, f. *the mind; the understanding; (the reasoning faculty as distinguished from* anĭmus, *the seat of feelings and passions.)* Anĭmo et mente, *with the whole soul.*

Mensis, is, m. *a month.*

Mentio, ōnis, f. (memĭni,) *a mention* or *a speaking of.*

Mentior, īri, ītus sum, tr. dep. *to lie; to assert falsely; to feign; to deceive.*

Mercātor, ōris, m. (mercor,) *a merchant; a trader.*

Mercatūra, æ, f. (id.) *merchandise; trade.*

Mercātus, ûs, m. (id.) *a market; a mart; a fair; an emporium; a sale.*

Merces, ēdis, f. (mereo,) *wages; a reward; a price.*

Mercurius, i, m. *Mercury, the son of Jupiter and Maia. He was the messenger of the gods.*

Mereo, ēre, ui, ĭtum, intr. & tr. *to deserve; to gain; to acquire.*

Mereor, ēri, ĭtus sum, intr. & tr. dep. *to deserve; to earn.*

Mergo, mergĕre, mersi, mersum, tr. *to sink; to dip in,* or *under.*

Meridiānus, a, um, adj. *southern; south; at noon-day;* from

Meridies, iēi, m. (medius, & dies,) *noon; mid-day; south.*

Merĭtò, adv. *with reason; with good reason; deservedly.*

Merĭtum, i, n. (mereo,) *merit; desert.*

Mersi. *See* Mergo.

Mersus, a, um, part. (mergo.)

Merŭla, æ, f. *a blackbird.*

Merx, cis, f. *merchandise.*

Messis, is, f. (meto,) *the harvest; a reaping.*

Meta, æ, f. (meto, āre,) *a pillar in the form of a cone; a goal; a limit.*

Metagonium, i, n. *a promontory in the northern part of Africa.*

Metallum, i, n. *metal; a mine.*

Metanīra, æ, f. *the wife of Celeus, king of Eleusis.*

Metellus, i, m. *the name of an illustrious family at Rome.*

Metior, metīri, mensus sum, tr. dep. *to measure.*

Metius, i, m. (Suffetius,) *an Alban general, put to death by Tullus Hostilius.*

Meto, metĕre, messui, messum, tr. *to reap; to mow.*

Metuo, metuĕre, metui, tr. & intr. *to fear;* from

Metus, ûs, m. *fear.*

Meus, a, um, pro. 121, (ego,) *my; mine.*

Micipsa, æ, m. *a king of Numidia.*

Mĭco, āre, ui, intr. *to move quickly,* or *with a quivering, tremulous motion, as the tongue of a serpent; to glance; to shine; to glitter. See* dimĭco.

Midas, æ, m. *a king of Phrygia, distinguished for his wealth.*

Migro, āre, āvi, ātum, intr. *to remove; to migrate; to wander.*

Mihi. *See* Ego.

Miles, ĭtis, c. (mille, properly, *one of a thousand;*) *a soldier; the soldiery.*

Milētus, i, f. *the capital of Ionia, near the borders of Caria.*

Militia, æ, f. (miles,) *war; military service.*

Milĭto, āre, āvi, ātum, intr. (id.) *to serve in war.*

Mille, n. ind. (in sing.) *a thousand:* millia, um, pl.—mille, adj. ind. 104, 5.

Milliarium, i, n. (mille, sc, passuum, 909,) *a milestone; a mile,* or 5000 *feet:* ad quintum milliarium urbis, *to the fifth milestone of the city,* i. e. *within five miles of the city.*

Miltiădes, is, m. *a celebrated Athenian general, who conquered the Persians.*

Milvius, i, m. *a kite.*

Minæ, ārum, f. pl. (mineo, *to hang over;*) *projecting points; battlements;* commonly, *threats.*

Minātus, a, um, part. (minor.)

Minerva, æ, f. *the daughter of Jupiter, and goddess of war and wisdom.*

Minĭmè, adv. (sup. of parum,) *least; at least; not at all.*

Minĭmus, a, um, adj. (sup. of parvus, 113,) *the least; the smallest.*

Ministerium, i, n. (minister,) *service; labor.*

Minium, i, n. *red lead; vermilion.*

Minor, āri, ātus sum, tr. dep. & intr. *to project; to reach upwards; to threaten; to menace.*

Minor, ōris, adj. (comp. of parvus, 113,) *less; smaller; weaker.*

Minos, ōis, *a son of Europa, and king of Crete.*

Minuo, minuĕre, minui, minūtum, tr. (minus,) *to diminish.*

Minùs, adv. (minor,) (comp. of parum,) *less:* quò minùs, *or* quomĭnus, *that—not.*

Miracŭlum, i, n. (miror,) *a miracle; a wonder.*

Mirabĭlis, e, adj. (id.) *wonderful; astonishing.*

Mirātus, a, um, part. (miror,) *wondering at.*

Mirè, adv. (mirus,) *wonderfully; remarkably.*

Miror, āri, ātus sum, tr. dep. *to wonder at; to admire;* from

Mirus, a, um, adj. *wonderful; surprising.*

Misceo, miscēre, miscui, mistum *or* mixtum, tr. *to mingle; to mix.*

Miser, ĕra, ĕrum, adj. (erior, errĭmus,) *miserable; unhappy; wretched; sad.*

Miserātus, a, um, part. (misĕror.)

Misereor, miserēri, miserĭtus, *or* misertus sum, tr. dep. (miser,) *to have compassion; to pity.*

Misĕret, miseruit, miserĭtum est, imp. (misereo, fr. miser,) *it pitieth:* me misĕret, *I pity.*

Misericordia, æ, f. (misericors, from misereo & cor,) *pity; compassion.*

Misĕror, āri, ātus sum, tr. dep. (miser,) *to pity.*

Misi. *See* Mitto.

Mistus & mixtus, a, um, part. (misceo.)

Mithridātes, is, m. *a celebrated king of Pontus.*

Mithridatĭcus, a, um, adj. *belonging to Mithridates; Mithridatic.*

Mitis, e, adj. § 21, II., (ior, issĭmus,) *mild; meek; kind; humane.*

Mitto, mĭttĕre, misi, missum, tr. *to send; to throw; to bring forth; to produce; to afford:* mittĕre se in aquam, *to plunge into the water.*

Mixtus. *See* Mistus.

Modĭcus, a, um, adj. (modus,) *moderate; of moderate size; small.*

Modius, i, m. *a measure; a half bushel.* 908, 4.

Modò, adv. *now; only; but:* modò—modò, *sometimes—sometimes:* conj. (*for* si modò *or* dummŏdo,) *provided that; if only.*

Modus, i, m. *a measure;* same

as modius, (908, 4,) *a manner; a way; degree; limit; moderation.*
Mœnia, um, n. pl. (munio,) *the walls of a city, furnished with towers and battlements for defence.*
Mœnus, i, m. *the Maine, a river of Germany, and a branch of the Rhine.*
Mœrens, tis, part. from
Mœreo, mœrēre, intr. *to be sad; to mourn.*
Mœris, is, m. *a lake in Egypt.*
Moles, is, f. *a mass; a bulk; a burden; a weight; a pile.*
Molestus, a, um, adj. (moles,) (ior, issĭmus,) *irksome; severe; troublesome; oppressive; unwelcome.*
Mollio, īre, īvi, ītum, tr. *to soften; to moderate;* from
Mollis, e, adj. (ior, issĭmus,) *soft; tender.*
Molossi, ōrum, m. pl. *the Molossians, a people of Epīrus.*
Momordi. *See* Mordeo.
Monens, tis, part. from
Moneo, ēre, ui, ĭtum, tr. *to advise; to remind; to warn; to admonish;* hence,
Monimentum, *or* -umentum, i, n. (moneo,) *a monument; a memorial; a record;* and
Monĭtor, ōris, m. *a monitor.*
Mons, tis, m. *a mountain; a mount.*
Monstro, āre, āvi, ātum, tr. (moneo,) *to show; point out.*
Mora, æ, f. *delay.*
Morbus, i, m. *a disease.*
Mordax, ācis, adj. (comp.) *biting; sharp; snappish;* fr.
Mordeo, mordēre, momordi, morsum, tr. *to bite.*
Mores. *See* Mos.
Moriens, tis, part. from
Morior, mori & morīri, mortuus sum, intr. dep. 220, *to die.*
Moror, āri, ātus sum, intr. dep. *to delay; to tarry; to stay; to remain;* tr. nihil moror, *I care not for; I value not.*
Morōsus, a, um, adj. comp. (mos,) *morose; peevish; fretful.*
Mors, tis, f. *death.*
Morsus, ûs, m. (mordeo,) *bite; biting.*
Mortālis, e, adj. (mors,) *mortal.*
Mortuus, a, um, part. (morior,) *dead.*
Mos, mōris, m. *a manner; a way; a custom:* more, *after the manner of; like:* mores, *conduct; deportment; manners; customs.*
Mossyni, ōrum, m. p. *a people of Asia Minor, near the Euxine.*
Motus, ûs, m. (moveo,) *motion:* terræ motus, *an earthquake.*
Motus, a, um, part. from
Moveo, movēre, movi, motum, tr. *to move; to stir; to excite.*
Mox, adv. *soon; soon after; by and by.*
Mucius, i, m. (Scævŏla,) *a Roman, celebrated for his fortitude.*

Muliebris, e, adj. *womanly; female;* from

Mulier, ĕris, f. *a woman.*

Multitūdo, ĭnis, f. (multus,) *a multitude.*

Multo, *or* -cto, āre, āvi, ātum, tr. (multa, *or* mulcta, from mulgeo,) *to punish by deprivation; to fine; to impose a fine; to sentence to pay a fine.*

Multò, & Multùm, adv. *much:* multò, *by far.*

Multus, a, um, adj. *much; many.*

Mummius, i, m. *a Roman general.*

Mundus, i, m. (mundus, *neat, orderly,*) *the world; the universe.*

Muniendus, a, um, part. from

Munĭo, īre, īvi, ītum, tr. *to build a wall or fortress; to fortify:* viam, *to open* or *prepare a road.*

Munus, ĕris, n. *an office; service; duty; a gift; a present; a favor; a reward for service;* (distinguished from donum, *a free gift.*)

Murālis, e, adj. *pertaining to a wall:* corōna, *the mural crown, given to him who first mounted the wall of a besieged town;* from

Murus, i, m. *a wall; a wall of a town, garden,* or *other enclosed place.*

Mus, muris, m. *a mouse.*

Musa, æ, f. *a muse; a song.*

Musca, æ, f. *a fly.*

Muscŭlus, i, m. dim, (mus,) *a little mouse.*

Musĭce, es, & Musĭca, æ, f. (musa,) *music; the art of music;* hence,

Musĭcus, a, um, adj. *musical.*

Muto, āre, āvi, ātum, tr. (moveo,) *to change; to transform.*

Mygdonia, æ, f. *a small country of Phrygia.*

Myrmecĭdes, is, m. *an ingenious artist of Milētus.*

Myndius, i, m. *a Myndian; an inhabitant of Myndus.*

Myndus, i, f. *a city in Caria, near Halicarnassus.*

Mysia, æ, f. *a country of Asia Minor, having the Propontis on the north, and the Ægean sea on the west.*

N.

Nabis, ĭdis, m. *a tyrant of Lacedæmon.*

Næ, adv. *verily; truly.*

Nactus, a, um, part. (nanciscor,) *having found.*

Nam, conj. *for; but.*

Nanciscor, nancisci, nactus sum, tr. dep. (nancio, not used,) *to get; to find; to meet with.*

Narbonensis, e, adj. Narbonensis Gallia, *one of the four divisions of Gaul, in the south-eastern part, deriving its name from the city of Narbo,* now *Narbonne.*

Naris, is, f. *the nostril.*

Narro, āre, āvi, ātum, tr. *to relate; to tell; to say.*

Nascor, nasci, natus sum, intr. dep. *to be born; to grow; to be produced.*

Nascĭca, æ, m. *a surname of Publius Cornelius Scipio.*

Nasus, i, m. *the nose.*

Natālis, e, adj. (nascor,) *natal:* dies natālis, *a birthday.*

Natans, tis, part. from

Nato, āre, āvi, ātum, intr. freq. (no,) *to swim; to float.*

Natu, abl. sing. m. *by birth:* natu minor, *the younger:* minĭmus, *the youngest:* major, *the elder:* maxĭmus, *the oldest;* § 26, 6.

Natūra, æ, f. (nascor,) *nature; creation; power;* hence,

Naturālis, e, adj. *natural.*

Natus, a um, part. (nascor,) *born:* octoginta annos natus, *born eighty years;* i. e. *eighty years old;* hence,

Natus, i, m. *a son.*

Naufragium, i, n. (navis & frango,) *a shipwreck.*

Nauta, æ, *and* navĭta, æ, (navis,) m. *a sailor.*

Navālis, e, adj. (navis,) *naval; belonging to ships.*

Navigabĭlis, e, adj. (navĭgo,) *navigable.*

Navigatio, ōnis, f. (id.) *navigation;* and

Navigium, i, n. *a ship; a vessel;* from

Navĭgo, āre, āvi, ātum, tr. (navis & ago,) *to steer, navigate,* or *direct a ship; to navigate; to sail:* navigātur, imp. *navigation is carried on; they sail.*

Navis, is, f. *a ship.*

Ne, conj. *not; lest; lest that; that—not:* ne quidem, *not even.*

Ne, conj. enclitic: *whether; or:* (In direct questions the translation is commonly omitted, Id. 56, 3d.)

Nec, conj. (nè & que,) *and not; but not; neither; nor.*

Necessarius, a, um, adj. (necesse,) *necessary:*—subs. *a friend.*

Necessĭtas, ātis, f. (id.) *necessity; duty.*

Neco, āre, āvi *or* ui, ātum, tr. *to kill; to destroy; to slay.*

Nefas, n. ind. (ne & fas,) *impiety; wrong; wickedness.*

Neglectus, a, um, part. from

Neglĭgo, -ligĕre, -lexi, -lectum, tr. (nec & lego,) *to neglect; not to care for; to disregard.*

Nego, āre, āvi, ātum, tr. (*probably,* ne & aio,) *to deny; to refuse: equal to* dico ut non, *to declare that not.*

Negotium, i, n. (nec & otium,) *business; labor; pains; difficulty:* facĭli *or* nullo negotio, *with little* or *no trouble; easily.*

Nemo, ĭnis, c. (ne & homo,) *no one; no man.*

Nemus, ŏris, n. *a forest; a grove; (but not consecrated as* lucus.)

Nepos, ōtis, m. *a grandson.*

Neptūnus, i, m. *the god of the sea, son of Saturn and Ops.*

Nequāquam, adv. (ne & quaquam,) *by no means.*

Neque, conj. (ne & que,) *and—not; neither; nor.*

Nequeo, īre, īvi, ītum, intr. irr. (ne & queo, § 83, 3,) *I can not; I am not able.*

Nequis, -qua, -quod, *or* -quid, pro. (ne & quis,) § 35, *lest any one; that no one* or *no thing.*

Nereis, ĭdis, f. *a Nereid; a sea-nymph. The Nereids were the daughters of Nereus and Doris.*

Nescio, īre, īvi, ītum, tr. (ne & scio,) *to be ignorant of; not to know; can not.*

Nestus, i, m. *a river in the western part of Thrace.*

Neuter, tra, trum, adj. (ne & uter,) *neither of the two; neither.*

Nicomēdes, is, m. *a king of Bithynia.*

Nidifĭco, āre, āvi, ātum, intr. (nidus & facio,) *to build a nest.*

Nidus, i, m. *a nest.*

Niger, gra, grum, adj. (nigrior, nigerrĭmus,) *black.*

Nihil, n. ind. *or* Nihĭlum, i, n. (ne & hilum,) *nothing:* nihil habeo quod, *I have nothing on account of which; i. e. I have no reason why.*

Nihilomĭnus, adv. (nihilo minus, *less by nothing;*) *nevertheless.*

Nilus, i, m. *the Nile; the largest river of Africa.*

Nimius, a, um, adj. (nimis, *too much;*) *too great; excessive; immoderate.*

Nimiùm, & Nimiò, adv. (id.) *too much.*

Ninus, i, m. *a king of Assyria.*

Niŏbe, es, f. *the wife of Amphīon, king of Thebes.*

Nisi, conj. (ne & si,) *unless; except; if not.*

Nisus, i, m. *a king of Megăris, and the father of Sylla.*

Nitĭdus, a, um, adj. comp. (niteo,) *shining; bright; clear.*

Nitor, ōris, m. (niteo,) *splendor; gloss; brilliancy.*

Nitor, niti, nisus & nixus sum, dep. *to strive.*

Nix, nivis, f. *snow.*

No, nare, navi, natum, intr. *to swim.*

Nobĭlis, e, adj. (ior, issĭmus,) (nosco,) *known; noted; noble; celebrated; famous; of high rank;* hence,

Nobilĭtas, ātis, f. *nobility; the nobility; the nobles; a noble spirit; nobleness.*

Nobilĭto, āre, āvi, ātum, tr. (id.) *to ennoble; to make famous.*

Noceo, ēre, ui, ĭtum, intr. *to injure; to harm.*

Noctu, abl. sing. monoptot, *by night; in the night time.*

Nocturnus, a, um, adj. (noctu,) *nightly; nocturnal.*

Nodus, i, m. *a knot; a tumor.*

Nola, æ, f. *a city of Campania.*

Nolo, nolle, nolui, intr. irr. (non & volo, § 83, 5,) *to be unwilling:* noli facĕre, *do not:* noli esse, *be not;* Id. 87.

Nomădes, um, m. pl. *a name given to those tribes who wander from place to place, with their flocks and herds, having no fixed residence.*

Nomen, ĭnis, n. *a name; fame.*

Non, adv. *not.*

Nonagesĭmus, a, um, adj. ord. *the ninetieth.*

Nonne, adv. (non & ne, *a negative interrogative,*) *not?* as, nonne fecit? *has he not done it?*

Nonnĭhil, n. ind. (non nihil, *not nothing;* i. e., *something.*

Nonnĭsi, adv. (non & nisi,) *only; not; except.*

Nonnullus, a, um, adj. (non & nullus,) *some.*

Nonus, a, um, num. adj. *the ninth.*

Nos. *See* Ego.

Nosco, noscĕre, novi, notum, tr. *to know; to understand; to learn.*

Noster, tra, trum, pro. *our;* 121.

Nota, æ, f. (nosco,) *a mark.*

Notans, tis, part. from

Noto, āre, āvi, ātum, tr. (nota,) *to mark; to stigmatize; to observe.*

Notus, a, um, part. (fr. nosco,) *known.*

Novem, ind. num. adj. pl. *nine.*

Novus, a, um, adj. (sup. issĭmus, § 26, 5,) *new; recent; fresh.*

Nox, noctis, f. *night:* de nocte, *by night.*

Noxius, a, um, adj. (noceo,) *hurtful; injurious.*

Nubes, is, f. *a cloud.*

Nubo, nubĕre, nupsi & nupta sum, nuptum, intr. *to cover with a veil; to marry; to be married;* (used only of the wife.)

Nudātus, a, um, part. *laid open; stripped; deprived;* from

Nudo, āre, āvi, ātum, tr. *to make naked; to lay open;* from

Nudus, a, um, adj. *naked; bare.*

Nullus, a, um, gen. ius, adj. (non ullus,) *no; no one.*

Num, interrog. adv. in *indirect* questions, *whether?* in *direct* questions, commonly omitted. *See* Ne, and Id. 56, 3d.

Numa, æ, m. (Pompilius,) *the second king of Rome, and the successor of Romulus.*

Numantia, æ, f. *a city of Spain, besieged by the Romans for twenty years.*

Numantīni, ōrum, m. pl. *Numantines; the people of Numantia.*

Numen, ĭnis, n. (nuo,) *a deity; a god.*

Numĕro, āre, āvi, ātum, tr. *to count; to number; to reckon;* from

Numĕrus, i, m. *a number.*

Numidiæ, ārum, m. pl. *the Numidians.*

Numidia, æ, f. *a country of Africa.*

Numĭtor, ōris, m. *the father of Rhea Sylvia, and grandfather of Romulus and Remus.*

Nummus, i, m. *money.*

Nunc, adv. *now:* nunc etiam, *even now; still.*

Nuncŭpo, āre, āvi, ātum, tr. (nomen & capio,) *to name; to call.*

Nunquam, (ne & unquam,) adv. *never.*

Nuntiātus, a, um, part. from

Nuntio, *or* -cio, āre, āvi, ātum, tr. (nuntius,) *to announce; to tell.*

Nuptiæ, ārum, f. pl. (nubo,) *nuptials; marriage; a wedding.*

Nusquam, adv. (ne & usquam,) *no where; in no place.*

Nutriendus, a, um, part. *to be nourished.*

Nutrio, īre, īvi, ītum, tr. *to nourish.*

Nutrītus, a, um, part.

Nutrix, īcis, f. (nutrio,) *a nurse.*

Nympha, æ, f. *a nymph; a goddess presiding over fountains, groves,* or *rivers,* &c.

O.

O! int. *O! ah!*

Ob, prep. *for; on account of; before.*

Obdormisco, -dormiscĕre, -dormīvi, intr. inc. (ob & dormisco,) *to fall asleep; to sleep.*

Obdūco, -ducĕre, -duxi, -ductum, tr. (ob & duco,) *to draw over; to cover over.*

Obductus, a, um, part. *spread over; covered over.*

Obedio, īre, īvi, ītum, intr. (ob & audio,) *to give ear to; to obey; to comply with; to be subject to.*

Obeo, īre, īvi & ii, ĭtum, tr. & intr. (ob & eo,) *to go to; to discharge; to execute; to die;* (i. e. mortem *or* supremum, diem obīre.)

Oberro, āre, āvi, ātum, (ob & erro,) *to wander; to wander about.*

Obĭtus, ûs, m. (obeo,) *death.*

Objaceo, ēre, ui, ĭtum, intr. (ob & jaceo,) *to lie against* or *before; to be opposite.*

Objectus, a, um, part. *thrown to* or *in the way; exposed.*

Objicio, -jicĕre, -jēci, -jectum, tr. (ob & jacio,) *to throw before; to throw to; to give; to object; to expose.*

Oblīgo, āre, āvi, ātum, tr. (ob

& ligo,) *to bind to; to oblige; to obligate.*

Oblīquè, adv. *indirectly; obliquely;* from

Oblīquus, a, um, adj. (ob & liquis,) *oblique; indirect; sidewise.*

Oblītus, a, um, part. *forgetting; having forgotten;* from

Obliviscor, oblivisci, oblītus sum, tr. dep. (ob & lino,) *to forget.*

Obnoxius, a, um, adj. (ob & noxius,) *obnoxious; subject; exposed to; liable.*

Obruo, -ruĕre, -rui, -rŭtum, tr. (ob & ruo,) *to rush down headlong against; to overwhelm; to cover; to bury.*

Obrŭtus, a, um, part. *buried; covered; overwhelmed.*

Obscūro, āre, āvi, ātum, tr. (obscūrus,) *to obscure; to darken.*

Obsĕcro, āre, āvi, ātum, tr. (ob & sacro,) *to beseech; to conjure.*

Obsĕquor, sĕqui, secūtus sum, intr. dep. (ob & sequor,) *to follow; to serve; to obey; to humor.*

Observo, āre, āvi, ātum, tr. (ob & servo,) *to keep before the mind; to observe; to watch.*

Obses, ĭdis, c. (obsideo,) *a hostage.*

Obsessus, a, um, part. *besieged;* from

Obsideo, -sidēre, -sēdi, -sessum, tr. (ob & sedeo,) *to sit before* or *opposite;* hence, *to besiege; to invest; to blockade;* hence,

Obsidio, ōnis, f. *a siege.*

Obsidionālis, e, adj. *belonging to a siege; obsidional:* corōna, *a crown given to him who had raised a siege.*

Obstetrix, īcis, f. *a midwife.*

Obtestātus, a, um, part. from

Obtestor, āri, ātus sum, tr. dep. (ob & testor,) *to call solemnly to witness; to conjure; to beseech; to entreat.*

Obtineo, -tinēre, -tinui, -tentum, tr. (ob & teneo,) *to hold; to retain; to obtain:* obtĭnet sententia, *the opinion prevails.*

Obtŭlit. *See* Offĕro.

Obviàm, adv. (ob & viam,) *in the way; meeting; to meet:* fio *or* eo obviàm, *I meet; I go to meet.*

Occasio, ōnis, f. (ob & cado,) *an occasion; a good opportunity.*

Occāsus, ûs, m. (id.) *the descent; the setting of the heavenly bodies; evening; the west.*

Occĭdens, tis, m. (id.) *the setting sun; evening; the west.*

Occidentālis, e, adj. (id.) *western; occidental.*

Occīdo, occidĕre, occīdi, occīsum, tr. (ob & cædo,) *to beat; to kill; to slay; to put to death.*

Occĭdo, occidĕre, occĭdi, occāsum, intr. (ob & cado,) *to fall; to fall down; to set.*

Occisūrus, a, um, part. (occīdo.)

Occīsus, a, um, part. (occīdo.)

Occœcātus, a, um, part. from

Occœco, āre, āvi, ātum, tr. (ob & cœco,) *to blind; to dazzle.*

Occulto, āre, āvi, ātum, tr. freq. (occŭlo,) *to conceal; to hide.*

Occultor, āri, ātus sum, pass. *to be concealed; to hide one's self.*

Occŭpo, āre, āvi, ātum, tr. (ob & capio,) *to occupy; to seize upon; to take possession of before another.*

Occurro, -currĕre, -curri & -cucurri, -cursum, intr. (ob & curro,) *to meet; to go to meet; to run to meet; to encounter.*

Oceănus, i, m. *the ocean; the sea.*

Octaviānus, i, m. (Cæsar,) *the nephew and adopted son of Julius Cæsar, called, after the battle of Actium, Augustus.*

Octāvus, a, um, num. adj. (octo,) *eighth.*

Octingenti, æ, a, num. adj. pl. (octo & centum,) *eight hundred.*

Octo, ind. num. adj. pl. *eight.*

Octoginta, ind. num adj. pl. (octo,) eighty.

Ocŭlus, i, m. *an eye.*

Odi, odisse, def. pret. § 84, 1, Obs. 2, *to hate; to detest.*

Odium, i, n. *hatred.*

Odor, ōris, m. *a smell:* pl. odōres, *odors; perfumes.*

Odōror, āri, ātus sum, tr. dep. (odor,) *to smell.*

Œneus, ei & eos, m. *a king of Calydon, and father of Meleăger and Dejanīra.*

Œnomāus, i. m. *the name of a celebrated gladiator.*

Œta, æ, m. *a mountain in Thessaly, on the borders of Doris.*

Offĕro, offerre, obtŭli, oblātum, tr. irr. (ob & fero,) *to bring before; to offer; to present.*

Officīna, æ, (opificīna, from opĭfex,) *a work-shop; an office.*

Officio, -ficĕre, -fēci, -fectum, tr. (ob & facio,) *to act in opposition; to stand in the way of; to injure; to hurt.*

Officium, i, n. (i. e. opificium, fr. ops & facio,) *a kindness; duty; an obligation; politeness; civility; attention.*

Olea, æ, f. *an olive-tree.*

Oleum, i, n. *oil.*

Olim, adv. *formerly; sometime.*

Olor, ōris, m. *a swan.*

Olus, ĕris, n. *herbs; pot-herbs.*

Olympia, æ, f. *a town and district of the Peloponnēsus, upon the Alpheus.*

Olympĭcus, a, um, adj. *Olym-*

pic; pertaining to Olympia.

Olympius, a, um, adj. *Olympian; pertaining to Olympus* or *to Olympia.*

Olympus, i, m. *a high mountain between Thessaly and Macedon.*

Omen, ĭnis, n. *an omen; a sign.*

Omnis, e, adj. *all; every; every one:* omnes, *all:* omnia, *all things:* sine omni discordiâ, *without any discord.*

Onus, ĕris, n. *a burden; a load.*

Onustus, a, um, adj. comp. (onus,) *laden; full of.*

Opĕra, æ, f. (opus,) *labor; pains:* dare opĕram, *to do one's endeavor; to devote one's self to.*

Opĕror, āri, ātus sum, intr. dep. (opĕra,) *to labor; to work.*

Opīmus, a, um, adj. (ops, is,) (ior, sup. *wanting;* § 26, 6,) *fat; rich; fruitful; dainty.*

Oportet, ēre, uit, imp. *it behoves; it is meet, fit,* or *proper; it is a duty; we ought.*

Oppĭdum, i, n. *a walled town; a town.*

Oppōno, -ponĕre, -posui, -posĭtum, tr. (ob & pono,) *to place opposite; to oppose; to set against.*

Opportūnus, a, um, adj. (ior, issĭmus,) (ob & portus, *with a harbor near,* or *opposite,* hence,) *seasonable; commodious; convenient; favorable.*

Opposĭtus, a, um, part. *opposite; opposed.*

Opprĭmo, -primĕre, -pressi, -pressum, tr. (ob & premo,) *to press down,* or *against; to oppress; to overpower; to subdue.*

Oppugnātus, a, um, part. from

Oppugno, āre, āvi, ātum, tr. (ob & pugno,) *to fight against; to assault; to besiege; to attempt to take by force; to storm.*

(Ops, nom., not in use, § 18, 12,) opis, gen. f. *aid; help; means; assistance:* opes, pl. *wealth; riches; resources; power.*

Optĭmè, adv. (sup. of benè,) *very well; excellently; best.*

Optĭmus, a, um, adj. (sup. of bonus,) (opto,) *most desirable; best; most worthy.*

Optio, ōnis, f. *a choice; an option;* from

Opto, āre, āvi, ātum, tr. *to desire.*

Opulens, & opulentus, a, um, adj. (ior, issĭmus,) *rich; opulent; wealthy;* fr. ops.

Opus, ĕris, n. *a work; a labor.*

Opus, subs. & adj. ind. *need.*

Ora, æ, f. *a coast; a shore.*

Ora, pl. *See* Os.

Oracŭlum, i, n. (oro,) *an oracle; a response.*

Orans, tis, part. (oro.)

Oratio, ōnis, f. (oro,) *a discourse; an oration.*

Orātor, ōris, m. (oro,) *an orator; an ambassador.*

Orbātus, a, um, part. (orbo,) *bereaved* or *deprived of.*

Orbēlus, i, m. *a mountain of Thrace or Macedonia.*

Orbis, is, m. *an orb; a circle:* in orbem jacēre, *to lie round in a circle:* orbis, *or* orbis terrārum, *the world.*

Orbo, āre, āvi, ātum, tr. (orbus,) *to deprive; to bereave of.*

Orcus, i, m. *Pluto, the god of the lower world; the infernal regions.*

Ordĭno, āre, āvi, ātum, tr. *to set in order; to arrange; to ordain.*

Ordo, ĭnis, m. *order; arrangement; a row:* ordĭnes remōrum, *banks of oars.*

Oriens, tis, m. (orior,) sc. sol, *the place of sun-rising; the east; the morning.*

Oriens, part. (orior.)

Orientālis, e, adj. (id.) *eastern.*

Orīgo, ĭnis, f. *source; origin:* origĭnem ducĕre, *to derive one's origin;* from

Orior, orīri, ortus sum, intr. dep. 220, Note, 8; *to arise; to begin; to appear.*

Ornamentum, i, n. (orno,) *an ornament.*

Ornātus, ûs, m. *an ornament;* fr.

Orno, āre, āvi, ātum, tr. *to adorn; to deck; to furnish; to equip.*

Oro, āre, āvi, ātum, tr. (os,) *to beg; to entreat.*

Orōdes, is, m. *a king of Parthia, who took and destroyed Crassus.*

Orpheus, eï & eos, m. *a celebrated poet and musician of Thrace;* § 15, 13.

Ortus, a, um, part. (orior,) *having arisen; risen; born; begun.*

Ortus, ûs, m. (id.) *a rising; east.*

Os, oris, n. *the mouth; the face.*

Os, ossis, n. *a bone.*

Ossa, æ, m. *a high mountain in Thessaly.*

Ostendŏ, -tendĕre, -tendi, -tensum, & -tentum, tr. (ob & tendo,) *to stretch* or *hold before; to show; to point out; to exhibit.*

Ostia, æ, f. *a town, built by Ancus Marcius, at the mouth of the Tiber;* from

Ostium, i, n. *a mouth of a river.*

Ostrea, æ, f. ostrea, ōrum, pl. n. *an oyster.*

Otium, i, n. *leisure; quiet; ease; idleness.*

Otos, i, m. *a son of Neptune,* or of *Aloeus.*

Ovis, is, f. *a sheep.*

Ovum, i, n. *an egg.*

P.

P. *an abbreviation of* Publius.

Pabŭlum, i, n. (pasco,) *food for cattle; fodder.*

Paciscor, pacisci, pactus sum, tr. & intr. (pango, *to fix* or *settle;* hence,) *to make a compact; to form a treaty; to bargain; to agree.*

Pactōlus, i, m. *a river of Lydia, famous for its golden sands.*

Pactum, i, n. (paciscor,) *an agreement; a contract:* quo pacto, *in what manner; how.*

Pactus, a, um, part. (paciscor.)

Padus, i, m. *the largest river of Italy,* now *the Po.*

Pæne, (*see* Pene,) adv. *almost.*

Palea, æ, f. *chaff.*

Palma, æ, f. *the palm of the hand; a palm-tree.*

Palpĕbra, æ, f. (palpo,) *the eye-lid:* pl. *the eye-lashes.*

Palus, ūdis, f. *a marsh; a swamp; a lake;* hence,

Paluster, palustris, palustre, adj. *marshy.*

Pan, Panis, m. (Acc. Pana,) *the god of shepherds.*

Pando, pandĕre, pandi, pansum & passum, tr. *to open; to expand; to spread out.*

Panionium, i, n. *a sacred place near mount Mycăle in Ionia.*

Panis, is, m. *bread.*

Panthēra, æ, f. *a panther.*

Papirius, i, m. *the name of several Romans.*

Papȳrus, i. and Papȳrum, i, n. *an Egyptian plant* or *reed, of which paper was made; the papyrus.*

Par, paris, adj. *equal; even; suitable.*

Parātus, a, um, part. and adj. (ior, issĭmus,) (paro,) *prepared; ready.*

Parcæ, ārum, f. pl. *the Fates.*

Parco, parcĕre, peperci *or* parsi, parsum *or* parcĭtum, intr. *to spare.*

Pardus, i, m. *a male panther.*

Parens, tis, c. (pario,) *a parent; father; mother; creator; author; inventor.*

Pareo, ēre, ui, intr. *to come near; to be at hand;* hence, *to obey; to be subject to.*

Paries, ĕtis, m. *a wall* (of a house.)

Pario, parĕre, pepĕri, partum, tr. *to bear; to bring forth; to cause; to produce; to obtain; to gain:* ovum, *to lay an egg.*

Paris, ĭdis, *or* ĭdos, m. (§ 15,13,) *a son of Priam, king of Troy, and brother of Hector.*

Parĭter, adv. (par,) *in like manner; equally; at the same time.*

Parnassus, i, m. *a mountain of Phocis, whose two summits were sacred to Apollo and Bacchus, and upon which the Muses were fabled to reside.*

Paro, āre, āvi, ātum, tr. *to prepare; to provide; to procure; to obtain; to equip:* parāre insidias, *to lay plots against.*

Paropamīsus, i, m. *a ridge of*

mountains in the north of India.

Pars, tis, f. *a part; a share; a portion; a region; a party:* in utrâque parte, *on each side:* magnâ ex parte, *in a great measure; for the most part.*

Parsimonia, æ, f. (parco,) *frugality.*

Parthus, i, m. *an inhabitant of Parthia; a Parthian.*

Particŭla, æ, f. dim. (pars,) *a particle; a small part.*

Partiendus, a, um, part. (partior.)

Partim, adv. (pars,) *partly; in part.*

Partior, īri, ītus sum, tr. dep. (pars,) *to divide; to share.*

Partus, a, um, part. (pario.)

Partus, ûs, m. (id.) *a birth; offspring.*

Parum, adv. (minûs, minĭmè, 234,) *little; too little.*

Parvŭlus, a, um, dim. adj. *small; very small;* from

Parvus, a, um, adj. (minor, minĭmus, 113,) *small* or *little; less; the least.*

Pasco, pascĕre, pavi, pastum, tr. & intr. *to give food to; to feed; to graze.*

Pascor, pasci, pastus sum, tr. & intr. dep. *to feed; to graze; to feed upon.*

Passer, ĕris, m. *a sparrow.*

Passim, adv. (passus, fr. pando,) *here and there; every where; in every direction.*

Passūrus, a, um, part. (patior.)

Passus, a, um, part. (patior,) *having suffered.*

Passus, a, um, part. (pando,) *stretched out; hung up; dried:* uva passa, *a raisin.*

Passus, ûs, m. (id.) *a pace; a measure of 5 feet:* mille passuum, *a mile,* or 5000 *feet.* 909.

Pastor, ōris, m. (pasco,) *a shepherd.*

Patefacio, facĕre, fēci, factum, tr. (pateo & facio,) *to open; to disclose; to discover; to detect.*

Patefīo, fiĕri, factus sum, pass. irr. § 83, Obs. 3, p. 188, *to be laid open* or *discovered.*

Patefactus, a, um, part. *opened; discovered.*

Patens, tis, part. & adj. *lying open; open; clear;* from

Pateo, ēre, ui, intr. *to be open; to stand open; to extend.*

Pater, tris, m. *a father:* patres, *fathers; senators:* paterfamilias, patrisfamilias, § 18, 9, *the master of a family; a housekeeper;* hence,

Paternus, a, um, adj. *paternal.*

Patientia, æ, f. *patience; hardiness;* from

Patior, pati, passus sum, tr. dep. *to suffer; to endure; to let; to allow.*

Patria, æ, f. (patrius, fr. pater,) *one's native country; one's birth-place.*

Patrimonium, i, n. (pater,) *patrimony; inheritance.*

Patrocinium, i, n. *patronage;* from

Patrōnus, i, m. (pater,) *a patron; protector.*

Patruēlis, is, c. (patruus,) *a cousin (by the father's side.)*

Pauci, æ, a, adj. pl. (paucus sing. seldom used,) *few; a few.*

Paulătim, adv. (paulus,) *gradually; little by little.*

Paulò, *or* Paullò, adv. (id.) *a little.*

Paulŭlùm, adv. *a little.*

Paullus, *or* Paulus, i. m. *a* cognōmen *or surname in the Æmilian tribe.*

Pauper, ĕris, adj. (ior, rĭmus,) *poor;* hence,

Pauperies, ēi, f. *poverty;* and

Paupertas, ātis, f. *poverty; indigence.*

Paveo, pavēre, pavi, intr. *to fear; to be afraid.*

Pavo, ōnis, c. *a peacock.*

Pax, pacis, f. *peace.*

Pecco, āre, āvi, ātum, intr. *to do wrong; to commit a fault; to sin.*

Pecto, pectĕre, pexi & pexui, pexum, tr. *to comb; to dress.*

Pectus, ŏris, n. *the breast.*

Pecunia, æ, f. (pecus, *the first coin in Rome being stamped with a sheep;) money; a sum of money.*

Pecus, ŭdis, f. *a sheep; a beast.*

Pecus, ŏris, n. *cattle (of a large size;) a herd; a flock.*

Pedes, ĭtis, c. (pes & eo,) *one who goes on foot; a foot-soldier.*

Pelăgus, i, n. *the sea.*

Peleus, i, m. *a king of Thessaly, the son of Æăcus, and father of Achilles.*

Pelias, æ, m. *a king of Thessaly and son of Neptune.*

Peligni, ōrum, m. pl. *a people of Italy, whose country lay between the Aternus and the Sagrus.*

Pelion, i, n. *a lofty mountain in Thessaly.*

Pellicio, -licĕre, -lexi, -lectum, tr. (per & lacio,) *to allure; to entice; to invite.*

Pellis, is, f. *the skin.*

Pello, pellĕre, pepŭli, pulsum, tr. *to drive away; to banish; to expel; to dispossess; to beat.*

Peloponnēsus, i, f. *a peninsula of Greece,* now called *the Morea.*

Pelusium, i, n. *a town of Egypt.*

Pendens, tis, part. *hanging; impending.*

Pendeo, pendēre, pependi, pensum, intr. *to hang.*

Pene, adv. *almost; nearly.*

Penetrāle, is, n. *the inner part of a house;* fr. penetralis, fr.

Penĕtro, āre, āvi, ātum, (penĭtus,) tr. *to go within; to penetrate; to enter.*

Penēus, i, m. *the principal river of Thessaly, flowing between Ossa and Olympus.*

Peninsŭla, æ, f. (pene & insŭla,) *a peninsula.*

Penna, æ, f. *a feather; a quill; a wing.*

Pensĭlis, e, adj. (pendeo,) *hanging; pendent.*

Penuria, æ, f. *want; scarcity.*

Peperci. *See* Parco.

Pepŭli. *See* Pello.

Pepĕri. *See* Pario.

Per, prep. *by; through; for; during; along.*

Pera, æ, f. *a wallet; a bag.**

Perăgro, āre, āvi, ātum, intr. (per & ager,) *to travel through; to go through* or *over,* (sc. the *field* or *country.*)

Percontor & -cunctor, āri, ātus sum, tr. dep. (per & contor,) *to ask; to inquire.*

Percunctātus, a, um, part. (percunctor.)

Percussor, ōris, m. *one who wounds; a murderer; an assassin;* from

Percutio, -cutĕre, -cussi, -cussum, tr. (per & quatio,) *to strike; to wound:* secūri, *to behead.*

Perdĭtè, adv. *very; vehemently; exceedingly; desperately;* from

Perdĭtus, a, um, part. & adj. (perdo,) *ruined; lost; undone; desperate.*

Perdix, īcis, f. *a partridge.*

Perdo, -dĕre, -dĭdi, -dĭtum, tr. (per & do,) *to ruin; to lose; to destroy.*

Perdūco, -ducĕre, -duxi, -ductum, tr. (per & duco,) *to lead to,* or *through to.*

Perductus, a, um, part. *brought; led; conducted.*

Peregrinatio, ōnis, f. *foreign travel; a residence in a foreign country;* from

Peregrinus, a, um, adj. (peregrè, *and that from* per & ager,) *foreign.*

Perennis, e, adj. (per & annus,) *lasting through the year; continual; lasting; unceasing; everlasting; perennial.*

Pereo, -īre, -ii, -ĭtum, intr. irr. (per & eo,) *to perish; to be slain; to be lost.*

Perfidia, æ, f. *perfidy;* from

Perfĭdus, a, um, adj. (per & fides,) *breaking faith; perfidious.*

Pergămum, i, n., & -us, i, f., -a, ōrum, pl. n. *the citadel of Troy;* also, *a city of Mysia, situated upon the river Caïcus, where parchment was first made, hence called* Pergamēna.

Pergo, pergĕre, perrexi, perrectum, intr. (per & rego,) *to go straight on; to advance; to continue.*

Perĭcles, is, m. *an eminent orator and statesman of Athens.*

Periculōsus, a, um, adj. (comp.) *full of danger; dangerous; perilous; hazardous;* from

Pericŭlum, & Perīclum, i, n. (perior, obsol. *whence* experior, *to try;* hence,) *an experiment; a trial; danger; peril.*

Peritūrus, a, um, part. (pereo.)

Perītus, a, um, adj. (ior, issĭmus,) (perior,) *experienced; skillful.*

Permeo, āre, āvi ātum, intr. (per & meo,) *to go through; to flow through; to penetrate; to permeate.*

Permisceo, -miscēre, -miscui, -mistum & -mixtum, tr. (per & misceo,) *to mix thoroughly; to mingle.*

Permistus, a, um, part. *mixed; mingled; confused.*

Permitto, -mittĕre, -mīsi, -missum, tr. (per & mitto,) *to grant; to allow; to permit; to commit; to intrust; to give leave to; to grant.*

Permutatio, ōnis, f. *exchange; change;* from

Permūto, āre, āvi, ātum, tr. (per & muto,) *to change; to exchange.*

Pernicies, ēi, f. (pernĕco,) *destruction; extermination;* hence,

Perniciōsus, a, um, adj. (ior, issĭmus,) *pernicious; hurtful.*

Perpendo, -pendĕre, -pendi, -pensum, tr. (per & pendo,) *to weigh; to ponder; to consider.*

Perpĕram, adv. *wrong; amiss; rashly; unjustly; absurdly; falsely.*

Perpetior, -pĕti, -pessus sum, tr. dep. (per & patior,) *to endure; to bear; to suffer.*

Perpetuus, a, um, adj. (perpes,) *perpetual; constant.*

Perrexi. *See* Pergo.

Persa, æ, m. *a Persian; an inhabitant of Persia.*

Persecūtus, a, um, part. from

Persĕquor, -sĕqui, -secūtus sum, tr. dep. (per & sequor,) *to follow closely; to pursue; to follow; to continue; to persevere in; to persecute.*

Perseus, ei & eos, m. *the son of Jupiter and Danăe;* also, *the last king of Macedon.*

Persĭcus, a, um, adj. *of Persia; Persian.*

Perspicio, -spicĕre, -spexi, -spectum, tr. (per & specio,) *to see through; to discern; to become acquainted with; to discover.*

Persuadeo, -suadēre, -suāsi, -suāsum, tr. (per & suadeo,) *to persuade.*

Perterreo, -terrēre, -terrui, -terrĭtum, tr. (per & terreo,) *to frighten greatly.*

Perterrĭtus, a, um, part. *affrighted; discouraged.*

Pertinacĭter, adv. (iùs, issĭmè,) *obstinately; constantly; perseveringly;* from

Pertĭnax, ācis, adj. (ior, issĭmus,) (per & tenax,) *obstinate; willful.*

Pertineo, -tinēre, -tinui, intr. (per & teneo,) *to extend; to reach to.*

Pervenio, -venīre, -vēni, -ventum, intr. (per & venio,) *to come to; to arrive at; to reach.*

Pervenītur, pass. imp. *one comes; they come; we come,* &c. Id. 67, Note.

Pervius, a, um, adj. (per & via,) *pervious; which may be passed through; passable.*

Pes, pedis, m. *a foot.*

Pessum, adv. *down; under foot; to the bottom:* ire pessum, *to sink.*

Pestilentia, æ, f. (pestīlens, fr. pestis,) *a pestilence; a plague.*

Petens, tis, part. (peto.)

Petitio, ōnis, f. *a petition; a canvassing or soliciting for an office;* from

Peto, ĕre, īvi, ītum, tr. *to ask; to request; to attack; to assail; to go to; to seek; to go for; to bring.*

Petra, æ, f. *the metropolis of Arabia Petræa.*

Petræa, æ, f. (Arabia,) *Arabia Petræa, the northern part of Arabia, south of Palestine.*

Petulantia, æ, f. (petulans, *forward,* fr. peto,) *petulance; insolence; mischievousness; wantonness.*

Phæax, ācis, m. *a Phæacian,* or *inhabitant of Phæacia,* now *Corfu. The Phæacians were famous for luxury.*

Phalĕræ, ārum, f. pl. *the trappings of a horse; habiliments.*

Pharos, i, f. *a small island at the western mouth of the Nile, on which was a tower or light-house, esteemed one of the seven wonders of the world.*

Pharsālus, i, m. *a city of Thessaly.*

Pharnăces, is, m. *a son of Mithridates, king of Pontus.*

Phasis, ĭdis & is, f. *a town and river of Colchis, on the east side of the Euxine.*

Phidias, æ, m. *a celebrated Athenian statuary.*

Philæni, ōrum, m. pl. *two Carthaginian brothers, who suffered themselves to be buried alive, for the purpose of establishing the controverted boundary of their country.*

Philippi, ōrum, m. pl. *a city of Macedon, on the confines of Thrace.*

Philippĭcus, a, um, adj. *belonging to Philippi.*

Philippĭdes, æ, m. *a comic poet.*

Philippus, i, m. *Philip; the father of Alexander;* also, *the son of Demetrius.*

Philomēla, æ, f. *a nightingale.*

Philosophia, æ, f. *philosophy.*

Philosŏphus, i, m. *a philosopher; a lover of learning and wisdom.*

Phineus, i, m. *a king of Arcadia, and priest of Apollo.*

Phocæi, ōrum, m. pl. *the Phocæans; inhabitants of Pho-*

cæa, a maritime city of Ionia.

Phocis, ĭdis, f. *a country of Greece.*

Phœnīce, es, f. *Phœnicia, a maritime country of Syria, north of Palestine.*

Phœnix, īcis, m. *a Phœnician.*

Phryx, ygis, m. *a Phrygian; an inhabitant of Phrygia.*

Picentes, ium, m. pl. *the inhabitants of Picenum.*

Picēnum, i, n. *a country of Italy.*

Pictus, a, um, part. (pingo,) *painted; embroidered:* picta tabŭla, *a picture; a painting.*

Piĕtas, ātis, f. (pius,) *piety; filial duty.*

Pignus, ŏris, n. *a pledge; a pawn; security; assurance.*

Pila, æ, f. *a ball.*

Pileus, i, m. *a hat; a cap.*

Pilus, i, m. *the hair.*

Pindărus, i, m. *Pindar, a Theban, the most eminent of the Greek lyric poets.*

Pingo, pingĕre, pinxi, pictum, tr. *to represent by lines and colors; to paint; to depict; to delineate; to draw:* acu, *to embroider.*

Pinguis, e, adj. (ior, issĭmus,) *fat; fertile; rich.*

Pinna, æ, f. *a wing; a fin.*

Piræeus, ĕi, m. *the principal port and arsenal of Athens.*

Pirāta, æ, m. *a pirate.*

Piscātor, ōris, m. (piscor, from piscis,) *a fisherman.*

Piscis, is, m. *a fish.*

Pisistrătus, i, m. *an Athenian tyrant, distinguished for his eloquence.*

Pistrīnum, i, n. (pinso, *to bruise;*) *a mill.*

Pius, i, m. *an* agnōmen, *or surname of Metellus.*

Pius, a, um, adj. *dutiful,* or *affectionate to parents; pious.*

Placeo, ēre, ui, ĭtum, intr. *to please:* sibi, *to be vain* or *proud of; to plume one's self.*

Placet, placuit, *or* placĭtum est, imp. *it pleases; it is determined; it seems good to.*

Placĭdus, a, um, adj. (ior, issĭmus,) (placeo,) *placid; quiet; still; tranquil; mild; gentle.*

Plaga, æ, f. *a blow; a wound:* plagæ, pl. *nets; toils.*

Planè, adv. (planus,) *entirely; totally; plainly; clearly.*

Planta, æ, f. *a plant.*

Platănus, i, f. *the plane-tree.*

Platea, æ, f. *a species of bird, the spoonbill, the heron.*

Plato, ōnis, m. *an Athenian, one of the most celebrated of the Grecian philosophers.*

Plaustrum, i, n. *a cart; a wagon.*

Plebs, and Plebes, is, f. *the people; the common people; the plebeians.*

Plecto, plectĕre, tr. *to strike; to punish.*

Plecto, plectĕre, plexui and

plexi, plexum, tr. *to plait; to twist; to weave.*

Plerusque, plerăque, plerumque, adj. (mostly used in the pl.) *most; the most; many.*

Plerùmque, adv. *commonly; generally; for the most part; sometimes.*

Plinius, i, m. *Pliny; the name of two distinguished Roman authors.*

Plotinius, i, m. *See* Catiēnus.

Plumbeus, a, um, adj. *of lead; leaden;* from

Plumbum, i, n. *lead.*

Pluo, pluĕre, plui *or* pluvi, intr. *to rain:* pluit, *it rains.*

Plurĭmus, a, um, adj. (sup. of multus,) *very much; most; very many.*

Plus, uris, adj. (n. in sing., comparative of multus,) § 21, 4 Exc.) *more:* pl. *many.*

Plùs, adv. (comparative of multùm,) *more; longer.*

Pluto, ōnis, m. *a son of Saturn, and king of the infernal regions.*

Pocŭlum, i, n. *a cup.*

Poēma, ătis, n. *a poem.*

Pœna, æ, f. *satisfaction given or taken for a crime; punishment; a punishment.*

Pœnĭtet, ēre, uit, imp. (poeniteo, and that from poena,) *it repents:* pœnĭtet me, *I repent.*

Pœnus, a, um, adj. *belonging to Carthage; Carthaginian:* subs. *a Carthaginian.*

Poēta, æ, m. *a poet.*

Pol, adv. *by Pollux; truly.*

Pollex, ĭcis, m. (polleo,) *the thumb; the great toe.*

Pollĭceor, ēri, ĭtus sum, tr. dep. (liceor,) *to promise;* hence,

Pollicĭtus, a, um, part.

Pollux, ūcis, m. *a son of Leda, and twin brother of Castor.*

Polyxēna, æ, f. *a daughter of Priam and Hecuba.*

Pomĭfer, ĕra, ĕrum, adj. (pomum & fero,) *bearing fruit:* pomifĕræ arbŏres, *fruit-trees.*

Pompa, æ, f. *a procession; pomp; parade.*

Pompeiānus, a, um, adj. *belonging to Pompey.*

Pompeius, i, m. *Pompey; the name of a Roman* gens, *or clan.*

Pompilius, i, m. *See* Numa.

Pomum, i, n. *an apple; any fruit fit for eating, growing upon a tree.*

Pondus, ĕris, n. (pendo,) *a weight.*

Pono, ponĕre, posui, posĭtum, tr. *to place; to put; to set.*

Pons, tis, m. *a bridge.*

Pontius, i, m. (Thelesīnus,) *a general of the Samnites.*

Pontus, i, m. *a sea; the deep sea: by* Synecdŏche, *the Euxine* or *Black sea;* also, *the kingdom of Pontus, on the south side of the Euxine.*

Poposci. *See* Posco.

Popŭlor, āri, ātus sum, tr. dep.

(popŭlo for depopŭlo, from popŭlus,) *to lay waste; to depopulate;* from

Popŭlus, i, m. *the people; a nation; a tribe:* pl. *nations; tribes.*

Porrectus, a, um, part. from

Porrĭgo, igĕre, exi, ectum, tr. (porro, *or* pro & rego,) *to reach* or *spread out; to extend; to offer.*

Porsĕna, æ, m. *a king of Etruria.*

Porta, æ, f. (porto,) *a gate.*

Portans, tis, part. (porto.)

Portendo, -tendĕre, -tendi, -tentum, tr. (porro, *or* pro & tendo,) *to show what will be hereafter; to presage; to forbode; to portend; to betoken.*

Portĭcus, ûs, f. (porta,) *a portico; a gallery; a porch.*

Porto, āre, āvi, ātum, tr. *to carry; to bear;* hence,

Portus, ûs, m. *a port; a harbor.*

Posco, poscĕre, poposci, tr. *to demand; to request earnestly; to ask as wages.*

Posĭtus, a, um, part. (pono,) *situated.*

Possessio, ōnis, f. *possession;* &

Possessor, ōris, m. *a possessor; an occupant;* from

Possĭdeo, -sidēre, -sēdi, -sessum, tr. (potis & sedeo,) *to possess.*

Possum, posse, potui, intr. irr. (potis & sum, § 83, 2,) *to be able; I can.*

Post, prep. *after:*—adv. *after; after that; afterwards.*

Postea, adv. (post & ea, *after these things;*) *afterwards.*

Postĕrus, (m. not used,) ĕra, ĕrum, adj. § 26, 2. (erior, rēmus,) (post,) *succeeding; subsequent; next:* in postĕrum, (*supply* tempus,) *for the future:* postĕri, ōrum, *posterity.*

Postis, is, m. (posĭtus, fr. pono,) *a thing set up; a post.*

Postquam, adv. (post & quam,) *after; after that; since.*

Postrēmò, & -ùm, adv. *at last; finally;* from

Postrēmus, a, um, adj. (sup. of postĕrus,) *the last:* ad postrēmum, *at last.*

Postŭlo, āre, āvi, ātum, tr. (posco,) *to ask; to ask for; to demand,* (as a right.)

Postumius, i, m. *the name of a Roman* gens *or clan.*

Posui. *See* Pono.

Potens, tis, adj. (ior, issĭmus,) *being able; powerful;* (possum.)

Potentia, æ, f. (potens,) *power; authority; government.*

Potestas, ātis, f. (potis,) *power;* (*civil power,* as distinguished from imperium, *military command.*)

Potio, ōnis, f. (poto,) *a drink; a draught.*

Potior, īri, ītus sum, intr. dep. (potis,) *to get; to possess; to obtain; to enjoy; to gain possession of.*

Potissĭmùm, adv. (sup. of potiùs,) *principally; chiefly; especially.*

Potītus, a, um, part. (potior,) *having obtained.*

Potiùs, adv. comp. (sup. potissĭmùm,) *rather.*

Poto, potāre, potāvi, potātum, *or* potum, tr. *to drink; to drink hard;* (see bibo.)

Potuisse. *See* Possum.

Potus, ûs, m. (poto,) *drink.*

Præ, prep. *before; for; in comparison of,* or *with.*

Præaltus, a, um, adj. comp. (præ & altus,) *very high; very deep,* (comparatively.)

Præbeo, ēre, ui, ĭtum, tr. (præ & habeo,) *to offer; to supply; to give; to afford:* speciem, *to exhibit the appearance of:* usum, *to serve for.*

Præcēdens, tis, part. from

Præcēdo, -cedĕre, -cessi, -cessum, intr. (præ & cedo,) *to go before; to precede.*

Præceptor, ōris, m. (præcipio,) *a preceptor, master,* or *teacher.*

Præceptum, i, n. (præcipio,) *a precept; a doctrine; advice.*

Præcīdo, -cidĕre, -cīdi, -cīsum, tr. (præ & cædo,) *to cut off.*

Præcipio, -cipĕre, -cēpi, -ceptum, tr. (præ & capio,) *to seize* or *take before;* hence, *to prescribe; to command.*

Præcipĭto, āre, āvi, ātum, tr. (præceps,) *to throw down headlong; to precipitate; to throw.*

Præcipuè, adv. *especially; particularly;* from

Præcipuus, a, um, adj. (præcipio,) *especial; distinguished; the chief; the principal.*

Præclārè, adv. *excellently; famously; gloriously;* from

Præclārus, a, um, adj. (præ & clarus,) *very clear* or *bright; famous.*

Præclūdo, -cludĕre, -clūsi, -clūsum, tr. (præ & claudo,) *to close beforehand; to stop; to shut up.*

Præco, ōnis, m. *a herald.*

Præda, æ, f. *booty; the prey.*

Prædĭco, āre, āvi, ātum, tr. (præ & dico,) *to tell openly; to publish; to declare; to assert; to affirm: to praise.*

Prædīco, cĕre, xi, ctum, tr. (præ & dico,) *to predict; to foretell.*

Prædictus, a, um, part. *foretold.*

Prædor, āri, ātus sum, tr. dep. (præda,) *to plunder.*

Præfans, tis, part. from

Præfāri, fātus, def. 222, 4, *to tell before,* or *foretell; to announce; to predict.*

Præfĕro, -ferre, -tŭli, -lātum, tr. irr. (præ & fero,) *to bear before; to show; to prefer.*

Præfinio, īre, īvi, ītum, tr. (præ & finio,) *to appoint beforehand: to determine.*

Præfinītus, a, um, part.

Prælātus, a, um, part. (præfĕro).

Prælians, tis, part. (prælior.)

Præliătus, a, um, part. from

Prælior, āri, ātus sum, intr. dep. *to give battle; to engage; to fight.*

Prælium, i, n. *a battle.*

Præmium, i, n. *a reward; a price; a recompense.*

Præmitto, -mittĕre, -mīsi, -missum, tr. (præ & mitto,) *to send before.*

Præneste, is, n. *a city of Latium.*

Prænuntio, āre, āvi, ātum, tr. (præ & nuntio,) *to tell beforehand; to announce; to signify; to give notice.*

Præpăro, āre, āvi, ātum, tr. (præ & paro,) *to get beforehand; to make ready; to prepare; to make.*

Præpōno, -ponĕre, -posui, -posĭtum, tr. (præ & pono,) *to set before; to value more; to place over; to prefer.*

Præsens, tis, adj. *present; imminent;* part. of præsum.

Præsēpe, is, n. præsēpes & præsēpis, is, f. (præsepio,) *a manger; a crib.*

Præsidium, i, n. (præsideo,) *a garrison; defence.*

Præstans, tis, part. & adj. (ior, issĭmus,) (præsto,) *standing before;* hence, *excellent; distinguished;* hence,

Præstantia, æ, f. *superiority; an advantage; a preëminence.*

Præsto, stāre, stĭti, stĭtum and stātum, intr. & tr. (præ & sto,) *to stand before; to excel; to be superior; to surpass; to perform; to pay; to grant; to give; to render; to execute; to cause:* se, *to show* or *prove one's self:* præstat, imp. *it is better.*

Præsum, -esse, -fui, intr. irr. (præ & sum,) *to be over; to preside over; to have the charge* or *command of; to rule over.*

Prætendo, -tendĕre, -tendi, -tensum or tum, tr. (præ & tendo,) *to hold before; to stretch* or *extend before; to be opposite to; to pretend.*

Præter, prep. *besides; except; contrary to.*

Præterea, adv. (præter & ea,) *besides; moreover.*

Prætereo, īre, ii, ĭtum, tr. irr. § 83, 3, (præter & eo,) *to pass over* or *by; to go beyond; to omit; not to mention.*

Prætereundus, a, um, part. (prætereo.)

Præteriens, euntis, part. (prætereo.)

Præterĭtus, a, um, part. (prætereo,) *past.*

Præterquam, adv. *except; besides:* præterquam si, *except in case.*

Prætorius, i. m. (vir,) *a man who has been a prætor; one of prætorian dignity.*

Pratum, i, n. *a meadow; a pasture.*

Pravĭtas, ātis, f. *depravity;* fr.

Pravus, a, um, adj. (ior, issĭmus,) *depraved; bad.*

Precātus, a, um, part. (precor.)

Preci, -em, -e, f. (prex not used, § 18, 12,) *a prayer:* pl. preces (entire).

Precor, āri, ātus sum, tr. dep. (preci,) *to pray; to entreat.*

Premo, premĕre, pressi, pressum, tr. *to press; to urge; to grieve.*

Pretiōsus, a, um, adj. (ior, issĭmus,) *precious; valuable; costly;* from

Pretium, i, n. *a price; a ransom; a reward:* in pretio esse, *to be valued; to be in estimation:* pretium opĕræ, *worth while.*

Priămus, i, m. *Priam, the last king of Troy.*

Pridie, adv. (pri, for priōri, & die,) *the day before.*

Priēne, es, f. *a maritime town of Ionia.*

Primò & -ùm, adv. (sup. of priùs, 233,) *first; at first:* quam primûm, *as soon as possible.*

Primōris, e, adj. (primus,) *the first; the foremost:* dentes, *the front teeth.*

Primus, a, um, num. adj. (sup. of prior,) *the first.*

Princeps, ĭpis, adj. (primus & capio,) *the chief; the first:* principes, *the princes; the chiefs; chief men;* hence,

Principātus, ûs, m. *a government; principality.*

Prior, us, adj. (sup. primus, 113, 4,) *the former; prior; first.*

Priscus, i, m. *a cognōmen or surname of the elder Tarquin.*

Priùs, adv. (prior,) *before; first.*

Priusquam, adv. (priùs and quàm,) *sooner than; before that; before.*

Privātus, a, um, adj. (privo,) *private; secret:*—subs. *a private man.*

Pro, prep. *for; instead.*

Probabĭlis, e, adj. comp. (probo,) *that may be proved; probable; commendable.*

Proboscis, ĭdis, f. *proboscis; the trunk of an elephant.*

Procas, æ, m. *See* Silvius.

Procēdens, tis, part. from

Procēdo, -cedĕre, -cessi, -cessum, intr. (pro & cedo,) *to go forth; to proceed; to go forward; to advance; to go out.*

Procerĭtas, ātis, f. *stature; height; tallness; length;* from

Procĕrus, a, um, adj. (comp.) *tall; long.*

Proclāmo, āre, āvi, ātum, tr. (pro & clamo,) *to cry out; to proclaim.*

Proconsul, ŭlis, m. (pro & consul,) *a proconsul.*

Procreo, āre, āvi, ātum, tr. (pro & creo,) *to beget.*

Procul, adv. *far.*

Procūro, āre, āvi, ātum, tr. (pro & curo,) *to take care*

of; to manage; (viz. *for another.*)

Procurro, currĕre, curri & cucurri, cursum, intr. (pro & curro,) *to run forward; to extend.*

Prodigium, i, n. (prodīco,) *a prodigy.*

Prodĭtor, ōris, m. (prodo,) *a traitor.*

Prodĭtus, a, um, part. from

Prodo, -dĕre, -dĭdi, -dĭtum, tr. (pro & do,) *to give out; to betray; to relate; to discover; to disclose; to manifest.*

Prœlior. *See* Prælior.

Prœlium, i, n. *See* Prælium.

Profectus, a, um, part. also,

Proficiscens, tis, part. from

Proficiscor, icisci, ectus sum, intr. dep. (pro & faciscor, from facio,) *to go forward; to march; to travel; to depart; to go.*

Profiteor, -fitēri, -fessus sum, tr. dep. (pro & fateor,) *to declare; to avow publicly; to profess:* sapientiam, *to profess wisdom; to profess to be a philosopher.*

Profugio, -fugĕre, -fūgi, -fugĭtum, intr. (pro & fugio,) *to flee,* (scil. *before* or *from;*) *to escape;* hence,

Profŭgus, a, um, adj. *fleeing; escaping:*—subs. *a fugitive; an exile.*

Progredior, -grĕdi, -gressus sum, intr. dep. (pro & gradior,) *to go forward; to proceed; to advance.*

Progressus, a, um, part. *having advanced.*

Prohibeo, ēre, ui, ĭtum, tr. (pro & habeo,) *to keep off,* or *away; to prohibit; to hinder; to forbid;* hence,

Prohibĭtus, a, um, part.

Projicio, -jicĕre, -jēci, -jectum, tr. (pro & jacio,) *to throw away; to throw down; to throw.*

Prolābor, -lābi, -lapsus sum, intr. dep. (pro & labor,) *to fall down; to fall forward;* hence,

Prolapsus, a, um, part. *having fallen.*

Prolāto, āre, āvi, ātum, tr. freq. (profĕro,) *to carry forward; to enlarge; to extend; to amplify.*

Proles, is, f. *a race; offspring.*

Prometheus, i, m. *the son of Iapĕtus and Clymĕne.*

Promittens, tis, part. from

Prommitto, -mittĕre, -mīsi, -missum, tr. (pro & mitto,) *to let go,* or *send forward; to promise; to offer.*

Promontorium, i, n. (pro & mons,) *a promontory; a headland; a cape.*

Promoveo, -movēre, -mōvi, -mōtum, intr. & tr. (pro & moveo,) *to move forward; to enlarge.*

Pronus, a, um, adj. *inclined; bending forward.*

Propāgo, āre, āvi, ātum, tr. (pro & pago,) *to propagate; to prolong; to continue.*

Prope, adv. & prep. (propiùs, proximè,) *near; near to; nigh.*

Propĕro, āre, āvi, ātum, intr. (propĕrus,) *to hasten.*

Propinquus, a, um, adj. comp. (prope,) *near; related:* propinqui, subs. *relations; kinsmen.*

Propior, us, adj. comp. § 26, 4, (sup. proximus,) *nearer.*

Propiùs, adv. *nearer;* comp. of prope.

Propōno, -ponĕre, -posui, -posĭtum, tr. (pro & pono,) *to set before; to propose; to offer.*

Propōnor, -pōni, -posĭtus sum, pass. *to be set before:* propositum est mihi, *It is proposed by me;* i. e. *I intend* or *purpose.*

Propontis, ĭdis, f. *the sea of Marmŏra.*

Proposĭtus, a, um, part. *proposed; put.*

Propriè, adv. *particularly; properly; strictly;* from

Proprius, a, um, adj. *peculiar; proper; one's own; special.*

Propter, prep. *for; on account of.*

Propulso, āre, āvi, ātum, tr. freq. (propello,) *to drive away; to ward off; to repel.*

Propylæum, i, n. *the porch of a temple; an entrance; the rows of columns leading to the Acropŏlis at Athens.*

Prora, æ, f. *the prow of a ship.*

Proscribo, -scribĕre, -scripsi, -scriptum, tr. (pro & scribo,) *to publish by writing; to proscribe; to outlaw; to doom to death and confiscation of goods.*

Prosecūtus, a, um, part. *having accompanied.*

Prosĕquor, -sĕqui, -secūtus sum, tr. dep. (pro & sequor,) *to follow after; to accompany; to attend; to follow; to celebrate:* honorĭbus, *to heap* or *load with honors; to honor.*

Proserpĭna, æ, f. *the daughter of Ceres and Jupiter, and wife of Pluto.*

Prospectus, ûs, m. (prospicio,) *a prospect; a distant view.*

Prospĕrè, adv. (prosper,) *prosperously; successfully.*

Prosterno, -sternĕre, -strāvi, -strātum, tr. (pro & sterno,) *to prostrate; to throw down.*

Prostrātus, a, um, part. (prosterno.)

Prosum, prodesse, profui, intr. irr. (pro & sum, § 83, 1,) *to do good; to profit.*

Protagŏras, æ, m. *a Greek philosopher.*

Protĕnus, adv. (pro & tenus,) *immediately; directly.*

Protēro, -terrĕre, -trīvi, -trītum, tr. (pro & tero,) *to trample upon; to tread down; to crush.*

Protractus, a, um, part. from

Protraho, -trahĕre, -traxi, -tractum, tr. (pro & traho,) *to protract; to prolong.*

Proveniens, tis, part. from

Provenio, -venīre, -vēni, -ventum, intr. (pro & venio,) *to come forth.*

Provincia, æ, f. (pro & vinco,) *a province.*

Provocatio, ōnis, f. *a calling forth; a challenge; a provocation;* from

Provŏco, āre, āvi, ātum, tr. (pro & voco,) *to call forth; to call out; to defy* or *challenge; to appeal.*

Proxĭmè, adv. (sup. of prope,) *nearest; very near; next to.*

Proxĭmus, a, um, adj. (sup. of propior,) *nearest; next.*

Prudens, tis, adj. (ior, issĭmus,) (provĭdens, fr. provideo,) *foreseeing; prudent; wise; expert;* hence,

Prudentia, æ, f. *prudence; knowledge.*

Pseudophilippus, i, m. *a false* or *pretended Philip, a name given to Andriscus.*

Psittăcus, i, m. *a parrot.*

Psophidius, a, um, adj. *of* or *belonging to Psophis; Psophidian.*

Psophis, ĭdis, f. *a city of Arcadia.*

Ptolemæus, i, m. *Ptolemy; the name of several Egyptian kings.*

Publĭcè, adv. (publĭcus,) *publicly; at the public expense; by public authority.*

Publicŏla, æ, m. (popŭlus & colo,) *a surname given to P. Valerius, on account of his love of popularity.*

Publĭcus, a, um, adj. (popŭlus,) *public:* in publĭcum procēdens, *going abroad* or *appearing in public:* subs. publĭcum, *the public treasury.*

Publius, i, m. *the* prænōmen *of several Romans.*

Pudibundus, a, um, adj. (pudeo,) *ashamed; bashful; modest.*

Puer, ĕri, m. *a boy; a servant.*

Puerīlis, e, adj. (puer,) *puerile; childish:* ætas, *boyhood; childhood.*

Pueritia, æ, f. (id.) *boyhood; childhood.*

Pugna, æ, f. (pugnus, *the fist;*) *a battle with fists; a close fight; a battle.*

Pugnans, tis, part. (pugno.)

Pugnātus, a, um, part. from

Pugno, āre, āvi, ātum, intr. (pugna,) *to fight:* pugnātur, pass. imp. *a battle is fought; they fight.*

Pulcher, ra, rum, adj. (chrior, cherrĭmus,) *fair; beautiful; glorious;* hence,

Pulchritūdo, ĭnis, f. *fairness; beauty.*

Pullus, i, m. *the young of any animal.*

Pulsus, a, um, part. (pello.)

Pulvillus, i, m. (Horatius,) *a Roman consul in the first year of the republic.*

Punĭcus, a, um, adj. *Punic; belonging to Carthage; Carthaginian.*

Punio, īre, īvi, ītum, tr. (pœna,) *to punish.*

Punītus, a, um, part. (punio.)

Pupillus, i, m. (dim. fr. pupŭlus, and that fr. pupus,) *a young boy; a pupil; a ward; an orphan.*

Puppis, is, f. *the stern of a ship.*

Purgo, āre, āvi, ātum, tr. *to purge; to purify; to clear; to clean; to excuse.*

Purpŭra, æ, f. *the purple muscle; purple;* hence,

Purpurātus, a, um, adj. *clad in purple:* purpurāti, pl. *courtiers; nobles.*

Purpureus, a, um, adj. (id.) *purple.*

Purus, a, um, adj. (ior, issĭmus,) *pure; clear.*

Pusillus, a, um, adj. (dim. fr. pusus,) *small; weak; little; very small.*

Puteus, i, m. *a well; a pit.*

Puto, āre, āvi, ātum, tr. *to think.*

Putresco, putrescĕre, putrui, intr. inc. (putreo,) *to rot; to decay.*

Pydna, æ, f. *a town of Macedon.*

Pygmæi, ōrum, m. *the Pygmies, a race of dwarfs inhabiting a remote part of India* or *Ethiopia.*

Pyra, æ, f. *a funeral pile.*

Pyrămis, ĭdis, f. *a pyramid.*

Pyrenæus, i, m., & Pyrenæi, ōrum, m. pl. *Pyrenees, mountains dividing France and Spain.*

Pyrrhus, i, m. *a king of Epīrus.*

Pythagŏras, æ, m. *a Grecian philosopher, born at Samos.*

Pythagorēus, i, m. *a Pythagorean; a follower or disciple of Pythagoras.*

Pythia, æ, f. *the priestess of Apollo at Delphi.*

Pythias, æ, m. *a soldier of Philip, king of Macedon.*

Q.

Q., *or* Qu., *an abbreviation of* Quintus.

Quadragesĭmus, a, um, num. adj. ord. *the fortieth;* from

Quadraginta, num. adj. pl. ind. *forty.*

Quadriennium, i, n. (quatuor & annus,) *the space of four years.*

Quadrīga, æ, & pl. æ, ārum, f. (quadrijŭgæ, quatuor & jugum,) *a four-horse chariot; a team of four horses.*

Quadringentesĭmus, a, um, num. adj. ord. *the four hundredth;* from

Quadringenti, æ, a, num. adj. pl. *four hundred.*

Quadrŭpes, pĕdis, adj. (quatuor & pes,) *having four feet; four-footed.*

Quærens, tis, part. from

Quæro, quærĕre, quæsīvi, quæsītum, tr. *to ask; to seek for; to inquire; to search:* quærĭtur, *it is asked; the inquiry is made;* hence,

Quæstio, ōnis, f. *a question.*

Quæstor, ōris, m. (quæsītor,

id.) *a quæstor; a treasurer; an inferior military officer who attended the consuls.*

Quæstus, ûs, m. (id.) *gain; a trade.*

Qualis, e, adj. *of what kind; as; such as; what.*

Quàm, conj. & adv. *as; how;* after comparatives, *than.*

Quamdiu, *or* Quandiu, adv. (quam & diu,) *as long as.*

Quamquam, *or* Quanquam, conj. *though; although.*

Quamvis, conj. (quam & vis, fr. volo,) *although.*

Quando, adv. *when; since.*

Quantò, adv. *by how much; as.*

Quantopĕre, adv. (quanto & opĕre,) *how greatly; how much.*

Quantùm, adv. *how much; as much as.*

Quantus, a, um, adj. *how great; as great; how admirable; how striking.*

Quantuslĭbet, quantalĭbet, quantumlĭbet, adj. (quantus & libet,) *how great soever; ever so great.*

Quapropter, adv. (qua & propter,) *wherefore; why.*

Quare, adv. (quâ & re,) *wherefore; for which reason; whence; therefore.*

Quartus, a, um, num. adj. ord. *the fourth.*

Quasi, adv. (*for* quamsi,) *as if; as.*

Quatriduum, i, n. (quatuor & dies,) *a space of four days.*

Quatuor, num. adj. pl. ind. *four.*

Quatuordĕcim, num. adj. pl. ind. (quatuor & decem,) *fourteen.*

Que, enclitic conj. (always joined to another word, and draws the accent to the syllable preceding it,) *and; also.*

Queo, īre, īvi, ĭtum, intr. irr. § 83, 3; *to be able; I can.*

Quercus, ûs, f. *an oak.*

Queror, queri, questus sum, tr. dep. *to complain.*

Questus, a, um, part. *complaining; having complained.*

Qui, quæ, quod, rel. pro. 125; *who; which; what;* used interrogatively, *who? which? what?*

Quì, adv. *how; in what manner.*

Quia, conj. *because.*

Quicunque, quæcunque, quodcunque, rel. pro. 131, 1, *whosoever; whatsoever; every one.*

Quidam, quædam, quoddam & quiddam, pro. 131, 1, *a certain one; a certain person* or *thing:* quidam homĭnes, *certain men.*

Quidem, adv. *indeed; truly; at least.*

Quin, conj. *but; but that.*

Quinctius, i, m. (Titus,) *a Roman general.*

Quindĕcim, num. adj. pl. ind. (quinque & decem,) *fifteen.*

Quingentesĭmus, a, um, num. adj. ord. *the five hundredth;* from

Quingenti, æ, a, num. adj. pl. (quinque & centum,) *five hundred.*

Quinquagēni, æ, a, num. adj. pl. dist. (quinquaginta,) *every fifty; fifty.*

Quinquagesĭmus, a, um, num. adj. (id.) *fiftieth.*

Quinquaginta, num. adj. pl. ind. *fifty.*

Quinque, num. adj. pl. ind. *five.*

Quinquies, num. adv. *five times.*

Quintò, adv. *the fifth time.*

Quintus, a, um, ord. num. adj. *the fifth.*

Quintus, *or* Quinctius, i, m. *a Roman surname.*

Quippe, conj. *for; since.*

Quis, quæ, quod, *or* quid, interrog. pro. *who? what?* quid, *why?*

Quisnam, *or* Quinam, quænam, quodnam, *or* quidnam, pro. 131, 2, *who; what.*

Quisquam, quæquam, quodquam, *or* quidquam, *or* quicquam, pro. *any one; any thing:* nec quisquam, *and no one.*

Quisque, quæque, quodque, *or* quidque, pro. *each; every; whosoever; whatsoever.*

Quisquis, quidquid, *or* quicquid, rel. pro. 131, Obs. 1, *whoever; whatever.*

Quivis, quævis, quodvis, *or* quidvis, pro. (qui *and* vis,) *whosoever; whatsoever; any one.*

Quò, adv. *that; to the end that; whither:* quò—eò, *for* quanto—tanto, *by how much—by so much;* or *the more—the more.*

Quòd, conj. *that; because.*

Quomĭnùs, adv. (quò & minùs,) *that—not.*

Quomŏdo, adv. (quo & modo,) *how; by what means.*

Quondam, adv. *formerly; once.*

Quoniam, conj. (quum & jam,) *since; because.*

Quoque, conj. *also.*

Quot, adj. ind. pl. *how many.*

Quotannis, adv. (quot & annus,) *annually; yearly.*

Quotidie, adv. (quot & dies,) *every day; daily.*

Quoties, adv. *as often as; how often.*

Quum, *or* Cùm, adv. *when:* quum jam, *as soon as:*—conj. *since; although.*

R.

Radius, i, m. *a staff; a ray; a rod.*

Radix, īcis, f. *a root; the foot* or *base of a mountain.*

Ramus, i, m. *a branch; a bough.*

Rana, æ, f. *a frog.*

Rapīna, æ, f. *rapine; plunder;* from

Rapio, rapĕre, rapui, raptum, tr. *to hurry away by force; to rob; to seize; to plunder.*

Raptor, ōris, m. (rapio,) *one who seizes or takes away by violence; a robber.*

Raptūrus, a, um, part. (rapio.)

Raptus, a, um, part. (rapio,) *seized; robbed; carried off.*

Rarĭtas, ātis, f. (rarus,) *rarity.*

Rarò, adv. *rarely; seldom;* fr.

Rárus, a, um, adj. *rare; few.*

Ratio, ōnis, f. (reor,) *a reason.*

Ratis, is, f. *a raft; a ship; a boat.*

Ratus, a, um, part. (reor,) *thinking; having thought.*

Rebello, āre, āvi, ātum, intr. (re & bello,) *to renew a war; to rebel; to revolt.*

Recēdo, -cedĕre, -cessi, -cessum, intr. (re & cedo,) *to recede; to yield; to retire; to withdraw.*

Recens, tis, adj. comp. *new; recent; fresh:*—adv. *recently; lately; newly:* recens nati, *new-born children.*

Receptus, a, um, part. (recipio.)

Receptūrus, a, um, part. (recipio.)

Recessus, ûs, m. (recēdo,) *a recess; a corner.*

Recipio, -cipĕre, -cēpi, -ceptum, tr. (re & capio,) *to take back; to receive; to take; to recover:* anĭmam, *to come to one's self again; to recover one's senses:* se, *to return.*

Recognosco, -noscere, -nōvi, -nĭtum, tr. (re & cognosco,) *to recognize; to know again; to betake one's self.*

Recollĭgo, -ligĕre, -lēgi, -lectum, tr. (re, con & lego,) *to gather up again; to recollect; to recover.*

Recondĭtus, a, um, part. from

Recondo, dĕre, dĭdi, dĭtum, tr. (re & condo,) *to put together again; to lay up; to hide; to conceal.*

Recordor, āri, ātus, tr. dep. (re & cor,) *to call back to mind; to recollect; to remember.*

Recreo, āre, āvi, ātum, tr. (re & creo,) *to bring to life again; to restore; to refresh.*

Rectè, adv. (iùs, issĭmè,) *right; rightly;* from

Rectus, a, um, adj. (ior, issĭmus,) (rego,) *straight; upright; right; direct.*

Recupĕro, āre, āvi, ātum, tr. (recipio,) *to recover; to regain.*

Reddĭtus, a, um, part. from

Reddo, -dĕre, -dĭdi, -dĭtum, tr. (re & do,) *to give back; to return; to give; to make; to render; to restore; to cause:* verba, *to repeat:* anĭmam, *to die:* voces, *to imitate.*

Redeo, -īre, -ii, -ĭtum, intr. irr. (re & eo,) *to go back; to return.*

Rediens, euntis, part. *returning.*

Redĭgo, -igĕre, -ēgi, -actum, tr. (re & ago,) *to bring back; to reduce:* in potestātem, *to bring into one's power.*

Redimendus, a, um, part. from

Redĭmo, -imĕre, -ēmi, -emptum, tr. (re & emo,) *to take back; to buy back; to redeem; to ransom.*

Reducendus, a, um, part. from

Redūco, -ducĕre, -duxi, -ductum, tr. (re & duco,) *to lead* or *bring back:* in gratiam, *to reconcile.*

Refĕrens, tis, part. *requiting; returning; conferring;* from

Refĕro, -ferre, -tŭli, -lātum, tr. irr. (re & fero,) *to bring back:* gratiam *or* gratias, *to requite a favor; to show gratitude:* beneficium, *to requite a benefit:* victoriam, *to bring back victory,* i. e. *to return victorious:* imagĭnem, *to reflect the image; to resemble.*

Refluens, tis, part. from

Refluo, -fluĕre, -fluxi, -fluxum, intr. (re & fluo,) *to flow back.*

Refugio, -fugĕre, -fūgi, -fugĭtum, intr. (re & fugio,) *to fly back; to flee; to retreat.*

Regia, æ, f. (sc. domus, from regius,) *a palace.*

Regīna, æ, f. (rex,) *a queen.*

Regio, ōnis, f. (rego,) *a region; a district; a country.*

Regius, a, um, adj. (rex,) *royal; regal; the king's.*

Regnatūrus, a, um, part. from

Regno, āre, āvi, ātum, intr. (regnum,) *to rule; to govern.*

Regnātur, pass. imp. *it is ruled by kings.*

Regnum, i, n. (rex,) *a kingdom; empire; dominion; reign; government; rule.*

Rego, regĕre, rexi, rectum, tr. *to direct* or *lead in a straight course; to rule.*

Regredior, -grĕdi, -gressus sum, intr. dep. (re & gradior,) *to turn back; to return.*

Regressus, a, um, part. *having returned.*

Regŭlus, i, m. *a distinguished Roman general in the first Punic war.*

Relātus, a, um, part. (refĕro.)

Relictūrus, a, um, part. (relinquo.)

Relictus, a, um, part. (id.)

Religio, ōnis, f. (relĭgo,) *what is binding* or *obligatory; religious scruple* or *hindrance;* hence, *religion; sacredness; sanctity; reverence; religious rites.*

Relinquo, -linquĕre, -līqui, -lictum, tr. (re & linquo,) *to leave behind; to desert; to quit; to abandon.*

Reliquiæ, ārum, f. pl. *the relics; the remains;* from

Relĭquus, a, um, adj. (relinquo,) *the rest; the remainder; the other.*

Remaneo, -manēre, -mansi, -mansum, intr. (re & maneo,) *to remain behind.*

Remedium, i, n. (re & medeor,) *a remedy.*

Remitto, -mittĕre, -mīsi, -missum, tr. (re & mitto,) *to send back; to remit.*

Removeo, -movēre, -mōvi, -mōtum, tr. (re & moveo,) *to move back*, or *away; to remove.*

Remus, i, m. *an oar.*

Remus, i, m. *the twin brother of Romŭlus.*

Renovātus, a, um, part. from

Renŏvo, āre, āvi, ātum, tr. (re & novo,) *to make anew; to renew.*

Renuntio, āre, āvi, ātum, tr. (re & nuntio,) *to bring back word; to inform; to report; to declare; to announce.*

Reor, reri, ratus sum, intr. dep. *to think; to suppose; to believe.*

Repăro, āre, āvi, ātum, tr. (re & paro,) *to get* or *procure again; to renew; to repair.*

Repentè, adv. (repens, fr. repo,) *suddenly.*

Reperio, -perīre, -pĕri, -pertum, tr. (re & pario,) *to find; to discover; to invent.*

Repĕto, -petĕre, -petīvi, -petītum, tr. (re & peto,) *to demand back.*

Repleo, ēre, ēvi, ētum, tr. (re & pleo,) *to fill again; to fill up; to replenish.*

Repōno, -ponĕre, -posui, -posĭtum, tr. (re & pono,) *to place back* or *again; to restore; to replace.*

Reporto, āre, āvi, ātum, tr. (re & porto,) *to bring back; to gain* or *obtain.*

Repræsento, āre, āvi, ātum, tr. (re & præsento,) *to make present again; to represent; to paint; to depict.*

Repudio, āre, āvi, ātum, tr. (repudium,) *to repudiate; to reject; to slight; to disregard:* uxōrem, *to divorce.*

Requīro, -quirĕre, -quisīvi, -quisītum, tr. (re & quæro,) *to seek again; to demand; to require; to need.*

Res, rei, f. *a thing; an affair; a way; a kingdom; a government; a subject:* res gestæ, *actions; exploits:* res familiāris *or* domestĭca, *domestic affairs; property.*

Reservo, āre, āvi, ātum, tr. (re & servo,) *to keep back; to reserve; to keep for a future time.*

Resideo, -sidēre, -sēdi, intr. (re & sedeo,) *to sit; to sit down; to remain.*

Resīmus, a, um, adj. (re & simus,) *bent back; crooked.*

Resisto, -sistĕre, -stĭti, -stĭtum, intr. (re & sisto,) *to hold* or *keep back; to resist; to withstand.*

Resolvo, -solvĕre, -solvi, -solūtum, tr. (re & solvo,) *to untie again; to loosen; to unbind; to unloose; to dissolve.*

Respondeo, -spodēre, -spondi, -sponsum, tr. (re & spondeo,) *to answer again; to answer; to reply; to correspond:* respondētur, pass.

imp. *it is answered,* or *the reply is made.*

Responsum, i, n. (respondeo,) *an answer; a reply.*

Respublĭca, reipublĭcæ, f. § 18, 9, (res publĭca,) *the state; the government; the commonwealth.*

Respuo, -spuĕre, -spui, tr. (re & spuo,) *to spit out; to reject.*

Restituo, -stituĕre, -stitui, -stitūtum, tr. (re & statuo,) *to put* or *set up again; to restore; to replace; to rebuild:* aciem, *to cause the army to rally.*

Retineo, -tinēre, -tinui, -tentum, tr. (re & teneo,) *to hold back; to retain; to detain; to hinder.*

Revērâ, adv. (res & verus,) *truly; in very deed; in reality; in good earnest.*

Reverentia, æ, f. (revereor,) *reverence.*

Reversus, a, um, part. *having returned;* from

Reverto, -vertĕre, -verti, -versum, intr. (re & verto,) *to turn back; to return.*

Revertor, -verti, -versus sum, intr. dep. *to return.*

Reviresco, -virescĕre, -virui, intr. inc. (revireo,) *to grow green again.*

Revŏco, āre, āvi, ātum, tr. (re & voco,) *to call back; to recall.*

Revŏlo, āre, āvi, ātum, intr. (re & volo,) *to fly back; to fly off again.*

Rex, regis, m. (rego,) *a king.*

Rhadamanthus, i, m. *a lawgiver of Crete, and subsequently one of the three judges of the infernal regions.*

Rhæti, ōrum, m. pl. *the inhabitants of Rhætia, now the Grisons.*

Rhæa, æ, f. (Silvia,) *the mother of Romulus and Remus.*

Rhenus, i, m. *the river Rhine.*

Rhinocĕros, ōtis, m. *a rhinoceros.*

Rhipæus, a, um, adj. *Rhipæan* or *Rhiphæan:* montes, *mountains, which, according to the ancients, were found in the north of Scythia.*

Rhodănus, i, m. *the river Rhone.*

Rhodius, i, m. *an inhabitant of Rhodes; a Rhodian.*

Rhodŏpe, es, f. *a high mountain in the western part of Thrace.*

Rhodus, i, f. *Rhodes; a celebrated town, and island in the Mediterranean sea.*

Rhœtēum, i, n. *a city and promontory of Troas.*

Rhyndăcus, i, m. *a river of Mysia.*

Ridens, tis, part. *smiling; laughing at;* from

Rideo, dēre, si, sum, intr. & tr. *to laugh; to laugh at; to mock, to deride.*

Rigeo, ēre, ui, intr. *to be cold.*

Rigĭdus, a, um, adj. (comp.) (rigeo,) *stiff with cold; rigid; severe.*

Rigo, āre, āvi, ātum, tr. *to water; to irrigate; to bedew: to wet.*

Ripa, æ, f. *a bank,* (of a river.)

Risi. *See* Rideo.

Risus, ûs, m. (rideo,) *laughing; laughter.*

Rixor, āri, ātus sum, intr. dep. (rixa,) *to quarrel.*

Robur, ŏris, n. *oak of the hardest kind,* hence, *strength:* robur milĭtum, *the flower of the soldiers.*

Rogātus, a, um, part. *being asked;* from

Rogo, āre, āvi, ātum, tr. *to ask; to request; to beg; to entreat.*

Rogus, i, m. *a funeral pile.*

Roma, æ, f. *Rome, the chief city of Italy, situated upon the Tiber;* hence,

Romānus, a, um, adj. *Roman.*

Romānus, i, m. *a Roman.*

Romŭlus, i, m. *the founder and first king of Rome:* Romŭlus Silvius, *a king of Alba.*

Rostrum, i, n. (rodo,) *a beak; a bill; a snout;* also, *the beak of a ship; a stage,* or *pulpit.*

Rota, æ, f. *a wheel.*

Rotundus, a, um, adj. (rota,) *round.*

Ruber, rubra, rubrum, adj. (rior, errĭmus,) *red.*

Rudis, e, adj. (ior, issĭmus,) *rude; unwrought; uncultivated; new; uncivilized.*

Ruīna, æ, f. (ruo,) *a ruin; a downfall; a fall.*

Rulliānus, i, m. *a Roman general, who commanded the cavalry in a war with the Samnites.*

Rumpo, rumpĕre, rupi, ruptum, tr. *to break* or *burst asunder; to break off; to break down; to violate.*

Ruo, uĕre, ui, utum, intr. & tr. *to run headlong; to fall; to be ruined; to hasten down; to rush; to throw down; to tear up.*

Rupes, is, f. *a rock; a cliff.*

Ruptus, a, um, part. (rumpo,) *broken; violated.*

Rursus, adv. *again.*

Rus, ruris, n. *the country; a farm;* hence,

Rustĭcus, a, um, adj. *rustic; belonging to the country.*

Rustĭcus, i, m. *a countryman.*

Rutilius, i, m. *a Roman consul.*

S.

Sabīni, ōrum, m. *the Sabines, a people of Italy.*

Sacer, sacra, sacrum, adj. (sup. errĭmus, § 26, 5,) *sacred; holy; divine; consecrated.*

Sacerdos, ōtis, c. (sacer,) *a priest; a priestess.*

Sacra, ōrum, m. pl. (id.) *religious service; sacrifice; sa-*

cred rites; religious observances.

Sacrifĭcans, tis, part. (sacrifĭco,) *sacrificing; offering sacrifices.*

Sacrificium, i, n. *a sacrifice;* from

Sacrifĭco, āre, āvi, ātum, tr. (sacer & facio,) *to sacrifice.*

Sæpè, adv. (iùs, issĭmè,) *often; frequently.*

Sævio, īre, ii, ītum, intr. (sævus,) *to rage; to be cruel.*

Sævĭtas, ātis, f. *cruelty; severity; savageness; barbarity;* from

Sævus, a, um, adj. (ior, issĭmus,) *cruel; severe; fierce; inhuman; violent.*

Saginātus, a, um, part. from

Sagīno, āre, āvi, ātum, tr. *to fatten.*

Sagitta, æ, f. *an arrow.*

Saguntīni, ōrum, m. pl. *the Saguntines; the inhabitants of Saguntum.*

Saguntum, i, n. *a town of Spain.*

Salio, salīre, salui & salii, intr. *to spring; to leap.*

Salsus, a, um, adj. (sallo, *to salt;* obsol. from sal,) *salt; sharp.*

Salto, āre, āvi, ātum, intr. freq. (salio,) *to dance.*

Salūber, -bris, -bre, adj. (brior, berrĭmus,) (salus,) *wholesome; salubrious; healthy;* hence,

Salubrĭtas, ātis, f. *salubrity; healthfulness.*

Salum, i, n. properly, the agitated motion of the sea: hence, *the sea.*

Salus, ūtis, f. *safety; salvation; health;* hence,

Salūto, āre, āvi, ātum, tr. *to wish health to;* hence, *to salute; to call.*

Salvus, a, um, adj. (salus,) *safe; preserved; unpunished.*

Samnītes, ium, m. pl. *the Samnites, a people of Italy.*

Sanctus, a, um, adj. comp. (sancio,) *holy; blameless.*

Sanguis, ĭnis, m. *blood.*

Sapiens, tis, (part. sapio, properly, *tasting; knowing by the taste;* hence,) adj. (ior, issĭmus,) *wise:*—subs. *a sage; a wise man;* hence,

Sapientia, æ, f. *wisdom; philosophy.*

Sapio, ĕre, ui, intr. (*to taste; to discern;* hence,) *to be wise.*

Sarcĭna, æ, f. (sarcio,) *a pack; a bundle.*

Sardinia, æ, f. *a large island in the Mediterranean sea, west of Italy.*

Sarmătæ, ārum, m. *the Sarmatians, a people inhabiting the north of Europe and Asia.*

Sarpēdon, ŏnis, m. *a son of Jupiter and Europa.*

Satelles, ĭtis, m. *a satellite; a guard; a body-guard.*

Satiātus, a, um, part. from

Satio, āre, āvi, ātum, tr. *to satiate; to satisfy;* from

Satis, adj. & adv. (comp. satius, *better;*) *enough; sufficient; sufficiently; very; quite.*

Satur, ŭra, ŭrum, adj. (ior, issĭmus,) (satio,) *satiated; full.*

Saturnia, æ, f. *a name given to Italy;* also, *a citadel and town near Janiculum.*

Saturnus, i, m. *the father of Jupiter.*

Saucio, āre, āvi, ātum, tr. (saucius,) *to wound.*

Saxum, i, n. *a rock; a stone.*

Scævŏla, æ, m. (Mucius,) *a brave Roman soldier.*

Scateo, ēre, intr. *to gush forth like water from a spring;* hence, *to be full; to abound.*

Scamander, dri, m. *a river of Troas, which flows from Mount Ida into the Hellespont.*

Scaurus, i, m. *the surname of several Romans.*

Scelestus, a, um, adj. (ior, issĭmus,) *wicked;* from

Scelus, ĕris, n. *an impious action; a crime; wickedness:* by metonymy, *a wicked person. See* Facinus.

Scena, æ, f. *a scene; a stage.*

Schœneus, i, m. *a king of Arcadia* or *Scyros, and father of Atalanta.*

Scheria, æ, f. *an ancient name of the island Corcyra,* or *Corfu.*

Scientia, æ, f. *knowledge;* from

Scio, īre, īvi, ītum, tr. *to know; to understand.*

Scipio, ōnis, m. *a distinguished Roman family:* Scipiōnes, *the Scipios.*

Scopŭlus, i, m. *a high rock; a cliff.*

Scorpio, ōnis, m. *a scorpion.*

Scotia, æ, f. *Scotland.*

Scriba, æ, m. *a writer; a secretary; a scribe;* from

Scribo, scribĕre, scripsi, scriptum, tr. *to write:* scribĕre leges, *to prepare laws.*

Scriptor, ōris, m. *a writer; an author.*

Scriptūrus, a, um, part. (scribo.)

Scriptus, a, um, part. (scribo.)

Scrutor, āri, ātus sum, tr. dep. (scruta,) *to search into; to trace out.*

Scutum, i, n. *a shield.*

Scylla, æ, f. *the daughter of Nisus.*

Scyros, i, f. *an island in the Ægean sea.*

Scythes, æ, m. *an inhabitant of Scythia; a Scythian.*

Scythia, æ, f. *a vast country in the north of Europe and Asia.*

Scythĭcus, a, um, adj. *Scythian.*

Seco, secāre, secui, sectum, tr. *to cut.*

Secēdo, -cedĕre, -cessi, -cessum, intr. (se & cedo,) *to go aside; to secede; to withdraw.*

Sectātus, a, um, part. *having followed* or *attended;* from

Sector, āri, ātus sum, tr. dep. freq. (sequor, 227, Obs. 1,) *to follow; to pursue; to accompany; to attend; to strive after.*

Secŭlum, and Sæcŭlum, i, n. *an age; a period of time.*

Secum, (se & cum, § 28, 4,) *with himself; with herself; with itself; with themselves.*

Secundus, a, um, adj. comp. (sequor,) *the second; prosperous:* res secundæ, *prosperity.*

Secūris, is, f. (seco,) *an axe.*

Secūtus, a, um, part. (sequor.)

Sed, conj. *but.*

Sedĕcim, num, adj. ind. pl. (sex & decem,) *sixteen.*

Sedeo, sedēre, sedi, sessum, intr. *to sit; to light upon.*

Sedes, is, f. (sedes,) *a seat; a residence; a settlement:* regni, *the seat of government.*

Seditio, ōnis, f. (se, *aside,* and eo,) *sedition; a rebellion; an insurrection.*

Sedŭlus, a, um, adj. (sedeo,) *diligent.*

Seges, ĕtis, f. *a crop; a harvest.*

Segnis, e, adj. (ior, issĭmus,) *dull; slow; slothful, sluggish.*

Sejungo, -jungĕre, -junxi, -junctum, tr. (se & jungo,) *to divide; to separate.*

Selucia, æ, f. *a town of Syria, near the Orontes.*

Semel, adv. *once:* plùs semel, *more than once.*

Semĕle, es, f. *a daughter of Cadmus and Hermione, and mother of Bacchus.*

Semen, ĭnis, n. *seed.*

Semirămis, ĭdis, f. *a queen of Assyria, and wife of Ninus.*

Semper, adv. *always;* hence,

Sempiternus, a, um, adj. *everlasting.*

Sempronius, i, m. *the name of a Roman gens or clan:* Sempronius Gracchus, *a Roman general.*

Sena, æ, f. *a town of Picenum.*

Senātor, ōris, m. (senex,) *a Senator.*

Senātus, ûs, & i, m. (senex,) *a senate.*

Senecta, æ, *or* Senectus, ūtis, f. (senex,) *old age.*

Senescens, tis, part. from

Senesco, senescĕre, senui, intr. inc. *to grow old; to wane;* from seneo, and that from

Senex, is, c. *an old man* or *woman:*—adj. *old:* (comp. senior, sometimes major natu,) § 26, 6.

Senŏnes, um, m. pl. *a people of Gaul.*

Sensi. *See* Sentio.

Sensus, ûs, m. (sentio,) *sense; feeling.*

Sententia, æ, f. *an opinion; a proposition; a sentiment;* from

Sentio, sentīre, sensi, sensum, tr. *to feel; to perceive; to be sensible of; to observe; to suppose.*

Sepăro, āre, āvi, ātum, tr. (se & paro,) *to separate; to divide.*

Sepelio, sepelīre, sepelīvi, sepultum, tr. *to bury; to inter.*

Sepes, is, f. *a hedge; a fence.*

Septem, num. adj. ind. pl. *seven.*

Septentrio, ōnis, m. *the Northern Bear; the North.*

Septies, num. adv. *seven times.*

Septĭmus, a, um, num. adj. ord. (septem,) *the seventh.*

Septingentesĭmus, a, um, num. adj. *the seven hundredth.*

Septuagesĭmus, a, um, num. adj. *the seventieth;* from

Septuaginta, num. adj. ind. pl. *seventy.*

Sepulcrum, i, n. (sepelio,) *a sepulchre; a tomb.*

Sepultūra, æ, f. (id.) *burial; interment.*

Sepultus, a, um, part. (sepelio,) *buried.*

Sequăna, æ, m. *the Seine, a river in France.*

Sequens, tis, part. from

Sequor, sequi, secūtus sum, tr. dep. *to follow; to pursue.*

Secūtus, a, um, part. (sequor.)

Serēnus, a, um, adj. (comp.) *serene; tranquil; clear; fair; bright.*

Sergius, i, m. *the name of several Romans.*

Sermo, ōnis, m. (sero,) *speech; a discourse; conversation.*

Serò, (seriùs,) adv. *late; too late.*

Sero, serĕre, sevi, satum, tr. *to sow; to plant.*

Serpens, tis, c. (serpo, *to creep,*) *a serpent; a snake.*

Sertorius, i, m. *a Roman general.*

Serus, a, um, adj. (comp.) *late.*

Servilius, i, m. *the name of a Roman family:* Servilius Casca, *one of the murderers of Cæsar.*

Servio, īre, īvi, ītum, intr. (servus,) *to be a slave; to serve, (as a slave).*

Servitium, i, n. *or* Servĭtus, ūtis, f. (id.) *slavery; bondage.*

Servius, i, m. (Tullius,) *the sixth king of Rome.*

Servo, āre, āvi, ātum, tr. *to preserve; to guard; to watch; to keep;* hence,

Servus, i, m. *a slave; a servant.*

Sese, pro. acc. and abl. § 28, Obs. 4, *himself; herself; themselves.*

Sestertium, i, n. *a sestertium,* or *a thousand sesterces.* 907.

Sestertius, i, m. *a sesterce,* or *two and a half asses.* 906 & 907.

Sestos, i, *or* -us, i, f. *a town of Thrace, on the shores of the Hellespont, opposite to Abydos.*

Seta, æ, f. *a bristle.*

Setīnus, a, um, adj. *Setine; belonging to Setia, a city of Campania, near the Pontine Marshes, famous for its wine.*

Setōsus, a, um, adj. (seta,) *full of bristles; bristly.*

Sex, num. adj. ind. pl. *six.*

Sexagesĭmus, a, um, num. adj. ord. (sex,) *the sixtieth.*

Sexaginta, num. adj. ind. pl. (sex,) *sixty.*

Sexcentesĭmus, a, um, num. adj. ord. (sex & centum,) *the six hundredth.*

Sextus, a, um, num. adj. ord. (sex,) *the sixth.*

Si, conj. *if; whether:* si quando, *if at any time.*

Sic, adv. *so; thus; in such a manner.*

Siccius, i, m. (Dentātus,) *the name of a brave Roman soldier.*

Siccus, a, um, adj. *dry:* siccum, *dry land:* in sicco (loco), *in a dry place:* (arĭdus, *thoroughly dry; parched.*)

Sicilia, æ, f. *Sicily, the largest island in the Mediterranean.*

Sicŭlus, a, um, adj. *Sicilian:* fretum, *the straits of Messina.*

Sicut, & Sicŭti, adv. (sic ut,) *as: as if.*

Sidon, ōnis, f. *a maritime city of Phœnicia.*

Sidonius, a, um, adj. *belonging to Sidon; Sidonian.*

Sidus, ĕris, n. *a star.*

Signifĭco, āre, āvi, ātum, tr. (signum & facio,) *to make* or *give a sign; to designate; to mark; to express; to signify; to give notice; to imply* or *mean.*

Signum, i, m, *a sign; a token; a statue; a standard; colors.*

Silens, tis, part. (sileo,) *silent; keeping silence.*

Silentium, i, n. (sileo,) *silence.*

Silēnus, i, m. *the foster-father and instructor of Bacchus.*

Sileo, ēre, ui, intr. *to be silent; to conceal.*

Silva, *or* Sylva, æ, f. *a forest; a wood.*

Silvia, æ, f. (Rhea,) *the mother of Romulus.*

Silvius, i, m. *a son of Æneas, the second king of Alba:* Silvius Procas, *a king of Alba, the father of Numitor and Amulius.*

Simia, æ, f. (simus,) *an ape.*

Simĭlis, e, adj. (ior, lĭmus, § 26, 1,) *similar; like;* hence,

Similĭter, adv. (similiùs, similĭmè,) *in like manner.*

Simplex, ĭcis, adj. comp. (sine plicâ, *without a fold; open; plain;*) hence, *simple; artless; open; plain; single.*

Simŏis, entis, m. *a river of Troas, flowing into the Scamander.*

Simonĭdes, is, m. *a Greek poet, born in the island of Cea.*

Simul, adv. *at the same time; at once; together; as soon as:* simul—simul—*as soon as,* or *no sooner than.*

Simulăcrum, i, n. (simŭlo,) *an image; a statue.*

Sin, conj. *but if.*

Sine, prep. *without.*

Singulāris, e, adj. *single; sin-*

gular; distinguished; extraordinary: certāmen singulāre, *a single combat;* from

Singŭli, æ, a, num. adj. pl. *each; one by one; every:* singŭlis mensĭbus, *every month.*

Sinister, tra, trum, adj. (comp. irr. § 26, 2,) *left.*

Sino, sinĕre, sivi, situm, tr. (for sio, obsol.) *to permit.*

Sinus, ûs, m. *a bosom; a bay; a gulf.*

Siquis, siqua, siquod *or* siquid, pro. *if any one; if any thing.*

Siquando, adv. (si & quando,) *if at any time; if ever.*

Sitio, īre, ii, intr. & tr. *to thirst; to be thirsty; to desire earnestly.*

Sitis, is, f. *thirst.*

Situs, a, um, part. & adj. (sino,) *placed; set; situated; permitted.*

Sive, conj. *or; or if; whether.*

Sobŏles, is, f. (subŏles, sub & oleo,) *a sprig* or *shoot; offspring.*

Sobrius, a, um, adj. *sober; temperate.*

Socer, ĕri, m. *a father-in-law.*

Sociālis, e, adj. (socius,) *pertaining to allies; social; confederate.*

Sociĕtas, ātis, f. *society; alliance; intercourse; partnership;* from

Socius, i, m. *an ally; a companion.*

Socordia, æ, f. (socors, fr. se & cor,) *negligence; sloth.*

Socrătes, is, m. *the most eminent of the Athenian philosophers.*

Sol, solis, m. *the sun.*

Soleo, ēre, ĭtus sum, n. pass. § 78, *to be wont; to be accustomed:* solēbat, *used.*

Solĭdus, a, um, adj. (ior, issĭmus,) *whole; solid; entire.*

Solitūdo, ĭnis, f. (solus,) *a desert; a wilderness; a solitary place.*

Solĭtus, a, um, part. (soleo,) *accustomed; usual.*

Sollers, tis, adj. (sollus, *whole,* not used, & ars,) *ingenious; inventive; cunning; skillful; shrewd.*

Sollertia, æ, f. (sollers,) *sagacity; skill; shrewdness.*

Solon, ōnis, m. *the lawgiver of the Athenians, and one of the seven wise men of Greece.*

Solstitium, i, n. (sol & sisto,) *the solstice, particularly the summer solstice, in distinction from* bruma, *the winter solstice; the longest day.*

Solum, i, n. *the earth; the soil; land.*

Solùm, adv. *alone; only;* fr.

Solus, a, um, adj. § 20, 4; *alone.*

Solūtus, a, um, part. from

Solvo, solvĕre, solvi, solūtum, tr. *to loose; to dissolve; to melt; to answer.*

Somnio, āre, āvi, ātum, intr. *to dream;* from

Somnium, i, n. *a dream;* from

Somnus, i, m. *sleep.*

Sonĭtus, ûs, m. *a sound; a noise;* from

Sono, āre, ui, ĭtum, intr. *to sound; to resound;* from

Sonus, i, m. *a sound.*

Sorbeo, -ēre, -ui, tr. *to suck in; to absorb.*

Soror, ōris, f. *a sister.*

Sp., *an abbreviation of* Spurius.

Spargo, spargĕre, sparsi, sparsum, tr. *to sprinkle; to strew; to scatter; to sow.*

Sparsi. *See* Spargo.

Sparsus, a, um, part.

Sparta, æ, f. *Sparta* or *Lacedæmon, the capital of Laconia.*

Spartăcus, i, m. *the name of a celebrated gladiator.*

Spartānus, i, m. *a Spartan.*

Sparti, ōrum, m. pl. *a race of men said to have sprung from the dragon's teeth sowed by Cadmus.*

Spartum, i, n. *Spanish broom, a plant of which ropes were made.*

Spatiōsus, a, um, adj. *large; spacious;* from

Spatium, i, n. *a race ground;* (stadium,) *a space; room; distance.*

Species, ēi, f. (specio,) *an appearance.*

Spectacŭlum, i, n. *a spectacle; a show;* from

Specto, āre, āvi, ātum, tr. freq. (specio,) *to behold; to see; to consider; to regard; to relate; to refer.*

Specus, ûs, m. f. & n. *a cave.*

Spelunca, æ, f. *a cave.*

Spero, āre, āvi, ātum, tr. *to hope; to expect.*

Spes, ei, f. *hope; expectation; promise.*

Speusippus, i, m. *the nephew and successor of Plato.*

Sphinx, gis, f. *a Sphinx. The Egyptian Sphinx is represented as a monster having a woman's head on the body of a lion.*

Spina, æ, f. *a thorn; a sting; a quill; a spine; a backbone.*

Spirĭtus, ûs, m. *a breath;* fr.

Spiro, āre, āvi, ātum, intr. *to breathe.*

Splendeo, ēre, ui, intr. *to shine; to be conspicuous;* hence,

Splendĭdus, a, um, adj. (comp.) *splendid; illustrious;* and

Splendor, ōris, m. *brightness; splendor.*

Spolio, āre, āvi, ātum, tr. *to despoil; to strip; to deprive;* from

Spolium, i, n. *the skin of an animal; spoils; booty.*

Spondeo, spondēre, spopondi, sponsum, tr. *to pledge one's word; to promise; to engage.*

Sponsa, æ, f. (spondeo,) *a bride.*

Spontis, gen., sponte, abl. sing., f. § 18, 11; *of one's own accord; voluntarily; spontaneously; of himself; of itself.*

Spurius, i, m. *a* prænōmen *among the Romans.*

Squama, æ, f. *the scale of a fish.*

Stabŭlum, i, n. (sto,) *a stall; a stable.*

Stadium, i, n. *a stadium; a furlong; a measure of* 125 *paces; the race-ground.*

Stannum, i, n. *tin.*

Stans, stantis, part. (sto.)

Statim, adv. (sto,) *immediately.*

Statio, ōnis, f. (sto,) *a station; a picket or watch;* (by day,) navium, *roadstead; an anchoring place.*

Statua, æ, f. (statuo,) *a statue.*

Statuarius, i, m. *a statuary; a sculptor.*

Statuo, uĕre, ui, ūtum, tr. (statum, fr. sisto,) *to cause to stand; to set up; to determine; to resolve; to fix; to judge; to decide; to believe.*

Status, a, um, adj. (sto,) *fixed; stated; appointed; certain.*

Statūtus, a, um, part. (statuo,) *placed; resolved; fixed; settled.*

Stella, æ, f. (sto,) *a star; a fixed star.*

Sterĭlis, e, adj. (comp.) *unfruitful; sterile; barren.*

Sterto, ĕre, ui, intr. *to snore.*

Stipes, ĭtis, m. *a stake; the trunk of a tree.*

Stirps, is, f. *root; a stock; a race; a family.*

Sto, stare, steti, statum, intr. *to stand; to be stationary:* stare a partĭbus, *to favor the party.*

Stoĭcus, i, m. *a Stoic, one of a sect of Grecian philosophers, whose founder was Zeno.*

Stolidĭtas, ātis, f. *stupidity;* fr.

Stolĭdus, a, um, adj. (ior, issĭmus,) *foolish; silly; stupid.*

Strages, is, f. (sterno,) *an overthrow; slaughter.*

Strangŭlo, āre, āvi, ātum, tr. *to strangle.*

Strenuè, adv. (iùs, issĭmè,) *bravely; actively; vigorously; strenuously;* from

Strenuus, a, um, adj. (comp.) *bold; strenuous; brave; valiant.*

Strophădes, um, f. pl. *two small islands in the Ionian sea.*

Struo, struĕre, struxi, structum, tr. *to put together; to construct; to build:* insidias, *to prepare an ambuscade; to lay snares.*

Struthiocamēlus, i, m. *an ostrich.*

Strymon, ōnis, m. *a river which was anciently the boundary between Macedonia and Thrace.*

Studeo, ēre, ui, intr. *to favor;*

to study; to endeavor; to attend to; to pursue.

Studiōsè, adv. (studiōsus, fr. studium,) *studiously; diligently.*

Studium, i, n. *zeal; study; diligence; eagerness.*

Stultitia, æ, f. *folly;* from

Stultus, a, um, adj. (ior, issĭmus,) *foolish:* stulti, *fools.*

Stupeo, ēre, ui, intr. *to be torpid* or *benumbed; to be astonished at; to be amazed.*

Sturnus, i, m. *a starling.*

Suadendus, a, um, part. (suadeo.)

Suadens, tis, part. from

Suadeo, suadēre, suasi, suasum, tr. & intr. *to advise; to persuade; to urge.*

Suavĭtas, ātis, f. (suavis,) *sweetness; grace; melody.*

Suavĭter, adv. (viùs, vissĭmè,) (id.) *sweetly; agreeably.*

Sub, prep. *under; near to; near the time of; just before; at; in the time of.*

Subdūco, -ducĕre, -duxi, -ductum, tr. (sub & duco,) *to withdraw; to take away; to withhold;* hence,

Subductus, a, um, part.

Subeo, īre, īvi & ii, ĭtum, intr. irr. (sub & eo, § 83, 4,) *to go under; to submit to:* onus, *to take up* or *sustain a burden.*

Subĭgo, -igĕre, -ēgi, -actum, tr. (sub & ago,) *to subject; to subdue; to conquer.*

Subĭtò, adv. *suddenly;* from

Subĭtus, a, um, adj. (subeo,) *sudden; unexpected.*

Sublātus, a, um, part. (suffĕro,) *taken away; lifted up.*

Sublĕvo, āre, āvi, ātum, tr. (sub & levo,) *to lighten; to relieve; to raise up; to assist.*

Sublīmis, e, adj. comp. (sub. for supra, & limus,) *sublime; high in the air:* in sublīme, *aloft;* hence,

Sublīmè, adv. *aloft; in the air.*

Submergo, -mergĕre, -mersi, -mersum, tr. (sub & mergo,) *to sink; to overwhelm.*

Submergor, -mergi, -mersus sum, pass. *to be overwhelmed; to sink; hence,*

Submersus, a, um, part.

Subrīdens, tis, part. *smiling at.*

Subrideo, -ridēre, -rīsi, -rīsum, intr. (sub & rideo,) *to smile.*

Subsilio, -silīre, -silui & silii, intr. (sub & salio,) *to leap up; to jump.*

Substituo, -stituĕre, -stitui, -stitūtum, tr. (sub & statuo,) *to put in the place of another; to substitute.*

Subter, prep. *under.*

Subterraneus, a, um, adj. (sub & terra,) *subterranean.*

Subvenio, -venīre, vēni, -ventum, intr. (sub & venio,) *to come to one's assistance; to succor; to help.*

Subvŏlo, āre, āvi, ātum, intr. (sub & volo,) *to fly up.*

Succēdo, -cedĕre, -cessi, -ces-

sum, intr. (sub & cedo,) *to succeed; to follow;* hence,
Successor, ōris, m. *a successor.*
Succus, i, m. (sucus, fr. sugo,) *juice; sap; liquid.*
Suffĕro, sufferre, sustŭli, sublātum, tr. irr. (sub & fero,) *to take away; to undertake; to bear.*
Suffetius, i, m. (Metius,) *an Alban general, put to death by Tullus Hostilius.*
Sufficio, -ficĕre, -fēci, -fectum, intr. (sub & facio,) *to suffice; to be sufficient.*
Suffodio, -fodĕre, -fōdi, -fossum, tr. (sub & fodio,) *to dig under; to undermine.*
Suffossus, a, um, part.
Suffragium, i, n. (sub & frango,) *a broken piece; a shred; a ballet; suffrage; vote; choice.*
Sui, pro. gen. 117, & 118, 3, 1st, *of himself; of herself; of itself:* duæ sibi similes, *two like each other.*
Sulla, *or* Sylla, æ, m. *a distinguished Roman general.*
Sulpicius, i, m. (Gallus,) *a Roman, celebrated for his learning and eloquence, and for his skill in astrology.*
Sum, esse, fui, intr. irr. § 54, *to be; to exist:* terrōri esse, *to excite terror.*
Summus, a, um, adj. (*see* Supĕrus,) *the highest; greatest; perfect:* in summâ aquâ, *on the surface of the water.*
Sumo, sumĕre, sumpsi, sumptum, tr. *to take.*
Sumptus, a, um, part. (sumo.)
Sumptus, ûs, m. (id.) *expense.*
Supellex, supellectīlis, f. *furniture; household goods.*
Super, prep. *above; upon.*
Superbè, adv. iùs, issĭmè, (fr. superbus,) *proudly; haughtily.*
Superbia, æ, f. (superbus,) *pride; haughtiness.*
Superbio, īre, īvi, ītum, intr. *to be proud; to be proud of;* from
Superbus, a, um, adj. comp. *proud; the Proud, a surname of Tarquin, the last king of Rome.*
Superfluus, a, um, adj. (superfluo,) *superfluous.*
Superjăcio, -jacĕre, -jēci, -jactum, tr. (super & jacio,) *to throw upon; to shoot over.*
Superjactus, a, um, part. from superjacio; Sall.
Supĕro, āre, āvi, ātum, tr. (super,) *to surpass; to conquer; to excel; to vanquish.*
Superstitiōsus, a, um, adj. (superstitio, fr. supersto,) *superstitious.*
Supersum, -esse, fui, intr. irr. (super & sum,) *to be over; to remain; to survive.*
Supĕrus, a, um, adj. (superior; suprēmus, *or* summus, § 26, 2,) *above; high; upper.*
Supervacuus, a, um, adj. (super & vacuus,) *superfluous.*

Supervenio, -venīre, -vēni, -ventum, intr. (super & venio,) *to come upon; to come; to surprise suddenly.*

Supervŏlo, āre, āvi, ātum, intr. (super & volo,) *to fly over.*

Suppĕto, ĕre, īvi, ītum, intr. (sub & peto,) *to come to; to be at hand;* hence, *to suffice; to remain; to serve; to be sufficient.*

Supplex, ĭcis, adj. (sub & plico,) *suppliant.*

Supplicium, i, n. (id.) *a punishment.*

Suppōno, -ponĕre, -posui, -posĭtum, tr. (sub & pono,) *to put under; to substitute.*

Supra, prep. & adv. *above; before.*

Surēna, æ, m. *the title of a Parthian officer, and next in authority to the king.*

Surgo, surgĕre, surrexi, surrectum, intr. (surrego, fr. sub & rego,) *to rise.*

Sus, uis, c. *a swine; a hog.*

Suscipio, -cipĕre, -cēpi, -ceptum, tr. (sub & capio,) *to take* or *lift up; to undertake; to take upon; to engage in; to receive.*

Suspectus, a, um, part. & adj. (suspicio,) *suspected; mistrusted.*

Suspendo, -pendĕre, -pendi, -pensum, tr. (sub & pendo,) *to suspend; to hang; to hang up.*

Suspensus, a, um, part.

Suspicio, -spicĕre, -spexi, -spectum, tr. (sub & specio,) *to look at secretly; to look up; to suspect.*

Suspĭcor, āri, ātus sum, tr. dep. *to suspect; to surmise.*

Sustento, āre, āvi, ātum, tr. freq. *to sustain; to support:* sustentāre vitam, *to support one's self;* from

Sustineo, -tinēre, -tinui, -tentum, tr. (sub & teneo,) *to bear up; to carry; to sustain; to support.*

Sustollo, sustollĕre, sustŭli, sublātum, tr. *to lift up; to take away; to raise.*

Suus, a, um, pro. *his; hers; its; theirs;* 118, Obs. 3, Exc., & 121, Obs. 3.

Sylla. *See* Sulla.

Syllăba, æ, f. *a syllable.*

Sylva. *See* Silva.

Syphax, ācis, m. *a king of Numidia.*

Syracūsæ, ārum, f. pl. *Syracuse, a celebrated city of Sicily.*

Syria, æ, f. *a large country of Asia, at the eastern extremity of the Mediterranean sea.*

Syriăcus, a, um, adj. *Syrian; belonging to Syria.*

T.

T., *an abbreviation of* Titus.

Tabesco, tabescĕre, tabui, inc. (tabeo,) *to consume; to pine away.*

Tabŭla, æ, f. *a table; a tablet; a picture; a painting:* plumbea tabŭla, *a plate* or *sheet of lead.*

Taceo, ēre, ui, ĭtum, intr. *to be silent.*

Tactus, ûs, m. (tango,) *the touch.*

Tædet, tæduit, tæsum est *or* pertæsum est, imp. *to be weary of:* vitæ eos tædet, *they are weary of life.*

Tænărus, i, m. & um, i, n. *a promontory in Laconia,* now *cape Matapan.*

Talentum, i, n. *a talent; a sum variously estimated from* $860 *to* $1020.

Talis, e, adj. *such.*

Talpa, æ, c. *a mole.*

Tam, adv. *so; so much.*

Tamen, conj. *yet; notwithstanding; still; nevertheless.*

Tanāis, is, m. *a river between Europe and Asia,* now *the Don.*

Tanăquil, ĭlis, f. *the wife of Tarquinius Priscus.*

Tandem, adv. (tam & demum,) *at length; at last; finally.*

Tango, tangĕre, tetĭgi, tactum, tr. *to touch.*

Tanquam, *or* Tamquam, adv. (tam & quam,) *as well as; as if; like.*

Tantălus, i, m. *a son of Jupiter; the father of Pelops, and king of Phrygia.*

Tantò, adv. (tantus,) *so much.*

Tantopĕre, adv. (tantus & opus,) *so much; so greatly.*

Tantùm, adv. *only; so much;* from

Tantus, a, um, adj. *so great; such:* tanti, *of so much value:* tanti est, *it is worth the pains; it makes amends.*

Tardè, adv. (iùs, issĭmè,) (tardus,) *slowly.*

Tardĭtas, ātis, f. (tardus,) *slowness; dulness; heaviness.*

Tardo, āre, āvi, ātum, tr. *to make slow; to retard; to check; to stop;* from

Tardus, a, um, adj. (ior, issĭmus,) *slow; dull.*

Tarentīnus, a, um, adj. *Tarentine; of* or *belonging to Tarentum:* Tarentīni, *Tarentines; the inhabitants of Tarentum.*

Tarentum, i, n. *a celebrated city in the south of Italy.*

Tarpēia, æ, f. *the daughter of Sp. Tarpeius: she betrayed the Roman citadel to the Sabines.*

Tarpēius, a, um, adj. *Tarpeian:* mons, *the Tarpeian* or *Capitoline mount.*

Tarquinii, ōrum, m. pl. *a city of Etruria, whence the family of Tarquin derived their name.*

Tarquinius, i, m. *Tarquin; the name of an illustrious Roman family:* Tarquinii, ōrum, pl. *the Tarquins.*

Tartărus, i, m., & -a, ōrum, pl. n. *Tartarus; the infernal regions.*

Taurĭca, æ, f. *a large peninsu-*

la of the Black Sea, now *called the Crimēa,* or *Taurida.*

Taurus, i, m. *a high range of mountains in Asia.*

Taurus, i, m. *a bull.*

Taygĕtus, i, m. & -a, ōrum, pl. *a mountain of Laconia, near Sparta.*

Tectum, i, n. (tego,) *a covering; a roof; a house.*

Tectus, a, um, part. (tego,) *covered; defended.*

Teges, ĕtis, f. *a mat; a rug; a coverlet;* from

Tego, gĕre, xi, ctum, tr. *to cover; to defend;* hence,

Tegumentum, i, n. *a covering.*

Telum, i, n. *a missile; a weapon; a dart; an arrow.*

Temĕrè, adv. *at random; accidentally; rashly.*

Tempe, n. pl. indec. *a beautiful vale in Thessaly, through which the river Peneus flows.*

Temperies, iēi, f. *a season* or *space of time; temperateness; mildness; temperature.*

Tempestas, ātis, f. (tempus,) *a storm; a tempest.*

Templum, i, n. *a consecrated place; a temple.*

Tempus, ŏris, n. *time; a season:* ad tempus, *at the time appointed:* ex tempŏre, *without premeditation.*

Temulentus, a, um, adj. (temētum,) *drunken; intoxicated.*

Tendo, tendĕre, tetendi, tensum, tr. *to stretch; to stretch out; to extend;* intr. *to advance; to go.*

Tenĕbræ, ārum, f. pl. *darkness.*

Teneo, tenēre, tenui, tentum, tr. *to hold; to have; to keep; to possess; to know; to hold by a garrison:* portum, *to reach the harbor.*

Tentātus, a, um, part. from

Tento, āre, āvi, ātum, tr. freq. (teneo,) *to attempt; to try.*

Tentyrītæ, ārum, c. pl. *the inhabitants of Tentyra, a town and island in Upper Egypt.*

Tenuis, e, adj. (comp.) *thin; slender; light; rare.*

Tenus, prep. *up to; as far as.*

Tepesco, escĕre, ui, intr. inc. (tepeo,) *to grow warm* or *cool; to become tepid.*

Ter, num. adv. *thrice.*

Terentius, i, m. *a Roman proper name.*

Tergum, i, n. *the back; the farther side:* a tergo, *from behind:* ad terga, *behind.*

Termīno, āre, āvi, ātum, tr. *to bound; to limit; to terminate;* from

Termīnus, i, m. *a boundary; limit; an end; bounds.*

Terni, æ, a, num. adj. pl. (tres,) *three by three; three.*

Terra, æ, f. *the earth; a country; the land:* omnes terræ, *the whole world.*

Terreo, ēre, ui, ĭtum, tr. *to terrify; to scare; to frighten.*

Terrester, terrestris, terrestre, adj. (terra,) *terrestrial:* anĭmal terrestre, *a land animal.*

Terribĭlis, e, adj. comp. (terreo,) *terrible.*

Terrĭto, āre, āvi, ātum, tr. freq. (id.) *to terrify; to affright.*

Territorium, i, n. (terra,) *territory.*

Terrĭtus, a, um, part. (terreo.)

Terror, ōris, m. (id.) *terror; consternation; fear.*

Tertius, a, um, num. adj. ord. (tres,) *the third;* hence,

Tertiò, num. adv. *the third time.*

Testa, æ, f. (tosta, fr. torreo,) *an earthen vessel; a shell.*

Testamentum, i, n. (testor,) *a will; a testament.*

Testūdo, ĭnis, f. (testa,) *a tortoise.*

Tetĭgi. *See* Tango.

Teutŏnes, um, & Teutŏni, ōrum, m. pl. *a nation in the northern part of Germany, near the Cimbri.*

Texo, texĕre, texui, textum, tr. *to weave; to plait; to form; to construct.*

Thalămus, i, m. *a bed-chamber; a dwelling.*

Thales, is & ētis, m. *a Milesian, one of the seven wise men of Greece.*

Thasus, i, f. *an island on the coast of Thrace.*

Theātrum, i, n. *a theatre.*

Thebæ, ārum, f. pl. *Thebes, the capital of Bœotia;* hence,

Thebānus, a, um, adj. *Theban; belonging to Thebes.*

Thelesīnus, i, m. *a Roman proper name.*

Themistŏcles, is, m. *a celebrated Athenian general in the Persian war.*

Theodōrus, i, m. *a philosopher of Cyrēnæ.*

Thermōdon, ontis, m. *a river of Pontus.*

Theseus, i, m. *a king of Athens, and son of Ægeus, and one of the most celebrated heroes of antiquity.*

Thessalia, æ, f. *Thessaly; a country of Greece, south of Macedonia;* hence,

Thessălus, a, um, adj. *belonging to Thessaly; Thessalian.*

Thestius, i, m. *the father of Althæa.*

Thetis, ĭdis & ĭdos, f. *one of the sea nymphs; the wife of Peleus, and mother of Achilles.*

Theutobŏchus, i, m. *a king of the Cimbri.*

Thracia, æ, f. *Thrace; a large country east of Macedonia.*

Thracius, a, um, adj. *belonging to Thrace; Thracian.*

Thrasybūlus, i, m. *an Athenian general, celebrated for freeing his country from the thirty tyrants.*

Thus, thuris, n. *frankincense.*

Tibĕris, is, m. 90, 2, *the Tiber, a famous river of Italy.*

Tibi. *See* Tu.

Tibĭcen, ĭnis, m. (tibia & cano,) *one who plays upon the flute; a piper.*

Ticīnum, i, n. *a town of Cisalpine Gaul, where the Romans were defeated by Hannibal.*

Tigrānes, is, m. *a king of Armenia Major.*

Tigranocerta, ōrum, n. *a city of Armenia Major, founded by Tigrānes.*

Tigris, ĭdis, (*seldom* is,) c. *a tiger.*

Tigris, ĭdis & is, m. *a river in Asia.*

Timens, tis, part. from

Timeo, ēre, ui, intr. & tr. *to fear; to dread; to be afraid.*

Timĭdus, a, um, adj. comp. (timeo,) *timid; cowardly.*

Timor, ōris, m. (id.) *fear.*

Tinnītus, ûs, m. (tinnio,) *a tinkling.*

Tintinnabŭlum, i, n. (tintinno, *same as* tinnio,) *a bell.*

Titio, ōnis, m. *a brand; a firebrand.*

Titus, i, m. *a Roman* prænōmen.

Tolĕro, āre, āvi, ātum, tr. *to bear; to endure; to admit of.*

Tollo, tollĕre, sustŭli, sublātum, tr. *to raise; to pick up; to remove; to do away with.*

Tondeo, tondēre, totondi, tonsum, tr. *to clip; to shave; to shear.*

Tonitru, u, n. *thunder;* from

Tono, āre, ui, ĭtum, intr. *to thunder:* tonat, imp. *it thunders.*

Tormentum, i, n. (torqueo,) *an engine for throwing stones and darts.*

Torquātus, i, m. *a surname given to T. Manlius and his descendants.*

Torquis, is, d. (torqueo,) *a collar; a chain.*

Tot, ind. adj. *so many.*

Totĭdem, ind. adj. (tot itĭdem,) *the same number; as many.*

Totus, a, um, adj. § 20, 4, *whole; entire; all.*

Trabs, is, f. *a beam.*

Tractātus, a, um, part. from

Tracto, āre, āvi, ātum, tr. freq. (traho,) *to treat; to handle.*

Tractus, ûs, m. (traho,) *a tract; a country; a region.*

Tractus, a, um, part. (traho.)

Tradĭtus, a, um, part. from

Trado, -dĕre, -dĭdi, -dĭtum, tr. (trans & do,) *to give over,* or *up; to deliver; to give; to relate; to teach:* tradunt, *they report:* tradĭtur, *it is related: it is reported:* traduntur, *they are reported.*

Tragĭcus, a, um, adj. *tragic.*

Tragœdia, æ, f. *a tragedy.*

Traho, trahĕre, traxi, tractum, tr. *to drag; to draw:* bellum, *to protract* or *prolong the war:* liquĭdas, aquas trahĕre, *to draw along clear waters; to flow with a clear stream.*

Trajicio, -jicĕre, -jēci, -jectum, tr. (trans & jacio,) *to convey over; to pass* or *cross over.*

Trames, ĭtis, m. (trameo, i. e. trans meo, *to go over* or *along;*) *a path; a way.*

Trano, āre, āvi, ātum, intr. (trans & no,) *to swim over.*

Tranquillus, a, um, adj. (comp.) *tranquil; calm; serene.*

Trans, prep. *over; beyond; on the other side.*

Transactus, a, um, part. (transĭgo.)

Transeo, īre, ii, ĭtum, intr. irr. (trans & eo,) *to pass* or *go over.*

Transfĕro, -ferre, -tŭli, -lātum, tr. irr. (trans & fero,) *to transfer; to carry over:* se ad aliquem, *to go over to.*

Transfĭgo, -figĕre, -fixi, -fixum, (trans & figo,) *to run through; to pierce; to stab.*

Transfŭga, æ, c. (transfugio,) *a deserter.*

Transgredior, -grĕdi, -gressus sum, intr. dep. (trans & gradior,) *to go* or *pass over.*

Transĭgo, -igĕre, -ēgi, -actum, tr. (trans & ago,) *to transact; to finish; to spend.*

Transilio, -silīre, -silui & -silīvi, intr. (trans & salio,) *to leap over.*

Transitūrus, a, um, part. (transeo,) *about to pass over; to pass on.*

Translātus, a, um, part. (transfĕro.)

Transmarīnus, a, um, adj. (trans & mare,) *beyond the sea; foreign; transmarine.*

Transno. *See* Trano.

Transvĕho, -vehĕre, -vexi, -vectum, tr. (trans & veho,) *to carry over; to convey; to transport.*

Transvŏlo, āre, āvi, ātum, intr. (trans & volo,) *to fly over.*

Trasimēnus, i, m. *a lake in Etruria, near which the consul Flaminius was defeated by Hannibal.*

Trebia, æ, f. *a river of Cisalpine Gaul, emptying into the Po.*

Trecenti, æ, a, num. adj. pl. *three hundred;* hence,

Trecentesĭmus, a, um, num. adj. *the three hundredth.*

Tredĕcim, num. adj. pl. ind. (tres & decem,) *thirteen.*

Tres, tria, num. adj. pl. 104, 3, *three.*

Trevĭri, ōrum, m. pl. *a people of Belgium.*

Triangulāris, e, adj. (triangŭlum,) *triangular; three-cornered.*

Tribūnus, i, m, (tribus,) *a tribune.*

Tribuo, uĕre, ui, ūtum, tr. *to attribute; to give; to grant; to bestow; to commit.*

Tribūtum, i, n. (tribuo,) *a tri-*

bute; a tax; a contribution; an assessment.

Tricesĭmus, a, um, num. adj. (triginta,) *the thirtieth.*

Triduum, i, n. (tres & dies,) *the space of three days:* per triduum, *for three days.*

Triennium, i, n. (tres & annus,) *the space of three years.*

Trigemĭni, ōrum, m. pl. (tres & gemĭni,) *three brothers born at one birth.*

Triginta, num. adj. pl. ind. *thirty.*

Trinacria, æ, f. *one of the names of Sicily.*

Triptolĕmus, i, m. *the son of Celeus, king of Eleusis.*

Tristitia, æ, f. (tristis, *sad;*) *sorrow; grief.*

Triumphālis, e, adj. (triumphus,) *triumphal.*

Triumphans, tis, part. from

Triumpho, āre, āvi, ātum, intr. *to triumph;* from

Triumphus, i, m. *a triumph; a triumphal procession.*

Triumvir, vĭri, m. (tres & vir,) *one of three joint public officers; a triumvir.*

Troas, ădis, f. *a country of Asia Minor, bordering upon the Hellespont.*

Trochĭlus, i, m. *a wren.*

Troglodȳtæ, ārum, c. pl. *Troglodytes, a people of Ethiopia, who dwelt in caves.*

Troja, æ, f. *Troy, the capital of Troas;* hence,

Trojānus, a, um, adj. *Trojan.*

Trucīdo, āre, āvi, ātum, tr. (trux & cædo,) *to kill in a cruel manner; to butcher; to murder; to slay; to massacre.*

Trux, ucis, adj. *savage; cruel; fierce; stern; grim.*

Tu, subs. pro. *thou;* § 28.

Tuba, æ, f. (tubus, *a tube,*) *a trumpet.*

Tuber, ĕris, n. (tumeo,) *a bunch; a tumor; a protuberance.*

Tubĭcen, ĭnis, m. (tuba & cano,) *a trumpeter.*

Tueor, tuēri, tuĭtus sum, tr. *to see; to look to; to care for; to defend; to protect.*

Tugurium, i, n. (tego,) *a hut; a shed.*

Tuli. *See* Fero.

Tullia, æ, f. *the daughter of Servius Tullius.*

Tullius, i, m. *a Roman.*

Tullus, i, m. (Hostilius,) *the third Roman king.*

Tum, adv. *then; and; so; also:* tum—tum. *as well—as; both—and:* tum demum, *then at length.*

Tumultus, ûs, m. (tumeo,) *a noise; a tumult.*

Tumŭlus, i, m. (id.) *a mound; a tomb.*

Tunc, adv. *then.*

Tunĭca, æ, f. *a tunic; a close woolen garment, worn under the toga.*

Turbātus, a, um, part. *disturbed; confused; troubled;* from

Turbo, āre, āvi, ātum, tr. (turba,) *to disturb; to trouble; to put into confusion.*

Turma, æ, f. *a division of Roman cavalry, consisting of thirty men; a troop.*

Turpis, e, adj. (ior, issĭmus,) *base; disgraceful.*

Turpitūdo, inis, f. (turpis,) *baseness; ugliness.*

Turris, is, f. *a tower.*

Tuscia, æ, f. *a country of Italy, the same as Etruria.*

Tuscŭlum, i, n. *a city of Latium.*

Tuscus, a, um, adj. *Tuscan; belonging to Tuscany; Etrurian.*

Tutor, ōris, m. (tueor,) *a guardian; a tutor.*

Tutus, a, um, adj. (ior issĭmus,) (tueor,) *safe.*

Tuus, a, um, adj. pro. 121, (tu,) *thy; thine.*

Tyrannis, ĭdis & ĭdos, f. *tyranny; arbitrary power;* fr.

Tyrannus, i, m. *a king; a tyrant; a usurper.*

Tyrius, a, um, adj. *Tyrian;* Tyrii, *Tyrians; inhabitants of Tyre.*

Tyrrhēnus, a, um, adj. *Tyrrhenian* or *Tuscan; belonging to Tuscany.*

Tyrus, i, f. *a celebrated maritime city of Phœnicia.*

U.

Uber, ĕris, n. *an udder; a teat.*

Ubertas, ātis, f. (uber, *rich, fertile,*) *fertility; fruitfulness.*

Ubi, adv. *where; when; as soon as.*

Ubīque, adv. *every where.*

Ulciscor, ulcisci, ultus sum, tr. dep. *to take revenge; to avenge.*

Ullus, a, um, adj. § 20, 4, *any; any one.*

Ulterior, us, (ultĭmus,) § 26, 4; *further;* hence,

Ulteriûs, adv. *farther; beyond; longer.*

Ultĭmus, a, um, adj. (sup. of ulterior,) *the last.*

Ultra, prep. *beyond; more than:*—adv. *besides; moreover; further.*

Ultus, a, um, part. (ulciscor,) *having avenged.*

Ulysses, is, m. *a distinguished king of Ithaca.*

Umbra, æ, f. *a shade; a shadow.*

Umbro, āre, āvi, ātum, tr. (umbra,) *to shade; to darken.*

Unâ, adv. (unus,) *together.*

Unde, adv. *whence; from which.*

Undĕcim, num. adj. pl. ind. (unus & decem,) *eleven.*

Undenonagesĭmus, a, um, num. adj. (unus, de, and nonagessĭmus,) *the eighty-ninth.*

Undequinquaginta, num. adj. pl. ind. *forty-nine.*

Undetricesĭmus, a, um, num. adj. *twenty-ninth.*

Undevicesĭmus, a, um, num. adj. *nineteenth.*

Undeviginti, num. adj. *nineteen.*

Undīque, adv. *on all sides.*

Unguis, is, m. *a claw; a talon; a nail.*

Ungŭla, æ, f. *a claw; a talon; a hoof:* binis ungŭlis, *cloven footed.*

Unīcus, a, um, adj. (unus,) *one alone; sole; only.*

Unio, ōnis, m. *a pearl.*

Univ́ersus, a, um, adj. (unus & versus,) *whole; universal; all.*

Unquam, adv. *ever:* nec unquam, *and never.*

Unus, a, um, num. adj. § 20, 4; *one; only; alone.*

Unusquisque, unaquæque, unumquodque, adj. *each one; each;* § 37, Obs. 2.

Urbs, is, f. *a city; the chief city; Rome.*

Uro, urĕre, ussi, ustum, tr. *to burn.*

Ursus, i, m. *a bear.*

Usque, adv. *even; as far as; till; until.*

Usus, a, um, part. (utor.)

Usus, ûs, m. (id.) *use; custom; profit; advantage.*

Ut, conj. *that; in order that; so that:* adv. *as; as soon as; when.*

Utcunque, adv. (ut & cunque,) *howsoever; somewhat; in some degree.*

Uter, tra, trum, adj. § 20, 4; *which? which of the two?*

Uterque, trăque, trumque, adj. § 20, 4; (uter & que,) *both; (taken separately, see* ambo,) *each; each of the two.*

Utĭlis, e, adj. comp. (utor,) *useful.*

Utĭca, æ, f. *a maritime city of Africa, near Carthage.*

Utor, uti, usus sum, intr. dep. *to use; to make use of.*

Utrinque, adv. *on both sides.*

Utrùm, adv. *whether.*

Uva, æ, f. *a grape; a bunch of grapes:* passa, *a raisin.*

Uxor, ōris, f. (ungo,) *a wife.*

V.

Vaco, āre, āvi, ātum, intr. *to be free from;* hence,

Vacuus, a, um, adj. *empty; unoccupied; vacant; free; exempt:* vacuus viātor, *the destitute traveler.*

Vadōsus, a, um, adj. (comp.) *fordable; shallow;* from

Vadum, i, n. (probably from vado, *to go;*) *a ford; a shallow.*

Vagans, tis, part. (vagor.)

Vagīna, æ, f. *a scabbard; a sheath.*

Vagītus, ûs, m. *weeping; crying.*

Vagor, āri, ātus sum, intr. dep. *to wander about; to stray.*

Valeo, ēre, ui, intr. *to be well,* or *in health; to be strong; to avail; to be distinguished; to be eminent:* multum valēre, *to be very powerful:* vale, *farewell.*

Valerius, i, m. *a Roman proper name.*

Vallis, is, f. *a valley; a vale.*

Variĕtas, ātis, f. (varius,) *variety; change.*

Vario, āre, āvi, ātum, tr. *to change; to vary;* from

Varius, a, um, adj. *various; diverse.*

Varro, ōnis, m. (Marcus,) *a very learned Roman:* P. Terentius, *a consul, who was defeated by Hannibal.*

Vasto, āre, āvi, ātum, tr. *to lay waste; to ravage;* from

Vastus, a, um, adj. *waste; desert;* hence, *wide; vast; great.*

Vates, is, m. *a poet; a bard.*

Ve, conj. (enclitic, 242, Obs. 2,) *or;* also, intensive or negative inseparable particle, 239, Obs. 2.

Vecordia, æ, f. (vecors; *mad;*) *madness; folly.*

Vectus, a, um, part. (veho.)

Vehĕmens, tis, adj. (ior, issĭmus,) (ve intens. & mens,) *vehement; immoderate;* hence,

Vehementer, adv. (iùs, issĭmè,) *vehemently; greatly; very; much; violently.*

Veho, vehĕre, vexi, vectum, tr. *to bear; to carry; to convey.*

Veiens, tis, & Veientānus, i, m. *an inhabitant of Veii.*

Veii, ōrum, m. pl. *a city of Tuscany, memorable for the defeat of the Fabian family.*

Vel, conj. *or; also; even:* vel lecta, *even when read:* vel—vel, *either—or.*

Vello, vellĕre, velli, *or* vulsi, vulsum, tr. *to pluck.*

Vellus, ĕris, n. (vello,) *a fleece.*

Velox, ōcis, adj. (ior, issĭmŭs,) (volo, āre,) *swift; rapid; active.*

Velum, i, n. (vexillum,) *a sail.*

Velut, & Velŭti, adv. (vel & ut,) *as; as if.*

Venālis, e, adj. (venus, *sale;*) *venal; mercenary.*

Venans, tis, part. (venor.)

Venatĭcus, a, um, adj. (id.) *belonging to the chase:* canis, *a hound.*

Venātor, ōris, m. (venor,) *a huntsman.*

Vendĭto, āre, āvi, ātum, freq. *to sell;* from

Vendo, vendĕre, vendĭdi, vendĭtum, tr. (venum & do,) *to sell.*

Venenātus, a, um, adj. *poisoned; poisonous;* from venēno, and that from

Venēnum, i, n. *poison.*

Veneo, īre, ii, intr. irr. (for venum eo,) *to be exposed for sale; to be sold.*

Venĕtus, i, m. *or* Brigantīnus, *a lake between Germany and Switzerland, called the Boden sea, or lake of Constance.*

Venio, venīre, veni, ventum, intr. *to come; to advance.*

Venor, āri, ātus sum, tr. dep. *to hunt.*

Venter, tris, m. *the belly; the stomach.*

Ventus, i, m. *a wind.*

Venus, ûs, *or* i, m. (used only in the dat. acc. & abl.) *sale.*

Venus, ĕris, f. *the goddess of love and beauty.*

Ver, veris, n. *the spring.*

Verber, ĕris, n. *a whip; a rod; a blow; a stripe;* hence,

Verbĕro, āre, āvi, ātum, tr. *to strike.*

Verbum, i, n. *a word.*

Verè, adv. (iùs, issĭmè,) (verus,) *truly.*

Vereor, ēri, ĭtus sum, intr. dep. *to fear; to be concerned for.*

Vergo, vergĕre, versi, intr. (also tr.) *to tend to; to incline; to verge towards; to bend; to look.*

Verisimĭlis, e, adj. comp. (verum & simĭlis,) *like the truth; probable.*

Verĭtus, a, um, part. (vereor.)

Verò, conj. *but:*—adv. (verus,) *indeed; truly.*

Verōna, æ, f. *Verona, a city in the north of Italy.*

Versātus, a, um, part. from

Versor, āri, ātus sum, tr. dep. freq. (verto,) *to turn; to revolve; to dwell; to live; to reside; to be employed.*

Versus, a, um, part. (vertor.)

Versùs, prep. *towards.*

Vertex, ĭcis, m. (verto,) *the top; the summit; the crown of the head.*

Verto, tĕre, ti, sum, tr. *to turn; to change.*

Veru, u, n. 91, Note, *a spit.*

Verùm, conj. *but; but yet;* fr.

Verus, a, um, adj. (comp.) *true.*

Vescor, i, intr. dep. (esca,) *to live upon; to feed upon; to eat; to subsist upon.*

Vespĕri, *or* -è, adv. *at evening:* tam vespĕri, *so late at evening.*

Vesta, æ, f. *a goddess; the mother of Saturn;* hence,

Vestālis, is, f. (virgo,) *a Vestal virgin; a priestess consecrated to the service of Vesta.*

Vestibŭlum, i, n. *the porch; the vestibule.*

Vestigium, i, n. *a footstep; a vestige; a trace; a mark; a track.*

Vestio, īre, īvi, ītum, tr. *to clothe;* from

Vestis, is, f. *a garment; clothes.*

Vesŭlus, i, m. *a high mountain of Liguria, and a part of the Cottian Alps.*

Veterānus, a, um, adj. (vetus,) *old:*—subs. *a veteran.*

Veto, āre, ui, ĭtum, tr. *to forbid; to prohibit.*

Veturia, æ, f. *the mother of Coriolānus.*

Veturius, i, m. (Titus,) *a Roman consul, who was defeated by the Samnites at the Caudine Forks.*

Vetus, ĕris, adj. (veterior, veterrĭmus, § 26, 2,) *ancient; old:* veteres, *the ancients;* hence,

Vetustas, ātis, f. *antiquity; age.*

Vetustus, a, um, adj. comp. (id.) *old; ancient.*

Vexi. *See* Veho.

Via, æ, f. *a way; a course; a path; a journey;* hence,

Viātor, ōris, m. *a traveler.*

Vicēni, æ, a, distrib. num. adj. pl. (viginti,) *every twenty; twenty.*

Vicesĭmus, a, um, num. adj. (id.) *the twentieth.*

Vici. *See* Vinco.

Vicies, num. adv. *twenty times.*

Vicinĭtas, ātis, f. *the neighborhood; vicinity;* from

Vicīnus, a, um, (vicus,) adj. *near; neighboring.*

Vicīnus, i, m. (vicus,) *a neighbor.*

Vicis, gen., f. § 18, 13, *change; reverse; a place; a turn;* in vicem, *in turn; in place of; instead.*

Victĭma, æ, f. (vinco,) *a victim; a sacrifice.*

Victor, ōris, m. (vinco,) *a victor; a conqueror:* adj. *victorious;* hence,

Victoria, æ, f. *a victory.*

Victūrus, a, um, part. (from vivo.)

Victus, a, um, part. (vinco.)

Vicus, i, m. *a village.*

Video, vidēre, vidi, visum, tr. *to see; to behold.*

Videor, vidēri, visus sum, pass. *to be seen; to seem; to appear; to seem proper.*

Viduus, a, um, adj. (viduo, *to bereave;*) *bereaved; widowed:* mulier vidua, *a widow.*

Vigil, ĭlis, m. (vigeo,) *a watchman.*

Vigĭlans, tis, adj. (ior, issĭmus,) (vigĭlo,) *watchful; vigilant.*

Vigilia, æ, f. (vigil,) *a watching:*—pl. *the watch,* (by night.)

Viginti, num. adj. pl. ind. *twenty.*

Vilis, e, adj. *cheap; vile; bad; mean.*

Villa, æ, f. (vicus,) *a country-house; a country-seat; a villa;* hence,

Villĭcus, i, m. *an overseer of an estate; a steward.*

Villus, i, m. *long hair; coarse hair.*

Vincio, vincīre, vinxi, vinctum, tr. *to bind.*

Vinco, vincĕre, vici, victum, tr. *to conquer; to vanquish; to surpass.*

Vinctus, a, um, part. (vincio.)

Vincŭlum, i, n. (id.) *a chain:* in vincŭla conjicĕre, *to throw into prison.*

Vindex, ĭcis, c. *an avenger; a protector; a defender; an asserter;* from

Vindĭco, āre, āvi, ātum, tr. *to claim; to avenge:* in libertātem, *to rescue from slavery.*

Vindicta, æ, f. (vindĭco,) *vengeance; punishment.*

Vinum, i, n. *wine.*

Viŏla, æ, f. *a violet.*

Viŏlo, āre, āvi, ātum, tr. (vis,) *to violate; to pollute; to corrupt.*

Vir, viri, m. (vis,) *a man.*

Vireo, ēre, ui, intr. *to be green; to be verdant; to flourish.*

Vires. *See* Vis.

Virga, æ. f. (vireo,) *a rod; a small staff; a switch.*

Virgilius, i, m. *Virgil, a very celebrated Latin poet.*

Virginia, æ, f. *the daughter of Virginius.*

Virginius, i, m. *the name of a distinguished Roman centurion.*

Virgo, ĭnis, f. (vireo,) *a virgin; a girl; a maid.*

Virgŭla, æ, f. (dim. from virga,) *a small rod.*

Viriāthus, i, m. *a Lusitanian general who was originally a shepherd, and afterwards a leader of robbers.*

Viridomărus, i, m. *a king of the Gauls, slain by Marcellus.*

Virtus, ūtis, f. (vir,) *virtue; merit; excellence; power; valor; faculty.*

Vis, vis, f. § 15, 12, *power; strength; force:* vis homĭnum, *a multitude of men:* vim facĕre, *to do violence:* —pl. vires, ium, *power; strength.*

Viscus, ĕris, n. *an entrail:* viscĕra, pl. *the bowels; the flesh.*

Vistŭla, æ f. *a river of Prussia, which still bears the same name, and which was anciently the eastern boundary of Germany.*

Visurgis, is, m. *the Weser, a large river of Germany.*

Visus, a, um, part. (video.)

Visus, ûs, m. (video,) *the sight.*

Vita, æ, f. *life.*

Vitandus, a, um, part. (vito.)

Vitĭfer, ĕra, ĕrum, adj. (vitis & fero,) *vine-bearing.*

Vitis, is, f. (vieo,) *a vine.*

Vitium, i, n. *a crime.*

Vito, āre, āvi, ātum, tr. *to shun; to avoid.*

Vitupĕro, āre, āvi, ātum, tr. (vitium paro,) *to find fault with; to blame.*

Vivĭdus, a, um, adj. (comp.) *lively; vivid;* from

Vivo, vivĕre, vixi, victum, intr. *to live; to fare; to live upon;* hence,

Vivus, a, um, adj. *living; alive.*

Vix, adv. *scarcely.*

Vixi. *See* Vivo.

Voco, āre, āvi, ātum, tr. (vox,) *to call; to invite; to name.*

Volo, āre, āvi, ātum, intr. *to fly.*

Volo, velle, volui, tr. irr. § 83, 4; *to wish; to desire; to be willing.*

Volsci, ōrum, m. pl. *a people of Latium.*

Volŭcer, -cris, -cre, adj. (volo, āre,) *winged:*—subs. *a bird.*

Volumnia, æ, f. *the wife of Coriolānus.*

Voluntas, ātis, f. (volo,) *the will.*

Voluptas, ātis, f. (volŭpe, fr. volo,) *pleasure; sensual pleasure.*

Volutātus, a, um, part. from

Volūto, āre, āvi, ātum, tr. freq. (volvo,) *to roll.*

Volvo, vĕre, vi, ūtum, tr. *to roll; to turn.*

Votum, i, n. (voveo,) *a wish; a vow.*

Vox, vocis, f. *a voice; a word; an expression; an exclamation.*

Vulcānus, i, m. *Vulcan, the god of fire, the son of Jupiter and Juno.*

Vulgus, i, m. *or* n. *the common people; the populace; the vulgar.*

Vulnerātus, a, um, part. from

Vulnĕro, āre, āvi, ātum, tr. *to wound;* from

Vulnus, ĕris, n. *a wound.*

Vulpecŭla, æ, f. dim. (vulpes,) *a little fox.*

Vulpes, is, f. *a fox.*

Vultur, ŭris, m. *a vulture.*

Vultus, ûs, m. (volo,) *the countenance; the expression: the look.*

X.

Xanthippe, es, f. *the wife of Socrates.*

Xanthippus, i, m. *a Lacedæmonian general, who was sent to assist the Carthaginians in the first Punic war.*

Xenocrătes, is, m. *a philosopher of Chalcēdon; the successor of Speusippus in the* Academia.

Xerxes, is, m. *a celebrated king of Persia.*

Z.

Zama, æ, f. *a city of Africa.*

Zeno, ōnis, m. *a philosopher of Citium, a town of Cyprus, and founder of the sect of the Stoics.*

Zetes, is, m. *a son of Boreas.*

Zona, æ, f. *a girdle; a zone.*

Zone, es, f. *a city and promontory in the western part of Thrace, opposite to the island of Thasus.*

EXERCISES

IN LATIN COMPOSITION.

Exercises in Latin composition for beginners can not be too simple, nor can they be too soon commenced. They are capable, also, under proper management, of being made one of the most exciting and pleasing, as well as profitable parts of study, even to young pupils. Exercises in considerable variety, and in the simplest form, are furnished in the Grammar under each part of speech. As soon as the pupil begins to read and translate, suitable exercises in Syntax may be drawn from every lesson, and even from every sentence, in which he may be drilled orally with great advantage, by simply changing the subject from the singular to the plural, or from the plural to the singular, and again by changing the mood or tense of the verb, or the active form for the passive, and *vice versa.* These may be still further varied by expressing the same idea in the interrogative or negative form, through all the varieties of mood, tense, number, or person, as before.

When the learner has become expert in this exercise, he may advance a step farther, and select from several sentences of his lesson, or from the stock now laid up in his memory, such words as are capable of forming a new sentence; and this again may be varied *ad libitum,* as before. To illustrate this—Suppose that the lesson of the day contains the following simple sentence, "*Terra parit flores,*" "The earth produces flowers," and the class has become familiar with the inflection of the words in every part, then let them change the words to correspond to such English sentences as the following:

The earth produced flowers; the earth has produced—had produced—will produce—may produce—might produce, &c., flowers,—a flower. Flowers are produced—were produced—have been produced, &c. The earth does not—did not—will not—can not, &c., produce flowers. Flowers are not—were not, &c., produced by the earth. Are flowers produced—were flowers produced—have flowers been produced, &c., by the earth? Are not flowers produced—were not flowers produced by the earth? &c., (as before.) Then again it may be noticed to the pupil that *terræ*, in the plural, means "*lands*" or "*countries*," and so may have a plural adjective and a plural verb; thus, *Omnes, multæ, quædam terræ pariunt flores*, "All," "many," "some lands produce flowers," &c., through a similar variety as before. In this manner, and in many other ways which will occur to the mind of an active teacher, a class may be kept actively and even intensely, as well as profitably occupied for ten or fifteen minutes, with a few words which, in their various forms and uses, will be indelibly impressed on the mind, while the memory and judgment are trained to prompt and accurate exercise, and more real progress made in the study of the language than by a careless reading of many pages extended through a drawling recitation of several days.

As a weekly, semi-weekly, or even daily exercise, pupils might be encouraged at a very early period to furnish an exercise in writing, framed by themselves from the lesson of the preceding day; or they may be supplied with English sentences framed from the lesson by the teacher or some of the more advanced scholars, to be rendered into Latin. In doing this they require no dictionary, and are not perplexed to know what words to choose, as the words are all before them in the lesson from which the exercise is drawn, and they have only to make the necessary changes in number, mood, tense, voice, &c., requisite to express the ideas contained in the exercise to be turned into Latin, in which also they are assisted by the model before them in the lesson, and the knowledge obtained in its previous study and recitation.

The following are framed from the reading lessons at the places indicated, as specimens of the kind of exercises here intended. They rise in gradation from simple unconnected sentences to those of the nature of a continued narrative, and are sufficient to furnish a short semi-weekly exercise of this kind during the time necessary to go through the Reader. They will also form a good preparation for a systematic work on Latin composition, such as **BULLIONS' LATIN EXERCISES.**

EXERCISES IN SIMPLE SENTENCES.

Change the Latin words in the following sentences so as to correspond to the English following.

1. *Fortes laudabuntur, ignāvi vituperabuntur.*
"Brave men will be praised, cowardly men will be blamed."

Brave men are praised, the cowardly are blamed. Brave men have always (*semper*) been praised, cowardly men blamed. Men praise the brave and blame the cowardly. Do not (*nonne*[a]) men praise the brave and blame the cowardly? A cowardly man will not be praised. A brave man will not be blamed. We will praise the good. You should blame the cowardly Let us praise[b] the brave and blame the cowardly. Let the brave be praised. Blame the cowardly.

2. *Honos est præmium virtūtis.*
"Honor is the reward of virtue."

Honor will be the reward of virtue. Honor was, (has been, had been,) the reward of virtue. Is not honor[a] the reward of virtue? Honors will be the rewards of virtue. Will not honor always be[a] the reward of virtue? Let honor always be[a] the reward of virtue.

3. *Victi Persæ in naves confugērunt.*
"The Persians being conquered fled to their ships."

The Persians were conquered and fled[c] to their ships. When the Persians were conquered[d] they fled to their ships. We have conquered the Persians and they have fled to their ships. If we conquer[e] the Persians they will flee to their ships. If the Persians should be conquered[f] they will flee to their ships. They say that the Persians were conquered and fled to their ships.

4. *Delectavērunt me epistŏlæ tuæ.*
"Your letters have delighted me."

Your letters delight me. I am delighted with your letters. Have I not[a] always been delighted with your letters? Do my (*meæ*) letters delight you (*te*)? His (*ejus*) letters will always give us pleasure. Our (*nostræ*) letters do not delight him. He will be delighted with our letters.

---

[a] Id. 56, 3.
[b] Gr. 171, 1.
[c] Id. 115, 1.
[d] Gr. 631.
[e] Gr. 627, 2.
[f] Id. 77, 2.

The words of the following sentences selected from the Introductory Exercises, pp. 60–79, will be found in the paragraphs indicated by the numbers prefixed. As a further exercise these may be varied as in the preceding. Nos. 1, 2, 3, 4.

5. (1.) There are many kings in Europe. Europe has many kings. There have been many good kings. There are many suns and more stars. Cicero was a good man and a distinguished consul. (2.) A brave soldier is to be praised. (3.) An elephant walks. Many sparrows build nests. The partridge runs. (4.) Black sheep are not found every where. Africa produces lions. The Romans often burned their dead. A brave man is not always praised. The Romans overthrew Carthage and Corinth.

6. (5.) The bear wanders in the forest. A parrot imitates the human voice. (6.) A day has been lost. Flowers are produced by the earth. Athens was liberated by Miltiades (7.) Herds of wild asses roam (*erro*) in the forests (*sylva*) of Asia and Africa. The tracks of wild beasts are diligently traced out by dogs. The variety of languages in the army of Cyrus was very great. (8.) Animals covered with wool are stupid, but (*sed*) they are capable of bearing cold. Foolish people are not happy. The Gauls were very brave.[a] The lion is the bravest of animals.[d]

7. (9.) Plato and Socrates were highly esteemed. It is our custom[b] to value the good.[c] Good men[c] forget injuries and remember kindnesses. It is the custom of foolish men to forget kindnesses. (10.) Good men[c] are an honor to their country; they are just and benevolent to all.[c] Nero was an enemy to the human race. A good man (*vir*) will be dear to all, a wicked man (*homo*) to no one.

8. (11.) Various coverings have been given to animals. Nature has given avarice and ambition to man alone. (12.) The Romans for the most part burned their dead. Homer mentions embroidered garments. (13.) We sometimes find stags of a white color. We have need of philosophy. Men of noble birth are not always of a noble disposition. Men of depraved disposition are never happy (*nunquam felix*). Be content with few things and thou wilt be free from cares.

[a] Id. 24. [b] Gr. 364. R XII. [c] Id. 19. [d] Gr. 355, R. X.

9. (14.) Lions eat flesh. Silver and gold are found in Spain. Men easily want gold and silver, but (*sed*) not food. Africa abounds in lions. (16.) The Romans were sent under the yoke. The year was divided into twelve months by Numa Pompilius. (17.) Hunger and blows tame wild beasts. Nightingales change their color in autumn. One oration of Socrates was sold for twenty talents. (18.) Mithridates, king of Pontus, was received by Tigranes, king of Armenia.

10. (19.) I desire to live with you. They wished to sleep. Why do men desire to change their fortune? We ought to learn to despise wealth. We can not (we are not able) to suffer poverty. All men[a] desire to be loved. (20.) Men must die.[b] They had to fight.[b] The art of writing[c] was invented by the Phœnicians. Paper is useful for writing. (21.) Catiline entered into a scheme for raising an army and destroying the city.

11. (22.) The sun will set and the wolves will come forth (*evenio*) to plunder.[d] The civil wars were carried on by Marius and Sulla. All the nations of men have been and they will be carried off by the power of death. (23.) Your letters have often been read by me.[e] The crocodile lives many years. Glory is thought to follow virtue. Great things have been undertaken. Our strength will not always remain.

12. (24.) The disposition of wild beasts is sometimes more gentle than that of men. (25.) This is the four-horse chariot which was made of ivory and covered with the wings of a fly. Fruits are not produced by every field that is sown. Words are repeated by the parrots[e] which are sent from India. Men who are mindful of favors will receive (*recipio*) favors. (27.) The fig-tree is so large that it conceals troops of horsemen under it. Do you know[g] (*Num scis*) who painted[f] Alexander? Is it true[g] (*Verumne est*) that bulls are swallowed whole in India by serpents?[e] Do you know[g] how many (*quot*) men there are in the world? Tell us (*Doce*) when the world was made,[f] and how many worlds there are.[f]

[a] Id. 19.
[b] Id. 113.
[c] Id. 111.
[d] Id. 102.
[e] Gr. 530.
[f] Gr. 627, 5.
[g] Id. 56, 3.

13. (29.) There are some who live[a] happy; there are others who are never happy. Is there any one who has not read[a] Demosthenes? Who is there that has not heard[a] concerning Cæsar? (30.) It is related that in Latmos scorpions do not hurt strangers, but that they kill the natives. They say (*narrant*) that Virgil in his will ordered his poems to be burned, and that Augustus forbade it to be done. (31.) The approaching day is announced by the crowing of the cock. The city built by Cecrops was called Cecropia. It is now called Athens. Many when dying are troubled with the care of burial.

EXERCISES IN COMPOUND AND CONNECTED SENTENCES.

As an example of the way in which compound and connected sentences may be varied, the first fable, page 80, may be changed into the following forms and translated into Latin corresponding to the English in each.

14. Through fear of a kite a hawk was asked by the doves to defend[b] them. When he assented[c] and was received[c] into the dove-cote, greater havoc was made by him in one day than could have been done[d] by the kite in many (*multis*).

15. The doves were led (*ductæ sunt*) by fear of a kite to ask[e] a hawk that he would defend[d] them. It is said that he assented[b] and that, being received into the dove-cote, he caused a much greater slaughter of the doves in one day than the kite could have caused[d] in a long time.

16. The doves are said to have asked a hawk whether, if received into the dove-cote, he would defend[g] them from the kite. He assented and was received; but the slaughter made in one day by the hawk was greater than could have been committed[d] by the kite in a long time.

17. It is related (*narrātur*) that when the doves through fear of a kite requested the hawk to defend[b] them, he assented; and that being received into the dove-cote a great havoc was made of the doves in one day.

---

[a] Gr. 638.
[b] Gr. 627, 1, 3d, & Id. 84.
[c] Gr. 631.
[d] Id. 88.
[e] Id. 86.
[f] Id. 97, 1.
[g] Gr. 627, 5.
[h] Gr. 690, R. LX.

18. (p. 99, &c.) 1. A serpent, the son[a] of Mars, the keeper of a certain fountain in Bœotia, was killed by Cadmus,[b] the son of Agenor. For this reason (*ob hoc*) all his offspring were put to death, and he himself was turned into a serpent. 2. All who came into the kingdom of Amycus, the son of Neptune, were compelled to fight with him, and being conquered were killed. 5. Life is said to have been restored[c] to Hippolytus, the son of Theseus, by Æsculapius, the son of Apollo.

19. (p. 101, &c.) 10. It is said that Tantalus[d] was the son of Jupiter; and that because he told to men the things which he heard among the gods, he was placed in water in the infernal regions, and always thirsts. Others say, that he is tormented with perpetual fear, dreading the fall of a stone which hangs over his head.[e] 15. The first men are said to have been formed of clay by Prometheus,[b] the son[a] of Japetus. It is also said that fire was brought by him from heaven in a reed, and that he pointed out how it might be preserved by being covered[f] with ashes.

20. (p. 105, &c.) 19. Europa, the daughter of Agenor, was carried by Jupiter from Sidon to Crete. When Agenor sent his sons to bring her back,[g] he told them that unless their sister was found they should not return.[h] 21. Atalanta, the daughter of Schœneus, was very beautiful. When many sought her in marriage, the condition was proposed that he should take[h] her who should first surpass[i] her in running. 23. Niobe, the wife[a] of Amphion, the son[a] of Jupiter and Antiope, had seven sons and as many daughters, who were all slain by the arrows of Apollo and Diana; and Niobe herself was changed into a stone.

21. (p. 109, &c.) 1. Neither the actions nor the thoughts of men are concealed from the gods. 2. The laws of the Athenians are said to have been written by Solon. No man can be esteemed happy in this life, because even to his last day he is exposed to uncertain fortune. 5. It is said that Democritus,[l] to whom[m] great riches had been left by his father, gave nearly all his patrimony to his fellow-citizens.

[a] Gr. 251, R. I.
[b] Gr. 530.
[c] Id. 92.
[d] Gr. 676.
[e] Gr. 399, R. IV.
[f] Gr. 688.
[g] Gr. 627, 1, 2d.
[h] Gr. 627, 1, 3d.
[i] Gr. 656.
[k] Gr. 382.
[l] Gr. 671, R. LVIII.
[m] Gr. 522, R. III.

22. (p. 112, &c.) 20. They say that Socrates, who was judged by the oracle of Apollo to be the wisest of all men,[a] was the son of a midwife; and the mother of Euripides, the tragic poet, is said to have sold herbs. 21. A question being proposed to Homer by a fisherman, which he could not answer, he is said to have died of vexation. 22. Simonides when eighty years[b] old entered into a musical contest, and obtained the victory. He afterwards (*postea*) lived at Syracuse[c] on intimate terms with Hiero the king.

23. (p. 116, &c.) 42. When certain persons warned Philip, king of Macedon, to beware[d] of one Pythias, a brave soldier,[e] but displeased with him,[f] he is said to have asked whether, (*num*) if a part of his body were diseased,[g] he should cut[h] it off or take care of it. It is said that he[i] then called Pythias to him, supplied him with money, and that after that, none of the king's soldiers were more faithful than Pythias.[k] 52. When Dionysius was banished from Syracuse, it is said that he went (*eo*) to Corinth,[l] where he taught boys their letters.

24. (p. 120, &c.) 65. Corinth was taken by L. Mummius. All Italy was adorned with paintings and statues. It is said that of so great spoils he converted nothing to his own use; and that when he died, his daughter received a dowry from the public treasury. 66. A statue of Ennius the poet was ordered by Scipio Africanus to be placed in the tomb of the Cornelian gens, because the exploits of the Scipios had been rendered famous by his poems.

25. (123, &c.) 1. In ancient times, Saturn came to Italy and taught the Italians agriculture. A fort built by him near Janiculum, was called Saturnia. 2. Troy being overthrown, it is said that Æneas, the son of Anchises, came into Italy, and was kindly received[m] by Latinus, king of those regions; and that having received the daughter of Latinus in marriage, he built a city and called it Lavinia. Romulus and Remus, the sons of Rhea Sylvia, having been exposed by the order of Amulius, were taken up by Faustulus, the king's shepherd, and given to his wife to be nursed.

---

[a] Gr. 355, R. X.
[b] Gr. 565, R. XLI.
[c] Gr. 549.
[d] Gr. 627, 1, 3d, & Id. 84.
[e] Gr. 251, R. I.
[f] Gr. 382, R. XVI.
[g] Gr. 627, 2.
[h] Gr. 627, 5.
[i] Gr. 671, R. LVIII.
[k] Gr. 467, R. XXIV.
[l] Gr. 553.
[m] Id. 104.

26. (p. 126, &c.) 12. Rome was built by Romulus, and divided into thirty curiæ called by the names of the Sabine women carried off by the Romans. 13. Numa Pompilius, the second king of Rome, was born at Cures. By him[a] laws were given to the state,[b] many sacred rites were instituted, and the manners of the people were softened. He reigned forty-three years.[c] 14. In the reign of Tullus Hostilius, who succeeded Numa, war was declared against the Sabines, which was terminated by the battle[d] of the Horatii and the Curiatii.

27. (p. 129, &c.) 23. Rome was governed by kings two hundred and forty-three years.[c] 23. After that the people created two consuls, who should hold (*teneo*[e]) the government for a year.[c] Brutus, by whom the kings had been expelled, and Tarquinius Collatinus, were the first consuls. 24. War[f] having been raised against the city by Tarquin, Brutus was killed in the first battle.

28. (p. 132, &c.) 1. The bravest of the Romans[g] was challenged to single combat by a certain Gaul of extraordinary size[h] of body. The challenge was accepted by T. Manlius, a young man of noble family, (*genus*[h]) who killed the Gaul and stripped[i] him of his golden chain. It is believed (*creditur*) that both he[k] and his posterity, from this circumstance, were called[l] Torquati.[m] 2. In a new war with the Gauls it is related (*narrātur*) that another Gaul[k] of remarkable strength[h] challenged the bravest of the Romans[g] to fight with[n] him; that M. Valerius, a tribune of the soldiers, offered himself, and advanced armed; that a crow, which had perched on his right shoulder, struck at the eyes of the Gaul with his wings and talons, and that Valerius, the Gaul[f] being killed, received the name of Corvinus.

29. (p. 138, &c.) 2. Hannibal, the Carthaginian general, when nine years old was brought by his father to the altars[b] to swear[n] eternal hatred towards the Romans. 3. It is said that having left his brother[f] in Spain, he crossed the Alps

---

[a] Gr. 530.
[b] Gr. 522, R. III.
[c] Gr. 565, R. XLI.
[d] Gr. 542, R. XXXV.
[e] Gr. 641, R. II.
[f] Gr. 690, R. LX.
[g] Gr. 355, R. X.
[h] Gr. 339, R. VII.
[i] Gr. 514, R. XXXI.
[k] Gr. 671, R. LVIII.
[l] Id. 97, 4.
[m] Gr. 319, R. V.
[n] Gr. 619, R. LIII. & Id. 84.

with (*cum*) a large army and thirty elephants, and that the Ligurians joined themselves with him; that he conquered Scipio, and afterwards Sempronius Gracchus. Soon after he advanced to Tuscia, where having engaged in battle[a] near the lake Trasimenus, he conquered Flāminius the consul, and slew twenty-five thousand of the Romans.[b]

30. (142, &c.) 3. After Philip, king of Macedonia, died, his son Perseus prepared great forces, renewed the war against the Romans, and conquered P. Licinius, the Roman general who had been sent against him. He was afterwards conquered by Æmilius Paulus, the consul, near Pydna, and twenty thousand of his infantry were slain. 5. Carthage, though bravely defended[c] by its citizens, was taken and destroyed by Scipio, in the seven hundredth year after it was built, and in the six hundred and eighth year from the building of Rome.

31. (p. 145, &c.) 1. In the war carried on against Jugurtha, the Romans were in great fear that[d] the Gauls would again get possession of the city. For this reason Marius was made consul a third and a fourth time. In two battles, two hundred thousand of the enemy were slain, and eighty thousand taken prisoners. For this meritorious conduct, a fifth consulship was conferred on Marius, in his absence.[c] C. Marius and Qu. Catulus fought against the Cimbri and the Teutones, who had passed over into Italy, slew forty thousand, and took sixty thousand of his army near Verona.

32. (150, &c.) 6. Lucius Sergius Catiline is said to have been a man of a very noble family,[e] but of a most depraved disposition.[e] It is related (*tradĭtur*) that he and certain illustrious, but daring men, entered[f] into a conspiracy for destroying their country;[g] that he was driven from the city by Cicero, who was then consul, and his companions seized and strangled in prison. 7. Nearly all Gaul was conquered by Cæsar in the space of nine years. The war was afterwards carried into Britain, and the Germans were conquered in great battles.

[a] Gr. 690, R. LX.
[b] Gr. 355, R. X.
[c] Gr. 688.
[d] Gr. 633.
[e] Gr. 339, R. VI.
[f] Gr. 312, R. I.
[g] Id. 112, 3.

33. (p. 154, &c.) 1. The three parts into which the whole world was divided, are Europe, Asia, and Africa. The straits of Gibralter separate Europe from Africa. 2. The boundary of Europe on the east is the river Tanais and the Euxine sea; on the south the Mediterranean sea; on the west the Atlantic ocean. 3. Spain lies toward the west. It is rich and fertile. In the region of Bætica, men, horses, iron, lead, brass, silver, and gold abound. 4. The Phocæi, having left Asia,[a] sought new settlements in Europe.

34. (p. 157, &c.) 11. The country beyond the Rhine, as far as the Vistula, is inhabited by the Germans, who are said to carry on war with their neighbors, not that they may extend[b] their limits, but from the love[c] of war. 12. It is said that the Germans[d] do not pay much attention to agriculture. Their food (*cibus*) is milk, cheese, and flesh. They erect their houses near (*ad*) some spring, or plain, or forest; and after a while they pass on to another place. Sometimes also they pass the winter in caves.

35. (p. 161, &c.) 24. Greece is more celebrated than any other nation in[e] the world, both for the genius of its people, and for their study[f] of the arts of peace and of war. Many colonies were led from it unto all parts of the world. 25. Macedonia was rendered illustrious by the reign of Philip and Alexander, by whom both Greece and Asia were subdued to a very great extent; and the government, taken from the Persians,[g] was transferred to the Macedonians.

36. (p. 162, &c.) 29. No region in Greece is more renowned for the splendor[i] of its fame than Attica.[e] There Athens is built; a city[h] concerning which the gods are said to have contended. So many poets, orators, philosophers; so many men, illustrious in every species of excellence, were produced by no other city in the world. There the arts of peace were cultivated to such a degree, that her renown from these was even more conspicuous[i] than (*quam*) her glory in war. The harbor of Piræus, connected with the city by long walls, was fortified by Themistocles, and affords (*præbet*) a safe anchorage for ships.

---

[a] Id. 104, & 690, R. LX.
[b] Gr. 627, 1.
Gr. 542, R. XXXV.
[d] Gr. 671, R. LVIII.
[e] Gr. 467, R. XXIV.
[f] Gr. 535, R XXXIV.
[g] Gr. 522, R. III.
[h] Gr. 251, R. I.
[i] Gr. 627, 1, 1st.

37. (163, &c.) 30. It is said that Thebes, a most celebrated city, was surrounded with walls by Amphion, by the[a] aid[a] of music. It was rendered illustrious by the genius[b] of Pindar and the valor of Epaminondas. 31. The city of Delphi was renowned for the oracle of Apollo, which had great authority among all nations, and was enriched (made rich) with numerous and splendid presents from all parts of the world. It is said that the tops of Mount Parnassus, which hangs over the city,[c] are inhabited by the Muses.

38. (170, &c.) 48. It is believed that Troy, a city[d] renowned for the war[b] which it carried on with the whole of Greece for ten years,[e] was situated at the foot of Mount Ida. From this mountain, rendered illustrious by the judgment of Paris in the contest of the goddesses, flowed[f] the rivers Scamander and Simois. 49. The Carians are said to have been so fond of war, that they carried[g] on the wars of other people for hire. 50. The water of the river Cydnus is very clear[h] and very cold.[h]

39. (172, &c.) 54. Babylon, the capital of the Chaldean nation, was built by Semiramis or Belus. It is said that its walls,[m] built of burnt brick,[i] are thirty-two feet[k] broad, and that chariots[m] meeting each other pass without danger; that the towers are ten feet[l] higher than the walls. The tower of Babylon is said to have been twenty stadia in circumference. 56. India produces very large animals. No dogs are so large as those which are produced there. The serpents are said to be so monstrous that elephants are killed[g] by their bite[b] and the coiling round of their bodies.

[a] Gr. 530.
[b] Gr. 542, R. XXXV.
[c] Gr. 339, R. IV.
[d] Gr. 251, R. I.
[e] Gr. 565, R. XLI.
[f] Gr. 312, R. I.
[g] Gr. 627, 1, 1st.
[h] Id. 24.
[i] Gr. 541.
[k] Gr. 573, R. XLII.
[l] Gr. 579, R. XLIII.
[m] Gr. 671, R. LVIII.

[THE END.]

www.ingramcontent.com/pod-product-compliance
Lightning Source LLC
LaVergne TN
LVHW020213110826
845151LV00003B/697

* 9 7 8 1 4 2 5 5 3 4 1 1 0 *